ACCESS HACKS™

Ken Bluttman

O'REILLY®

Beijing · Cambridge · Farnham · Köln · Paris · Sebastopol · Taipei · Tokyo

Access Hacks™
by Ken Bluttman

Published by O'Reilly Media, Inc., 1005 Gravenstein Highway North,
Sebastopol, CA 95472.

O'Reilly books may be purchased for educational, business, or sales promotional use. Online editions are also available for most titles (*safari.oreilly.com*). For more information, contact our corporate/institutional sales department: (800) 998-9938 or *corporate@oreilly.com*.

Editors:	Mitch Tulloch Brian Sawyer	**Production Editor:**	Mary Anne Weeks Mayo
Series Editor:	Rael Dornfest	**Cover Designer:**	Hanna Dyer
Executive Editor:	Dale Dougherty	**Interior Designer:**	David Futato

Printing History:

April 2005:	First Edition.

 This book uses RepKover™, a durable and flexible lay-flat binding.

ISBN: 0-596-00924-0
[C]   [7/05 UV]

Contents

Credits

About the Author

Ken Bluttman has been hacking around with Access for years. Having honed his programming skills back when the PC was just becoming a household item, Ken found Access a joy to use, even back in earlier versions.

Besides Access, Ken excels at Excel and the other Office products, as well as SQL Server, web development, and VB/VB.NET development. No wonder he rarely sleeps.

Ken is also the author of *Developing Microsoft Office Solutions* (Addison Wesley) and *Excel Formulas and Functions for Dummies* (Wiley), as well as numerous print and web-based articles.

On the personal side, Ken is a musician and a nature lover. Have guitar, will travel to the woods. Ken lives in New York with his wife, son, dog, and several amphibians.

Visit Ken at his web site: *http://www.bluttman.com.*

Contributors

The following people contributed their hacks, writing, and inspiration to this book:

- Steve Conklin is an independent software developer and the owner of Ultra D.N.T. (Development, Networks, and Training) Technology Consulting, located in Queens, New York. He specializes in Access, Visual Basic/VB.NET, and MS-SQL Server development, and is releasing a line of PocketPC applications for the mobile professional. Steve has written several articles for *Access/VB/SQL Advisor* magazine and he teaches Microsoft Windows and Office courses at a New York City community college. He is available for development work and can be reached at *UltraDNT@Hotmail.com*.

- Steve Huff has been developing Access database applications for more than nine years. He has a computer science degree from Northern Kentucky University, where he is taking night courses toward a master's degree in information systems. He has been developing Microsoft Office solutions as a consultant working for SARCOM for more than seven years. Steve lives in Kentucky with his wife, Melissa. You can reach him through his web site: *http://www.huffs.us*.

- Kirk Lamb has been dabbling with Access for many years. Although his expertise is in boating, he knows a good database when he sees one. Kirk lives with his wife, Dill, in Washington state.

- Andrea Moss first got involved with Access when she designed a system to track insurance claims. Since then, she has applied her artistic skills to designing layout and color schemes for various GUIs, including Access forms and web sites. Along the way, she has picked up a few Access tricks of her own.

- Michael Schmalz works in banking and performs business and technology consulting in a variety of industries. He has been a technical editor for O'Reilly on Microsoft Office books. Michael has a degree in finance from Penn State. He lives with his wife and daughter in Pennsylvania.

- Simon St.Laurent is a web developer, network administrator, computer-book author, and XML troublemaker living in Ithaca, New York. His books include *XML: A Primer*, *XML Elements of Style*, *Building XML Applications*, *Cookies*, and *Sharing Bandwidth*. He is a contributing editor to XMLhack.com and an occasional contributor to XML.com.

- Margaret Levine Young has used small computers since the 1970s. She graduated from Unix on a PDP-11 to Apple DOS on an Apple II to DOS, Windows, and Unix on a variety of machines. She has done all kinds of jobs that involve explaining to people that computers aren't as mysterious as they might think, including managing the use of PCs at Columbia Pictures, teaching scientists and engineers what computers are good for, and writing and cowriting computer manuals and books, including *Understanding Javelin PLUS*, *The Complete Guide to PC-File*, *UNIX for Dummies*, and *The Internet for Dummies*. Margy has a degree in computer science from Yale University and lives with her husband and two children in Vermont.

Acknowledgments

This book is a collaborative effort. My thanks go to the contributors for providing great hacks that I am sure you will enjoy as much as I have.

Special thanks and appreciation go to my editor, Mitch Tulloch. Mitch has stuck with me through the thick and thin of getting this project completed. His patience and perseverance have been awesome. Mitch would like to thank MTS Communications Inc. (*http://www.mts.ca*) for providing Internet services for hosting his web site (*http://www.mtit.com*).

Thanks to Michael Schmalz for tech-reviewing the material and keeping on my back about early binding versus late binding and other pertinent topics dear to our profession.

Thanks to Brian Sawyer and the great O'Reilly team. Thanks to all of you.

Thanks to my agent, Neil Salkind, and the Studio B team. Neil called me one day last year to see if I would be interested in writing *Access Hacks*. Of course! And that's how I met Mitch Tulloch.

Thanks to the staff at Database Creations, Inc. (*http://www.databasecreations.com*) and FMS, Inc. (*http://www.fmsinc.com*) for providing copies of their outstanding products.

Last but not least, thanks to my wife Gayla and son Matthew. Working on a book is always stressful, and they have been real troopers in giving me space and time to complete the book. It's cute to see a seven-year-old becoming such a computer pro. Often, Matthew will sit on my lap and watch what I am typing. Now he is an Access expert in his own right.

Preface

Access really is an amazing product. Its power is vast, and yet its maintenance is low. In fact, in most installations it sits on the desktop and is maintenance-free. It's flexible enough to be used by one person or to run an entire company. It's a rapid application development (RAD) tool that outshines other such tools (such as Visual Basic) in time to development and ease of use.

Access is also a complete database application system. It incorporates both the back-end and front-end elements of a database, thereby eliminating the need to use two products to get your work done. Even so, its flexibility allows an Access database file to be just a back end or just a front end. Access can control data in external database systems such as SQL Server and Oracle.

Need I say more? I don't think you need any convincing to know what a great product Access is. Either you are using it already, or you are about to start. Well, here is some great news: this book is going to show you even more ways to use Access. Whether it's how to run Union queries, play video files in Access, view web sites within Access, or even control Access from another product, there are hacks here to tickle every fancy.

Access Hacks lets you move beyond the familiar tables, forms, and reports paradigm and get new insights into making your database applications more valuable and exciting. It's my pleasure to show you new ways to work with your favorite database product. So, fire up your computer, and let's get started!

Why Access Hacks?

The term *hacking* has a bad reputation in the press. They use it to refer to someone who breaks into systems or wreaks havoc with computers as their weapon. Among people who write code, though, the term *hack* refers to a "quick-and-dirty" solution to a problem, or a clever way to get something done. And the term *hacker* is taken very much as a compliment, referring to someone as being *creative*, having the technical chops to get things done. The Hacks series is an attempt to reclaim the word, document the good ways people are hacking, and pass the hacker ethic of creative participation on to the uninitiated. Seeing how others approach systems and problems is often the quickest way to learn about a new technology.

How to Use This Book

Access Hacks is not meant to be a sequential read, although I won't complain if you read it straight through, from cover to cover! The book contains 100 hacks, and each stands on its own merit. You can read them in any order. Some hacks have a common theme with other hacks, in which case the flow is duly noted. Other than that, just dig in, and see what interests you. One group of hacks might be what you need for today's project, and another group might be what you need tomorrow.

How This Book Is Organized

Each chapter in *Access Hacks* centers on a facet of Access. In this way, you can focus on areas in which you need a little inspiration. If you need help with queries and SQL, go to Chapter 5. If you want to learn some programming tricks, go to Chapter 8. In particular, here is what you'll find in each chapter:

Chapter 1, *Core Access*
> The first chapter covers the basics, from organizing database objects to working with data. In this chapter, you'll find nuggets about helping users, overcoming version incompatibility, and even how to work with any amount of data.

Chapter 2, *Tables*
> Tables are the core object of any database. In this chapter, you'll find hacks that show you how to move data between tables and how to reset AutoNumbering to begin with a number of your choice. Also, you will learn what system tables are and how to have them stay out of your way.

Chapter 3, *Entry and Navigation*
> This chapter focuses on users' needs. Besides storing data, a database system needs to make it easy for users to manage the data. Chapter 3 is chock-full of hacks that improve how users work with forms, which of course are the most common database objects users interact with.

Chapter 4, *Presentation*

Once data is entered and stored, the rest of the equation involves reporting. This chapter shows you new ways to work with reports. Learn how to use a watermark, provide sophisticated sorting, and provide conditional totals. Don't forget to check the hacks on creating a slide show and playing videos!

Chapter 5, *Queries and SQL*

Running queries is a big part of database work. Many of the hacks in this chapter take you beyond the basics of the query design grid. Immerse yourself in the SQL language itself as you discover Union queries, using the In and Not operators, and how to use custom functions in queries. There is even a hack that encourages you to query unrelated tables to return all combinations of data in two fields.

Chapter 6, *Multiuser Issues*

Certain issues exist only in a shared environment. In this chapter, you'll find hacks that provide workarounds for common problems. Learn how to end an unattended edit and how to distribute a database with no hassles.

Chapter 7, *External Programs and Data*

Access is easy to integrate with other programs and protocols. This chapter shows you many ways to use Access with other products, including Excel, Word, MySQL, and SQL Server. If you have an inkling of how to work with XML data, this chapter includes hacks for that. There is even a hack that shows you how to create Access tables without running Access.

Chapter 8, *Programming*

This chapter provides a number of programming techniques. It includes hacks for optimizing code, writing faster code, and protecting code. Other hacks provide minisolutions, such as a way to drill down to a specific record and to provide feedback during a long process.

Chapter 9, *Third-Party Applications*

This chapter previews a few third-party products that make your database work a breeze. Learn about products that create a database framework, document your database, and even provide data. Last but not least, this chapter provides an overview of a complete XML-based application solution.

Chapter 10, *The Internet*

The hacks in this chapter show you how to create HTML files from Access. With just a little editing with an HTML tool or in a text editor you can turn an Access report into the format you need. You'll find hacks in this chapter for putting a web browser directly on an Access form. Need to check your online investments? You can do so without leaving the database.

Conventions Used in This Book

The following is a list of the typographical conventions used in this book:

Plain text

> Indicates options, queries, and options entered using Access's graphical user interface (GUI), including table titles, cell identifiers, named ranges, menu titles, menu options, menu buttons, and keyboard accelerators (such as Alt and Ctrl).

Italics

> Indicates URLs, filenames, filename extensions, and directory/folder names. For example, a path in the filesystem appears as */Developer/ Applications*.

`Constant width`

> Shows code examples, the contents of files, console output, as well as the names of variables, commands, functions, macros, statements, command-line queries, and other code excerpts.

`Constant width bold`

> Highlights portions of code, typically new additions to old code.

`Constant width italic`

> Used in code examples and tables to show sample text to be replaced with your own values.

Color

> The second color indicates a cross reference within the text.

You should pay special attention to notes set apart from the text with the following icons:

 This is a tip, suggestion, or general note. It contains useful supplementary information about the topic at hand.

 This is a warning or note of caution, often indicating that your money or your privacy might be at risk.

The thermometer icons, found next to each hack, indicate the relative complexity of the hack:

 beginner   moderate   expert

Using Code Examples

This book is here to help you get your job done. In general, you can use the code in this book in your programs and documentation. You do not need to contact us for permission unless you're reproducing a significant portion of the code. For example, writing a program that uses several chunks of code from this book *does not* require permission. Selling or distributing a CD-ROM of examples from O'Reilly books *does* require permission. Answering a question by citing this book and quoting example code *does not* require permission. Incorporating a significant amount of example code from this book into your product's documentation *does* require permission.

We appreciate, but do not require, attribution. An attribution usually includes the title, author, publisher, and ISBN. For example: "*Access Hacks* by Ken Bluttman. Copyright 2005 O'Reilly Media, Inc., 0-596-00924-0."

If you feel your use of code examples falls outside fair use or the permission given here, feel free to contact us at *permissions@oreilly.com*.

Safari Enabled

 When you see a Safari® Enabled icon on the cover of your favorite technology book, that means the book is available online through the O'Reilly Network Safari Bookshelf.

Safari offers a solution that's better than e-books. It's a virtual library that lets you easily search thousands of top tech books, cut and paste code samples, download chapters, and find quick answers when you need the most accurate, current information. Try it for free at *http://safari.oreilly.com*.

How to Contact Us

We have tested and verified the information in this book to the best of our ability, but you might find that features have changed (or even that we have made mistakes!). As a reader of this book, you can help us improve future editions by sending us your feedback. Please let us know about any errors, inaccuracies, bugs, misleading or confusing statements, and typos that you find anywhere in this book.

Please also let us know what we can do to make this book more useful to you. We take your comments seriously and will try to incorporate reasonable suggestions into future editions. You can write to us at:

O'Reilly Media, Inc.
1005 Gravenstein Highway North
Sebastopol, CA 95472
(800) 998-9938 (in the United States or Canada)
(707) 829-0515 (international/local)
(707) 829-0104 (fax)

To ask technical questions or to comment on the book, send email to:

bookquestions@oreilly.com

The web site for *Access Hacks* lists examples, errata, and plans for future editions. You can find this page at:

http://www.oreilly.com/catalog/accesshks

For more information about this book and others, see the O'Reilly web site:

http://www.oreilly.com

Got a Hack?

To explore Hacks books online or to contribute a hack for future titles, visit:

http://hacks.oreilly.com

CHAPTER ONE

Core Access
Hacks 1–12

Access is used in many different situations, in many different ways, by a diverse group of people. Some are novices, while others have been using a single custom Access solution for years. Still others are sophisticated users who want to take advantage of the application's bells and whistles, or they are Access developers who make those bells and whistles ring and sing.

One thing all users and developers want is for Access to support their needs as efficiently as possible. This can require a little customization or a downright minisolution that's implemented inside Access and helps to support the purpose of the overall solution.

This chapter includes a collection of hacks you can implement directly within Access. You'll find hacks designed to help general users by making their experience more rewarding and more efficient. You'll also find hacks a power user can implement to expand the value of his custom Access application. You'll even find hacks that only a developer can implement. A little VBA goes a long way here.

HACK #1 Help Users Find the Objects They Need

Place shortcuts to pertinent objects in custom groups so that users don't have to wade through all the database objects.

The Access database window can be overwhelming to some users. Tables, queries, forms, reports; determining where to find objects you need within these object collections isn't exactly a user-friendly process. Besides, sometimes a user needs just a handful of objects to complete his work. And yet he might be confronted with considerably more objects than he needs.

Luckily, the Access database window allows you to create custom groupings in which you can place shortcuts to only the desired objects. Just as the

Windows desktop has shortcuts to folders, files, and applications, Access lets you make shortcuts to your database objects. And it's a cakewalk to do so!

The Plain Database Window

Your Access application might open to a *navigation*, or *main*, form. From there, users click their way through the application. But not all applications are made in this way. Figure 1-1 shows the plain database window in all its unimpressive glory. Some applications open to this functional but inefficient window.

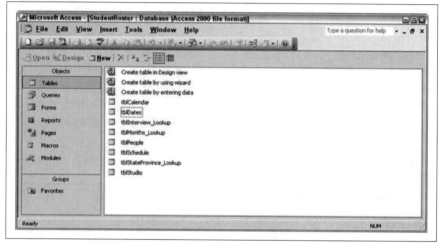

Figure 1-1. The standard Access database window

Of course, you can get to all the objects you need from here: click the Queries tab to find the queries you want to run, or click the Reports tab to find the reports you want to run. But you can avoid this drudgery. One great thing about the database window is the ability to make your own groups. In fact, it is clear that the database window does separate *objects* from *groups*. In Figure 1-1, on the left side of the database window, you can see a clear distinction of groups in the bottom half of the window.

Using Groups

By default, there is one Favorites group, in which you can place shortcuts to objects. It's easy to do; just find the object wherever it exists within the various tabs, and then click and drag it to the Favorites group. Figure 1-2 shows the result of doing just that. The Favorites group has been filled with shortcuts to some of the database objects. Note that these are *shortcuts*. The original objects are still where they belong within the object collections. You can delete a shortcut in the Favorites group, and the original object remains.

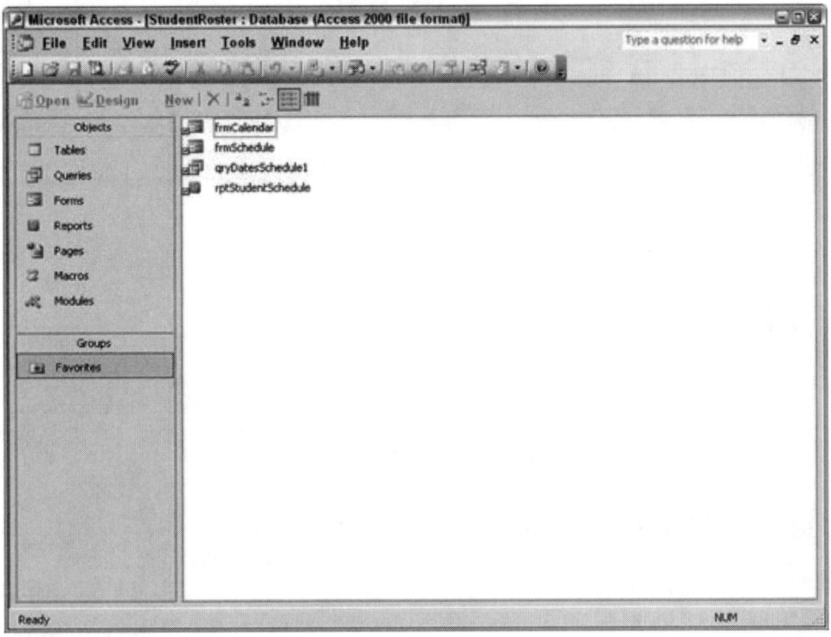

Figure 1-2. Placing shortcuts in the Favorites group

Clearly, using the Favorites group lets you focus user activity! However, you can also go a step further by adding additional groups for even better organization. How about a group for each user or type of user? For example, data entry operators and supervisors might use the same database application, but with different objects; the data entry operators might use certain forms, and supervisors or managers might use queries and reports to see overall activity.

It's easy to add a new group. Just right-click in the Groups area, select New Group from the list of options, and give the group a name. At this point you can drag objects to the new group. Figure 1-3 shows how two new groups have been added to the application. Each has its own list of shortcuts.

Another good point about groups is that the same objects can reside in more than one group. If you have a reason to place a shortcut to a particular report in three different groups, Access won't hold you back. In fact, you can even copy shortcuts from one group to another.

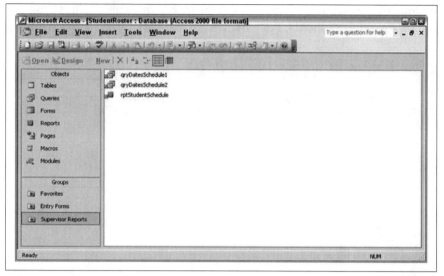

Figure 1-3. Creating and using a custom group

Personalize Your Access Application

Build personalization functionality so that users can set up the application in ways that work best for them.

There is no reason to limit all users to using an Access application in the same way. It's easy to overlook this capability because Access allows you to designate only one opening form in its startup options—that is, unless you tap into its database-opening events. Then, you can choose which form will open, what its properties are, and more. You can effectively make all facets of the application unique to a particular individual or profile. Here are a few items you can tailor this way:

Forms
Specify the opening form, how it's displayed, and what functionality it includes

Data sources
Specify which personalization tables, internal or external, are needed for each user's tasks

Reports
Show or hide details

This hack shows you how to use the AutoExec macro to run an opening function that delivers a personalized interface to the user. For this to work, you must first create a database table to store user preferences, and then, when the database starts up, you must be able to identify the user to the database. You can do this in a number of ways: for instance, a pop-up input box can ask for a name or initials (possibly with a password), a command-line switch can provide the user identity, or, if the Access security model is in use, the user ID can be made available through the CurrentUser property.

Storing Preferences

User preferences are stored in a table that has a field for each personalization facet. You determine which features to personalize. For example, a Long datatype field can store the preferred background color, a text field can store the name of the preferred opening form, and so on. Figure 1-4 shows such a table, aptly named Customized, with a few preferences filled in. The field name indicates the preference, and the actual value in the field is the setting.

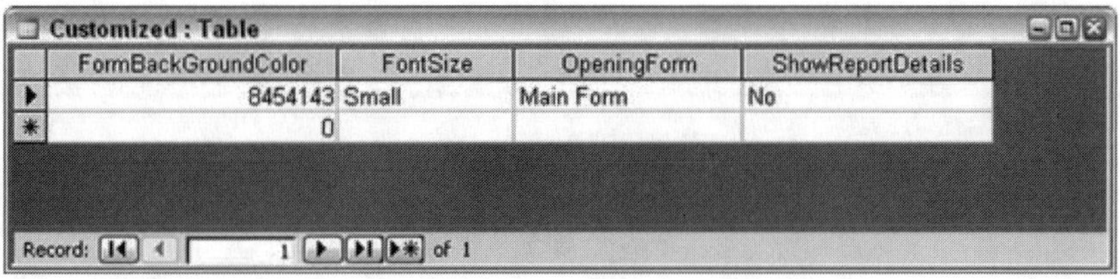

FormBackGroundColor	FontSize	OpeningForm	ShowReportDetails
8454143	Small	Main Form	No
0			

Record: 1 of 1

Figure 1-4. A table to hold single user preferences

This table is perfect for databases that are distributed to local client machines. In this configuration, only one user uses an instance of the database. Therefore, the table is structured to store the preferences of just a single user. A key point about the table is that it always has just a single record. That single record contains a field for each personalized item.

In a shared database configuration (such as when all users are using a network copy), the table needs to have an additional field to identify each user. The number of records this table ends up containing matches the number of users, plus one—that is, one record per user, plus a default record for the Admin user. Figure 1-5 shows this structure.

> It's a good idea to leave a record for the Admin user. This is the default Access user account and is present even when the security model isn't used. When no security login is used, the CurrentUser property defaults to Admin.

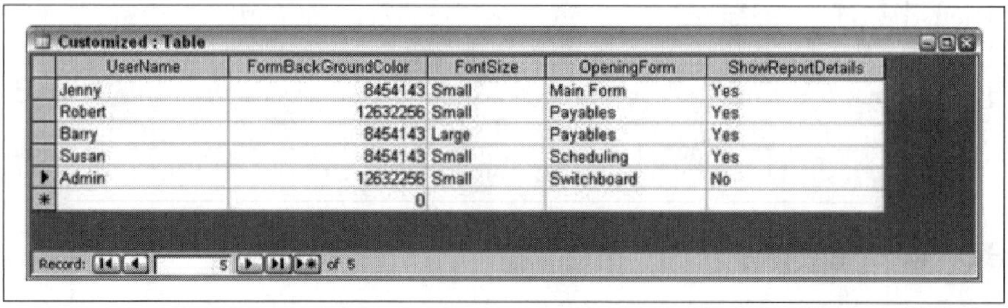

Figure 1-5. A table to hold multiple user preferences

All that's left to complete this hack is to give users a way to select their preferences. No, users aren't expected to enter such a cryptic thing as the numerical representation of a color! So, we'll use a form (what else!) to capture preferences. This unique form serves to just *manage* preferences; it has no other interaction with the database. Figure 1-6 shows the structure of such a form.

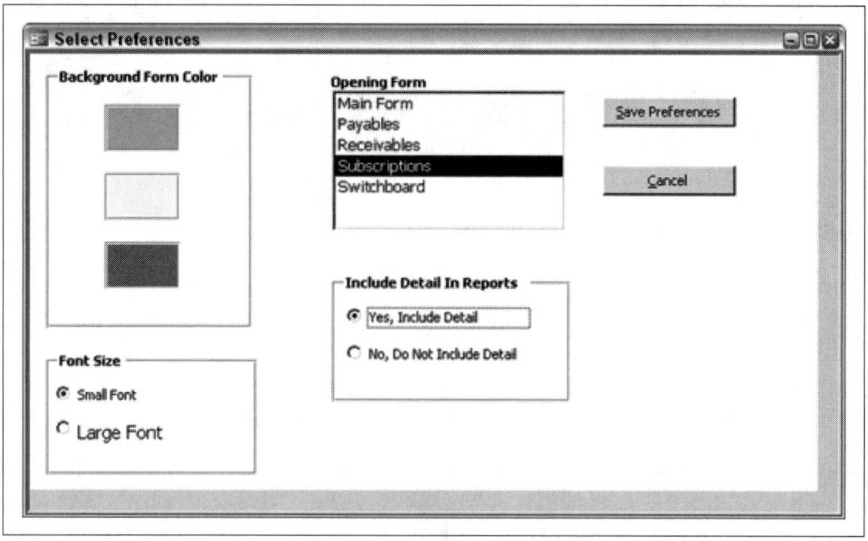

Figure 1-6. A form in which users select their preferences

Once the selections are made on the form, the Save Preferences button writes the preferences to the table. For a single-user table, a simple SQL insert does the trick, like this:

```
Update Customized Set FormBackGroundColor=8454143, FontSize='Small',
OpeningForm='Receivables', ShowReportDetails='No'
```

For the multiuser configuration, the extra field is in the SQL statement:

```
Update Customized Set FormBackGroundColor=8454143, FontSize='Small',
OpeningForm='Main Form', ShowReportDetails='Yes' Where UserName='Susan'
```

These SQL statements are assembled using the values of the form controls. ActiveX Data Objects (ADO) is used to update the values in the table. After the SQL statement is assembled, the Execute method of the Connection object runs the update:

```
Private Sub cmdSave()
  On Error GoTo err_end
  Dim conn As ADODB.Connection
  Set conn = CurrentProject.Connection
  Dim ssql As String
  ssql = "Update Customized Set " & _
    "FormBackGroundColor=" & _
    Me.groupFormColor & ", " & _
    "FontSize='" & _
    Choose(Me.groupFontSize, "Small", "Large") & "', " & _
    "OpeningForm='" & Me.lstForms & "', " & _
    "ShowReportDetails='" & _
    Choose(Me.groupReportDetail, "Yes", "No") & "'"
  conn.Execute ssql
  conn.Close
  Set conn = Nothing
  MsgBox "Preferences updated!"
  Exit Sub
err_end:
  conn.Close
  Set conn = Nothing
  MsgBox Err.Description
End Sub
```

Applying the Preferences

Just storing the preferences does nothing, so let's crack this application open a little wider. One of the preferences selects which form to display at startup. The AutoExec macro is used here to run a function that uses the last saved preference setting. As before, if this is a single-user installation, one type of table is used, but in a multiuser configuration, the username plays a role.

Here are two functions that can be called by the AutoExec macro. The AutoExec macro's RunCode action is used with the function name as the parameter. In either case, the DLookup function grabs the opening form preference and opens that form. The difference is in whether the DLookup function filters to a username. In the first function, it doesn't, but in the second function, it does:

```
Function open_up_single( )
  On Error GoTo err_end
  Dim myform As String
  myform = DLookup("OpeningForm", "Customized")
  If Not IsNull(myform) Then
    DoCmd.OpenForm myform
  Else
    DoCmd.OpenForm "Switchboard"
  End If
  Exit Function
err_end:
  MsgBox Err.Description
End Function

Function open_up_multi_user( )
  'On Error GoTo err_end
  Dim myform As String
  Dim username As String
  myform = _
    DLookup("OpeningForm", "Customized", "UserName ='" & _
    CurrentUser & "'")
  If Not IsNull(myform) Then
    DoCmd.OpenForm myform
  Else
    DoCmd.OpenForm "Switchboard"
  End If
  Exit Function
err_end:
  MsgBox Err.Description
End Function
```

Note that an If...Else block handles opening the default Switchboard form in case a null value is returned.

You need to implement how to use other types of preferences, such as including report details or using a different font size, when and where it makes sense for the given preference. For example, here's how you can change the background color of a form in the open event of the form:

```
Private Sub Form_Open(Cancel As Integer)
Me.Detail.BackColor = DLookup("FormBackGroundColor", "Customized")
End Sub
```

Using the Hack

All that's left now is to decide how to handle opening the customization form. You can make this action available on a toolbar, via a menu, or via a macro. A great idea is to put it into a custom group of commonly used objects. See "Help Users Find the Objects They Need" [Hack #1] to learn about making custom groups.

Work Fast and Avoid Typos

Save time and avoid mistakes by using simple keystrokes for entering the date, time, or other commonly used entries.

The mouse is nice, but nothing beats getting around an application faster than keyboard shortcuts. Ctrl-C for copy, Ctrl-V for paste, and so on, are pretty familiar. How about keyboard shortcuts for entering the date, time, and other data? Using these shortcuts will save valuable time when you are in a rush to finish a project. And how often are you not in a rush?

Know Thy Shortcuts

Table 1-1 summarizes useful keyboard shortcuts to use within your Access applications. This isn't an exhaustive list of keyboard shortcuts—not by a long shot! You can use the Access Help system to find all the shortcuts. The ones presented in Table 1-1 are specific shortcuts for entering data.

Table 1-1. Keyboard shortcuts for entering data

Action	Keyboard shortcut
Enter the current time.	Ctrl-:
Enter the current date.	Ctrl-;
Insert data from the same field in the previous record.	Ctrl-'
Insert the default value for the field.	Ctrl-Alt-spacebar
Insert a new line in a text or memo field.	Ctrl-Enter
Enter a new record.	Ctrl-+
Paste the contents of the Windows clipboard.	Ctrl-V

These shortcuts are quite handy. Have you ever forgotten the current date when you had to enter it in a field? Well, all you need to remember now is the keyboard shortcut to enter the current date. Which brings us to the next point...

Remember Where to Reference Shortcuts

It takes time to memorize a group of shortcuts, so the next best thing is to boil it down to memorizing just one. The twist here is to have the list of keyboard shortcuts available on a form that you can easily display using—you guessed it—a keyboard shortcut. However, you need to create this shortcut.

Using the AutoKeys Macro

The AutoKeys macro lets you assign database actions to custom keyboard shortcuts. You can assign actions to the function keys, to key combinations such as Ctrl-A, and to the Insert and Delete keys. You must follow a strict syntax, however: a carat (^) represents the Ctrl key, and a plus sign (+) represents the Shift key. You enter regular keys verbatim, and you enclose function keys and special keys (Insert and Delete) in braces ({}). Here are a few examples:

- ^A sets an action to Ctrl-A.
- {F9} sets an action to the F9 function key.
- +{F9} sets an action to Shift-F9.
- {INSERT} sets an action to the Insert key.

When you set a custom shortcut to an existing default shortcut, the custom shortcut overrides the default one. Therefore, you can override common keyboard shortcuts, such as Ctrl-V (paste), and instead provide your own.

The syntax statements are placed in the Macro Name column, and the appropriate actions are set in the Action column. The only other requirement is that the macro is actually named AutoKeys.

Figure 1-7 shows a form that lists the keyboard shortcuts. The form is based on a table that holds the shortcuts and their descriptions in two respective fields. An alternative is to just use label controls in which the shortcuts and descriptions have been entered.

Keyboard Shortcuts		
Description	**Keyboard Shortcut**	
Enter the current time	CTRL + Shift + :	
Enter the current date	CTRL + ;	
Insert data from the same field in the previous record	CTRL + '	
Insert the default value for the field	CTRL + ALT + Spaceba	
Insert a new line in a text or memo field	CTRL + Enter	
Enter a new record	CTRL ++	
Paste the contents of the Windows clipboard	CTRL + V	

Figure 1-7. A quick-reference form for keyboard shortcuts

A function key is easy enough to remember. F9 is a good one to target because it isn't commonly used. By contrast, F1 isn't a great choice because it's the standard for entering the Help system. To establish a custom keyboard shortcut, use the special AutoKeys macro. The AutoKeys macro is activated at startup in the same fashion as the AutoExec macro.

Figure 1-8 shows the AutoKeys macro set up with a few custom keyboard shortcuts. Pressing F9 opens the frmKeyboardShortcuts form shown in Figure 1-7.

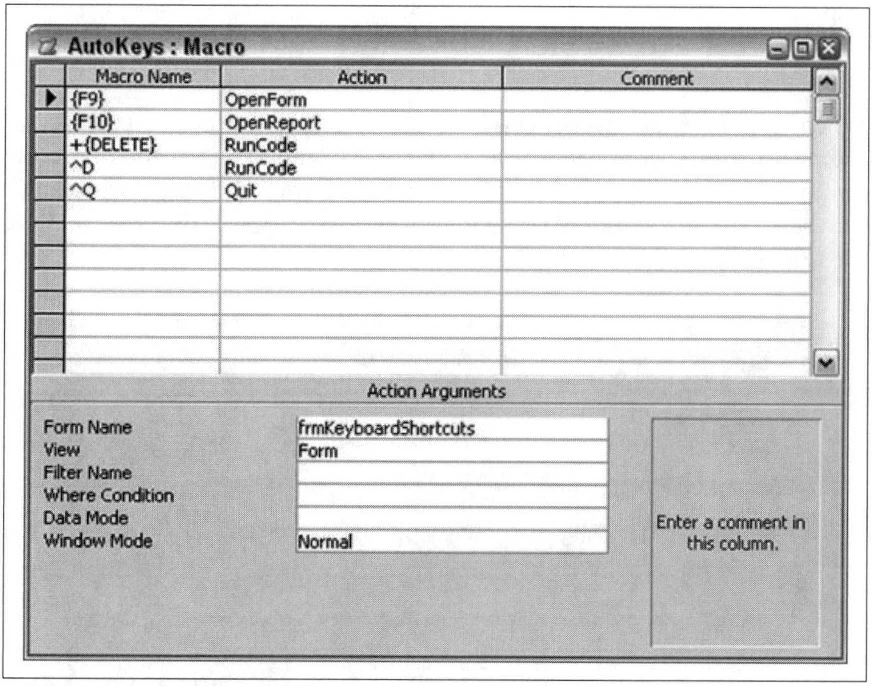

⬚ AutoKeys : Macro			
Macro Name	Action	Comment	
▶ {F9}	OpenForm		
{F10}	OpenReport		
+{DELETE}	RunCode		
^D	RunCode		
^Q	Quit		

Action Arguments

Form Name	frmKeyboardShortcuts
View	Form
Filter Name	
Where Condition	
Data Mode	
Window Mode	Normal

Enter a comment in this column.

Figure 1-8. Using the AutoKeys macro to set up custom keyboard shortcuts

HACK
#4

Optimize Data Changes

Avoid having to propagate data changes manually throughout related tables by establishing cascading updates and deletes.

The one constant you can count on is change. Why not plan for this eventuality in your applications? Take a real example: a customer changes her name. If you are in business long enough, this is something you will need to accommodate in your database.

Data changes need to be propagated in two ways. If the data isn't used as a table key or a foreign key, you need to change the data in all the places it resides in your tables. Hopefully, your data resides in only one place! A correctly modeled database holds a piece of data, such as a customer name, in just one place. If you do have such a piece of data in a few places, however, you presumably have a reason for doing this. Applications grow over time and often are handled by a succession of developers. It happens.

If you have database applications in which the same data is found all over the place, a brush up on data modeling is in order.

What about data that exists in table keys? This can be a frustrating change to propagate if many child tables use the data as the foreign key. That is, it will be frustrating unless you plan your relationships with cascading updates.

When creating relationships between tables, one option is to establish cascading updates. Figure 1-9 shows two tables of data. The tblCustomers table on top has customer information. The values in the key field, CustomerID, are the initials of the actual company names. In the lower tblInvoices table, the CustomerID serves as the foreign key.

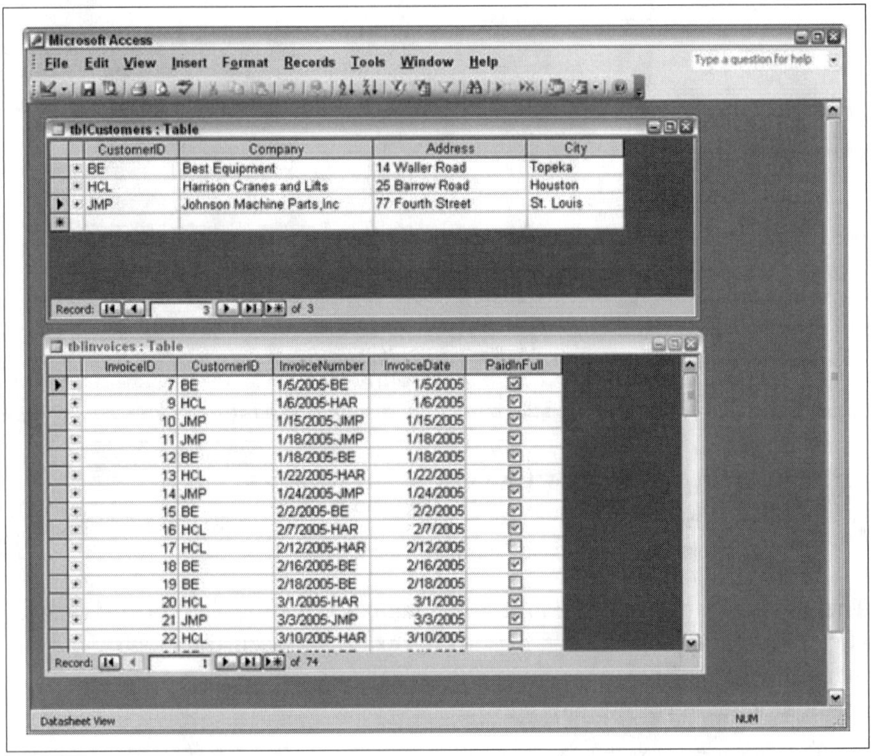

Figure 1-9. Related tables

Figure 1-10 confirms the relationship between the tables. A line leads from the CustomerID field in tblCustomers to the CustomerID field in tblInvoices. The number 1 on the tblCustomers table side of the line indicates that tblCustomers is the parent table. The infinity symbol (∞) above where the line meets the tblInvoices table indicates that tblInvoices is the child table. This is a *one-to-many* relationship. The tblInvoices table has other relationships as well.

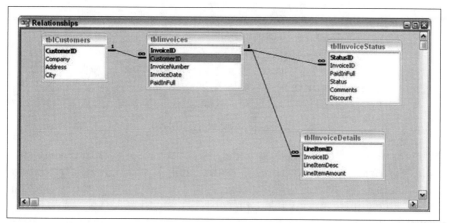

Figure 1-10. The Relationships window

The Edit Relationships dialog box, shown in Figure 1-11, is where you set relationships. To open the dialog in the Relationships window, double-click on a line that connects two tables. Note the Cascade Update Related Fields checkbox. When this box is checked, changing the value in the key field of the parent table automatically changes the values in the related field in the child table. This is a good thing! When a customer changes her name, all you have to do is change the value in the key. All the occurrences of the value in the child table automatically change to the new value.

In the example shown in Figure 1-9, if Best Equipment changes its name to Best Tools, the CustomerID value should be changed to BT. Making this change once in the tblCustomers table automatically updates all related records in the tblInvoices table.

 Another option in the Edit Relationships dialog box (Figure 1-11) is to establish cascading deletes. The Cascade Delete Related Records setting ensures that when you delete a record in the parent table, all related records in child tables are also deleted. When this option isn't set, you have to delete the records in the child table first, and then you can delete the records in the parent table.

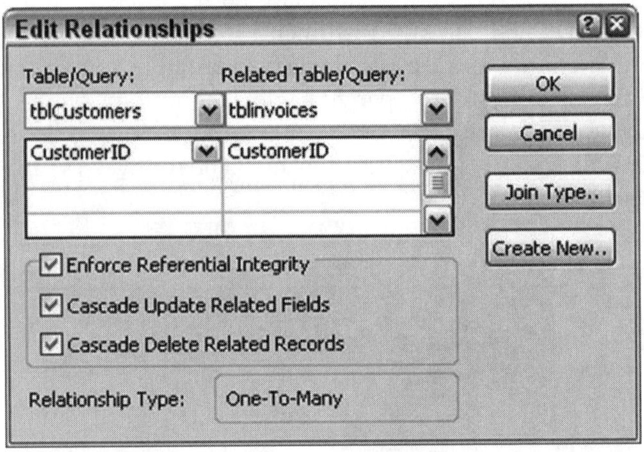

Figure 1-11. Selecting to use cascading updates and deletes

If the option to have cascading updates isn't set, you have to change each table's records separately. You can do that only if you remove the relationship first because Access doesn't let you change the values in the key field in either table if there are any related records. Trying to make an update in that way is quite messy.

HACK #5   Transfer Data Between Versions of Access

Say goodbye to version incompatibility issues.

Microsoft has released more than half a dozen versions of Access over the years. Some people and organizations buy into each upgrade, some skip around, and some hold on for dear life to the one they have been using since the previous century! The version doesn't matter when you or your organization work in a vacuum, but when you exchange data with external companies, version incompatibility can rear its ugly head.

Let's say you have Access 2003 and you send a database filled with your orders to a vendor. The vendor has Access 95. Uh-oh! The vendor can't open your database.

One of the recent data technologies initiated throughout the computing world is the use of XML and other platform-neutral protocols. This purportedly removes data incompatibility. XML is nice, but only the most recent versions of Access can read XML.

The way to share data is via a tried-and-true, low-key, low-tech method: export and save your data as text. Although they vary in terms of how text can be saved—delimited, type of delimiter character, text qualifier, fixed-width, and so on—all versions of Access can read and write text files. Figure 1-12 shows the Export Text Wizard, in which you set your text export options. When you initiate to export an Access table or query and select text as the type, the wizard starts up.

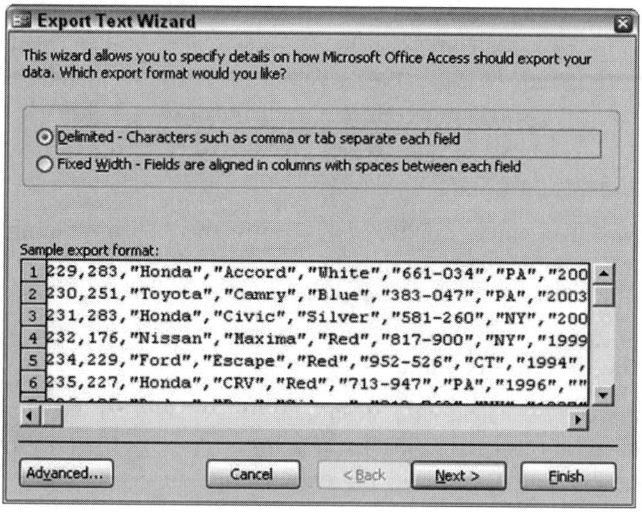

Figure 1-12. Using the Export Text Wizard

Admittedly, exporting and importing text isn't an ideal approach, especially when you have to export or import many tables of data. But it sure beats losing business because your client can't open your database.

XML has paved the way for easy data exchange among versions and systems. XML support is decent enough in Access 2003, less so in Access 2002 and Access 2000. If working with text files just doesn't seem right for your needs, you can always use XML. A separate external XML parser does the trick.

See Also

- "Provide Complete XML Control to Any Version of Access" **[Hack #87]**
- "Use Access as an XML Database" **[Hack #95]**

HACK
#6

Organize and Enhance Your Macros

Optimize and reduce the number of macros using the optional name and condition columns.

Macros are often used for small automations—usually for tasks that aren't too complex or sophisticated because VBA is available to handle the heavy processing. Let's think that way no more. Actually, macros can handle a decent amount of intelligent processing and, in fact, have a condition-testing ability similar to the If...Then structure in VBA. This hack shows you how to transform a single macro into a multipurpose workhorse.

Conditional Macro Actions

Macros have but a single mandatory column: the Action column. A macro can have one or more actions. However, macros also have an optional Condition column, in which a little entry can go a long way toward adding some punch to the process. When you're designing a macro, use the View menu to display the Condition column.

A condition can test a field value, evaluate the result returned by a function, and even use the returned value from a message box. Conditions also can use Boolean logic, incorporating *and/or*-type logic in the condition testing.

Figure 1-13 shows a macro in which a series of actions occur when the macro is run. A few of the actions run only when their condition is met. For instance, the End of Month function and the End of Month report are included in the processing only when it is the first day of the month (presumably tallying up figures about the month that just ended). Using the Day and Now functions takes care of testing for the first day of the month.

The Employee Bonus report runs only when a condition tested with a DLookup function is true.

The unconditional actions in the macro always run. Even when the actions with unmet conditions are passed over, the macro continues to run and doesn't stop prematurely.

Creating Macro Groups

Macros can also be organized into groups, known as *macro groups*. By creating macro groups, you can reduce the number of overall macros and keep similar macro actions together in one place. The key difference between a macro and a macro group is the use of the optional Macro Name column.

When you're designing macros, use the View menu to display the Macro Name column. Figure 1-14 shows a macro group named RunReport. The

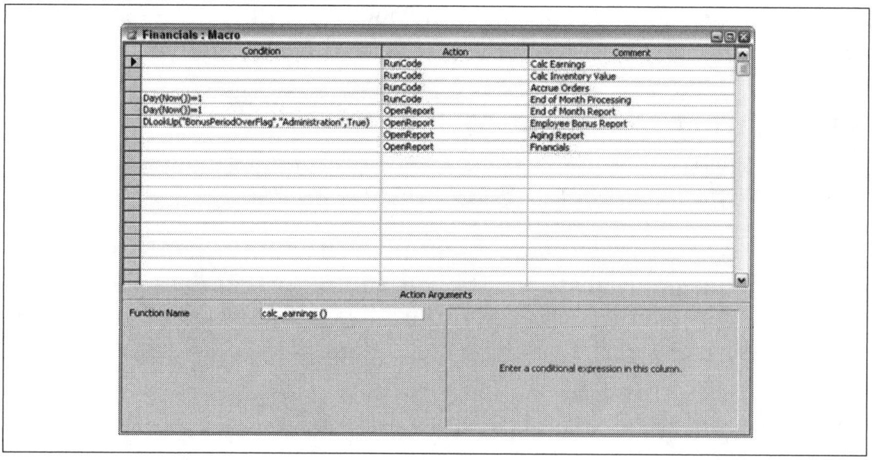

Figure 1-13. Using conditions in a macro

macro group handles the task of opening a number of individual reports. An important point, though, is that these reports won't open at the same time. Each macro name exists as a separate macro within the larger group.

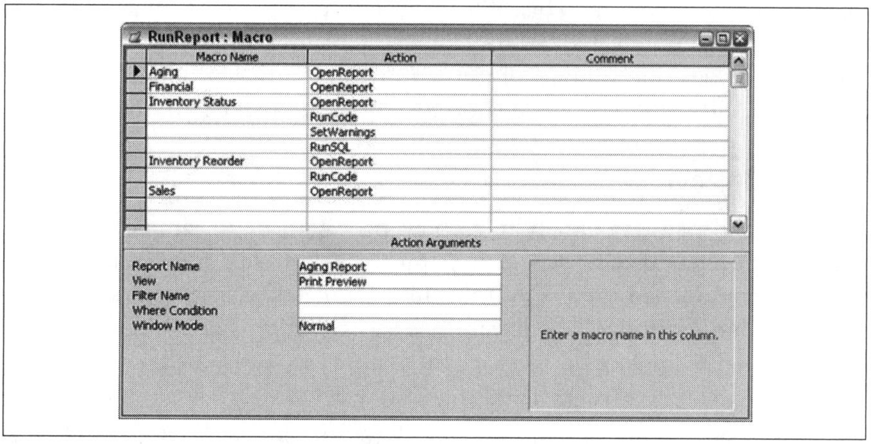

Figure 1-14. Using the Macro Name column

When a particular action needs to be initiated, you use the name of the macro group, a dot qualifier, and the name in the Macro Name column, like this:

```
DoCmd.RunMacro "RunReport.Inventory Status"
```

The point where the action starts is the row with the macro name. Successive actions will run until another macro name is encountered. Not all rows require a value in the Macro Name column. This is the beauty of macro groups. One cohesive design houses any number of smaller action sets. The benefit is a cleaner and easier-to-manage macro implementation.

Rid Your Database of Clutter

#7

Implement an object-use log to clean up an overloaded database by analyzing user actions and then deleting never-used objects.

Some Access database applications just get plain ugly. If you have ever browsed through a database with dozens and dozens of forms and reports, you know what I am referring to. This is often the result of a user community turned loose: forms for every point and purpose; a report for each day of the week; and then some.

Adding insult to injury, you can't easily tell which objects the users are actually using. Luckily, there is a way to reign in the application and reduce the clutter.

The goal is to find out which objects are no longer being used. Often, users create forms or reports that they use once and never look at again. Once you've identified which objects are no longer being used, you can delete them from the database. This will likely improve the performance of the database and certainly reduce its memory footprint after you compact it. The trick to deleting unused objects is to create a list of objects that are being used and then to delete the objects that didn't make it on the list.

Tracking Object Use

All forms and reports contain an open event. By putting a simple code routine into all open events, you can populate a log with the names of the objects being opened. Before you do this, you need to create a log table to store the object names. This doesn't need to be fancy; indeed, the log table can have just a single field to store the names. Optional fields can store a timestamp, the type of object, and so forth.

Figure 1-15 shows the design of such a table. It comprises two fields: one captures the object name, and the other captures the object type. The table receives a record each time an object is opened.

To append a record to the log table, an object must have a little bit of code in its open event. Here is a snippet that would go into the open event of a form named Customers:

```
Private Sub Form_Open(Cancel As Integer)
    Dim conn As ADODB.Connection
    Set conn = CurrentProject.Connection
    Dim ssql As String
```

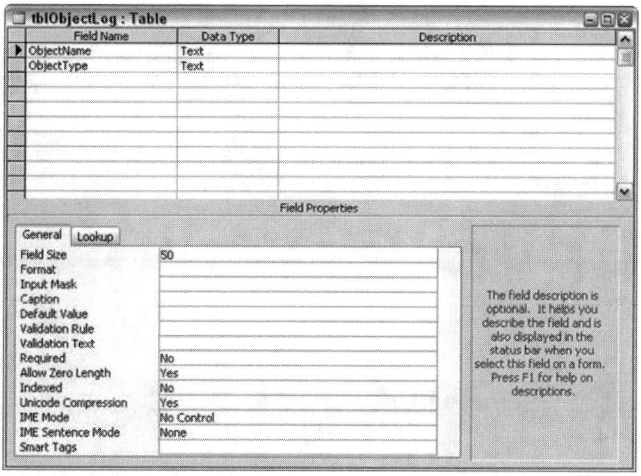

Figure 1-15. A table for logging objects as they are opened

```
    ssql = "Insert Into tblObjectLog Values ('Customers', 'Form')"
    conn.Execute ssql
    conn.Close
    Set conn = Nothing
End Sub
```

When the form is opened, a record is written into the log with the form's name and object type. You should put similar code into the open event of all forms and reports. Then let your users use the database again, and watch the log table begin to fill up. After a reasonable amount of time—a week, a month, whatever makes sense—examine the log table. You will see numerous entries. If a timestamp field was not used, you will see quite a number of duplicate records. Use a Select query with a Group By aggregate clause to view the results without seeing duplicates.

Identifying Unused Objects

Figure 1-16 displays a query of the Object log table. The listed objects represent the definitive list of objects users are opening. You can compare this list to the full list of forms and reports in the database, and you can safely delete the forms and reports that aren't on the list as long as you're comfortable that enough time has passed. Don't forget to compact the database after deleting the objects!

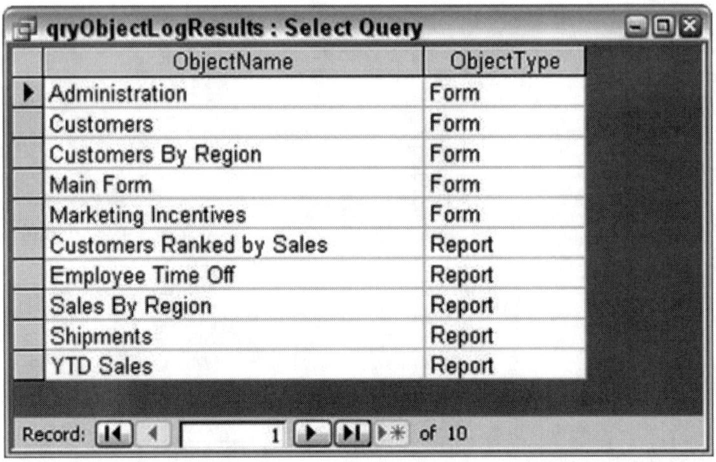

qryObjectLogResults : Select Query

ObjectName	ObjectType
Administration	Form
Customers	Form
Customers By Region	Form
Main Form	Form
Marketing Incentives	Form
Customers Ranked by Sales	Report
Employee Time Off	Report
Sales By Region	Report
Shipments	Report
YTD Sales	Report

Record: 1 of 10

Figure 1-16. Reviewing used database objects

Hacking the Hack

Part of this hack concerns the necessity to add code to the opening routine of all the forms and reports. What a manual hassle! However, you can automate this task. Here is an example of code that updates the open events of all the reports in the database:

```
Public Sub insert_open_report_event()
  ' !! Make sure all reports are closed before running !!
  Dim rpt As AccessObject
  For Each rpt In CurrentProject.AllReports
    DoCmd.OpenReport rpt.Name, acViewDesign
    With Reports(0).Module
      On Error Resume Next
      open_proc_start = .ProcBodyLine("Report_Open", vbext_pk_Proc)
      If Error <> 0 Then
        'has no open event, so create one
        Err.Clear
        open_proc_start = .CreateEventProc("Open", "Report")
      End If
      .InsertLines open_proc_start + 1, _
        "Dim conn as ADODB.Connection"
      .InsertLines open_proc_start + 2, _
        "Set conn =CurrentProject.Connection"
      .InsertLines open_proc_start + 3, _
        "Dim ssql as String"
      .InsertLines open_proc_start + 4, _
        "ssql = ""Insert Into tblObjectLog Values('" & _
        Reports(0).Name & "', 'Report')"""
      .InsertLines open_proc_start + 5, _
        "conn.Execute ssql"
```

```
    .InsertLines open_proc_start + 6, _
        "conn.Close"
    .InsertLines open_proc_start + 7, _
        "Set conn = Nothing"
   End With
   DoCmd.Close acReport, Reports(0).Name, acSaveYes
  Next
  MsgBox "All Reports Updated"
 End Sub
```

This code routine works with the module behind the report. This is actual VBA that writes VBA—kinda neat! Basically, each report is opened in Design mode; code is then inserted into the report's code module. You can develop a similar routine to work with forms, too; you'll need to address the AllForms collection instead of the AllReports collection.

HACK #8   Protect Valuable Information

Protect your data using the read-only command-line switch so that users can't edit the data.

Creating a desktop shortcut to a database provides a behind-the-scenes benefit. Specifically, you can use command-line switches that are unseen by all but the technically curious.

In this manner, it is easy to set up a shortcut to open a database in read-only mode and, thus protect your data and design elements. To do this, add the /ro switch at the end of the target string in the desktop shortcut. Note that the full target string isn't just the path to the database; it needs to start with the path to the Access executable, followed by the database path, followed by the switch.

Using Access 2003, which by default is in the standard *Program Files/ Microsoft Office/Office 11* directory, the full target string looks like this:

```
"C:\Program Files\Microsoft Office\OFFICE11\MSACCESS.EXE"
"C:\Sales Summaries\Sales2005.mdb" /ro
```

When the desktop shortcut is clicked, the database opens in read-only mode. A confirmation message is presented at startup, shown in Figure 1-17. Data can't be added, deleted, or edited.

This is a great way to disseminate information without concern for data integrity issues. Distributing the database application in such a way that a desktop shortcut is created or updated guarantees that the database opens in just the way you intended.

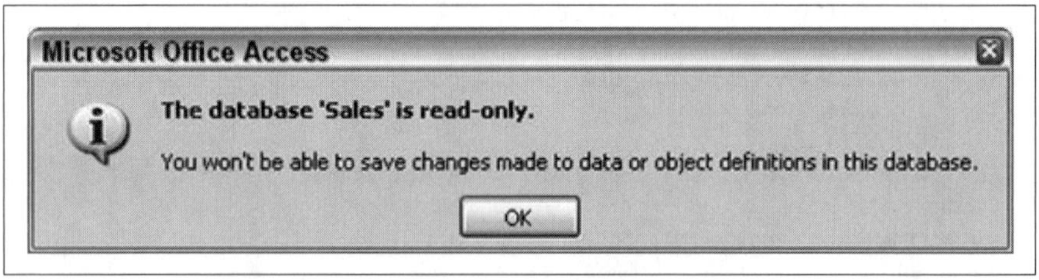

Figure 1-17. A reminder about the read-only status

But Just in Case

Of course, a half-savvy user can just start up Access and open the database via the Open dialog, thus bypassing the desktop shortcut. The database is then opened in full read/write mode, unless a gotcha is in place to prevent this.

To handle this, you can place a simple SQL Insert operation in the database's opening routine, and you can include an extra table in the database for just this purpose. If the operation succeeds, the user is warned to use the desktop shortcut (as shown in Figure 1-18), and the database closes.

Figure 1-18. Catching users who try to skip using the desktop shortcut

The Code

Here's the routine that tests a SQL Insert:

```
Public Function test_mode( )
  On Error GoTo err_end
  Dim conn As ADODB.Connection
  Set conn = CurrentProject.Connection
  Dim ssql As String
  ssql = "Insert Into tblModeTest Values ('test')"
  conn.Execute ssql
  conn.Close
  Set conn = Nothing
```

```
    'if got this far then database is not in read only mode
    'tell user, then quit
    MsgBox "Database must be opened through desktop shortcut"
    DoCmd.Quit
    Exit Function
err_end:
    'all is well, an error was expected
End Function
```

There is a twist to this: the database is supposed to be in read-only mode, so the optimal outcome is that the operation will fail instead of succeed. An error trap is implemented in the routine, so if the error is triggered, all is well, and no action is taken. If the insert succeeds, the warning is displayed, and the Quit method closes the database. This routine should be called by the AutoExec macro so that it runs immediately when the database opens.

Work with Any Amount of Data

Plan a multiple-database architecture to house any amount of data—gigabytes, even terabytes!

The only size limit in Access is that a table can't contain more than 1GB of data. Well, if that's it, there is a lot of opportunity here. Access isn't cut out for incredibly large stores of data, granted, but that's not the point. If SQL Server or Oracle isn't going to be installed at your place of business for another year, take advantage of Access's flexible architecture to work with any amount of data.

The technique is simply to make a plan for how to structure the data among multiple database files and tables. There is no rule that says an Access application must reside completely in a single Access file. An Access application can be split into a front end and a back end. That is, the forms, reports, and queries stay in the front end, and the data itself is put into a separate file. The data tables are then linked to the front end. This is standard fare, the quintessential client/server in its simplest execution, shown here in Figure 1-19.

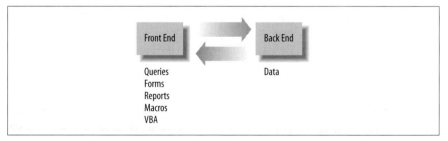

Figure 1-19. A simple front-end/back-end configuration

Splitting Up Data

There is no reason to be limited to a single file on the back end. The organization of and facts about the data will drive the decisions concerning how it can be parsed into smaller data stores. For example, if you are working with a large customer base, you can split the data from one data table into 26 tables—one for each letter of the alphabet. Figure 1-20 shows such a configuration.

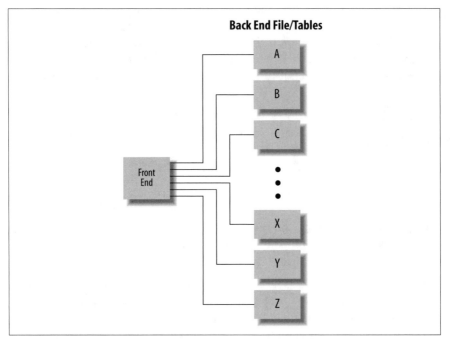

Figure 1-20. *Using multiple databases on the back end*

An alternative is to split a customer list by city, state, province, or other geographic delimiter. Again, this allows you to take an overwhelmingly large set of data and turn it into manageably smaller (albeit still large) stores of data.

Splitting the data is the key to this hack. Analyze the data, and come up with a game plan. Perhaps the data is date-based. You can split it up by month, day, or whatever makes sense.

Working with Split Data

There is an unwelcome side effect to splitting data. In a relational system, you lose the simplicity of relying on the established relationships when data is split out to additional tables. Picture this: you have a master table of customers and a related table of customer purchases. You split the customers into 10 smaller tables. What happens to the relationship? You can work around this problem in two ways.

One way is to relate the purchases table to all 10 master tables. The other is to leave out the relationships altogether and instead incorporate behind-the-scenes processing to wed data back together as needed by front-end activity.

This isn't as complicated as it might sound. In a nutshell, VBA and ADO work together to find customers and purchases that match based on whatever criteria are being selected in the front end. A workable approach to find purchases that match a criterion is to create a recordset or array of records from the purchases table, and then run these records against the 10 customer tables while looking for a match on the key fields. No, this isn't an eloquent or particularly efficient way of processing data. However, it enables Access to work with gigabytes or more of data, and that is the measure of success in this case.

HACK #10 Find Database Objects in a Snap

Use the description property to prevent users from being overwhelmed by sifting through cryptic-sounding forms, queries, and reports.

Many of us follow naming conventions when creating database objects. Among the developer community, we have come to recognize and take for granted that tbl, frm, rpt, and other prefixes are part and parcel of our work. For example, tblStaff is a table, frmAdmin is a form, and rptContacts is a report.

However, when you complete a database with several objects that are named in this way, it's a challenge to the average database user to understand the names. Figure 1-21 shows a perfect example of a database with several forms.

There is a way to resolve this dilemma, and it doesn't mean developers have to change their naming habits. All database objects can be given a *description*. The best thing is that you can enter descriptions for objects directly in the database window without having to open an object in Design mode.

In the database window, just right-click an object, and from the menu that appears, click Properties. A small dialog box opens for you to enter a natural-sounding description, as shown in Figure 1-22.

After you enter descriptions for all the objects, just be sure to list the database objects in List view instead of Icons view. This makes the descriptions visible. Figure 1-23 shows how the group of forms in Figure 1-21 is now understandable.

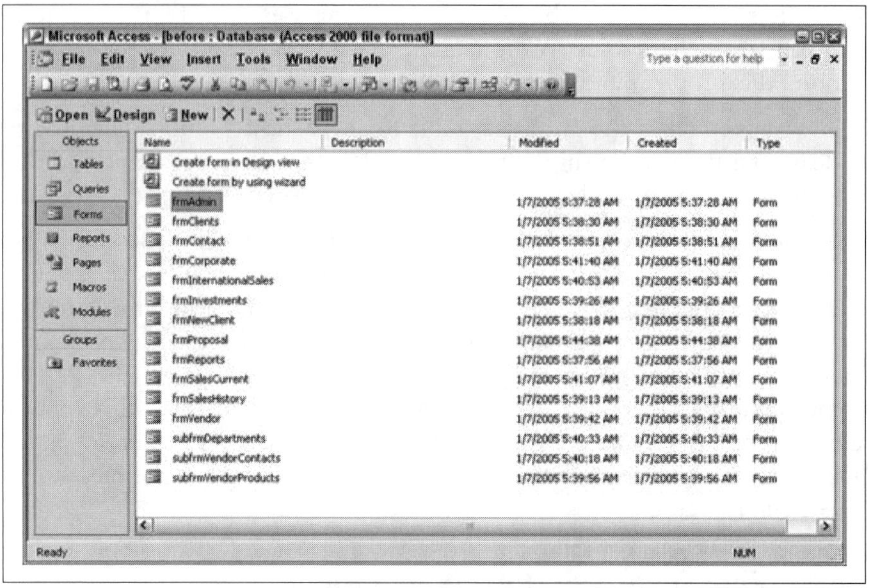

Find Database Objects in a Snap

Figure 1-21. Cryptic form names that can stump a user

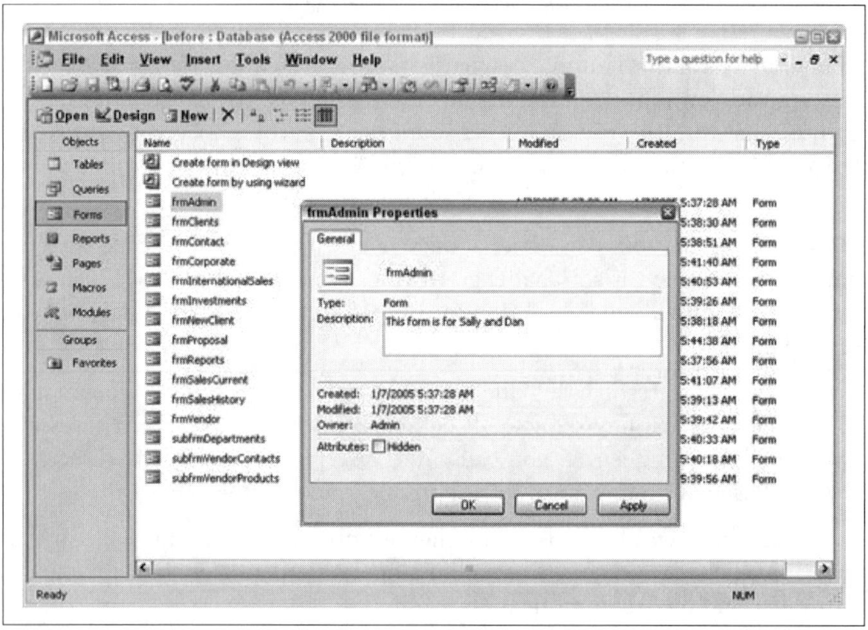

Figure 1-22. Entering a description

A neat thing about this approach is that you can even use a warning message so that users know not to open an object. This is particularly helpful in

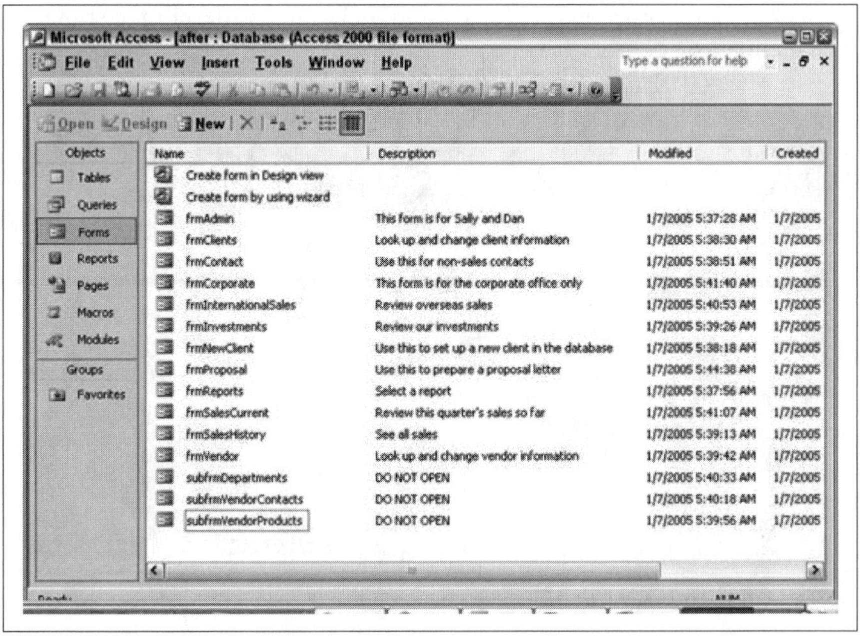

Figure 1-23. Selecting a form by its description

the case of subforms. Users shouldn't open subforms directly because they appear inside other forms. The description tells users not to open them.

—Kirk Lamb

HACK #11 Use a Junction Table

Correctly model a many-to-many relationship.

It's easy to fall into the trap of assuming all relationships are of the *one-to-many* type. It's true that many data relationships do follow the one-to-many paradigm. For example, one person has zero or more telephone numbers. However, not all data is meant to be modeled in this way.

A perfect example of data that appears to fit the one-to-many model, but doesn't, is the relationship between instructors and students. On the one hand, one instructor does have many students, thereby proving a one-to-many relationship exists. On the other hand, one student has many instructors—which is also a one-to-many relationship. So, what is the problem?

Figure 1-24 shows one way to model instructors and students. The instructor table occupies the *one* spot and the student table occupies the *many* spot. Instructors and students get together for appointments. This model works but emphasizes that instructors are of a different level than students, which might not be true.

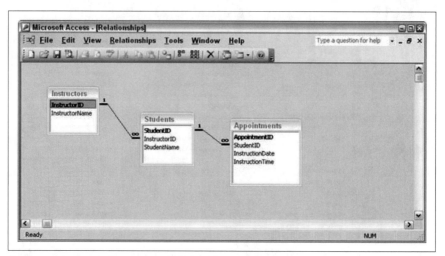

Figure 1-24. An inefficient one-to-many relationship

In Figure 1-24, the student table is also required to have the instructor ID as the foreign key. This is acceptable, but now look at the appointments table; it considers appointments as belonging to students, but appointments belong to both instructors and students.

Figure 1-25 shows how to resolve the dilemma in the data model. Because appointments belong to both instructors and students, that is how the model should look. The appointments table serves as a *junction* table between instructors and students.

A junction table becomes the *many* table for two or more other tables. All the key fields of the *one* tables become foreign keys in the junction table. Any other pertinent fields are included in the junction table. In this example, the junction table has fields for the date and time the instructor and student will meet. Also, the student table no longer has the instructor ID as a foreign key. In this example, instructors and students have no hierarchy; therefore, it makes sense that one doesn't serve as a *many* to the other.

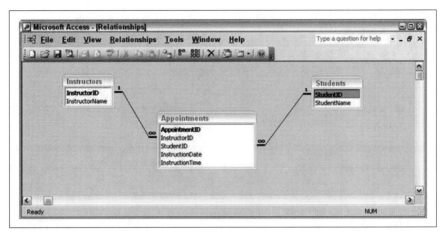

Figure 1-25. A better model

Stop the Database from Growing

Use the Compact on Close option to keep a database from getting too big.

Access databases are notorious for their ability to grow in size. This is especially true as data is moved in and out. For example, when a database application regularly imports data, processes the data, and then exports it back out, the database can become huge, on the order of several megabytes in size. This can be the case even when the data moving in and out is of a reasonable size.

To shrink the database back to the size it should be, you need to *compact* the database. However, expecting users to compact their databases isn't a great idea, especially if your users aren't technically savvy. Luckily, Access includes an option to compact a database when it is closed. This option was not available in older versions of Access, but it is available in Access 2002 and Access 2003.

Figure 1-26 shows the Options dialog box (Tools → Options) with the General tab on top. Note the Compact on Close checkbox.

Access is unlike other products, such as SQL Server, in that it doesn't allow you to control the size of the database. Setting the database to compact each time it closes removes what has traditionally been a recurring problem with Access.

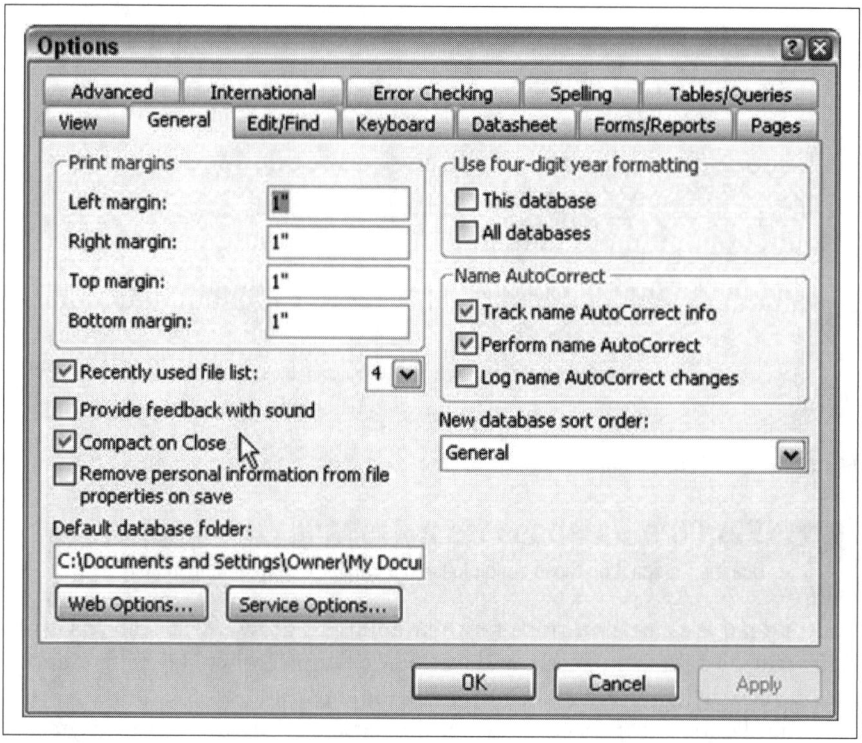

Figure 1-26. Selecting to compact on close

Tables
Hacks 13–18

Were it not for tables, we would have no place to store data! Tables are straightforward; they comprise rows and columns, or records and fields. So, what is there to hack?

Table design is one area in which a little customization goes a long way. Changing the default datatype and other properties speeds up development time. Without this intervention, text fields default to 50 characters. Is this a good size? That depends on your project.

Have you ever wished you could implement triggers the way SQL Server does? You can! Use the inherent events available to forms to get the same results.

Need to hide data? There's a hack for that, too!

HACK #13 Create an AutoNumber Field with a Custom Value

The AutoNumber field doesn't need to begin with a value of 1. You can override Access's default autonumbering scheme to better suit your requirements.

A great feature that Access brings to the table-creation process is the AutoNumber field. This field type places a value of 1 in the first record and automatically increases the value by 1 as records are added. It doesn't contain any significant or meaningful data. Its basic purpose is to become the key field and thereby provide uniqueness to the data records.

Just plop a field into the table design, and designate it as an AutoNumber field. Typically such a field has a name with ID or Num in it, such as CustomerID or RecordNum. Note that a table can have only one AutoNumber field.

All in all, AutoNumber is a great feature, but there is one gotcha: the value always starts at 1. Often, this isn't an issue because the field value really is unimportant. The fact that the values are *unique* is what matters more. But what if you need to use a self-incrementing number that starts at a different value? Can you do this? Of course!

Seeding AutoNumber with a Number of Your Choice

The AutoNumber field type doesn't have a property to specify the starting value. Figure 2-1 shows a table design. As you can see, the first field is an AutoNumber field, and its addressable properties fill the lower-left area of the table design window. Note that you have nowhere to input a default start value.

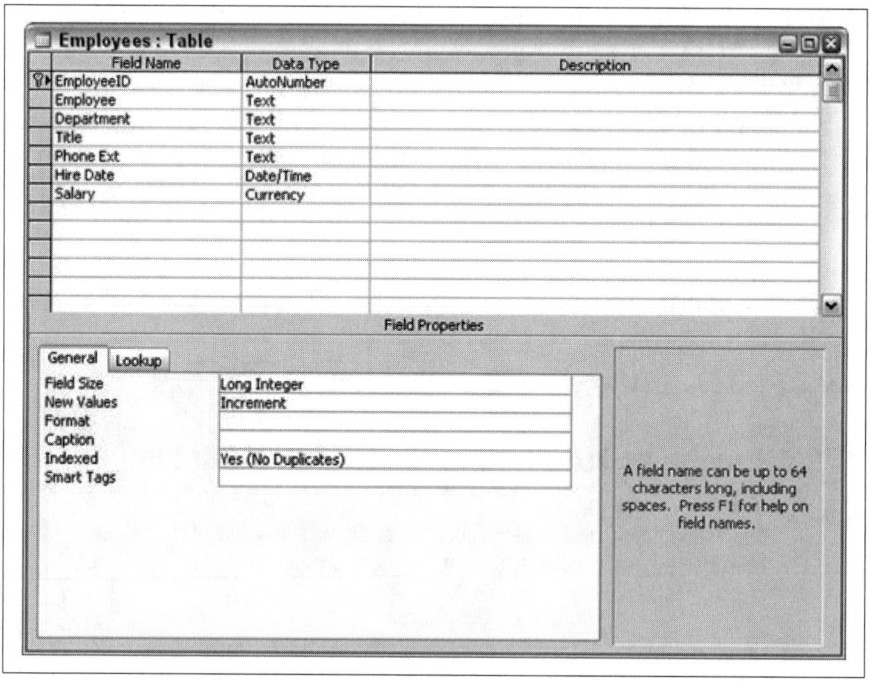

Figure 2-1. AutoNumber, an incrementing field type

To be clear, the table does contain a New Values property, but all it tells you is whether new values are incremented or are random. It tells you nothing about starting the increment at a value of your choice. So, the first record will have a value of 1 in the field, the second record will have a value of 2 in the field, and so on.

To override the default starting value of 1, you can use an Append query to insert a different starting value. After you have designed the table and are ready to use it, you must get the initial value in place. Figure 2-2 shows an Append query that specifically places a value in the AutoNumber field. That is, one record gets added to the table, with the AutoNumber field receiving the designated value.

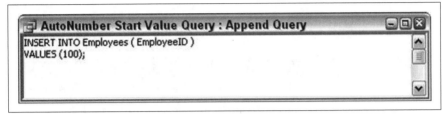

Figure 2-2. Using a query to set the beginning AutoNumber value

Note that you enter this query in the SQL view. That's because it's not obvious how to enter this query in the design view (the query grid), in which Append queries are typically used to append one table to another. This operation works by appending a value to a field in a table with no other table involved (in a pinch, you can design another table just to hold the value, but you don't have to do so).

Figure 2-3 shows the results of running the Append query. The Employees table was empty but now it contains its first record, and the AutoNumber value for that record is 100.

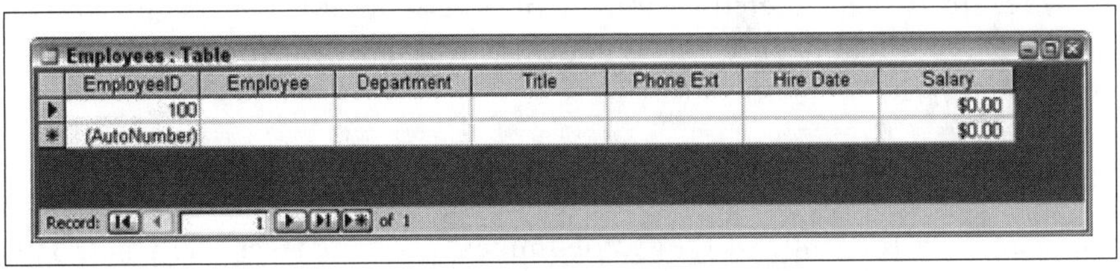

EmployeeID	Employee	Department	Title	Phone Ext	Hire Date	Salary
100						$0.00
(AutoNumber)						$0.00

Record: |◄◄| ◄ | 1 | ►|►I|►*| of 1

Figure 2-3. The first record with the designated starting AutoNumber value

Note that no other fields have been populated yet. If any other fields must have a value, you must populate them with appropriate values in the query. For example, you can modify the query to populate additional fields, such as Employee and Title, like this:

```
INSERT INTO Employees (EmployeeID, Employee, Title)
VALUES (100, 'John Smith', 'Supervisor');
```

Figure 2-4 shows the result of applying this new query. On the surface, this seems to take care of two birds with one stone—starting the AutoNumber with a value of your choice, yet without using a dummy record (as in Figure 2-3) to do so. However, this approach can be problematic. It's a little odd to populate the first record in this manner and then to populate all subsequent records via forms, processing, or other methods. The point is that it probably isn't practical to populate the first record in any method that differs from how other records are inserted.

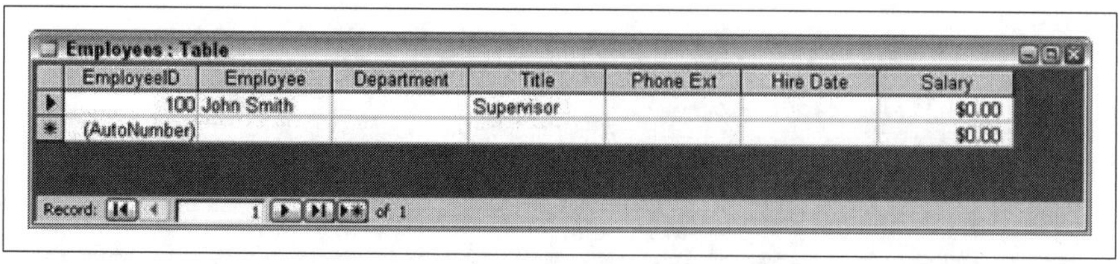

Figure 2-4. Using a query to fill the AutoNumber field, along with other fields

But how can you get the first record to have the desired starting AutoNumber value without having a dummy record as the first record in your table? The twist is to still populate the first record using a query, but to populate the AutoNumber field with a value of one less than the real starting value. You can then delete this record, and the AutoNumber will increment as subsequent records are added. This means the first real data record, entered in whatever way your system handles it, will have the first value of choice. The AutoNumber will just increment from there, as expected.

In the example shown in this hack, the query needs to populate the table with a single record, in which a value of 99 is given to the AutoNumber. That record is then deleted (manually or otherwise; it doesn't matter how). When the first real data record is added, it will have an AutoNumber value of 100.

Hacking the Hack

You can reset the value of the AutoNumber field whenever you want. This doesn't change the existing records. It lets new records be numbered starting from a new initial value. You just run the Append query, as shown in Figure 2-2 (adjusted as discussed to handle any other required fields), but reset the value to one that is higher than the highest value already in the table. For example, if the last record entered in the table has a value of 220, reset the count to something higher. Obviously, you would skip the next incremental number; otherwise, there would be no reason to reestablish where the increment begins.

This offers an interesting option for managing your data. What if a series of records in a table has some unobvious but related attribute? For example, you can reset the AutoNumber field to a new starting value at the start of each year. Then, each year's data will be easy to distinguish. For example, all records in the year 2005 might lie within the 5,000–5,999 range, all records for 2006 within the 6,000–6,999 range, and so on.

HACK #14 Copy Data Between Tables Without an Append Query

Use Paste Append to easily copy data across tables.

Access users often use an Append query to append records from one table to another. In a production environment in which data is always being shuffled around, using Append queries can become tedious. Each time you design one, you have to match the fields of the destination table with the fields of the source table. This is easy when the fields have the same name, but it takes manual intervention when the field names differ.

If you have designed and saved an Append query definition, and the source and destination tables never change in name or structure, all is well for you. However, if even a single extra character is misplaced or is missing in the field names, the query either bombs or asks you to fill in the value for the unidentifiable field. Neither is an option you can live with.

How can you deal with these accidents waiting to happen? Fortunately, you can copy data between tables in another way: use Paste Append.

Appending Across Tables

A paste method unique to Access, Paste Append appends the contents of the clipboard to a database table. The data has to match the table in structure, but it does *not* need to have matching field names. That right there improves on the tedious data entry involved when using the query grid. To be fair to Append queries, they do have an advantage of their own: an Append query can use criteria to append filtered sets of records. Paste Append, on the other hand, just appends everything. However, if the need to apply criteria isn't an issue, Paste Append has the advantage.

Figure 2-5 shows two tables: one contains existing customers, and the other contains a list of leads that have to be added to the list of existing customers. The records in the tblLeads table need to be added to the tblCustomers table. The field names aren't the same, although the field types and purposes match.

The simplest thing to do is to select all the records in tblLeads (Ctrl-A). Copy the records, go to the tblCustomers table, and use the Edit → Paste Append menu to enable Paste Append, as shown in Figure 2-6.

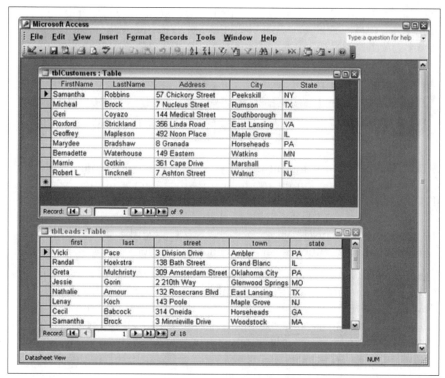

Figure 2-5. Appending similar data from one table to another

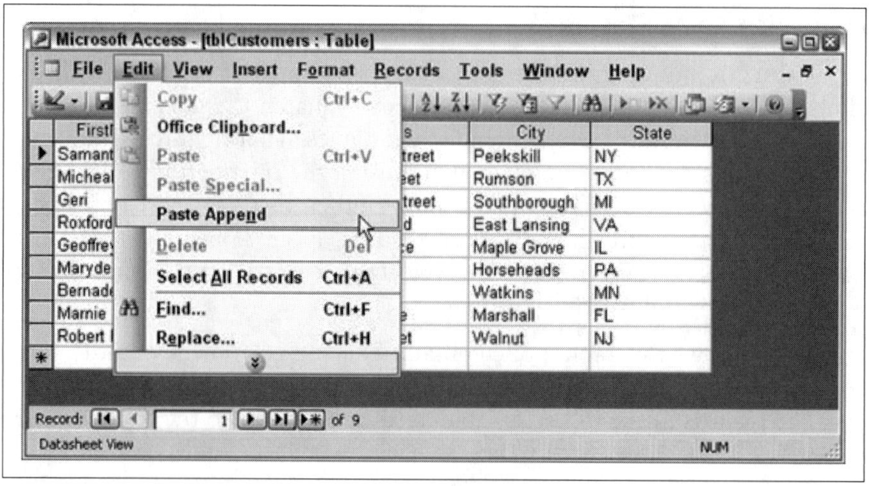

Figure 2-6. Using Paste Append

Note that the records are appended without concern for the field names. However, an alternative method is available that is easier still: the table with the records to be appended (tblLeads in this example) doesn't even have to be open! Just select and copy the table while it is closed. Do this directly in the database window. Then, open the table that receives the records (tblCustomers in this example), and use the Paste Append menu item as before.

This method has an issue, though. When the field names are the same, the method works like a charm. However, if at least one field name is different, the method still works, but the field names of the table being copied from might be inserted as a record!

Of course, by nature, field names are text-based, so if the table receiving the append contains fields that aren't text-based, Paste Append won't paste the field names. You might get an error about the datatype being wrong, but this is OK. Strange but true!

Finally, even when you know a record will appear that contains field names instead of data, the Paste Append method still might be preferable to creating an Append query because it is usually much easier to delete a single record from a table than it is to design a new query from scratch.

Appending Across Databases

The techniques in this hack work not just within a single database application, but also across databases. In other words, you can select and copy records from a table in one database and then append these records to a table in a different database. However, both databases must be open to make this possible.

Figure 2-7 shows two databases, side by side on the desktop.

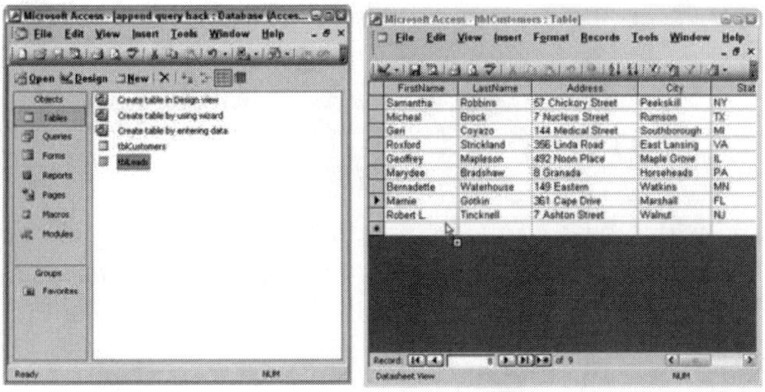

Figure 2-7. Appending data across databases

The tblLeads table, in the database on the left, is simply being dragged over to the open tblCustomers table in the database on the right. The tblLeads table is effectively being copied, not moved; the original stays in the first database. Letting go of the mouse button completes the append operation.

HACK #15 Steer Clear of System Tables

Avoid incorrect results by leaving system tables out of your table count and definition routines.

How many tables are in your database? You might think finding this out is as easy as counting how many tables are listed on the Tables tab of your database window. To that I respond, "Try again!"

Access uses a number of *system tables* to control its own internal workings. Usually, these additional tables are hidden, but they are there nonetheless. Figure 2-8 shows a database with some tables.

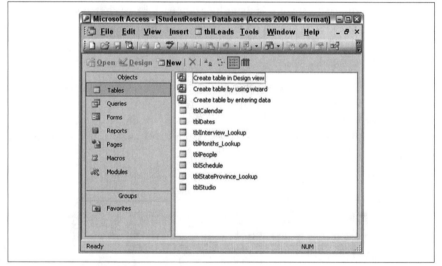

Figure 2-8. Tallying the tables

It looks like this database contains eight tables, doesn't it? Let's try getting a count in a different way. In the VB Editor, activate the Immediate window (Ctrl-G). Then, enter the following code snippet and press the Enter key:

```
?Application.CurrentData.AllTables.Count
```

Figure 2-9 shows the code and its results in the Immediate window. For the database in Figure 2-8, the result is 15, so Access is telling us the database actually contains 15 tables, although only eight are visible on the Tables tab.

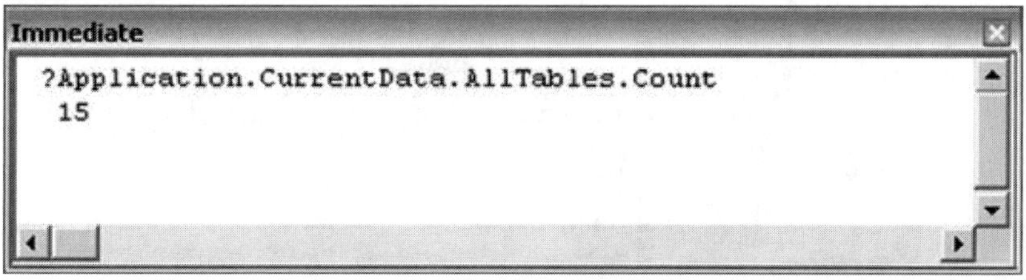

```
Immediate                                                    ☒
    ?Application.CurrentData.AllTables.Count                 ▲
    15


                                                            ▼
◄  ▌▌                                                       ►
```

Figure 2-9. Counting all the tables

The code snippet tells the truth, however: this database does indeed contain 15 tables. The ones you couldn't see before are the system tables. Let's display them!

Back in the database proper (not the VB Editor), use the Tools → Options menu to display the Options dialog box. Select the View tab. As shown in Figure 2-10, one of the options in the Show area is to display system objects. Select this checkbox to make the system tables visible.

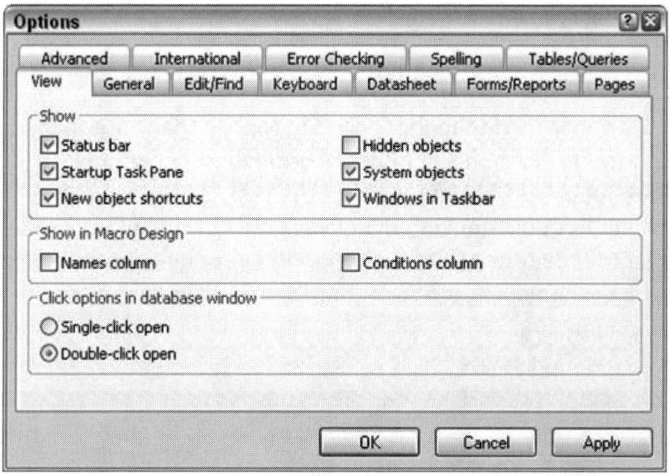

Figure 2-10. Selecting to show system objects

Now, looking at the Tables tab in Figure 2-11, you can see the system tables.

Note that all the system table names start with MSys. This is actually a useful attribute about these tables because it makes it easy to remove them from a table count.

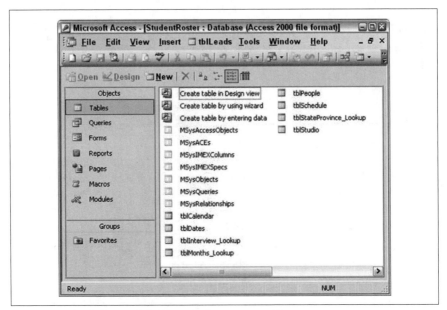

Figure 2-11. Displaying all tables, including system tables

The Code

But why does any of this matter? One reason is that an application might need to iterate through all the tables in a database—perhaps to add a property, to look for a field or data, to alter the table structure in some way, and so on. In such circumstances, the system tables must be avoided. Fortunately, a simple code routine easily handles this by purposely avoiding all tables that have names beginning with MSys, as follows:

```
Sub count_tables( )
'list tables in database
Dim table_num As Integer
Dim tbl_count As Integer
With Application.CurrentData
  For tbl_count = 1 To .AllTables.Count
    If Left(.AllTables(tbl_count - 1).Name, 4) <> "MSys" Then
      Debug.Print .AllTables(tbl_count - 1).Name
    End If
  Next tbl_count
End With
End Sub
```

This code routine cycles through all the tables in the database and writes the name of each table to the debug (Immediate) window, as long as the table's name doesn't start with MSys. To use this routine, replace the table names with any particular *per-table* processing you need.

Running the Code

Figure 2-12 shows the output of this routine. The Immediate window is filled with just the pertinent application data tables, and that's exactly what we need.

Figure 2-12. Listing just the data tables

By isolating the data tables from the system tables in this way, you can work with the data tables how ever you want, without worrying about crashing your application.

HACK #16 Hide Sensitive Information

Name tables with the USys prefix to prevent them from being visible.

Here's a quick and easy hack to hide data from prying eyes. Of course, any Access guru with enough notches in his belt will figure this one out. But ordinary users? Not likely. You can hide your tables using this approach and still retain full functionality in your application. Queries, forms, reports, macros, and code will still work, but anyone viewing the Tables tab won't find the tables you designate as hidden.

To do so, prefix your table names with USys. This acts as a flag to Access to treat the tables as a quasi-mix of system and user tables, and the ability is built in to hide or display them. Figure 2-13 demonstrates this procedure: a form is open and is clearly displaying data, but the Tables tab in the database window has no tables!

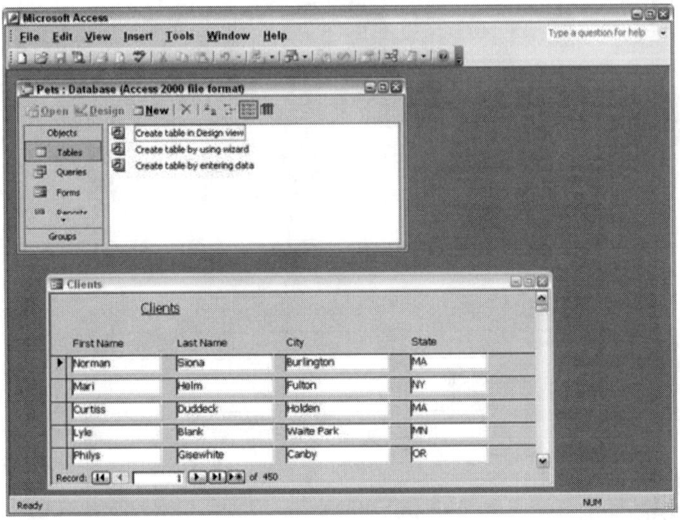

Figure 2-13. A form based on a hidden table

The form in Figure 2-13 has the record source property set to the USysClients table. In the Tools → Options → View menu, you'll find a setting for displaying system objects, as shown in Figure 2-14. Note that checking to display system objects makes USys tables visible.

Figure 2-15 shows all the system objects in their glory. The USys tables are there, as well as the MSys tables **[Hack #15]**.

> The prefix isn't case-sensitive. You can use USYS, USys, usys, and so on; they all work to differentiate a table.

An Alternative

Another way to hide objects in your database is to right-click a database object, which then displays a menu that includes a Properties option. Selecting this displays a Properties dialog, as shown in Figure 2-16. Checking the Hidden checkbox hides the object.

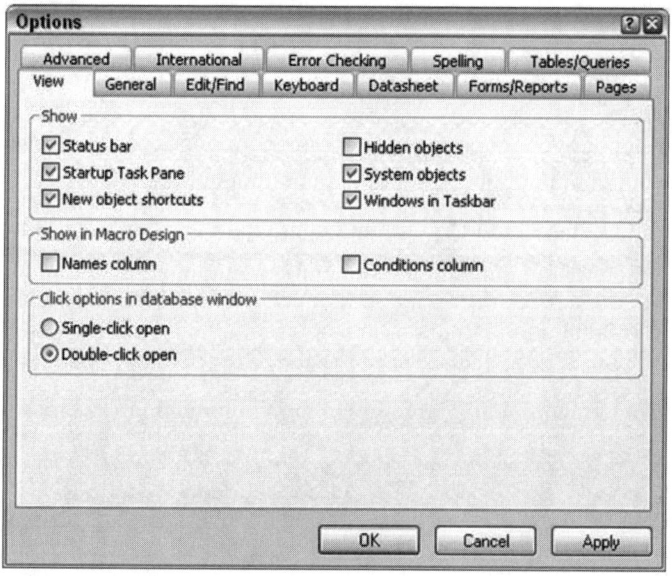

Figure 2-14. Selecting to display USys-prefixed tables

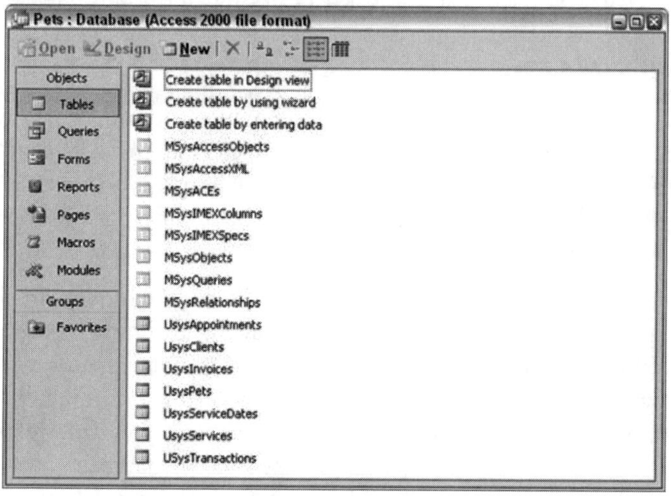

Figure 2-15. Displaying all USys and MSys tables

To display hidden objects, simply check "Hidden objects" in the Show section of the Options dialog box, as shown previously in Figure 2-14. But note that between prefixing object names with USys and setting the hidden

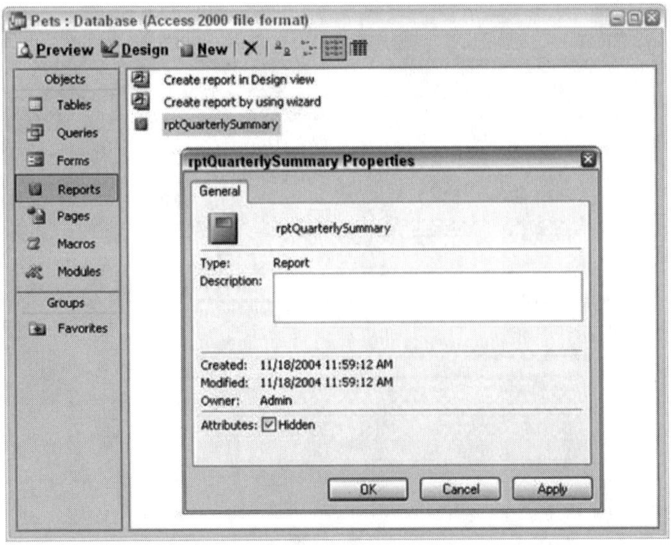

Figure 2-16. Setting the Hidden attribute

attribute, you've got enough capability to be a little smart *and* a little danger-ous. Just because you can't see objects doesn't mean they aren't there!

Hacking the Hack

Although this hack showed you how to hide tables and, therefore, avoid giv-ing users access to raw data, you can hide other database objects as well. Just prefix the names of queries, forms, reports, and so on, with USys, and they magically disappear. Or, set the hidden attribute in the Properties dia-log. It helps to write down the names first!

A really cool trick is to use the USys prefix, or to set the hidden attribute, for *all* database objects. As a result, anyone viewing the tabs in the database window will see absolutely nothing. By setting the Startup form to a form prefixed with USys, you can get the entire application running. As long as you are fully aware of how all the objects are named, you can create a com-plete application without a single visible object in the database window tabs. Of course, the objects become visible when they are opened, but by taking the correct measures to keep users out of your design elements, you can dis-tribute an *invisible* database.

Simulate Table Triggers

HACK #17

Incorporate the same functionality as SQL Server or Oracle in your Access application.

Access 2003 and earlier versions don't support table events. A *trigger* is a table event that you can fire on an insert, an edit, or a delete action—a valuable function. A useful example is to catch an edit before it completes and to store the original data—that is, store the original record somewhere else, such as in a backup table. This leaves you with a data audit trail. If for some reason the edited data is problematic, you can recall the original data.

This logic applies to deletes as well. Using triggers, you can hook into a delete and archive the data instead of just discarding it. In the case of inserts (such as new records being added to a table), data can be validated before being allowed into the table.

Unfortunately, Access doesn't let you do any of this directly from the point of view of the table itself. But you *can* do all of this when working through forms. Forms have plenty of events to hook into, and you can handle similar functionality as traditional triggers by working through forms instead of tables.

Setting Up an Audit Log

To demonstrate how all this works, let's add a new table to a database to mirror an existing data table and create an audit log of changes to the data table. We'll do this by using two additional fields: one to store the type of operation and one to store a timestamp. Figure 2-17 displays two tables: the data table (tblClients) and a table to store records from the first table just prior to them being edited or deleted (tblClientsAuditLog).

Here are a couple of points to consider:

- The log table contains two additional fields: Action and Timestamp.
- The ClientID field is the primary key in the data table, but it is purposely not set as a primary key in the log table. This is because the log table might hold multiple records that pertain to the same client (and therefore the same ClientID).

Checking Out the Form Events

Now you can use a standard form to view, add, edit, and delete records from the data table. Figure 2-18 shows a typical form based on the tblClients table.

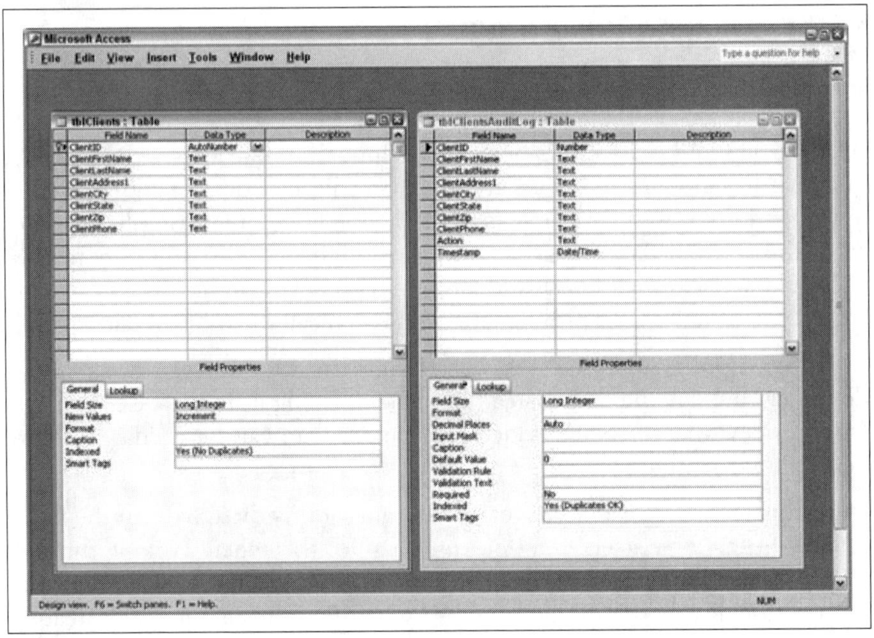

Figure 2-17. Using an audit log table to store records

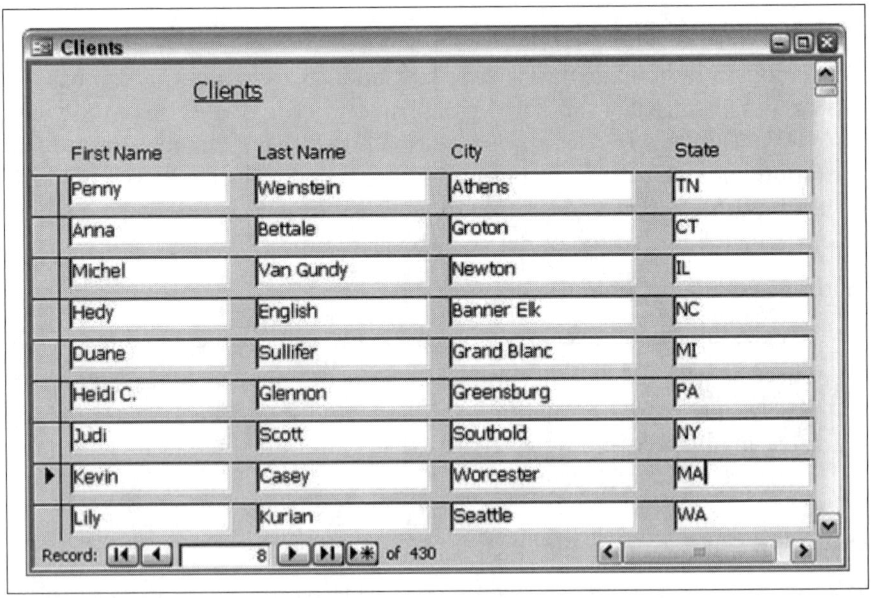

Figure 2-18. Inserts, updates, and deletes, done with a form

Of course, there is some code behind this form. Two events are tapped: the Before Update event and the Delete event. Before Update handles both inserts and updates, and Delete handles deletes. In particular, when an insert is made, the Before Update event validates the data (i.e., it checks to see if there is a last name). If the validation fails, the Cancel property is set to True, which causes the event to abort.

When an update (an edit) is made, the record receiving the change is written to the log table, prior to the change. This means the original data is kept intact. When a delete is made, the record that is to be deleted is also written to the log table, prior to the change.

The Code

Here is the code behind the form. The Action field in the log table receives one of two values: Update or Delete. The two event routines use a common function (build_sql):

```
Private Sub Form_BeforeUpdate(Cancel As Integer)
  On Error GoTo err_end
  Dim ssql As String
  Dim conn As ADODB.Connection
  Set conn = CurrentProject.Connection
  If NewRecord = False Then
    ssql = build_sql(ClientID, "Update")
    conn.Execute ssql
    conn.Close
    Set conn = Nothing
  Else
    If IsNull(ClientLastName) Or ClientLastName = "" Then
      MsgBox "Must provide name"
      Cancel = True
    End If
  End If
  Exit Sub
err_end:
  MsgBox Err.Description
End Sub

Private Sub Form_Delete(Cancel As Integer)
  On Error GoTo err_end
  Dim ssql As String
  Dim conn As ADODB.Connection
  Set conn = CurrentProject.Connection
  ssql = build_sql(ClientID, "Delete")
  conn.Execute ssql
  Exit Sub
err_end:
  MsgBox Err.Description
End Sub

Function build_sql(client_id As Long, operation As String) As String
  build_sql = "Insert Into tblClientsAuditLog Values ("
```

```
build_sql = build_sql & ClientID & ", "
build_sql = build_sql & "'" & _
DLookup("ClientFirstName", "tblClients", "ClientID=" & _
    client_id) & "', "
 build_sql = build_sql & "'" & _
DLookup("ClientLastName", "tblClients", "ClientID=" & _
    client_id) & "', "
  build_sql = build_sql & "'" & _
DLookup("ClientAddress1", "tblClients", "ClientID=" & _
    client_id) & "', "
  build_sql = build_sql & "'" & _
DLookup("ClientState", "tblClients", "ClientID=" & _
    client_id) & "', "
  build_sql = build_sql & "'" & _
DLookup("ClientCity", "tblClients", "ClientID=" & _
    client_id) & "', "
  build_sql = build_sql & "'" & _
DLookup("ClientZip", "tblClients", "ClientID=" & _
    client_id) & "', "
  build_sql = build_sql & "'" & _
DLookup("ClientPhone", "tblClients", "ClientID=" & _
    client_id) & "', "
 build_sql = build_sql & "'" & operation & "', "
 build_sql = build_sql & "#" & Now( ) & "#)"
End Function
```

Running the Code

The code runs when inserts, updates, and deletes are made using the form.
No particular additional action, such as clicking a button, is required. The
log table fills up with records as users do their thing. The log table keeps
track of all the changes and even stores multiple changes per client. The
build_sql function creates an Insert SQL statement. The statement will
include either Update or Delete as one of the values being written, the difference being which routine called the function (and passed the word *Update*
or *Delete* as an argument). The SQL string is handed back to the calling routine, from where the insert is run.

This certainly can be useful in the real world. For example, say a client
moves (an address edit), gets married (a name edit), starts buying from your
competitor (a delete!), and so on. Figure 2-19 shows the resulting log table
with some records. Each record displays the action and the timestamp.

The methods used in this hack simulate what SQL Server, Oracle, and other
database products provide in the way of triggers. Let's not allow the elite of
the database world to believe Access isn't up to snuff!

Between the client table and the log table are multiple records, and there is a
sequence to the records, thanks to the wonderful timestamp.

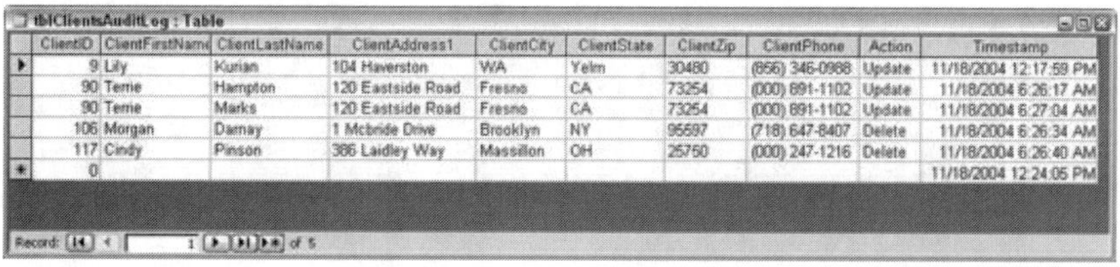
tblClientsAuditLog : Table

ClientID	ClientFirstName	ClientLastName	ClientAddress1	ClientCity	ClientState	ClientZip	ClientPhone	Action	Timestamp
9	Lily	Kurian	104 Haverston	WA	Yelm	30480	(856) 346-0968	Update	11/18/2004 12:17:59 PM
90	Terrie	Hampton	120 Eastside Road	Fresno	CA	73254	(000) 891-1102	Update	11/18/2004 6:26:17 AM
90	Terrie	Marks	120 Eastside Road	Fresno	CA	73254	(000) 891-1102	Update	11/18/2004 6:27:04 AM
106	Morgan	Darnay	1 Mcbride Drive	Brooklyn	NY	95597	(718) 647-8407	Delete	11/18/2004 6:26:34 AM
117	Cindy	Pinson	386 Laidley Way	Massillon	OH	25750	(000) 247-1216	Delete	11/18/2004 6:26:40 AM
0									11/18/2004 12:24:05 PM

Record: 1 of 5

Figure 2-19. Records copied to the audit log table before being updated or deleted

Hacking the Hack

This hack was written with the advantage of knowing the table structure and field types. Therefore, I knew ahead of time to place single quotes around text values in the `build_sql` function. When adapting this hack, you will probably know ahead of time what type of data to expect, but if you don't, you can tap into the ADOX library to determine datatypes.

ADOX provides a way to read through each field in a table and determine its type (as well as other properties). The following is a basic routine to read through a single table and have the name and type returned for each field:

```
Sub get_fields()
  Dim cat As ADOX.Catalog
  Set cat = New ADOX.Catalog
  Dim fld As ADOX.Column
  cat.ActiveConnection = CurrentProject.Connection
  For Each fld In cat.Tables("tblClients").Columns
    Debug.Print fld.Name & " " & fld.Type
  Next
  Set cat = Nothing
End Sub
```

Note that to use the ADOX library, you must set a reference. As with other references, go to the VB Editor and use the Tools → References menu to display the References dialog box, shown in Figure 2-20. The library is named *Microsoft ADO Ext. 2.7 for DDL and Security*. Check the appropriate checkbox, and click OK to close the dialog.

The routine returns a numerical constant for each field type. For example, a value of 202 indicates a Text field type (although properly noted as a variable-width character field in ADOX lingo). Use the Object Browser to view the `DataTypeEnum` constants to see what the numbers represent. This collection of datatype constants is available once the reference to ADOX is set. Figure 2-21 shows the Object Browser zeroed in on the list of datatype constants. For any constant, you can see the numerical representation at the bottom of the Object Browser.

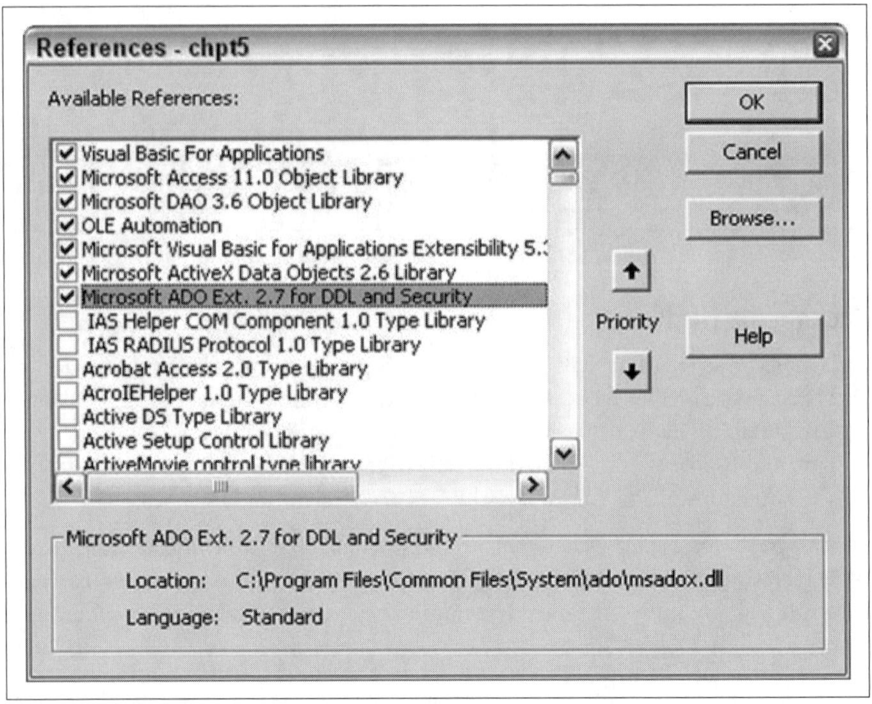

Figure 2-20. Setting a reference to ADOX

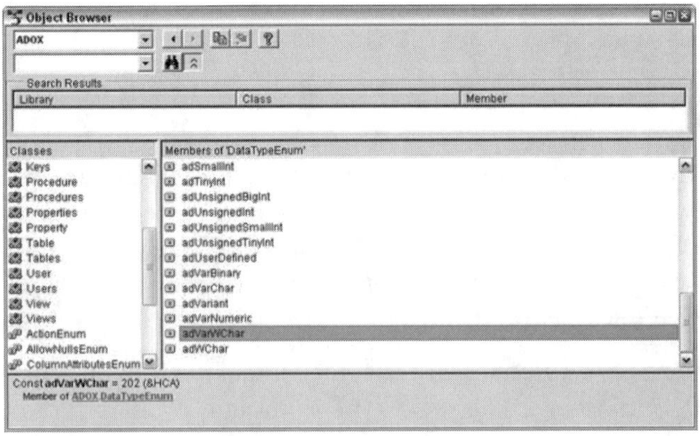

Figure 2-21. Reviewing datatype constants

Using Select Case or a set of If statements interspersed with the ADOX code in this section, you can write a routine that doesn't rely on knowing the field types ahead of time.

Create Tables Faster

Optimize table design by changing the design defaults to match your needs.

A Text field is 50 characters. A Number field is a long integer, and the default value is 0. Sound all too familiar? How often have you gone out of your way to alter these defaults? Well, with this hack, you no longer need to.

In the Options dialog box (Tools → Options), on the Tables/Queries tab, you'll find settings for selecting the default size for text fields, the default number type (integer, long, single, etc.) for number fields, and even the overall default type. Figure 2-22 shows this dialog box and the settings.

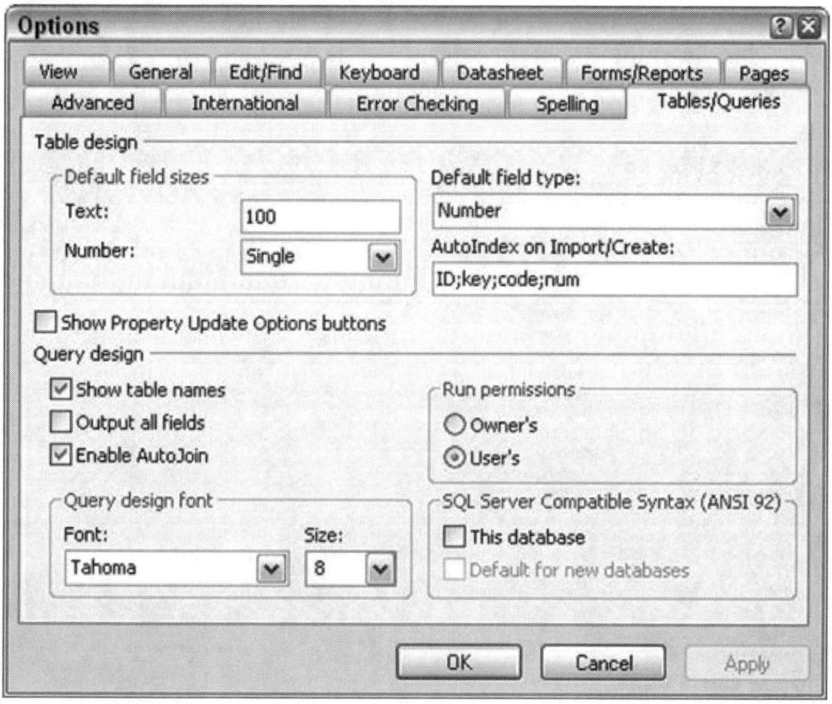

Figure 2-22. Changing field defaults

In Figure 2-22, the default Text field size has been changed to 100. This means that as new text fields are added to the design of a table, they will default to a size of 100. Also, the default Number type has been set to Single. As new number fields are added, they default to the Single datatype. The overall default field type is set to Number; therefore, as new fields are entered into a table design, they default to a Number field type—and that type will be of the Single number type.

Altering these design defaults can be quite useful. If, for example, you are designing a table that predominantly contains dates, set the default field type to Date/Time, and save yourself a lot of field-type selection. As you enter new fields, they will default to Date/Time. You will need to adjust only the minority of fields that aren't of this type.

Setting Default Values

The settings in the Options dialog box control field type settings but offer nothing to indicate default values. In other words, you can select Single as the default number type, but you can't specify that the field defaults to a value of 1.25 (for example) as new records are added to the table.

However, a setting is available in which you can indicate a default value. The field in the third row of the table being designed in Figure 2-23 has been manually set to 1.25, and this becomes the default value for the field.

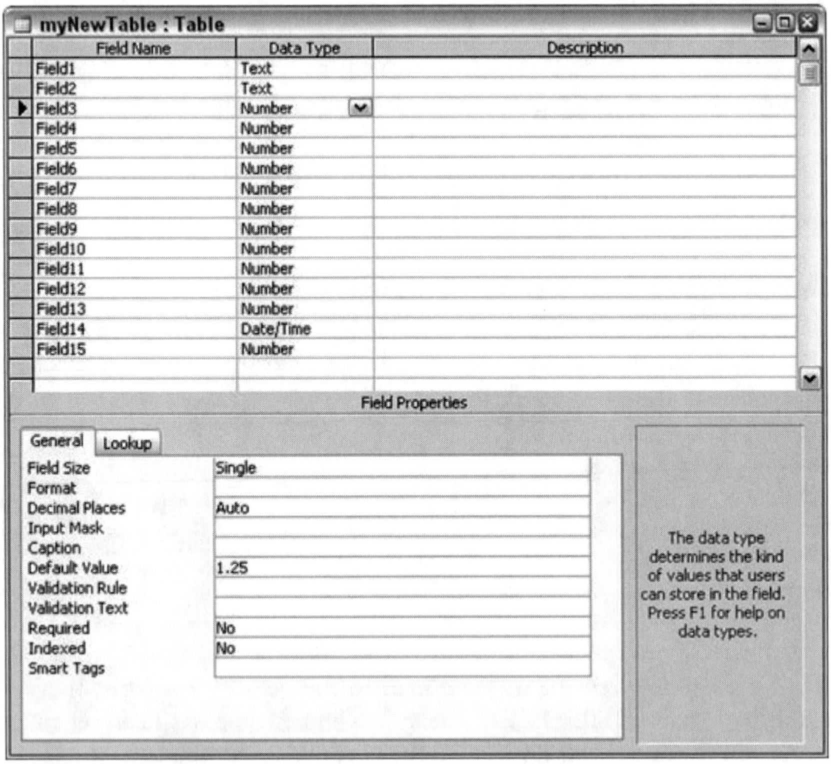

Field Name	Data Type	Description
Field1	Text	
Field2	Text	
Field3	Number	
Field4	Number	
Field5	Number	
Field6	Number	
Field7	Number	
Field8	Number	
Field9	Number	
Field10	Number	
Field11	Number	
Field12	Number	
Field13	Number	
Field14	Date/Time	
Field15	Number	

Field Properties

General | Lookup

Field Size	Single
Format	
Decimal Places	Auto
Input Mask	
Caption	
Default Value	1.25
Validation Rule	
Validation Text	
Required	No
Indexed	No
Smart Tags	

The data type determines the kind of values that users can store in the field. Press F1 for help on data types.

Figure 2-23. Setting a default field value

The Code

What if 100 other fields need to be set to such a default value? My fingers hurt just thinking about the manual entry that would be involved! Automating this task will be a lifesaver—well, at least a finger saver. A little code to the rescue!

```
Sub change_field_defaults()
   Dim cat As ADOX.Catalog
   Set cat = New ADOX.Catalog
   Dim fld As ADOX.Column
   cat.ActiveConnection = CurrentProject.Connection
   For Each fld In cat.Tables("myNewTable").Columns
     If fld.Type = adSingle Then
        fld.Properties("Default").Value = 1.25
     End If
   Next
   Set cat = Nothing
End Sub
```

This code uses the ADOX library **[Hack #17]** to work with the fields in the designated table. In this example, the table name is hardcoded, but it certainly can be passed as an argument. This code example cycles through the fields, and when a field type is designated as Single (indicated by the adSingle constant), its default value is set to 1.25.

You can expand this code routine to set default values for all possible field types. Even more, you can set default values for combinations of field types and field names. For example, a field named local_rate can be a single field type, which you can set it to a default value of .25; likewise, you cab set a field named national_rate, also a Single datatype, to have a default value of .5.

CHAPTER THREE

Entry and Navigation
Hacks 19–27

An application's success often rests on user acceptance. With this in mind, it makes sense to plan how to make your application's front-end experience as visually pleasing and user-friendly as possible.

Sometimes user experience is overlooked. Developers can spend oodles of time designing fields and tables, setting up relationships, writing tricky SQL, and so on. Does this mean anything to the typical user? Not one whit!

Let's face it. Access is more than just a database. It is a database with built-in front-end tools. Tables are the core of a database, but the ability to create forms and reports is the main job of a development platform. Access has both, so let's make the best of both.

The hacks in this chapter have been drummed up with the ordinary user in mind. Entering data is a major user activity, and these hacks make this often mind-numbing activity a little more pleasant.

HACK #19 Help Users Navigate Through Long Forms

Use Page Break controls and command buttons so that users won't have to scroll through long data-entry forms.

Information is wonderful. The more you know, the more you can do and plan for—unless you are the one stuck entering the data. Then, all you can plan on is a lot of typing and mousing around.

Figure 3-1 shows an entry form, and a rather long one at that. This entry form contains more entry fields than can reasonably fit onscreen, as evidenced by the scrollbar on the right of the form. Anyone using this form will need to scroll or tab through to the fields on the bottom.

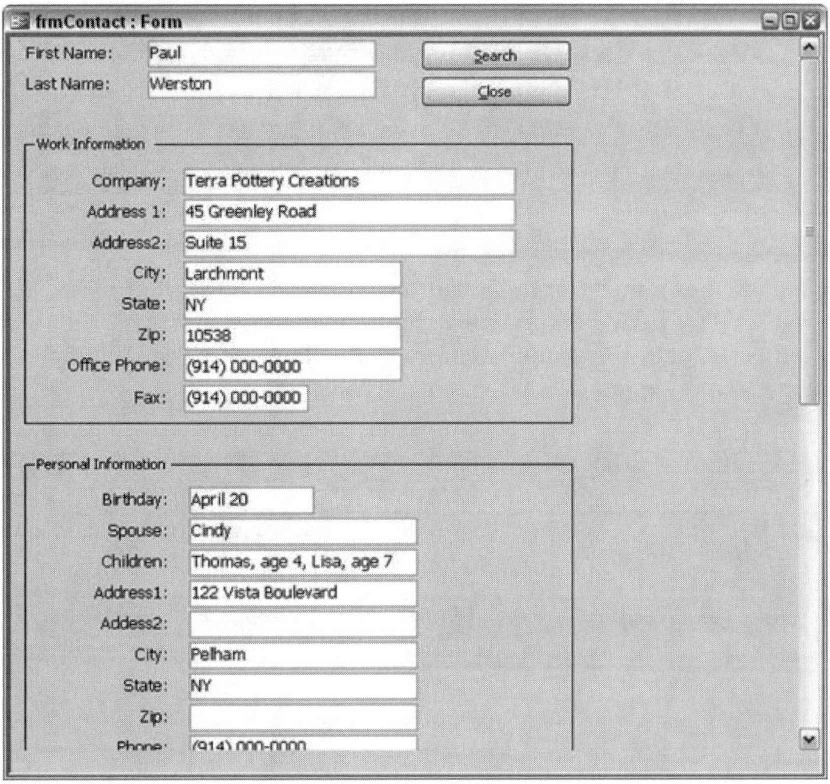

Figure 3-1. A form that takes a lot of entries

A tab control is great for managing a lot of controls on a form. However, this hack is based on a real-life situation. I once worked on a project in which data-entry operators were entering information from legal-size forms. The entry screen had to match the layout of the form.

The Page Up and Page Down keys on the keyboard make it easy to scroll up and down through the form, but you can't control how much scrolling will occur. The odds that pressing Page Up or Page Down will leave the form right where you need it are indeed small.

Luckily, you can get this to work properly. All you need to do is add *Page Break controls* to the form. What are Page Break controls, you ask? Figure 3-2 shows the Toolbox with the Page Break control pointed out. By placing page breaks strategically in the form design, you can get the Page Up and Page Down keys to scroll the form right to where you need it.

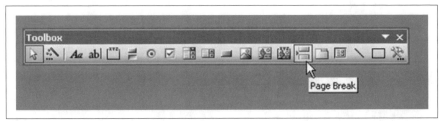

Figure 3-2. The Page Break control on the Toolbox

Figure 3-3 shows the form in Design mode. A Page Break control has been placed directly above the Personal Information section. This is a rather unobtrusive control. It simply appears as a string of dots in Design mode, and in View mode, you don't even see the control.

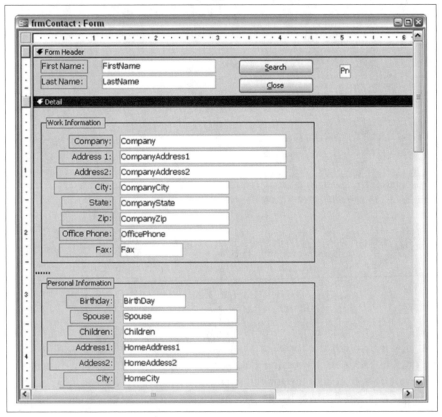

Figure 3-3. Adding Page Break controls

Now, when you use the Page Down key you will scroll the form directly to where the Page Break control resides. Figure 3-4 shows how the form easily scrolls to the Personal Information section.

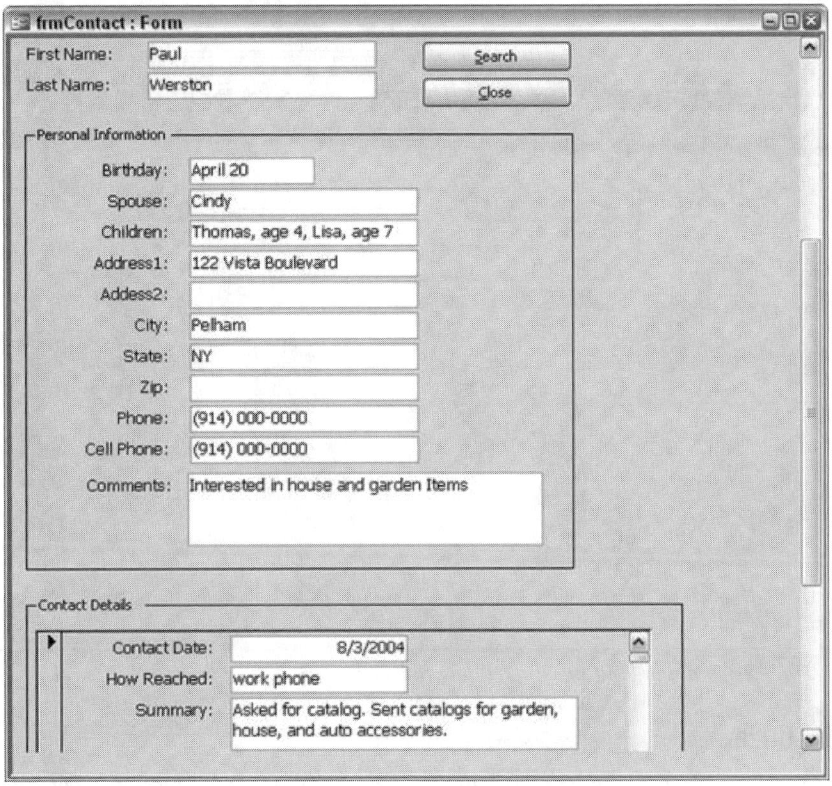

Figure 3-4. Smart scrolling

Smart Navigation

Using the Page Up and Page Down keys is an adequate way to scroll a form, but we can do better. Imagine this: a form has several segregated data areas, and you need to access them in random order. Having to press Page Up or Page Down several times to get the form to where you need it is a lot of work.

To avoid this problem, you can place a series of command buttons in the form header (or form footer). The header and footer are always visible because these sections are exempt from scrolling. Figure 3-5 shows the form in Design mode, with command buttons in the header that will let users scroll to where they want.

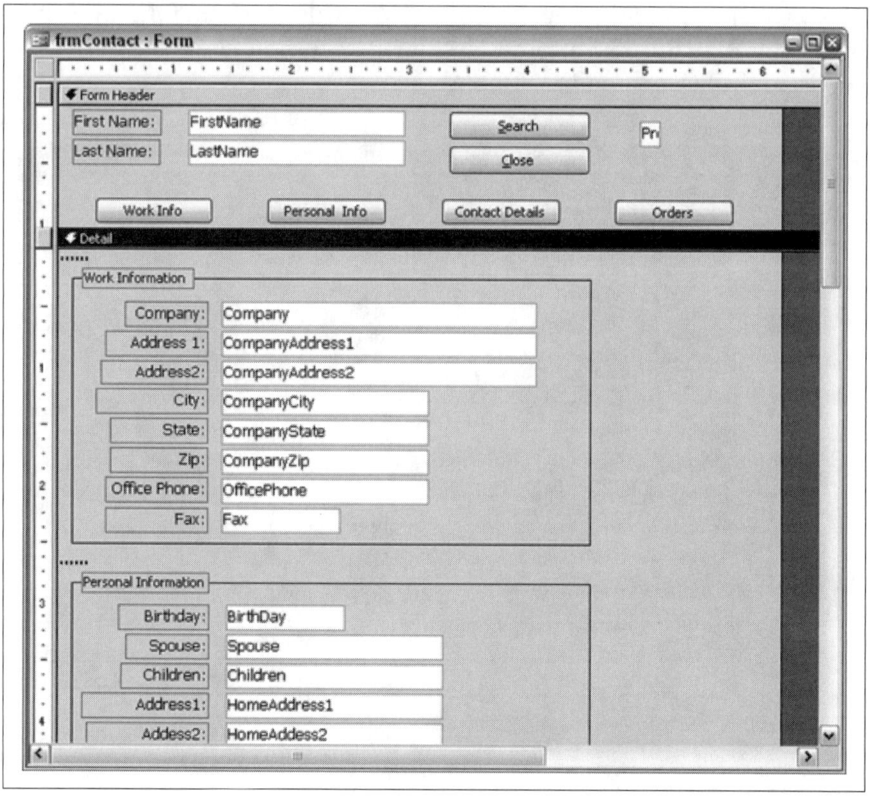

Figure 3-5. Command buttons to facilitate form navigation

The Code

The trick is for each button to simulate Page Up and Page Down keystrokes. The following code uses the SendKeys statement to accomplish this. The four new buttons on the form each initiate a series of SendKeys statements:

```
Private Sub cmdWorkInfo_Click()
'
' 4 SendKeys up, 1 SendKeys down
'
   navigate_form 4, 1
End Sub

Private Sub cmdPersonalInfo_Click()
'
' 4 SendKeys up, 2 SendKeys down
'
   navigate_form 4, 2
End Sub
```

```
Private Sub cmdContactDetails_Click()
'
' 4 SendKeys up, 3 SendKeys down
'
  navigate_form 4, 3
End Sub

Private Sub cmdOrders_Click()
'
' 4 SendKeys up, 4 SendKeys down
'
  navigate_form 4, 4
End Sub

Sub navigate_form(u As Integer, d As Integer)
  For form_up = 1 To u
    SendKeys "{PGUP}"
  Next form_up
  For form_down = 1 To d
    SendKeys "{PGDN}"
  Next form_down
End Sub
```

Each Click event sends the number of Page Up and Page Down keystrokes that are required to have the form scroll to the desired area. These simulated keystrokes access the Page Break controls placed earlier on the form. When a button is clicked, the routine immediately sends four Page Up keystrokes. The number of keystrokes is based on this particular example. The point is to get to the top of the form. Four Page Up keystrokes are needed only if the form is currently at the bottom page break, but using four regardless of the form's location doesn't present a problem.

The code then simulates the correct number of Page Down keystrokes. The number differs for each button—for each area being scrolled to. In other words, the Work Info button has one Page Down, the Personal Info button has two Page Downs, and so forth.

With this approach, any area of a long form is just a single click away, and it isn't necessary for users to go through the entire form.

HACK #20 Help Users Enter Additional Text

Place the insertion point at the end of the text in a text box so that additional entries land just where they should.

This technique makes so much sense, and yet it is often overlooked. Have you ever noticed that when you're editing data in a form, and you tab into a text box, the entire text is selected? Unfortunately, this default behavior makes the data vulnerable to accidental overwriting. Figure 3-6 shows the address text box fully selected. Assuming an edit is needed to *add* additional text (not to *replace* the text), the user must move his mouse to the end of the text and then click to deselect it.

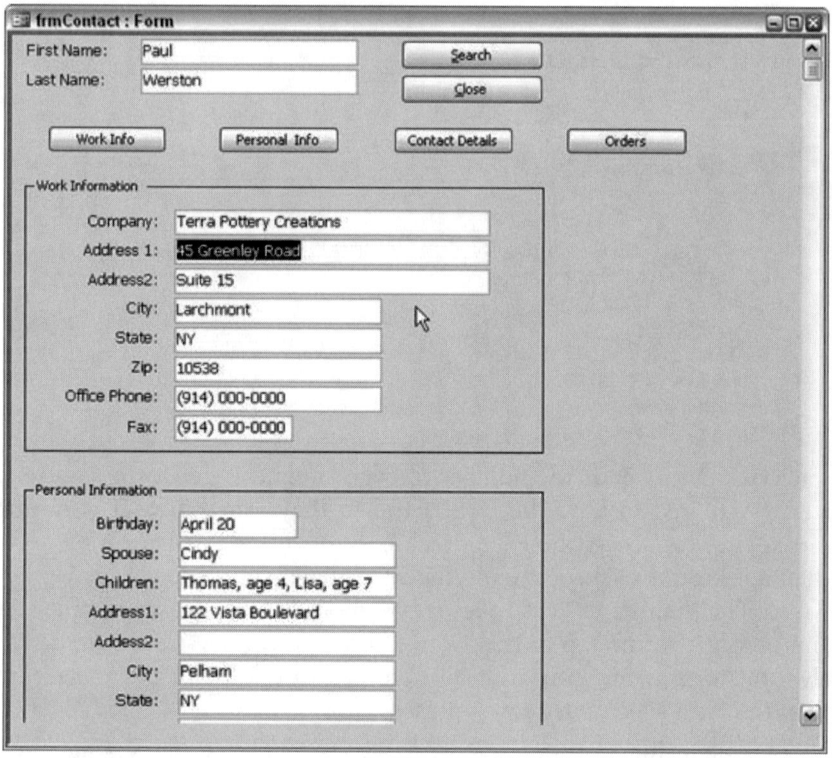

Figure 3-6. Automatically selected data, vulnerable to an accidental delete or overwrite

Wouldn't it be nice if the user didn't have to click first to deselect the text? Of course, there is a way to do this. It takes just a smattering of code.

Many controls, including text boxes, have an Enter event, which is triggered when the control is clicked or tabbed into. This is the event in which you can place code to move the cursor to the end of the text, before the user has a chance to enter any keystrokes. The following code snippet is based on the control being named CompanyAddress1:

```
Private Sub CompanyAddress1_Enter()
   Dim text_length As Integer
   text_length = Len(Me.CompanyAddress1)
   Me.CompanyAddress1.SelStart = text_length
End Sub
```

The length of the text is determined with the Len function, and then the SelStart property is set to the length. It's that simple.

You can add a routine such as this to all the text boxes in a form, if it makes sense to do so. Is data usually overwritten, or does it receive additional characters? Only you know your application, so only you can decide where to incorporate this code. In this example, some additional information has been added to the address, as shown in Figure 3-7.

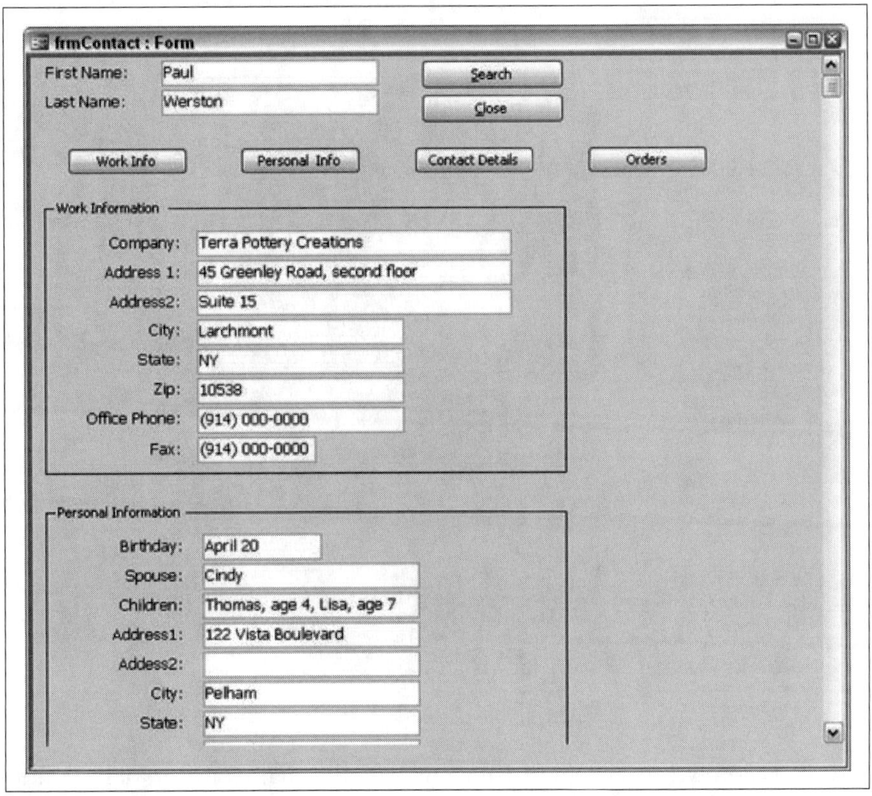

Figure 3-7. Information added, but not used to replace the existing text

The SelStart property has two related members: SelLength and SelText. Singly or in combination, three text selection properties give you fine control over handling text in a text box or combo box.

So far, this hack has shown you how to use SelStart to set where the entry will begin. But once I had to provide a user with an easy way to reverse last name/first name to first name/last name for a set of records. Names often include initials, middle names, and so forth. If you've ever written a name-parsing routine, you know how difficult it is to get the routine to handle all the variations found in names.

This was a one-shot deal, so it didn't make sense for me to create a long, drawn-out routine. Instead, I used the selection properties, and I left some of the work up to the user. Here's how it worked.

I presented the contact names that had to be reversed in a form, such as that shown in Figure 3-8.

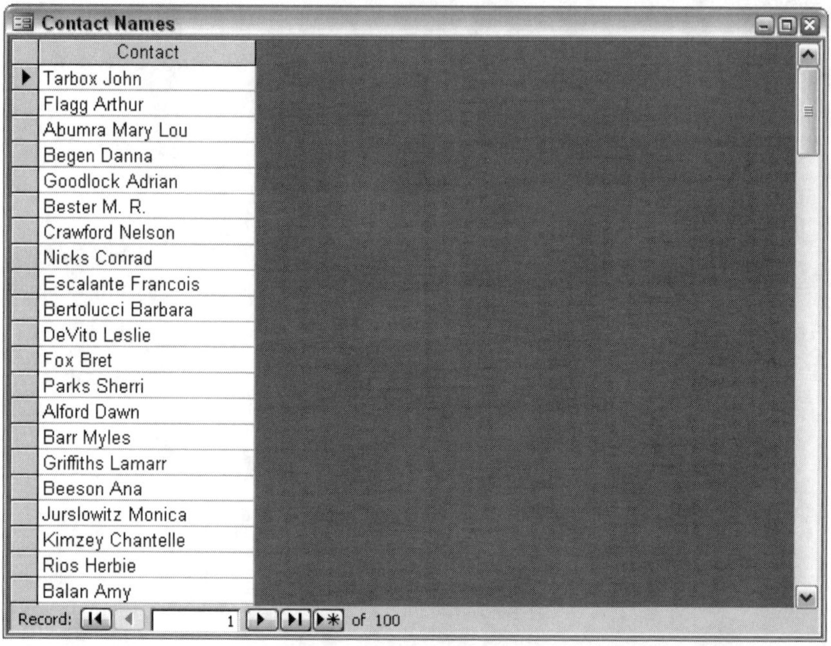

Figure 3-8. The names that needed to be reversed

The user simply selected the first name—or first name and initial, or first name and middle name, and so on—and then pressed either the Tab or the Enter key, as shown in Figure 3-9.

That's all it took! It worked by implementing the selection properties on the text box's Exit event. In this example, the text box is named Contact. The routine explained earlier, which uses the Enter event, is also used in this example:

```
Private Sub Contact_Enter( )
'
'remove selection effect
'and place insertion point at end
```

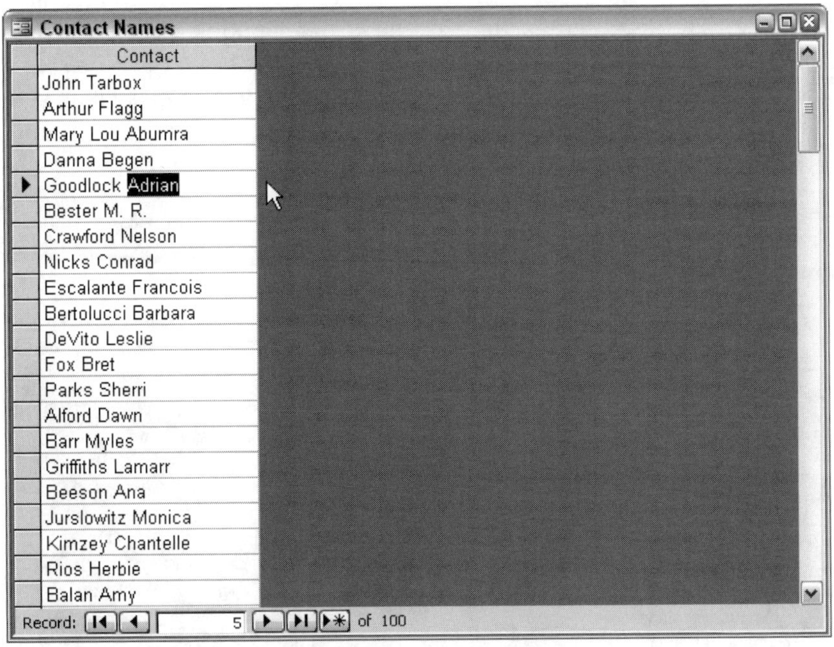

Figure 3-9. A first name selected

```
    Dim text_length As Integer
    text_length = Len(Contact)
    Contact.SelStart = text_length
End Sub

Private Sub Contact_Exit(Cancel As Integer)
'
'if there is selected text and the selection
'is less than the full text size then
'if the selection starts past the first position then
'move the selected text to the front
'
    Dim new_text As String
    If Contact.SelLength > 0 And _
       Contact.SelLength < Len(Contact) Then
          If Contact.SelStart > 1 Then
             new_text = Contact.SelText & " " & _
               Left(Contact, Len(Contact) - Contact.SelLength)
             Contact.Text = Trim(new_text)
          End If
    End If
End Sub
```

For convenience, the Enter event makes sure the text isn't selected at the beginning. The user selects the first name, and middle initial or middle name, if present, and then either tabs out of the text box or just presses the Enter key. This fires the Exit event, which tests the text to make sure something has been selected, it isn't the same length as the entire text, and it doesn't start at the beginning.

The routine then reverses the selected and unselected portions (the first name and the last name) and returns them to the text box. Figure 3-10 shows the result.

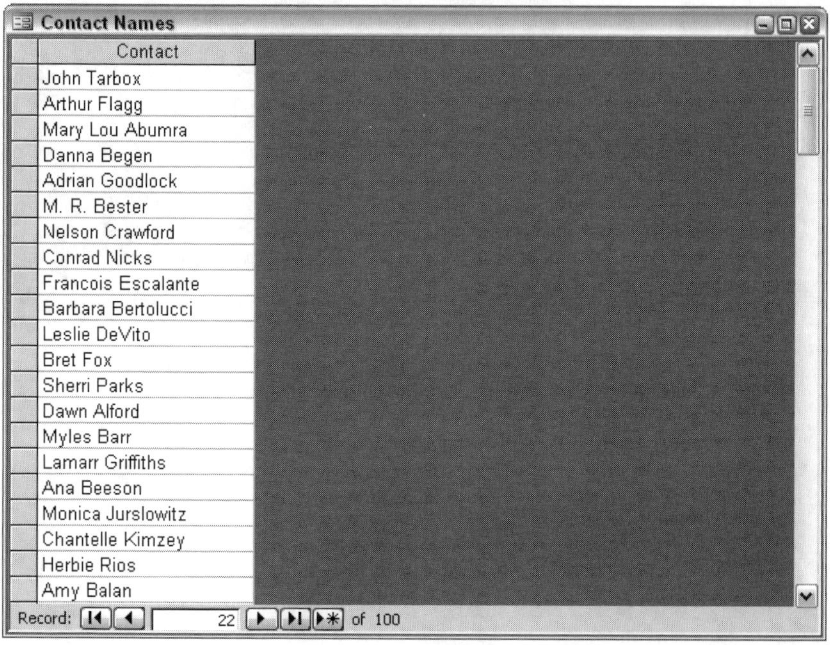

Figure 3-10. All the names reversed

The routine uses all three selection properties: SelStart, SelLength, and SelText. These properties give you all you need to work with selected portions of text. When you compare them to the equivalent text properties and methods—Text, Len, Left, Right, Mid, and so on—you can see that they give you quite a bit of control when manipulating text.

Let Users Add Custom Items to Predesigned Lists

Avoid forcing choices to existing list items only by adding a procedure to handle new values.

Users often choose items from an existing list via a combo box on a form. Sometimes, however, a user might need to enter into the combo box a value that isn't on the list. This can happen, for example, when the user is working with a new customer that he has not yet appended to a customer table, or when the user is correcting an existing list item that is misspelled.

The Limit To List property controls whether a new value is allowed entry in a combo box. If this property is set to No, users can enter new values into the combo box. This is fine, but with one caveat: if the new value is meant to become a permanent member of the list, just typing it into the combo box doesn't add it to the list.

If it makes sense for your application to let users permanently add values to a combo box's source list, you need to use a different technique. First, set the Limit To List property to Yes. (Yes, this means the new item won't be allowed, but read on!) The trick to this hack is to implement inclusion of the new item by tapping the On Not In List event, which works only when the Limit To List property is set to Yes.

Figure 3-11 shows a form in Design mode. The form has a combo box on it, and the property sheet shows the properties for the combo box, with the Limit To List property set to Yes.

When a user attempts to add a new value to the combo box, the On Not In List event fires. Within this event, a code routine handles adding the new value to the list.

The Code

The code is simple and straightforward. Two arguments are provided to the routine: NewData and Response. The event stub comes predesigned with these arguments, so you don't have to create them:

```
Private Sub cmbCustomers_NotInList(NewData As String, _
        Response As Integer)
    Dim ctl As Control
    Set ctl = Me.cmbCustomers
    Response = acDataErrAdded
    ctl.RowSource = ctl.RowSource & ";" & NewData
End Sub
```

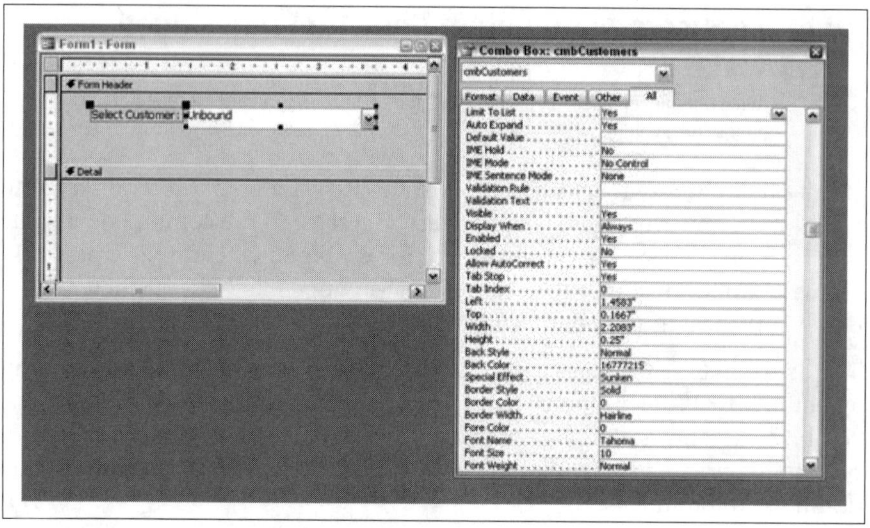

Figure 3-11. The Limit To List property set to Yes

The Response argument tells Access to override the behavior of not allowing a value to be added. The developer does this by setting the Response to the adDataErrAdded constant. The new data (supplied by the NewData argument) is then added to the Row Source.

Hacking the Hack

So far, this hack works on the premise that the Row Source Type is set to a Value List. If the Row Source Type is Table/Query, you need an append routine to place the new value in the underlying data store. In this case, the Not In List event appends the new value to the source table.

Here is an example of how to code the routine. This example assumes a source table named tblShippingMethods with a field named Shipping-Method:

```
Private Sub cmbShippingMethods_NotInList(NewData As String, _
        Response As Integer)
    Dim new_data As String
    Dim conn As ADODB.Connection
    Set conn = CurrentProject.Connection
    'double up any apostrophes before Insert
    new_data = Replace(NewData, "'", "''")
    Response = acDataErrAdded
    conn.Execute "Insert Into " & _
        "tblShippingMethods(ShippingMethod) Values('" & _
            new_data & "')"
End Sub
```

Populate and Sort Lists with Flair
Use these three clever techniques to populate and sort listbox controls.

Lists are integral to form design. True, not all forms need a list, but when they're applicable, selecting an item from a list is much easier than typing in the value. This also makes it easier to avoid typos.

This hack presents three ways to populate and sort listbox controls. In each example, the underlying tables and structure are key elements. The examples show how to sort alphabetically, but from two sources; how to sort based on a key value; how to sort on placement in the SQL statement; and even how to sort by tracking the popularity of the list items themselves! The SQL Union clause is a key factor to getting much of this to happen.

The Form

Figure 3-12 shows a form with three lists, aptly named List 1, List 2, and List 3.

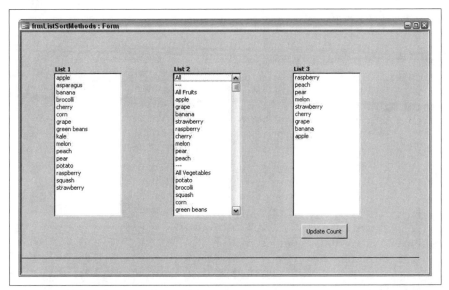

Figure 3-12. Three list controls on a form

Behind the scenes, two tables populate the list controls: tblFruits and tblVegetables, shown in Figure 3-13. Note that they share two common fields: SortNumber and ListItem. This common structure is put to good use, as you will see soon.

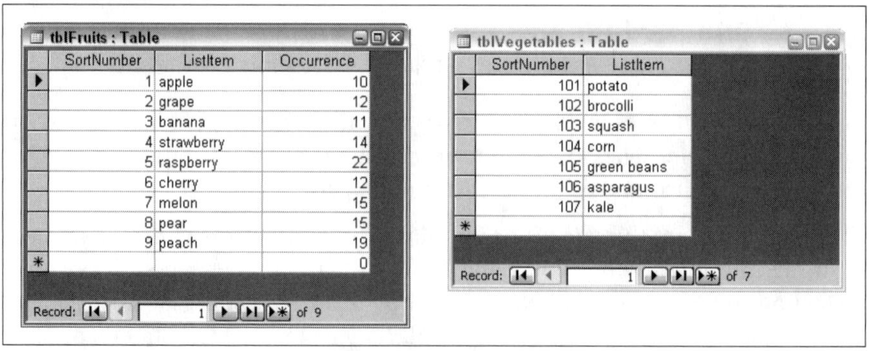

Populate and Sort Lists with Flair

Figure 3-13. Two tables used to populate the list controls

Populating a Listbox Alphabetically from Two Sources

List 1 displays the values from the two tables, sorted alphabetically as one larger list. The trick is to have the List control use the records of both tables in its Row Source property. You do this by combining the records of both tables in a Union query. Figure 3-14 shows the form in Design mode with the property sheet set to List 1.

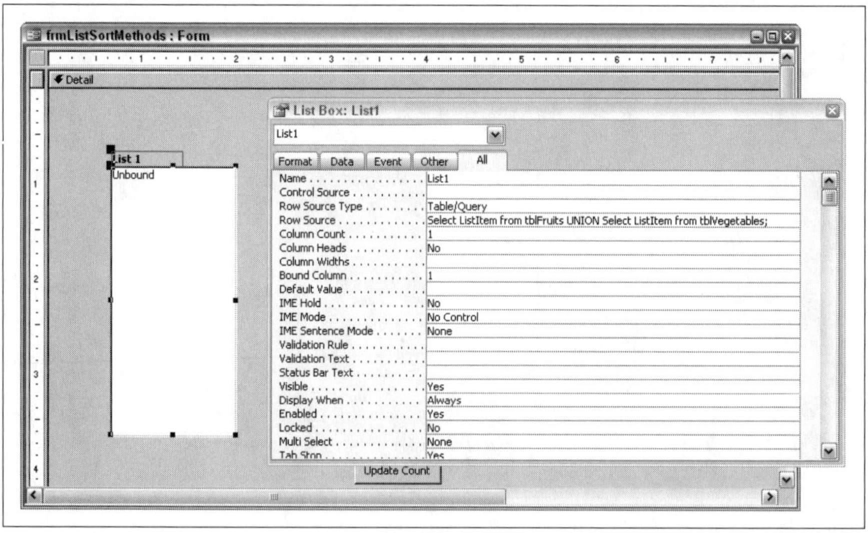

Figure 3-14. The Row Source property for List 1

The SQL statement in the Row Source property reads like this:

```
Select ListItem from tblFruits UNION Select ListItem from tblVegetables;
```

The Union clause allows the values from the two tables to be combined, given that the structure and datatype are the same. In other words, the

ListItem field from each table is addressed with the SQL statement. Querying the same number of fields in each Select statement with the Union query is a requirement. The query can't run if the number of fields being accessed from each table differs.

As a result the combined records are sorted as if they really come from one source (which technically is true via the Union query). Therefore, the distinction of fruits and vegetables is purposely lost, and instead, asparagus follows apple, broccoli follows banana, and so on.

This technique is useful when you need to present items in a list that come from more than one source. As discussed in the following section, you can bring together as many sources as you need with multiple Union clauses.

Controlling the Sort in a Listbox Populated from Multiple Sources

In Figure 3-12, List 2 shows the result of sorting fruits in a certain order and vegetables in a certain order. Additionally, the fruits and vegetables aren't sorted with each other. The list also includes separators and values not found in the source tables: All, All Fruits, and All Vegetables. How did all these items get into the list?

A Union query populates the listbox. The two sources—tblFruits and tblVegetables—are used, but instead of letting the list mix and sort the items alphabetically, the SortNumber field controls the sort.

A key point here is that the range of values for SortNumber in the tblFruits table is different from the range of values for SortNumber in the tblVegetables table. The Union operation actually does combine both sources into one sort, but the SortNumber field ranges keep the two lists apart in the listbox.

Figure 3-15 shows the form in Design mode with the property sheet set to List 2. The SQL statement that serves as the Row Source property is displayed in the Zoom box.

Here is the SQL statement:

```
Select "All" as a, -2 as SortNumber from tblFruits
Union Select "---"  as a, -1 as SortNumber from tblFruits
Union Select "All Fruits" as a, 0 as SortNumber from tblFruits
Union Select ListItem, SortNumber From tblFruits
Union Select "---" as a, 99 as SortNumber from tblVegetables
Union Select "All Vegetables" as a,
100 as SortNumber from tblVegetables
Union Select ListItem, SortNumber From tblVegetables
Order By SortNumber
```

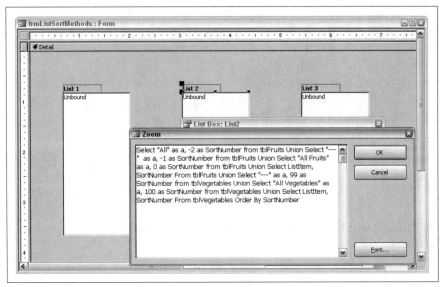

Figure 3-15. The Row Source property for List 2

Quite a bit is going on here. Overall, the SQL combines items from the source tables with items provided right within the SQL. All these tie together via the SortNumber field.

This SQL statement uses the Union clause several times, to make sure that all Select statements point to the same number of fields. In this example, that number is 2.

The SQL starts by getting the word All to the top of the list. This snippet forces the word All into the list:

```
Select "All" as a, -2 as SortNumber
```

The code snippet does this by giving the word All the lowest value of SortNumber—in this case, -2. To be clear, neither the word All nor the value -2 actually comes from an underlying table. However, their placement in the SQL follows the structure of all the other Select statements in the SQL, which allows them to be combined with the other values being accessed by the SQL.

The SQL uses Union to combine values from the tables with these on-the-fly values. A number of these values are in the SQL:

```
Select "All" as a, -2 as SortNumber from tblFruits
Select "---" as a, -1 as SortNumber from tblFruits
Select "All Fruits" as a, 0 as SortNumber from tblFruits
Select "---" as a, 99 as SortNumber from tblVegetables
Select "All Vegetables" as a, 100 as SortNumber from tblVegetables
```

All these parts of the SQL force the list to present a value: All, All Fruits, All Vegetables, or ---. None of these values comes from the tables. However, all of them are paired with a sort number, and this is what places them in their sequential place in the listbox.

Consider the sort numbers associated with these on-the-fly items, while considering the sort numbers of the items in the tables (see Figure 3-13). Sort numbers for the vegetables start at 101. Therefore, the All Vegetables item has been associated with the number 100. This forces it to appear in the list directly above the actual vegetables.

Keep in mind that a listbox such as this, with several possible items a user can select, also requires a related level of functionality to handle the user's selection. If a user selects a single fruit or vegetable, chances are the application will continue processing. However, what if a user selects All Fruits? Your processing will need to handle all the values in the tblFruits table.

Also note that you enter the separator characters (---) into the list for the sake of segregating parts of the lengthy list of items. This is rather pleasing for someone scrolling through a long list; however, a user can select the separators! Therefore, you need to ensure that user validation and feedback are in place in case this happens. Typically, if a user selects the separator characters, a message should appear alerting him to make another selection.

Sorting List Items by Popularity

It's not always easy to know ahead of time which items users will select most often from a list. You can use a Sort Number field to arrange list items in a way that seems best, but there is an even better way to do this.

Why not let user actions drive the way the list is sorted? Keeping in mind that it is easy to sort a list by a numerical field, logic dictates that the values in the numerical field should reflect the popularity of the list items.

This is easy to do by updating a list's Sort field each time it is selected. Figure 3-16 shows the form in Design mode with the property sheet set to List 3.

Here's the Row Source SQL statement for List 3:

```
SELECT Occurrence, ListItem FROM tblFruits ORDER BY Occurrence DESC;
```

This listbox uses the tblFruits table exclusively. This table has the additional Occurrence field, which drives the way items are sorted in the listbox. Note from the Row Source property that items are listed based on the Occurrence field values being in descending order.

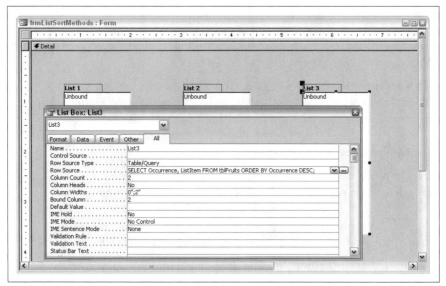

Figure 3-16. The Row Source property for List 3

To make sense of this, it is necessary to somehow update the values in the Occurrence field. This update occurs when you process the selected list value—in whatever way your processing works. For the purpose of this demonstration, a button has been placed on the form. Here's the Click event for the button:

```
Private Sub cmdUpdateCount_Click( )
   'get the current count for this item
   Dim selected_item_count As Integer
   If Not IsNull(Me.List3) Then
     selected_item_count = _
        DLookup("Occurrence", "tblFruits", "ListItem='" & Me.List3 & "'")
     'increase the count and update the table
     selected_item_count = selected_item_count + 1
     DoCmd.SetWarnings False
     DoCmd.RunSQL ("Update tblFruits Set Occurrence=" & _
        selected_item_count & " Where ListItem='" & Me.List3 & "'")
     Me.List3.Requery
   End If
End Sub
```

In a nutshell, the DLookup function finds the current value of the Occurrence field for the selected item and stores it in the selected_item_count variable. The value is incremented by 1, and a SQL Update statement writes the value back into the table, for the given item. Finally, the list is refreshed so that on the form the list will resort.

As a result, when items in the list are selected and processed, they float to the top of the list. You can see this by comparing the placement of items in List 3 in Figure 3-12 with the values of the Occurrence field in the tblFruits table in Figure 3-13. For example, raspberry is the first item in List 3 because it has the highest value in the Occurrence field.

HACK #23 Use Custom Controls on Your Forms

Move past standard Access controls, and discover new design possibilities.

If you develop enough Access applications, you begin to take the Toolbox for granted. You know all the controls and when to use them. But did you ever notice the Toolbox has a button that leads to more controls? Figure 3-17 shows where this button is located.

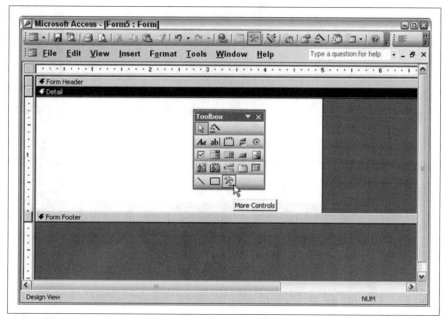

Figure 3-17. Finding additional controls

Clicking the More Controls button opens a list of new controls from which to select. I don't suggest testing all of them because I think that some aren't useful in Access. However, if you scroll to the Microsoft controls, you might find some interesting ones to try on a form. Let's see how we can use a few of these custom controls.

Adding a Custom Control to a Form

The list of controls will probably differ between computer systems, but it's a safe bet that you have the Microsoft Forms controls loaded on your computer because they are installed with Microsoft Office.

As an example, I placed a Microsoft Forms 2.0 spinbutton control on a form, as shown in Figure 3-18. I did this by simply selecting it from the long control list and then drawing on the form using the mouse.

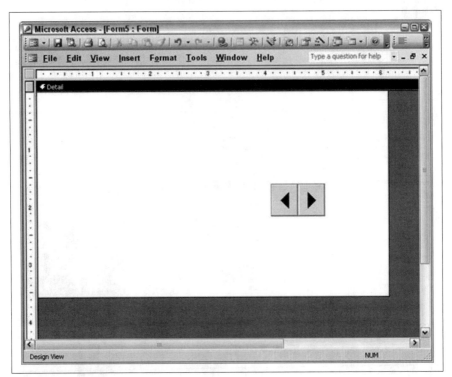

Figure 3-18. A spinbutton control on a form

The spinbutton control has minimum and maximum value properties that you can set. Therefore, you can use the spinner to cycle through from 1–100, 128–133, or whatever makes sense for your application. You can access the spinner's value from code in the same way you do for other controls.

Next, I put the Microsoft Date and Time Picker Control 6.0 on the form, as shown in Figure 3-19. This nifty control stays in a collapsed state until you click it. It then opens to a scrollable calendar. This is a great user enhancement; users don't have to enter dates manually when you put such a control as this on a form. And the good thing about this control is that it remains small when it's not in use.

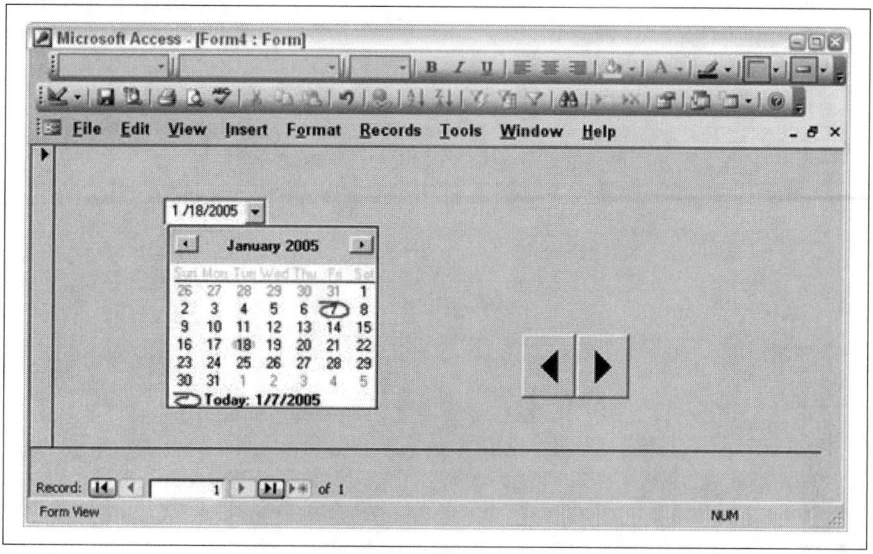

Figure 3-19. Making it easy to select a date

It's useful to become familiar with a few of the new controls and to think of them as part of your control toolbox. This opens the door to new ways to design forms, and it provides users with an enhanced experience.

See Also

- "Play Videos in Access Forms" [Hack #34]
- "Use a Browser Inside Access" [Hack #97]

HACK #24 Confirm Record Updates Before Saving
Give users a chance to review their edits before they save a record.

When you're working on a bound form, as you scroll through records, data changes are saved automatically. This behavior is normal and is often appreciated rather than questioned. However, sometimes it is prudent to interrupt this process and let a user review her work. Once the update happens, the original data is gone, unless other measures, such as backups, are in place.

One thing that works in our favor to control this is the Before Update event. By hooking into this event, you can ask the user whether she wants to complete the update. If the answer is no, you undo the changes.

Users should control whether they want to be prompted to confirm changes because the prompts can become annoying. A user might want this feature sometimes but not other times. Figure 3-20 shows a form with a checkbox in the upper-right section that acts as a flag indicating whether to confirm updates.

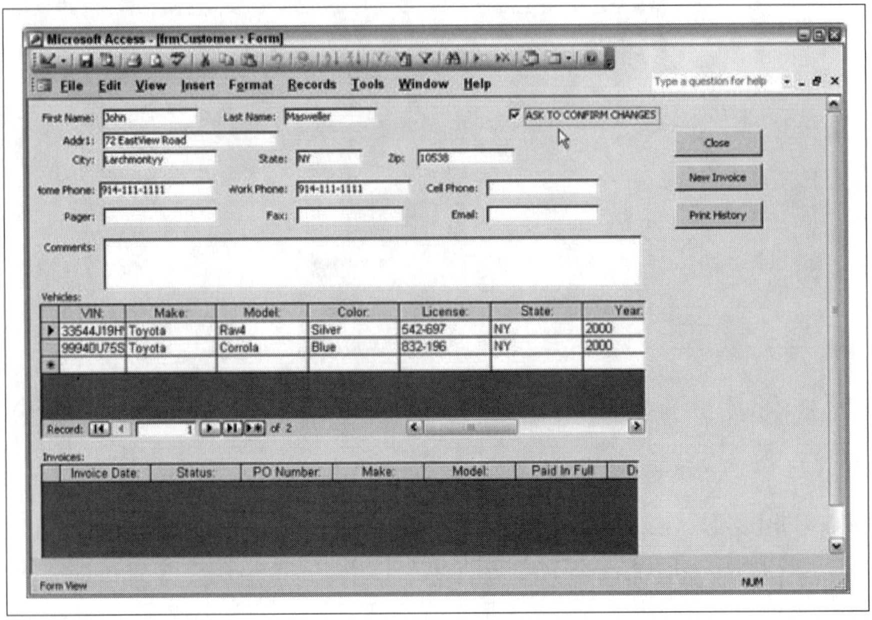

Figure 3-20. A checkbox to indicate whether to confirm updates

The Before Update event fires only when the data changes. In the event, the checkbox value is tested, and if the value is true, the user is prompted. Figure 3-21 shows the prompt.

If the user clicks Yes, the update proceeds. If she clicks No, an undo command runs, thereby dropping the changes to the data. Here is the event and the code:

```
Private Sub Form_BeforeUpdate(Cancel As Integer)
  If Me.chkConfirm = True Then
    proceed = MsgBox("Do you want to save the changes?", vbYesNo, _
      "Save Changes")
    If proceed = vbNo Then
      DoCmd.RunCommand acCmdUndo
    End If
  End If
End Sub
```

A key point to this hack is letting the user decide whether to be prompted. Being asked to confirm endless changes will quickly become a source of

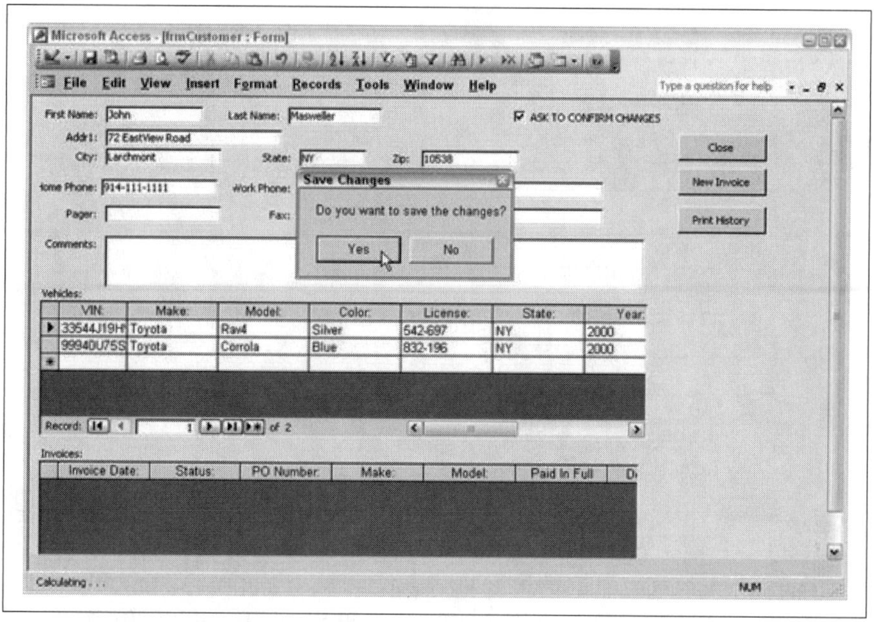

Figure 3-21. Confirming an update

frustration. The nice thing is that users can decide to turn on the feature when updating critical information, such as names and addresses, but turn off the feature when making changes to less important data.

Put a Clock on a Form
HACK #25

Give users the time and date, even for more than one time zone.

By combining a form's On Timer event, its timer interval, and the system clock, you can place a functional clock on a form.

Figure 3-22 shows a form with a clock in the header. Its placement in the header, and not in the details section, makes sense because it is unbound and isn't specific to any record in the detail.

You can go about your business moving through records, editing data, and so on; the time will just keep ticking away undisturbed.

Creating the Clock

The clock is easy to create. First, place a label control on the form. Then, set the form's timer interval to 1,000 (which equals one second). Finally, place a single line of code in the form's On Timer event:

```
Me.lblClock.Caption = Format(Now( ), "hh:mm:ss AMPM")
```

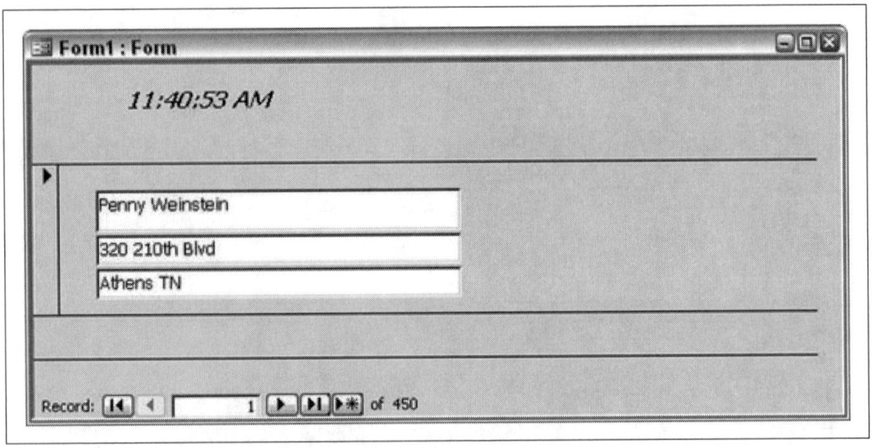

Figure 3-22. A form that tells the time

This assumes the label control is named lblClock. The Now function returns the system time, and the Format function gives the time a desirable look. The format isn't necessary, though. If you don't use it, the full date and time is returned. The format, as applied here, displays just the time; hh:mm:ss is a format for hours (hh), minutes (mm), and seconds (ss).

Hacking the Hack

You can do a lot to boost the clock's appeal and functionality. One idea is to display the time for cities in different time zones. Figure 3-23 shows a form with two clocks. One displays the time in New York, and the other displays the time in Chicago.

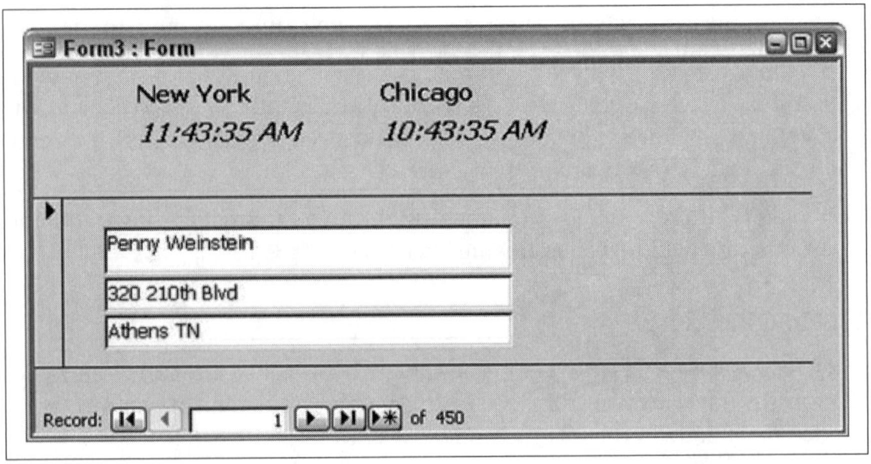

Figure 3-23. Two clocks on a form

Chicago is one hour behind New York. You account for the one-hour difference by applying the DateAdd function. Here is the updated On Timer event:

```
Me.lblClockNewYork.Caption = Format(Now( ), "hh:mm:ss AMPM")
Me.lblClockChicago.Caption = Format(DateAdd("h", -1, Now( )), _
    "hh:mm:ss AMPM")
```

DateAdd can add or subtract time. In this case, a value of -1 subtracts one hour.

Here's another idea: give the user a way to change the format. You accomplish this by using a public variable and the label control's DblClick event. When the form is opened, a public variable, named format_type in this example, is given a value of 1. Each time a user double-clicks the clock, the format_type variable increments. When it hits 4, it is set back to 1. The On Timer event tests the format_type variable and applies the particular format. Here is the full code behind the form that takes care of this:

```
Option Compare Database
Public format_type As String

Private Sub Form_Open(Cancel As Integer)
   format_type = 1
End Sub

Private Sub Form_Timer( )
Select Case format_type
  Case 1
     Me.lblClock.Caption = Format(Now( ), "hh:mm:ss AMPM")
  Case 2
     Me.lblClock.Caption = Format(Now( ), "hh:mm AMPM")
   Case Else
     Me.lblClock.Caption = Format(Now( ), "mm/dd hh:mm AMPM")
 End Select
End Sub

Private Sub lblClock_DblClick(Cancel As Integer)
   format_type = format_type + 1
   If format_type = 4 Then format_type = 1
End Sub
```

Now, a user can double-click the clock until it displays the date and time in a way that suits him. Of course, you can easily increase the number of available formats.

Be Tab-Smart

#26 Override a form's tab order so that users get to the entry boxes they need.

Setting the tab order is probably not the biggest thing on your mind when you design a form. It doesn't really require much planning or analysis.

Typically, you do it at the end, after all the controls are in place. To be honest, at times I've simply forgotten to set a tab order on my forms. But, of course, the user community lets me know when that happens.

So, I started thinking that if tab stops on a form are really important to users, why not go one step better and make the tab order work more intelligently. On some forms only some boxes receive entries. A smart way to tab through a form in this situation is to sense which entry boxes can be skipped.

This makes sense when the condition or entry into a text box is based on some understandable logic flow. For example, if you're entering information about a new customer, usually you fill in every field. However, when you're entering a piece of information on an existing customer, most likely you tab over several text boxes.

Figure 3-24 shows a form in which a selection has been made from a combo box. The combo box, named Status, has four choices: Enrolled, Walk-In, Phone, and Renewal.

In the Exit event of the combo box, a Select Case statement sets the focus to different form controls, depending on the selection made in the combo box. For example, a status of Walk-In is used for unregistered people who come in without an appointment. They need to be set up in the system, so the next entry box to go to is the Referral Source. By contrast, when an Enrolled person comes in, the next box to enter is Comments. Here is the code in the Exit event:

```
Private Sub status_Exit(Cancel As Integer)
Select Case status
  Case "Enrolled"
     Me.txtComments.SetFocus
  Case "Walk-In"
     Me.txtReferralSource.SetFocus
  Case "Renewal"
     Me.txtStudentFirstName.SetFocus
End Select
End Sub
```

The gist of this approach is that you can apply rules to the tab order based on what makes sense to the business. As another example, a database system at a car dealership should skip right over a section about what type of new car a customer wants to purchase if she is in the market for a used car. If the section about new cars contains 12 fields, the salesperson needs to tab through 12 unneeded boxes, unless a better method is in place. Instead, some other control on the form can act as a flag so that you can implement smart tabbing. Using the Exit events of controls is a great way to support this business workflow.

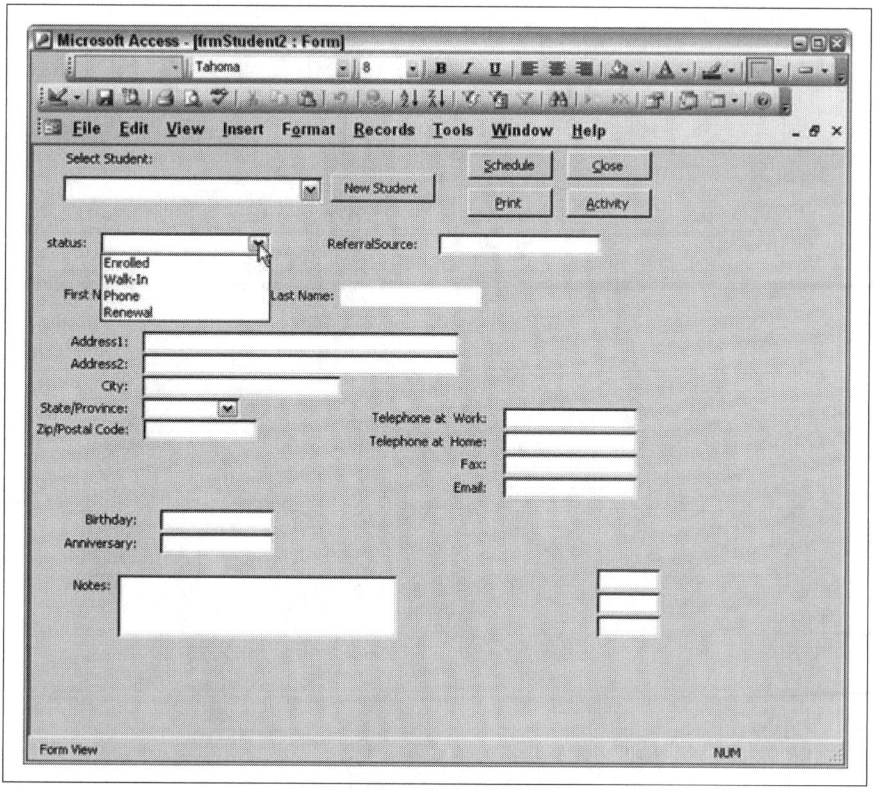

Figure 3-24. A combo box selection to drive the tab order

Highlight the Active Control

HACK #27

Provide a visual aid on a busy form by emphasizing the control that has the focus.

As you tab through a form and enter data, it is possible to get lost. The more controls on a form, the more likely this is to occur. This hack shows you how to keep the current entry box highlighted.

"Be Tab-Smart" **[Hack #26]** shows a way in which users can tab around the form in a sensible manner. That hack works with a little code put into a control's Exit event. This hack uses the Exit event, as well as the Enter event. In this hack, all controls that accept entry have code in both events.

Figure 3-25 shows the entry form with a border around the First Name entry box. As a user tabs through the form or clicks specific controls, the border will always appear around the active control. The border is displayed on only one control at a time.

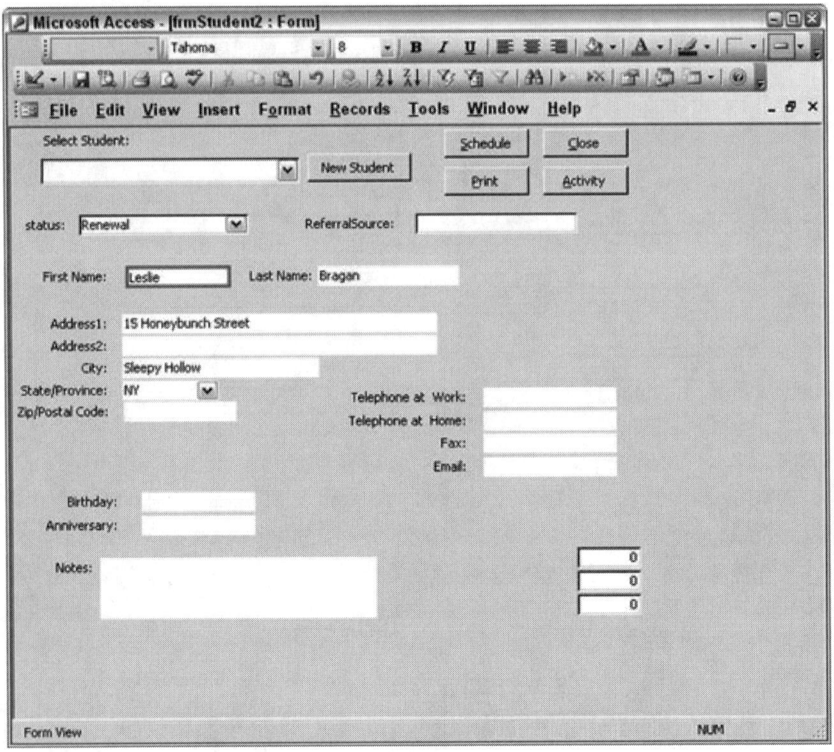

Figure 3-25. A border appearing around the active control

To get this to work, the controls on the form must have their Special Effect property set to Flat. You can use other settings that allow borders to be displayed, such as Shadow, but Flat seems to work best. When Shadow is used, and when the control loses the border, the control still retains the shadow part of the border, and that doesn't look right.

Figure 3-26 shows the code module behind the form. Two subroutines are at the top: active_control_enter and active_control_exit. These subroutines run when they're called by each control's Enter and Exit events. The active_control_enter subroutine sets the active control, whatever it is at the time, to have a thick, red border. The border style value of 1 indicates a solid border. The border width value of 2 indicates a thick border. Red is then set as the border color.

The active_control_exit subroutine has just a single line of code; it sets the border to transparent.

Figure 3-26. The code for turning a border on and off

Each time a control is entered, it means a different control was just exited. Therefore, these two subroutines fire in a pair. The Exit routine turns off the border for one control, and the Enter routine turns it on for another.

Using the technique in this hack ensures that users clearly see which control is active.

CHAPTER FOUR

Presentation

Hacks 28–39

As comprehensive as a database can be—with programmatic functionality, sophisticated queries, and other bells and whistles—you still need to be able to *communicate* facts about the data it contains. This is where forms and reports come into play. A decent database front end is critical for interaction between the database and us mere mortals. Access, of course, shines in this area.

The report designer in Access is a feature-rich development platform. It includes formatting tools, grouping and sorting options, a palette full of controls, and the ability to hook into events and muster up some coolness with VBA. Forms also have events, formatting options, and properties galore. Putting them all to use is beyond the scope of a single chapter. So instead, this chapter highlights some exciting ways to work with forms and reports.

You've already seen how to use forms to display database records. How about using a form to play a slideshow or movies? "Create a Slideshow in Access" [Hack #33] and "Play Videos in Access Forms" [Hack #34] show you how.

First impressions are usually the best. Make sure your reports are eye-poppers. A number of hacks in this chapter explain how to provide sophisticated grouping and formatting in reports. "Provide a Direct Link to a Report" [Hack #31] shows how a busy user can click a shortcut to print a report without fussing around with the database. "View Reports Embedded in Forms" [Hack #35] explains how to incorporate reports into forms.

HACK #28 Separate Alphabetically Sorted Records into Letter Groups

Tap the Prefix Characters property to gain new layout possibilities.

Sorting alphabetically is nothing new; in fact, it's rather old—one of the standard practices we take for granted. When you've got dozens or hundreds of printed records, though, it can be tedious to flip through report pages looking for a particular line item, even though they're in alphabetical order.

A neat thing to do is to segregate the records on a report alphabetically. Figure 4-1 shows a page from a report in which sorted records list repeatedly with *no* such segregation or break. The records are sorted—no question on that score—but the layout makes it challenging to flip to the approximate area you need to find.

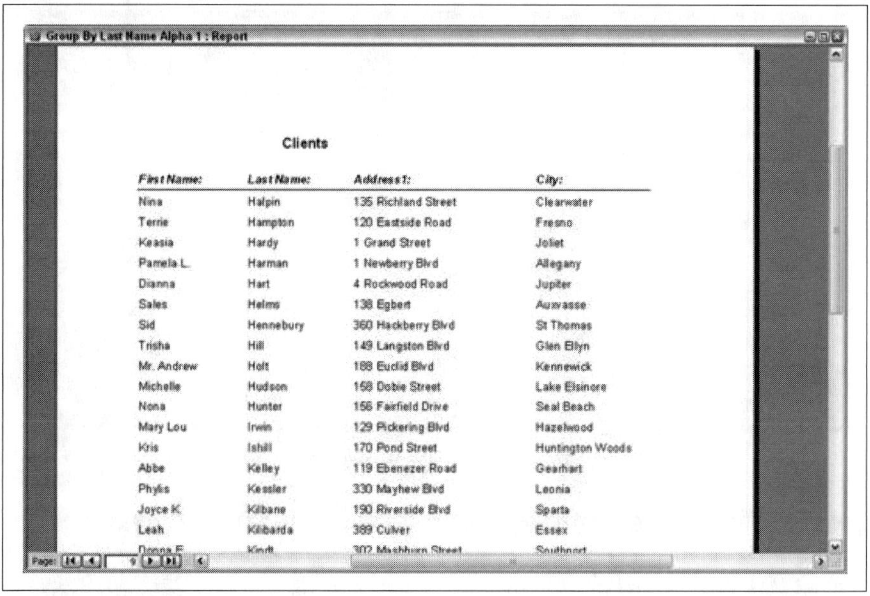

Figure 4-1. A report with a repetitive layout

The report's design is straightforward. The details section contains the fields that become the line items. The report in this format doesn't use groups, and that is why it is monotonous to look at. Figure 4-2 shows the design of the report.

Segregating by Letter

A way to break up the endless line-item listing is to add a group to the report. Figure 4-3 shows how the report's design has been altered to include a group.

The group is based on the ClientLastName field, which, of course, is the field being sorted on. Here are a few key points about how this group is being used:

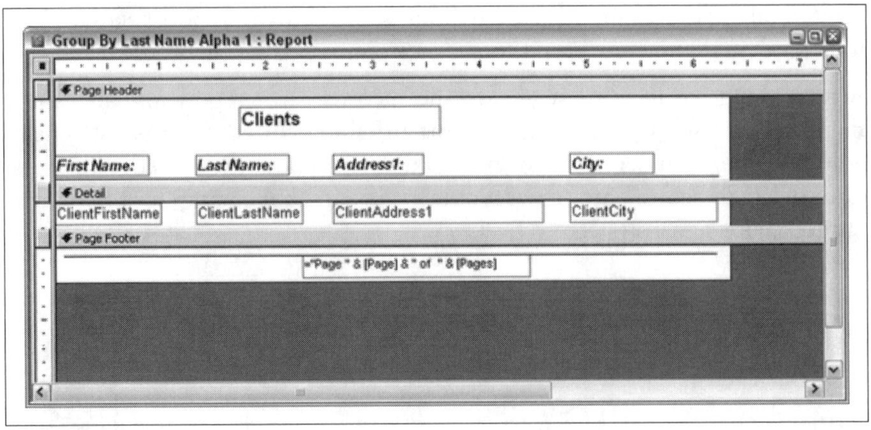

Figure 4-2. A report that doesn't use grouping and sorting

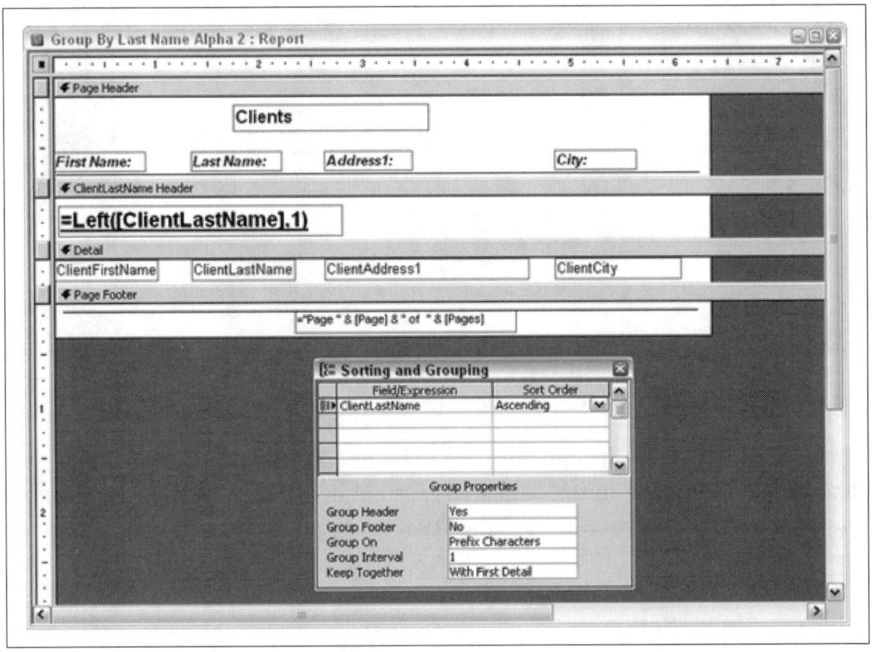

Figure 4-3. A report that uses grouping and sorting

- The group has a header. A footer isn't required. In the Sorting and Grouping dialog box, Group Header and Group Footer are set to Yes and No, respectively.

- In the Sorting and Grouping dialog box, the Group On property is set to Prefix Characters, and the Group Interval property is set to 1.

- In the group header itself, an unbound text box has been inserted, and its `Control Source` property is set to an expression.

When the report runs, the expression in the unbound text box forces the group break to occur on the letters of the alphabet, instead of on each occurrence of a last name. As a result, all the *A*s are together, all the *B*s are together, and so on. You accomplish this by using the `Left` function to return the first letter:

```
=Left([ClientLastName],1)
```

Figure 4-4 shows how the report segregates by letter.

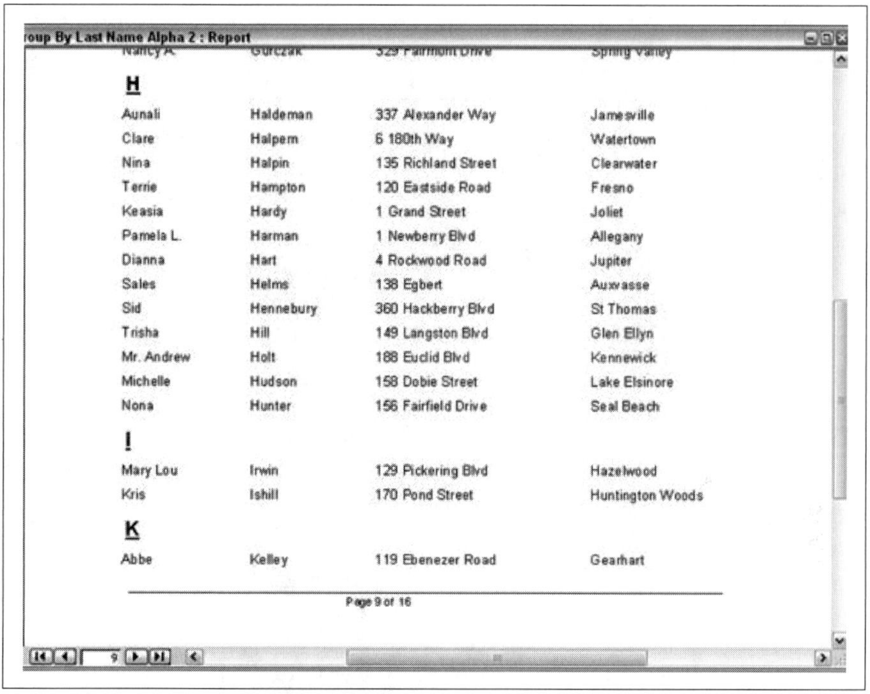

Figure 4-4. Clients broken out by first letter

The larger font, bold, and underline settings make the distinctions visually clear when thumbing through a report.

Hacking the Hack

Note that on the report page shown in Figure 4-4, none of the clients' last names start with the letter J. The fact that some records don't exist could be vital news to someone. I can just hear the boss yelling, "What happened to the Johnson account?" Such a reaction is based on expecting to see something that isn't there. The flip side to this is that missing records might be identified *only* by pointing out that no records have met a condition.

In particular, it would be useful if the report stated that no records were found for the letter J. We need a way to still display the alphabetic letter on the report, but in the current design, this won't ever happen. Any alphabetic letters that currently appear on the report are there because records in which the last name starts with the letter J *do* exist.

To get all letters to appear on the report, regardless of whether records beginning with those letters exist, include somewhere in the design a list of all the letters to be compared against. The approach used here is to relate the client table with a table of the letters, instead of basing the report on just the client table.

A table is added to the database with just one field: Letter. The table contains 26 records, for the letters A through Z. Figure 4-5 shows the table, named tblLetters.

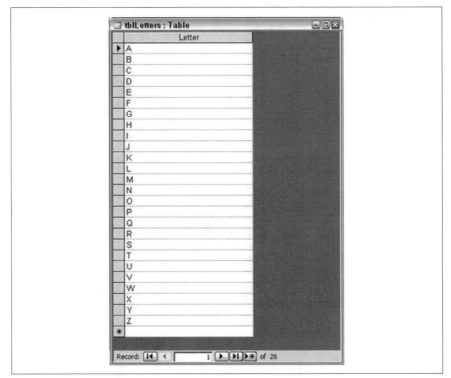

Figure 4-5. A table filled with letters of the alphabet

It's not a bad idea to include the digits 0–9 in the table as well, especially if you're working with the names of companies.

The report's Record Source property was previously set to the client table (tblClients). Now, though, the report's record source will be based on a query. Here is the SQL statement:

```
SELECT tblClients.ClientFirstName, tblClients.ClientLastName,
tblClients.ClientAddress1, tblClients.ClientCity, tblLetters.Letter
FROM tblClients RIGHT JOIN tblLetters ON
left(tblClients.ClientLastName,1) = tblLetters.Letter;
```

A key point about this statement is that a RIGHT JOIN is used to relate the tables. This ensures that all records from the letters table (tblLetters) will be present. In other words, every letter will be available to the report, even when no last names start with that letter.

The report's design also needs a slight change. The group is no longer based on the last name; instead, it's based on the Letter field. Also, a new expression is used in the unbound text box. Figure 4-6 shows these changes.

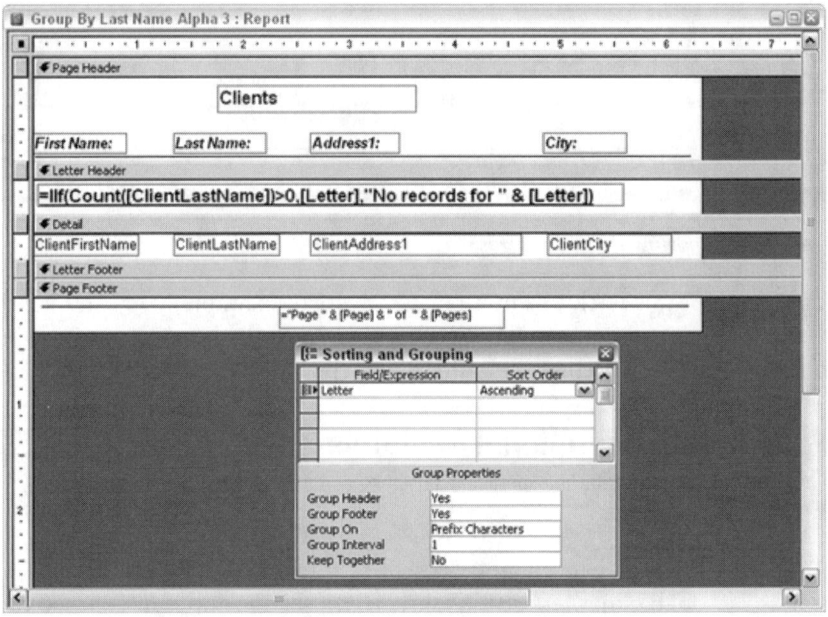

Figure 4-6. Grouping on the alphabet

The expression in the text box returns one of two possible statements. When at least one record contains a last name starting with a given letter, the letter is displayed. When no records contain a last name starting with the given letter, a message is displayed that no records were found for that letter. You accomplish this using the IIF and Count functions:

```
=IIf(Count([ClientLastName])>0,[Letter],"No records for " & [Letter])
```

As a result, this report has all the alphabetical letters as group headers, regardless of whether any records match, as shown in Figure 4-7.

Group By Last Name Alpha 3 : Report			
Trisha	Hill	149 Langston Blvd	Glen Ellyn
Nona	Hunter	156 Fairfield Drive	Seal Beach
Nina	Halpin	135 Richland Street	Clearwater
Dianna	Hart	4 Rockwood Road	Jupiter
Keasia	Hardy	1 Grand Street	Joliet
Sid	Hennebury	360 Hackberry Blvd	St Thomas
Mr. Andrew	Holt	188 Euclid Blvd	Kennewick
Aunali	Haldeman	337 Alexander Way	Jamesville
Sales	Helms	138 Egbert	Auxvasse
Terrie	Hampton	120 Eastside Road	Fresno
Clare	Halpern	6 180th Way	Watertown
I			
Mary Lou	Irwin	129 Pickering Blvd	Hazelwood
Kris	Ishill	170 Pond Street	Huntington Wood
No records for J			
K			
Dave	Konneker	102 Powhatton Way	Riverhead
Alberta	Kramer	7 Mariposa Way	Garberville
Lily	Kurian	104 Haverston	Yelm
Donna E.	Kindt	302 Mashburn Street	Southport
Page 9 of 16			

Page: 9

Figure 4-7. *Reporting that no records exist*

You can adapt this hack in a number of ways. For example, you can hide the details section, and you can alter the expression in the header to print a line only when no records exist. This alters the report to list exceptions only.

HACK #29 Create Conditional Subtotals

Split a grand total into pertinent business summaries using running sums and expressions.

A common request is to create two sets of totals for comparison. This, by itself, is reasonable in a report design; you can set a group that is based on a field that breaks on different values. A perfect example is data based on a year. If the report includes a Year field, you can include subtotals in the group footer. That is, you can get a summary (of whatever other fields) for each year.

But when you throw in the need to report totals on more than one condition, things start to get a bit messy. You can create two groups, but you must decide which group nests inside the other. That decision isn't always clear-cut. Added to this are various layout options. If you want to arrange these subtotals in any fashion other than underneath each other, you are out of luck—that is, unless you use running sums and calculated controls.

Figure 4-8 shows a report that displays grand totals for each year and, underneath them, the yearly grand totals separated by each state's contribution.

```
Visits 2003 2004 : Report

                    Customer Visits Per State, 2003 vs. 2004


                    2003                              2004

            Total Visits:   707              Total Visits:   890


        Total Visits in CT:   127        Total Visits in CT:   153
        Total Visits in MA:   80         Total Visits in MA:   93
        Total Visits in NY:   169        Total Visits in NY:   231
        Total Visits in NJ:   195        Total Visits in NJ:   246
        Total Visits in PA:   136        Total Visits in PA:   167


Page:  I◄  ◄     1   ►  ►I   ◄
```

Figure 4-8. Grand totals and subtotals

> Of course, you can create a report such as the one in Figure 4-8 using other methods; for instance, you could use a subreport instead. The running sums method outlined in this hack is only one method available for reporting totals on more than one condition.

This hack uses an example of a veterinary practice, which has data about visits to the practice over two years and clients who come from five different states. The report's record source is based on a Union query that combines two identical Select queries—identical, that is, except that one uses records for 2003 and the other uses records for 2004. The report's record source, therefore, is the following statement:

```
SELECT * FROM qryServiceDates_2003
Union SELECT * FROM qryServiceDates_2004
```

Figure 4-9 shows the qryServiceDates_2003 query. Each customer has zero or more pets, and each pet has zero or more visits. Bear in mind that the report reports on visits only. The type of pet isn't relevant, but the data model calls for the pets table (tblPets) to be included.

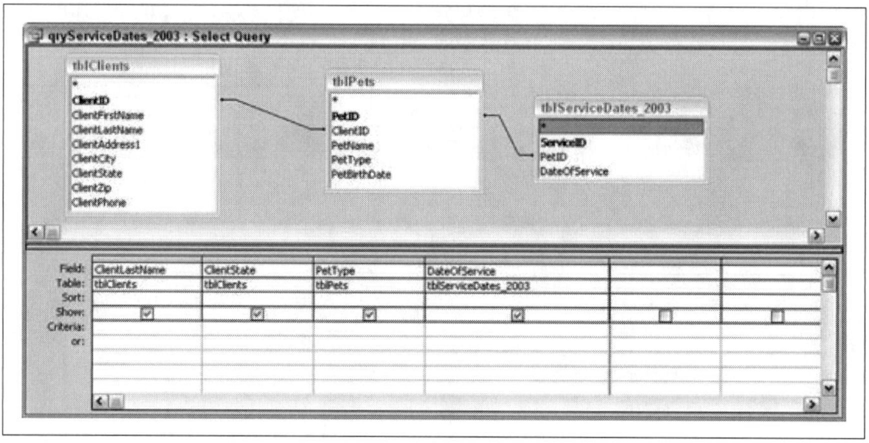

Figure 4-9. Querying information about visits

Using Running Sums

This report processes hundreds of records, but only the totals appear because the detail section's Visible property has been set to false. Even so, the details section plays a vital role in housing a set of text boxes that are used for running sums. Figure 4-10 shows the report design.create two sets of totals for comparison. This, by

In addition to actual data fields, the detail section contains 10 unbound text boxes, all of which have the Running Sum property set to Over All, as shown in the property sheet in Figure 4-10.

The 10 text boxes handle the 10 possible conditions. The data comprises two years and five states, for a total of 10 possible subtotals. Each unbound text box has a calculation for its control source. For example, the txtCT2004 text box contains this expression:

```
=IIf([ClientState]="CT" And Year([DateOfService])=2004,1,0)
```

This statement gets the running sum to increment only when the state is CT and the year is 2004. Each text box works in this way, with each incrementing on some variation of the two conditions, state and year.

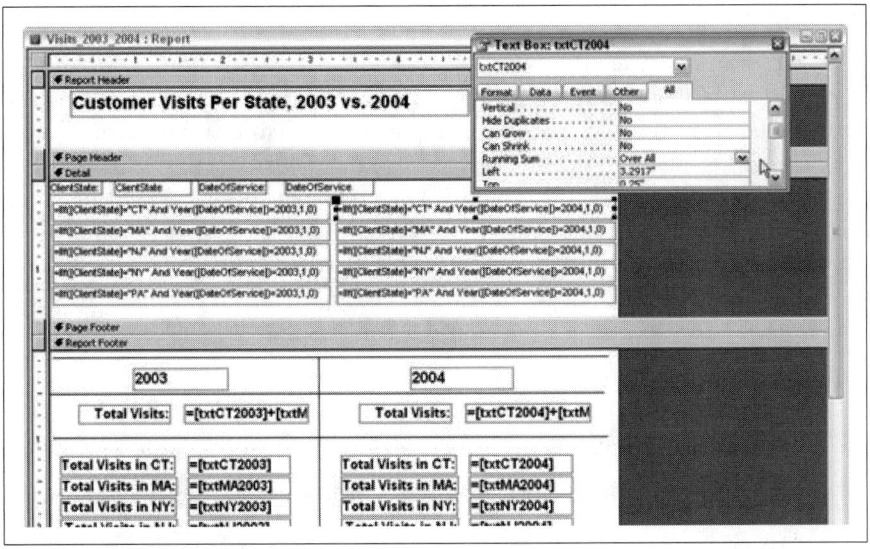

Figure 4-10. The Running Sum property set to Over All

The names of these text boxes are vital because they are referenced in other controls in the report footer. The names are txtCT2003, txtCT2004, txtMA2003, txtMA2004, and so on. All in all, five states are used: CT, MA, NY, NJ, and PA.

The report footer contains two areas, one for the summary of each year. The areas are separated visually with some line controls. There is no real setting to split the report footer.

All the text boxes in the report footer are unbound, and they reference the text boxes in the detail section. For example, the report footer text box that displays the total for CT for 2003 simply references the txtCT2003 running sum text box, with this statement:

```
=[txtCT2003]
```

The 10 summaries in the report footer that display a sum based on year and state all work in the same way. Each references a single text box from the detail section. The two grand totals in the footer, the ones based on total year, simply sum the associated five text boxes from the detail section. For example, the text box that displays the grand total for 2004 has this statement for its control source:

```
=[txtCT2004]+[txtMA2004]+[txtNY2004]+[txtNJ2004]+[txtPA2004]
```

By calculating totals in the detail section and then referencing those running sum text boxes, you can arrange the report's layout any way you wish.

Hacking the Hack

The data model shown in this hack (see Figure 4-9) includes a table with pets. What if the user wanted to report by year, state, *and* pet? Assuming the data includes 10 types of pets (cat, dog, bird, and so on), you would have 100 variations of conditions: that is, 2 years times 5 states times 10 pet types. You could create such a report using the steps described in this hack, but this would be tedious. A better approach with such a large number of conditions is to base the report on a Crosstab query. The example in "Summarize Complex Data" [Hack #45] uses the data model from this hack to show how such a query works.

See Also

- "Summarize Complex Data" [Hack #45]
- "Use Conditional Formatting to Point Out Important Results" [Hack #30]

HACK #30 Use Conditional Formatting to Point Out Important Results

Not only can you use the built-in conditional formatting feature, but you also can roll your own with a little VBA!

Why not add a little impact to important results or facts about your data? Instead of having a report display results textually, use a bit of formatting based on conditions in the data to draw readers' eyes directly to the important news. If the news is good, you can take all the credit and maybe get a promotion. If the news is bad, you can always use the "Don't shoot the messenger" line.

"Create Conditional Subtotals" [Hack #29] demonstrates how to create a report based on data that covers two years, with each year broken out as its own total. This is great for common analyses in which you're comparing results from one year to the next to see how much the data has changed (including whether the change was positive or negative).

Some reports, however, also print a third column indicating the percent change when the two values are compared. Although this isn't covered here, you can apply the conditional formatting explained in this hack to the percent change text boxes if you choose to include them.

Standard Conditional Formatting

Access provides a nice conditional formatting utility. With it you can easily change font attributes, foreground color, and background color properties when a specified condition is met. Figure 4-11 shows the Conditional Formatting dialog box. In this example, expressions have been entered for the conditions. Alternatively, you can base the conditions on actual data values.

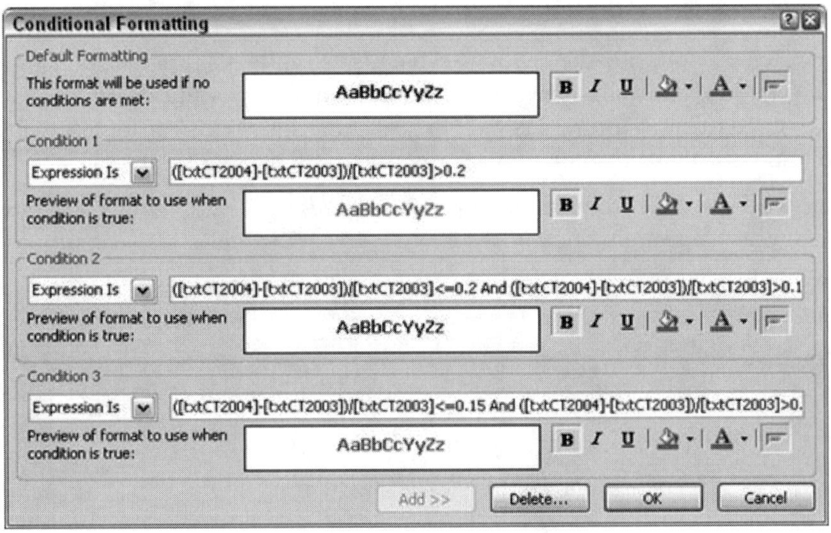

Figure 4-11. Font colors that change based on the condition

Use the Format → Conditional Formatting... menu to display the Conditional Formatting dialog box. The Conditional Formatting dialog box manages formatting for one control at a time. Therefore, you must select a control before you can access the menu. Also, the menu item is disabled unless conditional formatting can be applied to the selected control.

Figure 4-11 shows the conditional formatting that has been set up for the txtCT2004Total text box. In particular, for this control the following three formatting options have been set, to test for the difference in percentage between the 2003 and 2004 amounts:

Greater than 20%
```
([txtCT2004]-[txtCT2003])/[txtCT2003]>0.2
```

Greater than 15% and equal to or less than 20%
```
([txtCT2004]-[txtCT2003])/[txtCT2003]<=0.2 And _
        ([txtCT2004]-[txtCT2003])/[txtCT2003]>0.15
```

Greater than 10% and equal to or less than 15%
```
([txtCT2004]-[txtCT2003])/[txtCT2003]<=0.15 And _
        ([txtCT2004]-[txtCT2003])/[txtCT2003]>0.1
```

Each condition provides different formatting based on selections made in the Conditional Formatting dialog box. This works fine, but the three-condition limit might require another approach.

Conditional Formatting the VBA Way

By placing code into the report's event stubs, you can provide robust formatting—beyond what the standard conditional formatting feature allows. The standard formatting has two major limitations: you can test for three conditions only, and some of the formatting options aren't available.

The workaround is to just code up your own using VBA. Figure 4-12 shows the report; note that Total Visits for 2004 is set in italic and has a border around it.

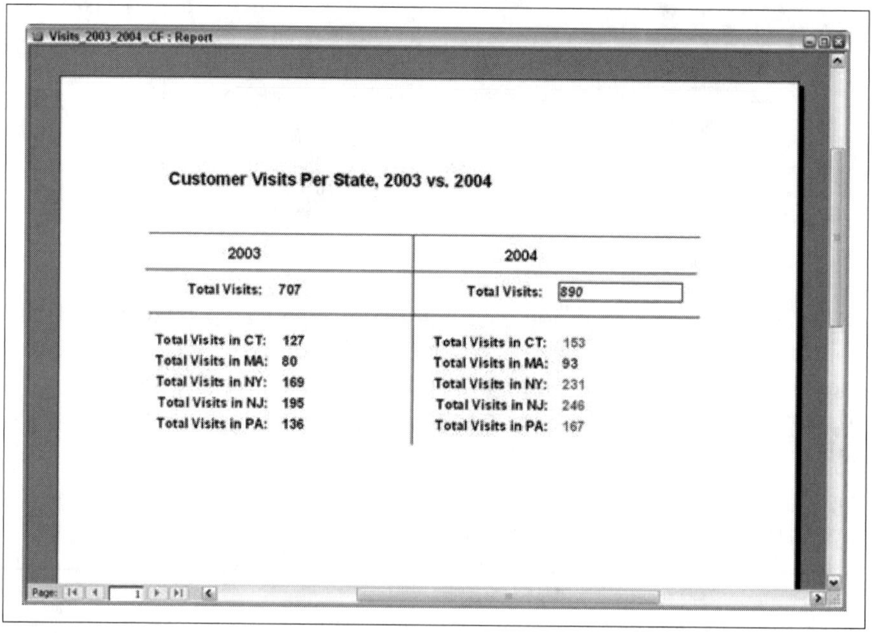

Figure 4-12. Conditional formatting applied through VBA code

This formatting was applied because a condition was met, based on what was tested in the code. This code has been placed in the report's ReportFooter_Print event:

```
Private Sub ReportFooter_Print(Cancel As Integer, PrintCount As Integer)
    Dim visits_change As Single
    visits_change = ([txt2004Total] - [txt2003Total]) / [txt2003Total]
    Select Case visits_change
        Case Is > 0.25
```

```
        Me.txt2004Total.Properties("ForeColor") = vbBlue
        Me.txt2004Total.Properties("Borderstyle") = 1
        Me.txt2004Total.Properties("BorderColor") = vbBlack
        Me.txt2004Total.Properties("FontItalic") = 1
      Case Is <= 0.25, Is > 0.2
        Me.txt2004Total.Properties("ForeColor") = vbBlue
      Case Is <= 0.2, Is > 0.15
        Me.txt2004Total.Properties("ForeColor") = vbGreen
      Case Is <= 0.15, Is > 0.1
        Me.txt2004Total.Properties("ForeColor") = vbMagenta
      Case Is <= 0.1, Is > 0
        Me.txt2004Total.Properties("ForeColor") = vbBlack
      Case Is <= 0
        Me.txt2004Total.Properties("Borderstyle") = 1
        Me.txt2004Total.Properties("BorderColor") = vbRed
    End Select
  End Sub
```

The code tests the percentage change and then uses a Select Case statement to apply different formatting based on the percentage change. Six conditions are provided, but you aren't limited in terms of number of conditions; use whatever number makes sense for your application. Also, the type of formatting is open to whatever you can control through VBA, which is just about everything.

HACK #31 Provide a Direct Link to a Report

Provide a desktop shortcut to a report so that users can completely skip the process of starting up the database.

What can be easier for a manager or a database-challenged individual than just skipping the process of opening the database? You can easily provide this functionality by including a shortcut directly to the report. The shortcut goes on the user's desktop.

Creating a Shortcut

To create such a shortcut, first open the database, and then right-click the desired report. The context menu includes a Create Shortcut... menu item, as shown in Figure 4-13.

When the user clicks the Create Shortcut... menu item, a dialog box pops up for her to select where to place the shortcut. The user's PC desktop will probably be filled in as the default, as shown in Figure 4-14.

After the user clicks the OK button, the desired shortcut is created. Clicking the shortcut starts up the database and opens the report, but unfortunately, the database stays open.

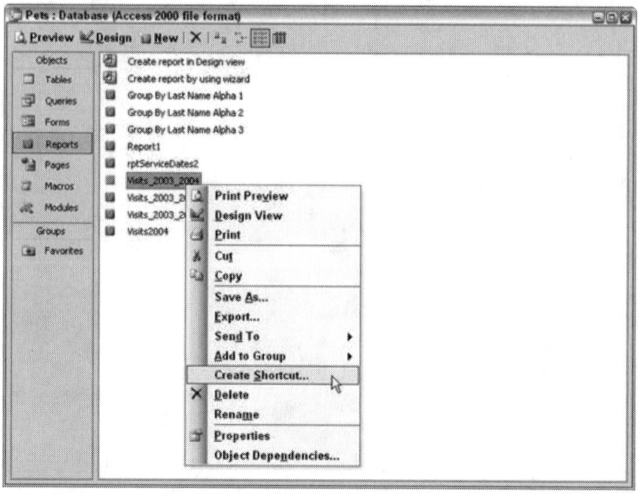

Figure 4-13. Creating a shortcut to a report

Figure 4-14. Selecting the location for the shortcut

Printing a Report and Closing the Database in One Click

A better approach is to enable the user to click the shortcut, print the report, and close the database afterward, all automatically via a single click. Sounds like a macro to me!

Figure 4-15 shows a simple macro that prints a report and then closes the database.

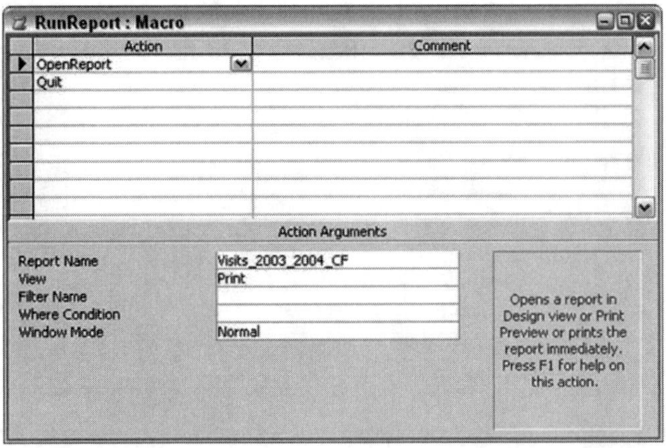

Figure 4-15. Using a macro to run the report and close the database

All that is necessary is the action to open the report. It's important that View is set to Print, not to Print Preview or Design. This sends the report directly to the printer instead of displaying it. The follow-up Quit action closes the database.

Note that if the report is usually generated with selections made on a form, you should create a shortcut to the form instead. You can create such short-cuts for any database object.

HACK #32   Protect Intellectual Property

Prevent misuse of confidential and copyrighted material by printing watermarks on reports.

If someone is bent on taking your intellectual property, you have no fool-proof way to prevent it. However, common sense dictates that we do our best to protect our assets. Often, putting some wording on the page or in the report header or footer saying the material is confidential serves this need. However, this method doesn't necessarily make the message stick out like a sore thumb.

An additional measure is to put *watermarks* on reports. A watermark sits right within the body of a report, page after page. It ends up underneath the actual text and is somewhat transparent; that way, it doesn't obscure the text, but it is evident enough to get the message across in a big way.

Figure 4-16 shows a report in which a watermark sits mixed in with the data. The word "Confidential" stretches diagonally from the lower left to the upper right. The text appears to sit on top of the watermark.

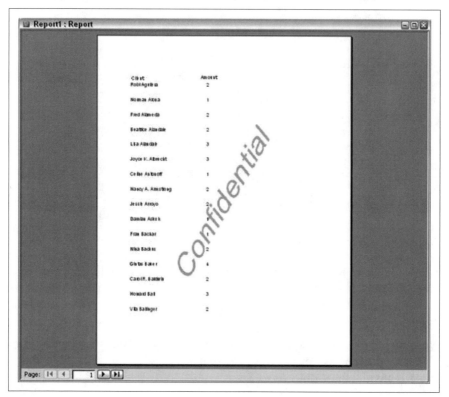

Figure 4-16. Using a watermark to get the message across

Making the Watermark

To create a watermark, you need to create a graphic that you will set to the Picture property on a report. You will need a graphics program to create a decent watermark. Several good graphics programs are available. I use an excellent, affordable program called Paint Shop Pro by Corel Corp. (*http://www.jasc.com*). Whichever graphics program you use, it must be able to do the following:

Work with text as a graphic
> You want to be able to stretch and orient the data.

Apply transparency settings
> The final graphic should be in the ballpark of 75% transparent. It's best to determine the actual setting via trial and error.

Specify the size of the graphic
> When creating the graphic, it's important to make it almost as large as the paper you are using. Whatever size you make the graphic is the size it appears on the report (based on a property setting described later in this hack).

Save the graphic as a .jpg, .bmp, and so on
> You can use any file format that can be used when tapping the Picture property on the report.

Creating such a graphic is beyond the scope of this hack, but for your information, the graphic in Figure 4-16 is 70% transparent and was saved as a *.jpg* file. The graphic is about 4×7 inches. Figure 4-17 shows how the graphics file appears on its own.

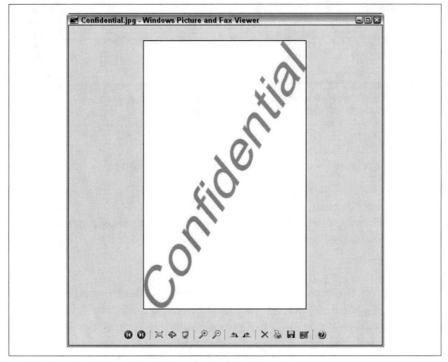

Figure 4-17. The watermark as a graphics file

Using the Watermark

Once you save the watermark as a file, go into the report's Design mode. In the property sheet, click the Picture property, and browse to select the graphics file, as shown in Figure 4-18.

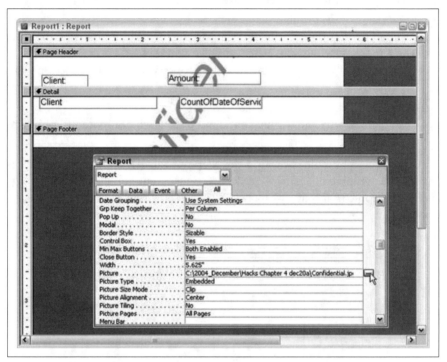

Figure 4-18. Setting the report's Picture property

A few other relevant settings work with the Picture property:

Picture Type
You have a choice of Embedded or Linked. Embedded is the correct choice here. Linked will attempt to open the graphic separately, which isn't the point of using a watermark.

Picture Size Mode
The choices are Clip, Stretch, and Zoom. Each treats how the graphic is placed on the report in a different manner. Experimenting with these settings is the best way to understand how they work. However, as mentioned earlier, if you sized the graphic correctly when you created it, use the Clip setting here. Following this approach helps to avoid having to guess your way through the picture's placement on the report.

Picture Alignment

You have five choices: Top Left, Top Right, Center, Bottom Left, and Bottom Right. Most people choose Center, but you might find a different setting serves your needs.

Picture Tiling

The settings are Yes and No. The No setting places the graphic once on the page. The Yes setting tiles the graphic, which creates a repeating pattern. Try both of them to see which is better for you. The Yes setting makes a busier-looking watermark, but perhaps that is what you want.

Picture Pages

This lets you designate on which pages the watermark will appear. The choices are All Pages, First Page, and No Pages. I hope you don't choose No Pages, or you won't see your watermark!

You also might have to change the Back Style property on the report. You might have to do this because the watermark appears under the text, and text boxes can take up more room than the actual text they display. Figure 4-19 demonstrates this dilemma. In the report, the rectangular shape of the text box covers up part of the watermark. You don't actually see the text box, but the rectangular shape becomes apparent when it's contrasted with the watermark underneath.

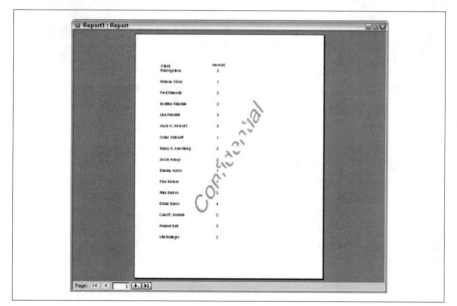

Figure 4-19. Text boxes covering up the watermark

To avoid this behavior, go into the design of the report. For any text boxes that sit over the watermark, change the Back Style property from Normal to Transparent. This forces the text boxes to display just the text, which is exactly the effect you want. Figure 4-20 shows how the report appears when the text boxes are transparent.

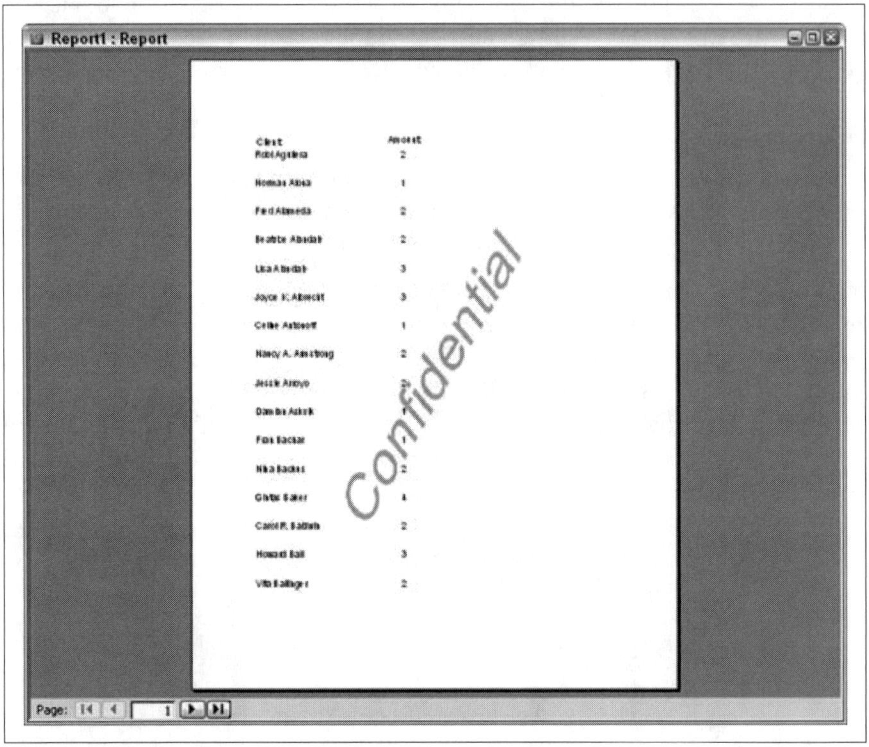

Figure 4-20. *The watermark, appearing through the text boxes*

Create a Slideshow in Access

Use images and the OnTimer event to create a controllable visual show.

Incorporating pictures into Access is a great thing. It provides a way to depict products, personnel, or any other items you want to show via pictures instead of via a textual description. Typically you do this by storing the paths to graphics files in a table field. In this manner, the graphics and the table data are connected. On a form, when a record is displayed, an image control can be updated with the graphic found at the related path.

This hack doesn't imitate such a data-based scenario. Instead, it works with an unbound form to display unbound graphics. You can mix the functionality described here with a data-bound solution. For example, while a form displays database records, the unbound graphics functionality could be incorporated into the form header or footer.

This hack uses the image control to display the graphics and shows how to update the graphics being displayed on a periodic basis, typically a few seconds. The hack also shows you how to let users drive the graphic display update on demand.

The Graphics

For the example in this hack, all the graphics are in the same directory. The directory is hardcoded in the code, but the code can easily be updated to handle multiple directories, passed paths from a dialog, and so on. For now, let's say that a group of *.jpg* files sit in a directory, as shown in Figure 4-21.

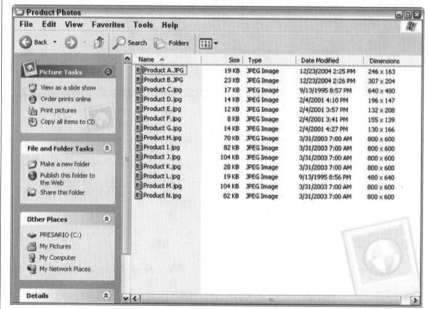

Figure 4-21. Picture files in a directory

Note that all the files don't have to be in the *.jpg* format. You also can use other graphics types, such as bitmaps (*.bmp*) and TIFF (*.tif*) files (this is also specified in the code).

The Form Design

Figure 4-22 shows the form in Design mode. It contains just a few controls: some buttons, a checkbox, and the image control. The image control has an initial picture, but this is overridden as the slideshow runs.

Figure 4-22. The design of the slideshow form

As you can see, the user can either run an automated slideshow or navigate through the graphics manually. The Next and Previous buttons allow the user to move forward and backward through the graphics while not in an automated mode. These buttons just cycle through a VBA collection of paths to the graphics, and the user can use them to update the image control's Picture property.

The checkbox is used to set the mode. If it's checked, the slideshow runs. Regardless of whether the user lets the graphics change automatically, she must press the Start button. This is a nice feature because it gives the user control over when to start the show. After all, someone might still be getting popcorn!

However, because there is a Start button, it makes sense to also have a Stop button. Clicking the Stop button merely changes the value of a Boolean-type public variable, named stop_show, from false to true.

The Code

A vital piece of this application is the use of the form's OnTimer event. In the following code, note that the Timer Interval has a setting of 2000. This tells the form to fire its OnTimer event every two seconds. You can change this value to accommodate other intervals:

```
Option Compare Database
Public stop_show As Boolean
Public pixpaths As Collection
Public pixnum As Integer
'
Private Sub Form_Open(Cancel As Integer)
'
'set initial properties
'
  Me.chkRunContinuous = False
  Me.cmdNext.Enabled = False
  Me.cmdPrevious.Enabled = False
End Sub
'
Private Sub cmdStart_Click()
'
'read paths of graphics into a collection
'displays the first graphic
'
  stop_show = False
  If Me.chkRunContinuous = False Then
    Me.cmdNext.Enabled = True
    Me.cmdPrevious.Enabled = True
  End If
  'replace with your path!!
  pix_path = "C:\Product Photos"
  Set pixpaths = New Collection
  Set fs = Application.FileSearch
  With fs
    .LookIn = pix_path
    .FileName = "*.jpg"
    If .Execute() > 0 Then
      For i = 1 To .foundfiles.Count
        pixpaths.Add Item:=.foundfiles(i)
      Next i
    Else
      MsgBox "No files found!"
    End If
  End With
  'load first pix
  Me.imgPixHolder.Picture = pixpaths(1)
  pixnum = 1
End Sub
'
Private Sub cmdNext_Click()
'
```

```
'advances to the next graphic
'cycles forward through collection
'
  If pixnum = pixpaths.Count Then
    pixnum = 1
  Else
    pixnum = pixnum + 1
  End If
  Me.imgPixHolder.Picture = pixpaths(pixnum)
End Sub
'
Private Sub cmdPrevious_Click()
'
'displays the previous graphic
'cycles backward through collection
'
  If pixnum = 1 Then
    pixnum = pixpaths.Count
  Else
    pixnum = pixnum - 1
  End If
  Me.imgPixHolder.Picture = pixpaths(pixnum)
End Sub
'
Private Sub cmdStop_Click()
'
'sets global variable to false
'disables Previous and Next buttons
'
  stop_show = True
  Me.cmdNext.Enabled = False
  Me.cmdPrevious.Enabled = False
End Sub
'
Private Sub Form_Timer()
'
'if the mode is to run continuously and the
'stop button has not been clicked, then keep cycling graphics
  If Me.chkRunContinuous = True _
    And stop_show = False Then cmdNext_Click
  End Sub
```

This code module contains a handful of routines. The form's Open event builds a collection of paths to the graphics, found within a specified directory. The specific directory and graphics file type are hardcoded. The FileSearch object uses these values to find the graphics files. You can expand this to look in more than one directory and/or for more than one file type. Read up on the FileSearch object in the Help system or on the Internet for more information.

The chkRunContinuous checkbox determines how the application will run. If it is unchecked, the Next and Previous buttons are used to navigate through the graphics. When the user clicks either button, the index to the collection is increased or decreased, and the `Picture` property of the image control is updated to the particular collection item.

If the user checks the chkRunContinuous checkbox, the Next and Previous buttons are disabled, and the slideshow runs on its own. The time that elapses between each graphic is based on the `Timer Interval`. The slideshow will run continuously until the user clicks the Stop button. When the Stop button is clicked, it sets the `stop_show` variable to `true`. This causes the `Timer` event to skip updating the graphic because the update occurs only when `stop_show` is `false`.

Hacking the Hack

You can enhance this basic slideshow in several ways. One thing to consider is that the graphics have no supporting text. Keeping an unbound approach, one way around this problem is to provide a way to display details about a graphic when it is clicked. The image control has a `Click` event, which you can use to return the value of the `Picture` property, as shown in Figure 4-23.

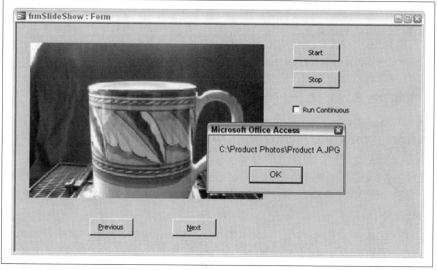

Figure 4-23. Taking advantage of the image control's Click event

Because the picture being displayed can provide its name, you can use the image control's `Click` event to find and display anything pertaining to the particular graphic. For example, because the graphic's filename can be isolated, you can gather additional information about the graphic from a text file or other source.

Of course, another approach is to simply bind the image control to paths stored in a table. Another field can then supply textual information about the picture in a text box. In fact, this is the more standard approach. I didn't point this out earlier because it requires more work to update the paths in table records than just once in the code. Also, if you adapt the code to work with a user-supplied path, of course the unbound approach makes more sense because there would be no preentered paths.

HACK #34   Play Videos in Access Forms

Deliver your message the multimedia way with the Windows Media Player.

Here's a really neat way to spice up your Access applications: play movies! Although this might seem a little too entertaining for "real" business use, consider that movies are one of the best vehicles for delivering information. You can incorporate movies into your database design in several ways. You can relate movie clips to data records, in which case the associated movie runs when a record is displayed. You can also have an unrelated movie play on demand (requiring a button click or some other way to initiate the movie to play).

To play movies you need to incorporate a control that can handle movie files. A number of these are available, most notably Windows Media Player, which is what this hack uses.

Putting the Player on the Form

First, you must add Windows Media Player to the form. Because this isn't a standard control, you must access it using the More Controls button on the toolbox, as shown in Figure 4-24.

Clicking the More Controls button displays a lengthy list of controls and libraries. Scroll down to find Windows Media Player, as shown in Figure 4-25.

After you click the control in the list, draw it on the form. Figure 4-26 shows a form in which Windows Media Player, a listbox, and a command button have been inserted. In this configuration, the listbox displays a list of movies from which to select; clicking the button plays the selected movie.

In Figure 4-26, the listbox is populated with paths to *.mpg* movie files. The listbox has two columns. The first column is the bound column, which

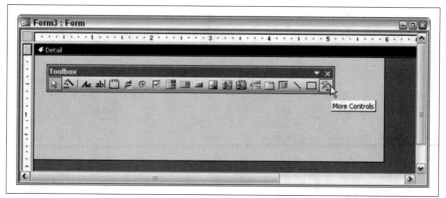

Figure 4-24. Looking for more controls

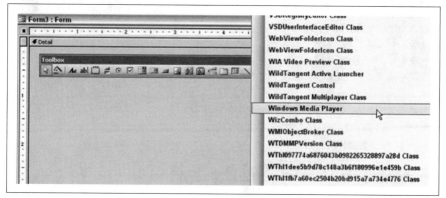

Figure 4-25. Selecting Windows Media Player

holds the paths to the movie files. Its width is set to zero, so it isn't displayed to the user. Instead, the second column, which contains friendly names for the movies, is displayed. When the user has selected a movie, she simply presses the command button to start the movie. This effectively is a simple playlist. Figure 4-27 shows the form in View mode before playing a movie.

Playing a Movie

So, just how does a movie play? Actually, it's quite simple: the path to a movie file is handed to Windows Media Player's URL property and the movie starts playing automatically. This example shows the button's code; it takes the path from the listbox and hands it to the player:

```
Private Sub cmdPlayMovie_Click( )
    If Not IsNull(Me.listMovies) Then
        Me.WMPlayer.URL = Me.listMovies
```

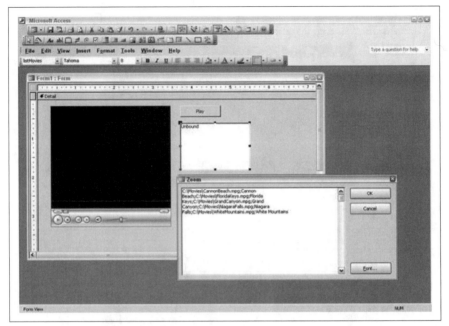

Figure 4-26. Form design with Windows Media Player

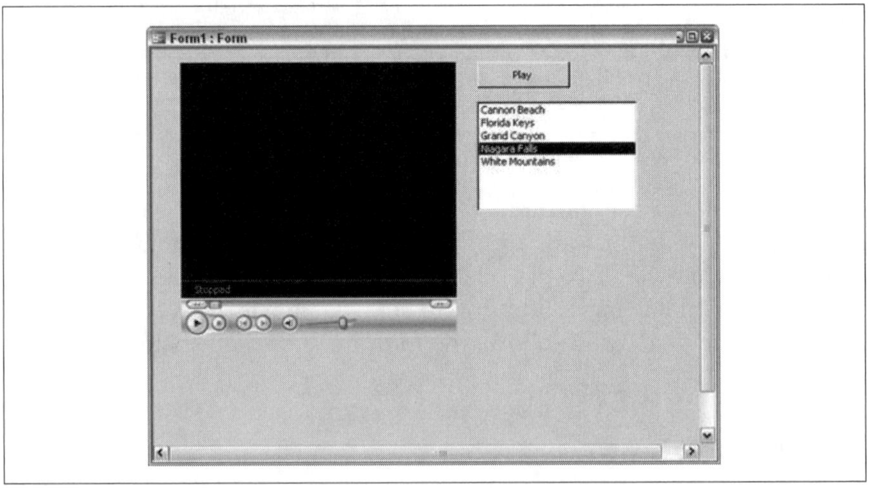

Figure 4-27. Selecting a movie

```
        Else
          MsgBox "First select a movie"
        End If
    End Sub
```

Starting, stopping, fast-forwarding, rewinding, and pausing are functions built into the player. These functions are available through the buttons on the player itself. This allows the user to work the movie in any needed fashion.

Windows Media Player has many events you can hook into. A little thought and creativity will go a long way toward integrating movies into your applications. This hack shows the basic way to implement a movie, but you can code around and work with the player in myriad ways.

See Also

- Windows Media Support Center (*http://support.microsoft.com/default. aspx?scid=fh;en-us;wmp*)

HACK #35 View Reports Embedded in Forms

Preview reports, whether current or historical, directly on the form you are working on.

Access is one of the most powerful reporting tools on the market. Beginning with Access 97, Microsoft introduced the ability to create snapshot reports that you can view with the free Snapshot Viewer, available for download from Microsoft (search for ActiveX Snapshot Viewer at *http://www. microsoft.com/downloads*).

Access database application developers can use the ActiveX Snapshot Viewer to customize the look and feel of their applications by displaying reports embedded in forms.

Creating the Form

The form is composed of a combo box and the ActiveX Snapshot Viewer. The combo box contains a list of all the reports in the database. When the form opens, the Load event executes the following code to fill the combo box with a listing of all available reports:

```
Private Sub Form_Load( )
Dim obj As AccessObject, dbs As Object
    Dim strList As String
    Set dbs = Application.CurrentProject
    For Each obj In dbs.AllReports
            strList = strList & obj.Name & ";"
    Next obj
    cboReports.RowSourceType = "Value List"
    cboReports.RowSource = strList
End Sub
```

To add the ActiveX Snapshot Viewer, select More Controls from the tool-box, as shown in Figure 4-28, scroll down, and select Snapshot Viewer Control 11.0. Note that depending on your version of Access, your control might be earlier than the 11.0 version.

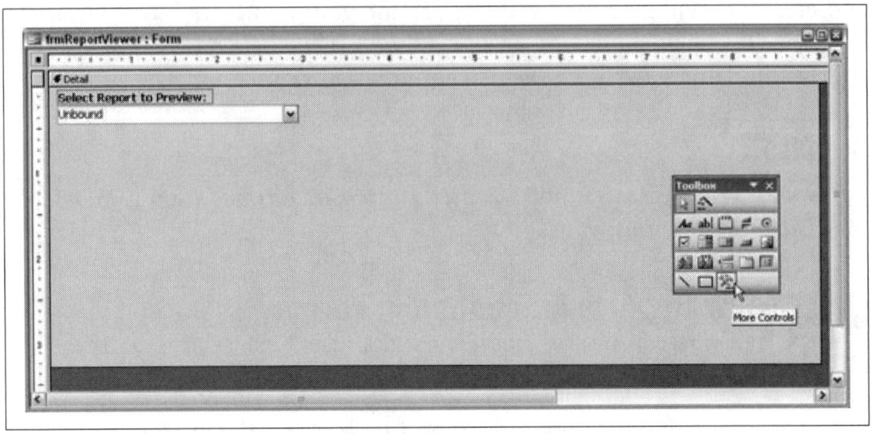

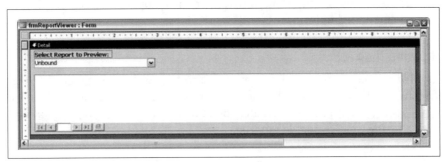

Figure 4-28. Adding the ActiveX Snapshot Viewer

Size the Snapshot Viewer Control to an approximate width that matches the size of the paper on which you will print the report. This helps avoid having to scroll left and right to see a report once it is displayed. Figure 4-29 shows the form design with the Snapshot Viewer Control in place.

Figure 4-29. Sizing the snapshot viewer

After adding the Snapshot Viewer Control, place the following code in the On Change event of the combo box. Make sure the name of the Snapshot Viewer on your form matches the name in the code:

```
Private Sub cboReports_Change( )
    DoCmd.OutputTo acOutputReport, cboReports, acFormatSNP, _
            Application.CurrentProject.path & "\temp.snp"
    SnapshotViewer1.SnapshotPath = _
```

```
        Application.CurrentProject.path & "\temp.snp"
    End Sub
```

In this example, a temporary snapshot report is created, called *temp.snp*, and it is placed in the directory in which the database is running. The *temp.snp* snapshot report is then loaded into the Snapshot Viewer. This *temp.snp* file is replaced each time a new selection is made. If you are running from a shared location with a multiuser database, make sure you store the temporary snapshot file on the local machine, not on the network; this avoids any multiuser issues.

As shown in Figure 4-30, the final form displays an invoice report that was selected from a combo box.

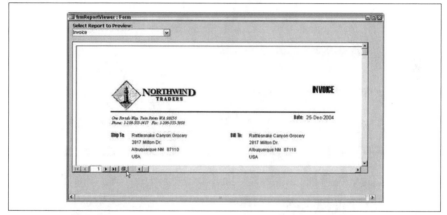

Figure 4-30. Displaying a report

This hack gives the application one place for users to select reports and view them before printing. Also note that the ActiveX Snapshot Viewer includes a Print button next to the navigation buttons.

Hacking the Hack

An advantage to saving reports as snapshots is they are static, as opposed to the dynamic reports you get with report objects in Access. You can save those reports in a folder and view them as historical reports with the Snapshot Viewer. You also can change the code to have a combo box that displays the report names from a given directory, which allows the user to select historical reports to view with the Snapshot Viewer.

—*Steve Huff*

Put Line Numbers on a Report

HACK #36

Use the Running Sum property to include an incremental counter in your report.

Sometimes you might want to include line numbers on a report. This is fairly easy to do. The trick is to include an unbound text box, set its Running Sum property to Over Group or Over All, and set its Control Source to the starting value.

Figure 4-31 shows a report in Design mode. The text box on the left is unbound and will display an incremental value when the report runs. The property shows how its control source is set to =1, the beginning value.

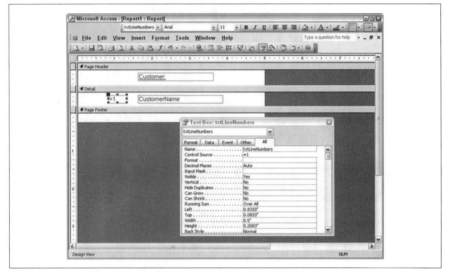

Figure 4-31. A text box to display line numbers

Figure 4-32 shows how the report looks when run.

The value placed in the Control Source property not only provides the seed value, but also serves as the increment value. When a value of 1 is used, the counting starts at 1 and increments by 1. You can use other values as well. For example, a value of 10 might be desirable, in which case the counting starts at 10 and increments by 10, as shown in Figure 4-33.

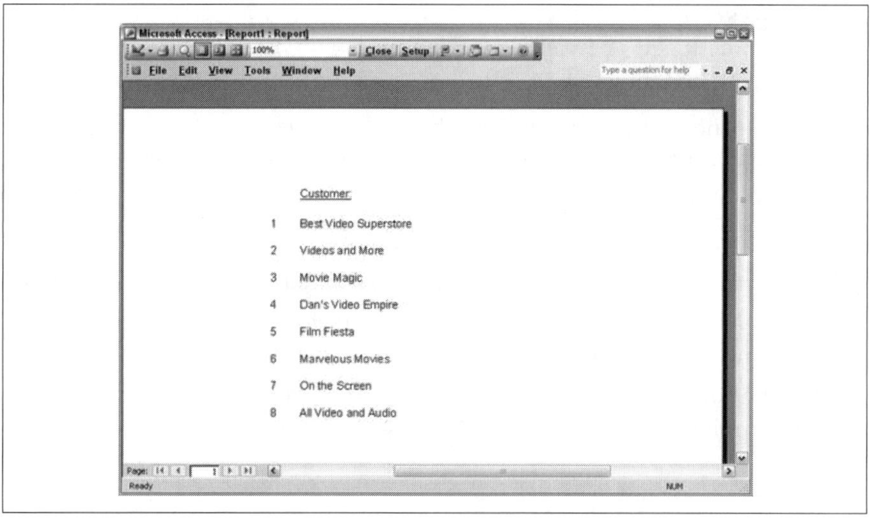

Figure 4-32. Displaying a report with line numbers

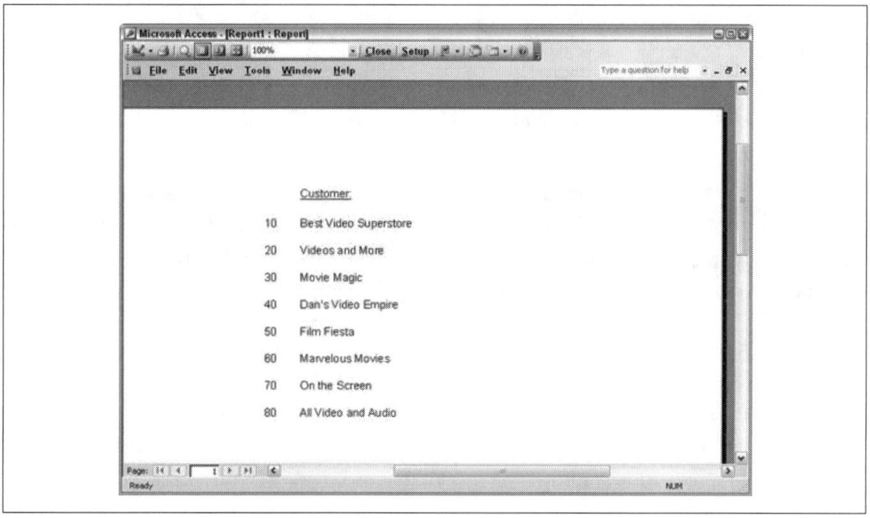

Figure 4-33. Lines counting by tens

Shade Alternating Lines on a Report

HACK #37

Go for the readability factor. Use alternating shaded lines to make a more pleasing presentation.

A quick way to make reports easier to read is to shade every other line. Although no direct property or method provides this feature, you can achieve the look with a little planning. To accomplish this, use an unbound text box to keep an incremental value. As line items are processed, the incrementing value toggles between even and odd. You can then use this toggle's values to your advantage.

The background color property of the report's details section is changed, depending on the value of the incremental running sum. When the value is odd, one color is applied. When the value is even, another color is applied.

You have to set a few properties for this to work:

- In the report's details section, an unbound text box is included. Its Control Source property is set to =1. Its Visible property is set to No. Set its name to txtRunningSum.

- Set the Back Style property of the text boxes and labels to Transparent. This applies to controls in the details section only.

The Code

In the details section's Format event, place this code:

```
Dim even_odd As Integer
Me.Detail.BackColor = vbWhite
even_odd = Me.txtRunningSum Mod 2
If even_odd = 0 Then
   Me.Detail.BackColor = vbYellow
End If
```

You use the Mod operator to determine whether the current running sum value is even or odd. Mod returns the remainder of a division operation. When an even number is divided by 2, the remainder is 0. The even_odd variable holds the result of the Mod operation.

The Results

The routine starts out by defaulting the background color to white. If the even_odd variable isn't 0, the background color is changed to yellow.

Figure 4-34 shows how the report looks when run.

Hacking the Hack

A couple of alternatives are available. If, for example, you have to shade every third line, you can test whether the running sum is a multiple of 3. Any multiple of 3 divided by 3 has no remainder.

Alternatively, you can use the RGB function to control the color. RGB is an acronym for red, green, blue. The function works by blending the three colors, each as a number between 0 and 255. Look up the RGB function in the

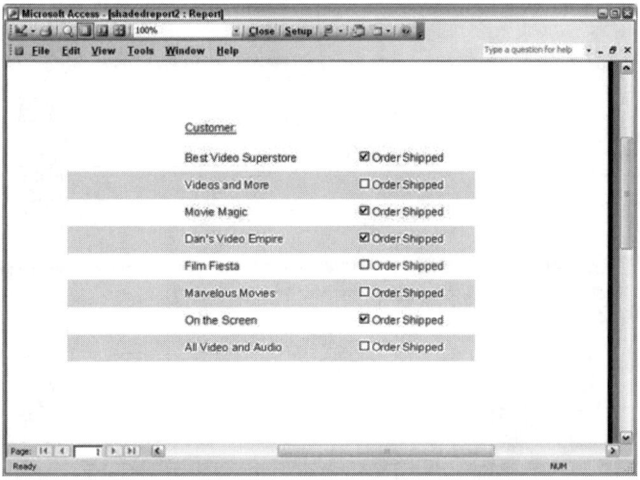

Figure 4-34. A report with alternate row shading

Access Help system; it's a great function to get familiar with. To use it in this hack, just change the BackColor property, like this:

```
Me.Detail.BackColor = RGB(200, 200, 200)
```

You will have to experiment with different settings, but here's a guide you can follow:

- Setting all three RGB argument functions to 0 creates black.
- Setting all three RGB argument functions to 255 creates white.

All other colors are available by applying varying values to the arguments.

HACK #38 Save Paper by Reducing Whitespace

Use the Can Shrink property to condense your reports.

Empty data fields in a long report can pose a problem when it comes time to print the report. Imagine a list of 1,000 contacts, and only half have a phone number entered into a phone number field. When you designed the report, you included the phone number field for contacts that have a phone number. However, when you print the report, you see 500 empty spaces representing the phone number fields of customers without phone numbers. When other data fields are empty as well, the situation just gets worse.

All told, this whitespace can account for 50 or more extra pages in the report, depending on how the report is laid out. Figure 4-35 shows a report that suffers from this problem. Some contact information is missing, yet room is still set aside for it.

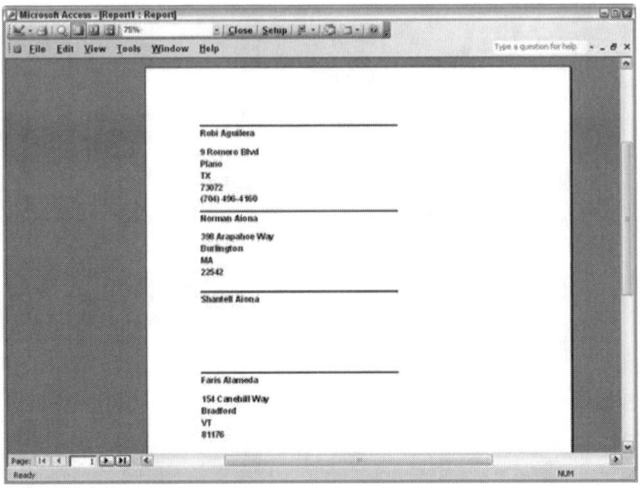

Save Paper by Reducing Whitespace

Figure 4-35. A waste of paper

Figure 4-36 shows the design of the report. The detail section contains a group of fields. As shown in Figure 4-35, some of the fields are empty.

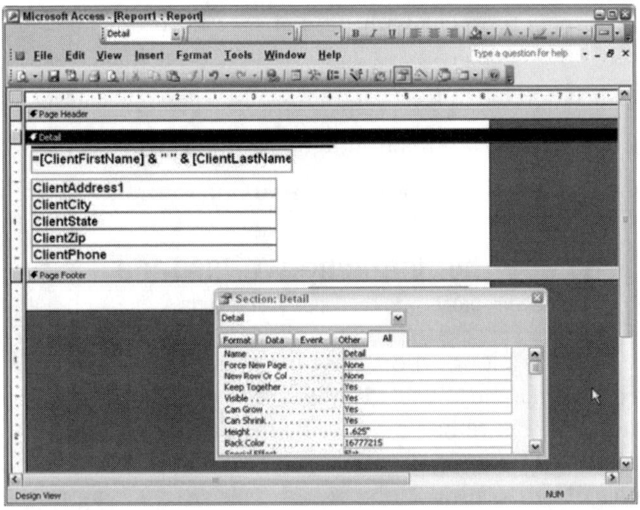

Figure 4-36. Setting the Can Shrink property

On the property sheet, set the Can Shrink property to Yes. Apply this to the fields in the detail section and to the detail section itself.

> When you use the Can Grow or Can Shrink properties, you must apply the settings to both the bound controls and the detail section.

With Can Shrink set to Yes, any empty data fields on this report won't take up space. Figure 4-37 shows the improved report.

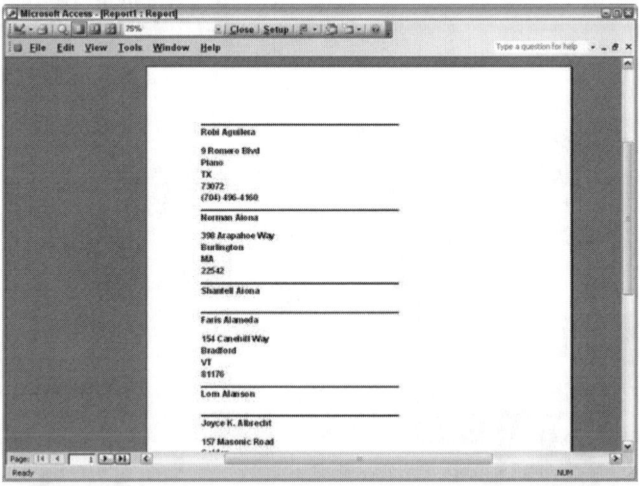

Figure 4-37. A more compact report

In that figure, you can see some contacts are missing a phone number, and others are missing all the data. In both cases, the amount of empty space shrinks. As you can see when comparing the report in Figure 4-37 with the one in Figure 4-35, even the first page displays more contacts. As wasteful whitespace is dropped, the number of pages on the report is reduced.

The Can Grow property provides the opposite functionality as well. When designing a report, place controls where they make the most sense. Occasionally, you might have more data than you can display in the field, given the size of the bound control. Setting Can Grow to Yes lets the field expand as needed to print all the data.

HACK #39 Include the Date, Time, and Page Count

Use common expressions to quickly insert necessary header and footer information.

It's always helpful to include a timestamp on a report, indicating when it was printed. This might be the only clue as to whether the information is up to date. Including page counts is also important. Having dozens of printed pages and not knowing the order in which they go can be quite frustrating.

Access provides an easy way to include these necessary and sometimes overlooked items. The Expression Builder contains a list of common expressions. While designing a report, the best way to display the Expression Builder is to first place an unbound text box in the report header or footer (or wherever makes sense) and then click the ellipses (...) next to the control source for the unbound text box. This opens up the Expression Builder, shown in Figure 4-38.

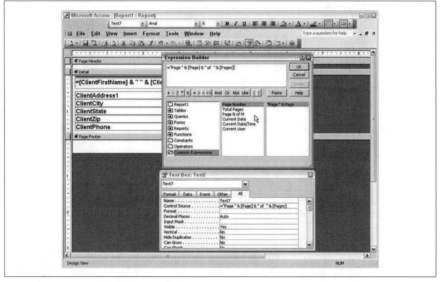

Figure 4-38. Using the Expression Builder to insert common expressions

The available common expressions include page numbers, date and time, and current user. The Page N of M setting is particularly useful because it not only states the page number but also provides a message such as "Page 15 of 40." Once you've selected the expression you want, click the OK button to insert the expression into the unbound text box. When the report runs, the page numbering (or other common expression) is included on the report.

CHAPTER FIVE

Queries and SQL
Hacks 40–54

You can accomplish a lot with the Access query grid. You can achieve even more by working directly in the SQL pane. Queries are categorized into two types: Select (passive) queries and Action queries. You use Select queries to pull data records out of tables. You use Action queries to do something with or to the data. You can run both types of queries in the query grid, but only up to a point. For example, to use a Union query you must use straight SQL statements. You also must use the SQL language for certain sophisticated Action queries.

In this chapter, you'll find all sorts of SQL activities going on, both in and out of the grid. For instance, "Return a Sample of Records" [Hack #40] shows how to return a small set of records using settings in the grid. Meanwhile, "Place a Grand Total in a Query" [Hack #43] is achieved with SQL.

All in all, these hacks show how to accomplish some cool and/or necessary tasks you might be hard-pressed to figure out how to do on your own. Decent knowledge of the SQL language pays off in spades as you work on your projects. The query grid shields you from learning SQL, but after a while, you probably will need to do things you can't do using the grid. Hopefully, the hacks in this chapter will get the brain gears turning and serve as a springboard to even more sophisticated database work.

HACK #40 Return a Sample of Records

Use the Top predicate to return a portion of your records without bias.

Most often, you use a Select query to return all the records that match certain criteria. Usually, this query returns a data set that is smaller than the table or tables upon which the query is built. That is, not all records match the criteria, and the number of records that do match is smaller than the underlying set of table data.

Sometimes, you might need only a sample of records that aren't based on the criteria or in which the criteria are irrelevant. This isn't the same as fine-tuning the criteria to limit the number of returned records. For example, statistical work might require a sample from which to infer facts about the whole data set. Regardless of whether the *population* data is a table or a filtered data set already based on some criteria, the point is that the next step of getting a sample is completed without any preconceived notion. This is where the SQL Top predicate comes in handy.

The Top predicate works in two ways:

- Returns a number of records
- Returns a percentage of records

Using the Top Predicate

The Top predicate allows you to isolate records from the top of a data set. If you want to get records from the bottom, first apply a reverse sort (i.e., descending instead of ascending). Either way, you will continuously get the same set of records each time you run the query. Later in this hack, we'll discuss a method for getting a true random sample.

Figure 5-1 shows a query in Design mode in which the query property sheet is used to indicate the number of records to return. The Top Values property has a few values from which to select. You can use one of these, or you can enter your own.

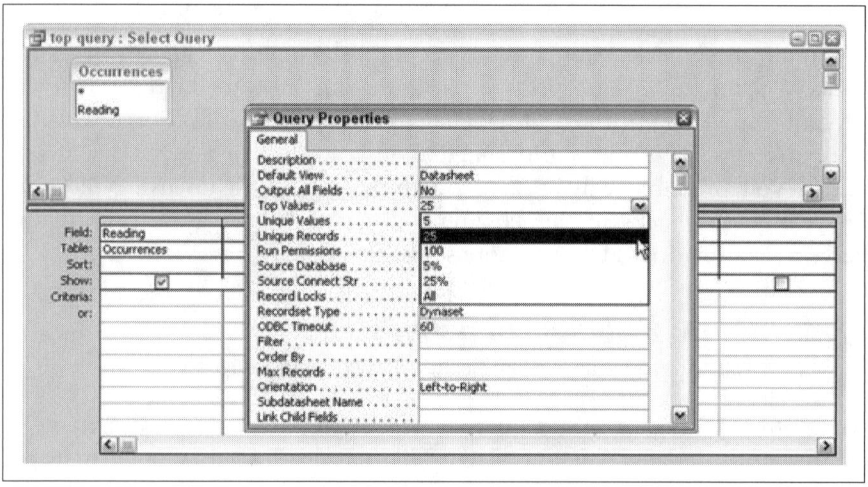

Figure 5-1. Selecting a value for the Top predicate

With 25 as the selected count to return, the query returns, no surprise, 25 records from the top of the data set, as shown in Figure 5-2.

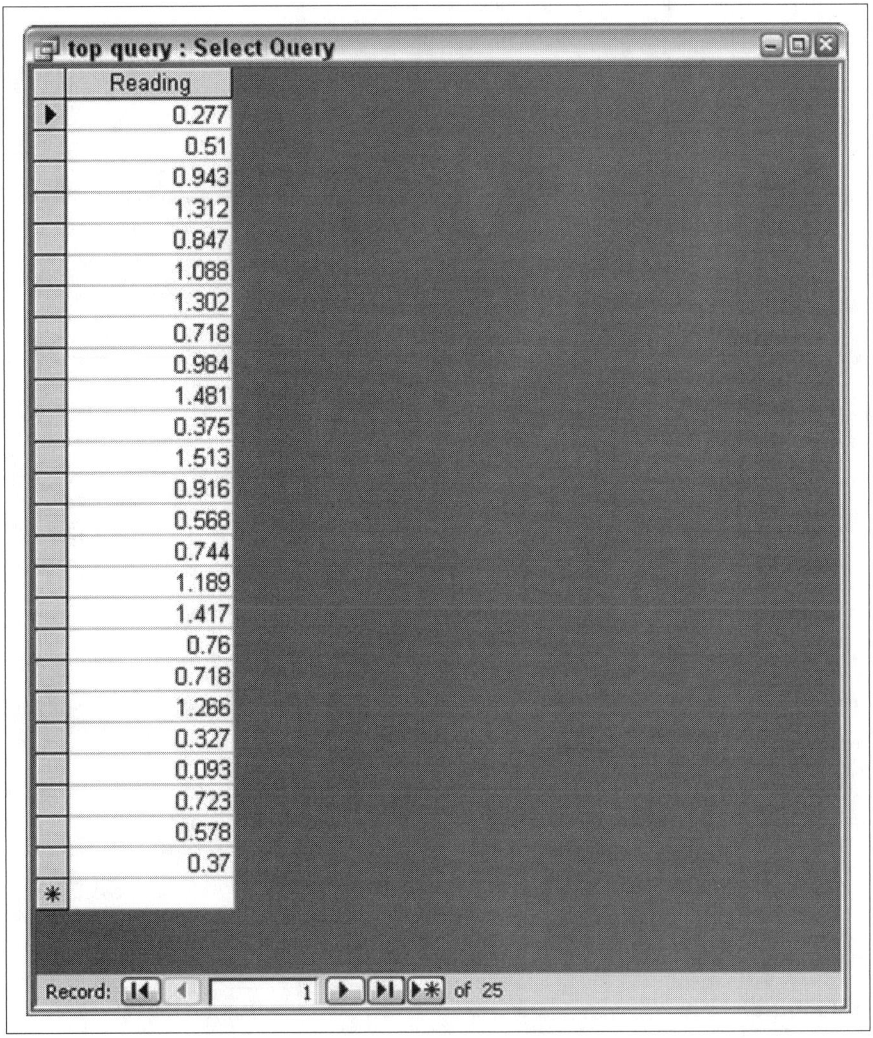

Figure 5-2. Returning the designated number of records

It's interesting to see the SQL the Access query grid generates. Switching to SQL view, here is what you see:

```
SELECT TOP 25 Occurrences.Reading
FROM Occurrences;
```

The Top predicate sits just after the Select statement and specifies the number of records to return.

To return a percentage of records, simply add the word Percent to the SQL statement, after the number:

```
SELECT TOP 25 PERCENT Occurrences.Reading
FROM Occurrences;
```

To indicate percent when using the query designer, add the percent sign (%) to the Top Values property, as shown in Figure 5-3.

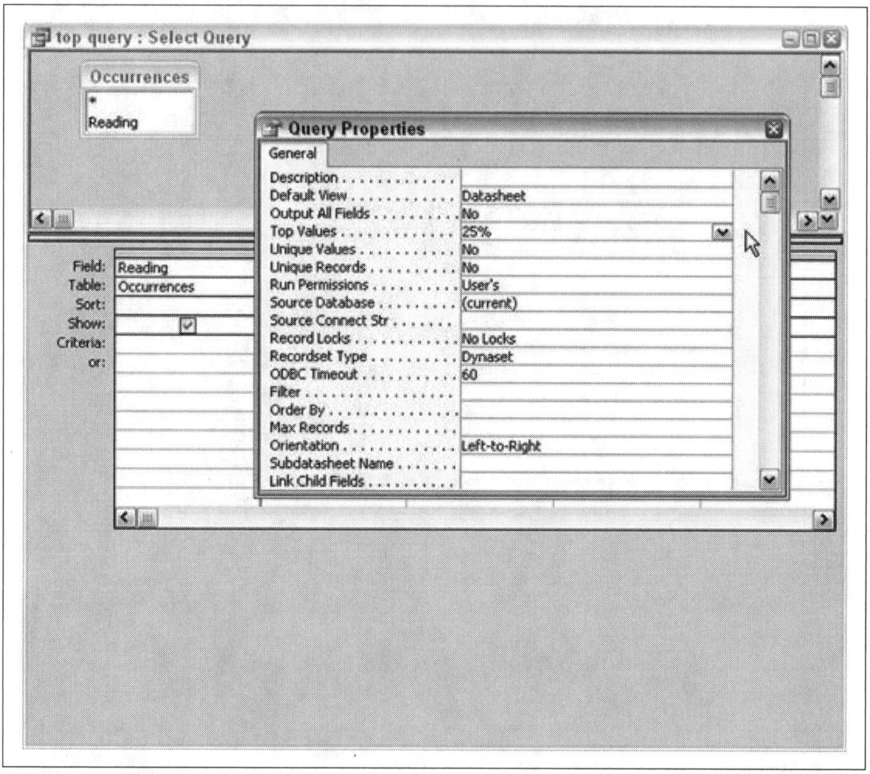

Figure 5-3. Indicating to return a percentage of records

Hacking the Hack

The Top predicate is great for grabbing a handful of records, but it will always grab the same records. Even when no sort is placed on the source data, the records still sit in the order in which they were placed in the table.

Returning a random set of records requires using the Rnd function. You apply this as a sort. Normally, a sort isn't what you want to use to return an unbiased data set, but sorting on a random value makes this a moot point. To make this work, alter the SQL statement to look like this:

```
SELECT TOP 25 Occurrences.Reading
FROM Occurrences
ORDER BY RND([Reading]);
```

Enter the name of the field as the argument for the Rnd function. Each time the query runs, a random selection of records is returned.

Create Bulletproof Insert Operations

Prevent failed append operations so that all the records make it into the table.

You use the SQL Insert statement to append records to a table. Although this usually works great, it is prone to issues that can make it bomb. This hack shows two things you can do to validate data before handing it off to an Insert operation. Before we discuss these validation methods, let's create a simple table, as shown in Figure 5-4.

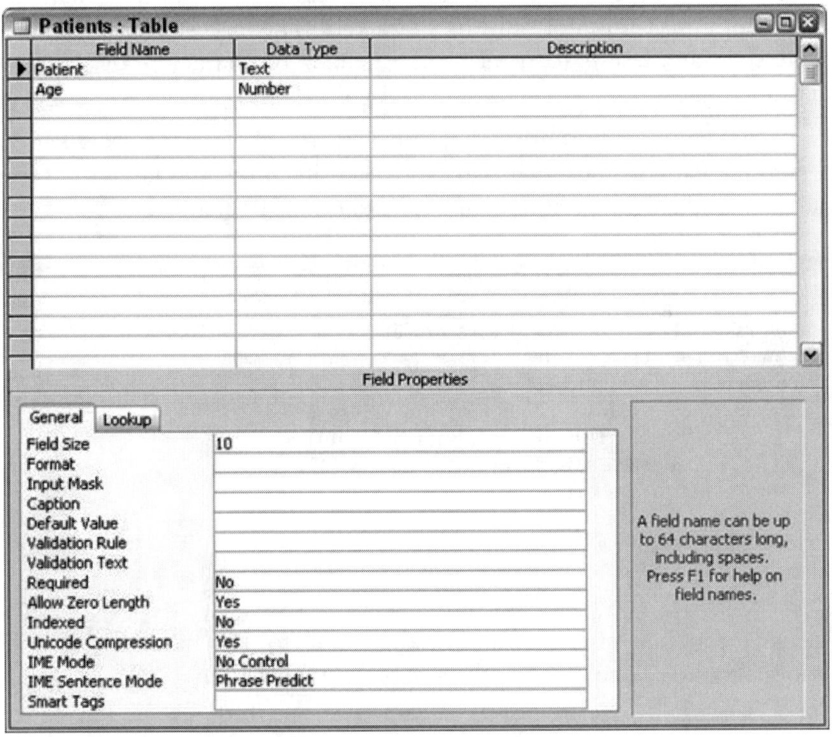

Figure 5-4. A table that accepts names and ages

The table has two fields:

Patient
    Meant to take just the first name; the length is set to 10.

Age
    The age of the patient.

Handling Excessive Text Length

One thing that can trip up an Insert is trying to stick data into a field when the data is longer than the field length. This is an issue only for text fields. Here is an Insert statement that works fine:

```
"Insert Into Patients (Patient, Age) Values ('Gary', 22)"
```

The name Gary fits in the Patient text field. Now, look at this statement:

```
"Insert Into Patients (Patient, Age) Values ('Bartholemew', 22)"
```

Uh-oh. The name Bartholemew is 11 characters long, but the Patient field can accept a maximum of only 10 characters. The easiest way to fix statements such as these is to truncate the text to 10 characters by using the Left function.

Here is a sample code routine that appends records from the NewPatients table to the Patients table. The Left function sits in the middle of the Insert statement and ensures that no name is longer than 10 characters:

```
Dim myDB As ADODB.Connection
Set myDB = CurrentProject.Connection
Dim rsNewPatients As ADODB.Recordset
Set rsNewPatients = New ADODB.Recordset
rsNewPatients.Open ("Select * from NewPatients"), myDB
Do Until rsNewPatients.EOF
  myDB.Execute ("Insert Into Patients Values ('" & _
     Left(rsNewPatients.Fields("Patient"), 10) & _
     "', " & rsNewPatients.Fields("Age") & ")")
rsNewPatients.MoveNext
Loop
rsNewPatients.Close
myDB.Close
Set myDB = Nothing
```

The Left function cuts the size of the name to 10 characters. Another option, of course, is to increase the size of the table field.

Watching Out for Apostrophes

Nothing disrupts an Insert faster than the odd apostrophe or single quotation mark. It's reasonable to have these in your data; after all, the name

O'Reilly has one. But in a SQL Insert, the single quote qualifies text. There-fore, without a little help, this Insert operation will fail:

```
"Insert Into Patients (Patient, Age) Values (Left('O'Reilly',10), 22)"
```

The problem is that as the statement is executed, the single quote before the letter O starts the text and the single quote after the letter O ends the text. This leaves the Reilly part of the name as unidentifiable.

Doubling up single quotes removes the problem, and the way to do this is to use the Replace function. Replace replaces each instance of a single quote with two single quotes. Here is the previous code routine modified to han-dle single quotes:

```
Dim myDB As ADODB.Connection
Set myDB = CurrentProject.Connection
Dim rsNewPatients As ADODB.Recordset
Set rsNewPatients = New ADODB.Recordset
rsNewPatients.Open ("Select * from NewPatients"), myDB
Do Until rsNewPatients.EOF
  myDB.Execute ("Insert Into Patients Values ('" & _
    Replace(rsNewPatients.Fields("Patient"), "'", "''") & _
    "', " & rsNewPatients.Fields("Age") & ")")
rsNewPatients.MoveNext
Loop
rsNewPatients.Close
myDB.Close
Set myDB = Nothing
```

Here is how to use the Replace function:

```
Replace(rsNewPatients.Fields("Patient"), "'", "''")
```

Replace works by testing a string of text for one or more characters. If the string is found, it is replaced with another string of one or more characters. The three function arguments are:

- The string being searched
- The characters being searched for
- The replacement string

All data coming from the NewPatients Patient field is tested for the single quote, and if it's found, the quote is replaced with two single quotes. This creates an acceptable SQL statement, and the insert can proceed.

Combining the Two Validations

I left the best for last. You need to test for both excessive length and apostro-phes. Can you test for both simultaneously? You bet! Just nest one function inside the other with the following code:

```
myDB.Execute ("Insert Into Patients Values ('" & _
  Left(Replace(rsNewPatients.Fields("Patient"), "'", "''"), 10) & _
  "', " & rsNewPatients.Fields("Age") & ")")
```

HACK #42 Find Unmatched Records on Multiple Field Keys

The Find Unmatched Query Wizard looks for unmatched records based on a single related field. You can adapt this query to work on more than one related field.

The easiest way to find records in one table that has no related records in another table is to use Access's built-in Find Unmatched Query Wizard. Figure 5-5 shows the New Query dialog box, which accesses the wizard.

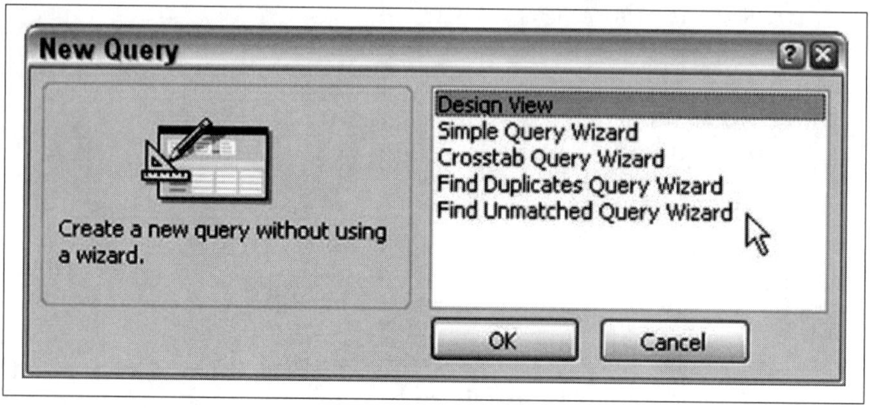

Figure 5-5. Starting up the Find Unmatched Query Wizard

A handful of wizard screens walk you through setting up the query. You select the two tables and even which way the query should work. For example, do you need to know which records in Table A have no related records in Table B? Or do you need to know which records in Table B have no related records in Table A? Either way, the key to making this possible is that the tables are related in the first place.

> Strictly speaking, the tables selected to be in an unmatched query don't have to be formally related, at least in regard to setting up a relationship in the Relationships window. It's just that the fields being matched should be housing the same data; otherwise, all records are returned as unmatched.

Tables can be related on single field keys or on multiple field keys. Unfortunately, the wizard lets you specify only a single field to relate the tables, as shown in Figure 5-6.

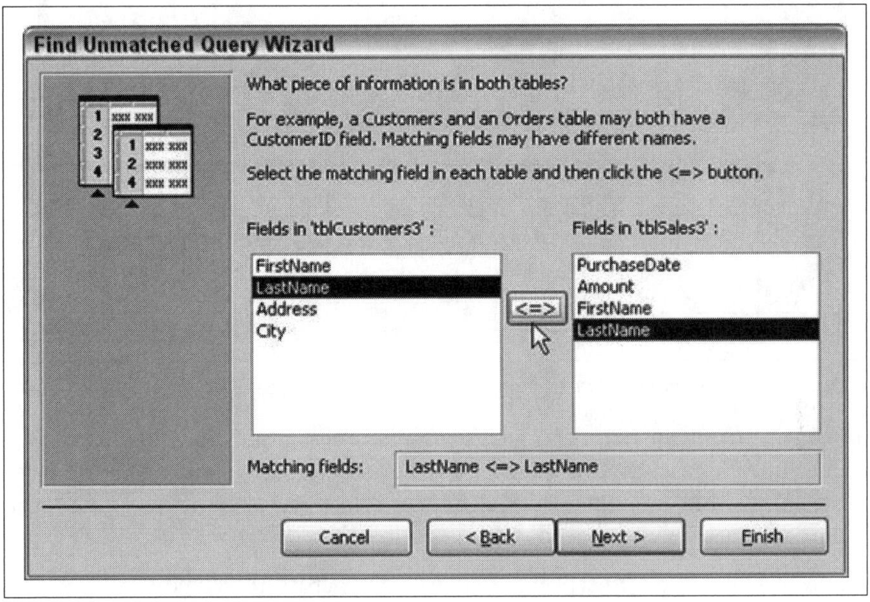

Figure 5-6. *Specifying a single field to be included for the match*

Select a single field from each table, on the left and right, and then click the button between the two tables to set the match the query will use. The wizard generates a query that is saved in the database. This is convenient because it allows you to reuse the query without having to recreate it. You also can change the query, which I'll describe next.

Reviewing the Query

The example used here finds which customers have no matching records in a sales table. Using the Find Unmatched Query Wizard, I can look for customers based on their last name alone. Figure 5-7 shows the query design the wizard generated.

The query uses a LEFT JOIN to return all records of customers whose last name field is Null in the sales table. The SQL looks like this:

```
SELECT tblCustomers3.FirstName, tblCustomers3.LastName
FROM tblCustomers3 LEFT JOIN tblSales3 ON
tblCustomers3.LastName = tblSales3.LastName
WHERE (((tblSales3.LastName) Is Null));
```

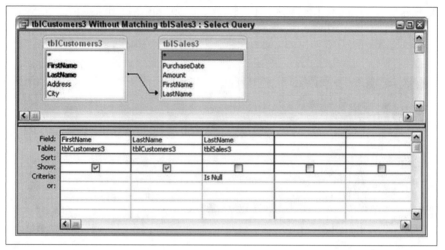

Figure 5-7. The unmatched query design

There is a problem here, though. Two customers might have the same last name. In that case, as long as one of the customers has a record in the sales table, any other customers with the same last name don't appear in the query's results, even if they should.

Figure 5-8 illustrates this point. Left to right across the screen are the customer table, the sales table, and the query that looks for customers that have no sales. Starting on the left, there are two customers with the same last name: Kam Winter and Muriel Winter. In the sales table, in the middle, Muriel Winter has a sales record. In the query result on the right, Kam Winter is *not* listed as a customer with no sales, even though Kam should be there.

Because the last name is all that is tested, all customers with the same name are skipped in the query results, as long as one of them has a sales record. This isn't acceptable.

Changing the Query

All you need to do is alter the query so that both the last name and the first name are tested. We do this in the query design, in either the grid or the SQL pane. Figure 5-9 shows how the query is designed now.

It's important to make sure a few things are changed correctly:

- You need to add a criterion that looks for Null in First Name.
- You need to add a second relationship between the tables, on the new included field. Look closely at the differences in how the tables in the

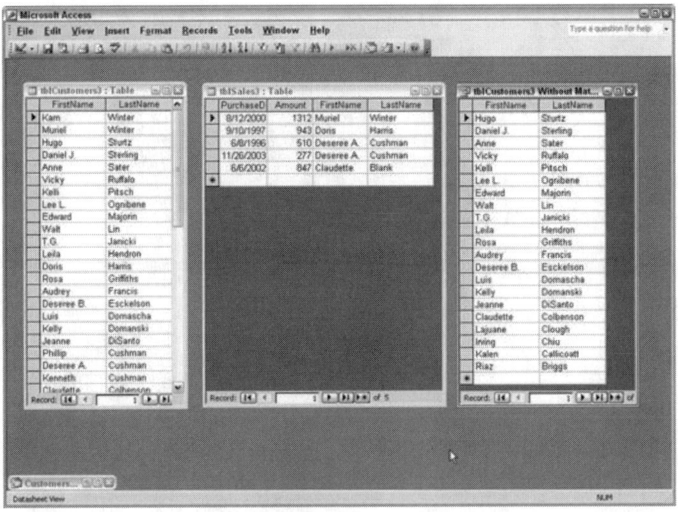

Figure 5-8. Reviewing tables and the unmatched query

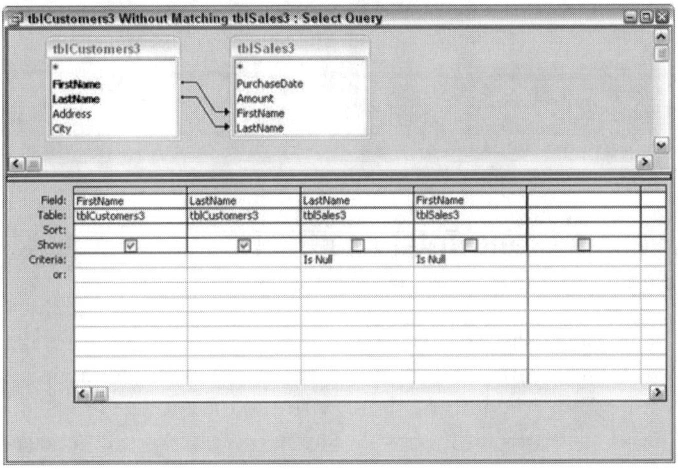

Figure 5-9. The unmatched query, now testing on two fields

query are related, comparing the design in Figure 5-7 with the design in Figure 5-9.

- You should uncheck the fields that come from the secondary table (the sales table in this example); that is, they should not appear in the output.

Figure 5-10 shows how the query returns Kam Winter as being a customer with no sales records. Some other customers appear in the result as well.

![The correct unmatched records window showing tblCustomers3 Without Matching tblSales3 : Select Query with FirstName and LastName columns]

tblCustomers3 Without Matching tblSales3 : Select Query

FirstName	LastName
Kam	Winter
Hugo	Sturtz
Daniel J.	Sterling
Anne	Sater
Vicky	Ruffalo
Kelli	Pitsch
Lee L.	Ognibene
Edward	Majorin
Walt	Lin
T.G.	Janicki
Leila	Hendron
Rosa	Griffiths
Audrey	Francis
Deseree B.	Esckelson
Luis	Domascha
Kelly	Domanski
Jeanne	DiSanto
Kenneth	Cushman
Phillip	Cushman
Claudette	Colbenson
Lajuane	Clough
Irving	Chiu
Kalen	Callicoatt
Riaz	Briggs

Record: 1 of 24

Figure 5-10. The correct unmatched records

HACK #43   Place a Grand Total in a Query

Use a Union query to combine raw data records with the data total.

Here's a neat way to list the records in a table and have the total appear at the bottom. First, create a Select query to return the table records; then use the Union statement to combine them with the data total. The Sum aggregate function handles returning the total. The assumption, of course, is that the data is numeric.

You need to enter this type of query in the SQL pane because the query grid doesn't support creating or displaying Union queries. Here is a sample SQL statement that combines sales records with the sum of the sales:

```
SELECT tblSales.Amount
FROM tblSales
UNION ALL SELECT Sum(tblSales.Amount) AS SumOfAmount
FROM tblSales;
```

Figure 5-11 shows the bottom of the returned query records. Sure enough, a grand total is in the last record.

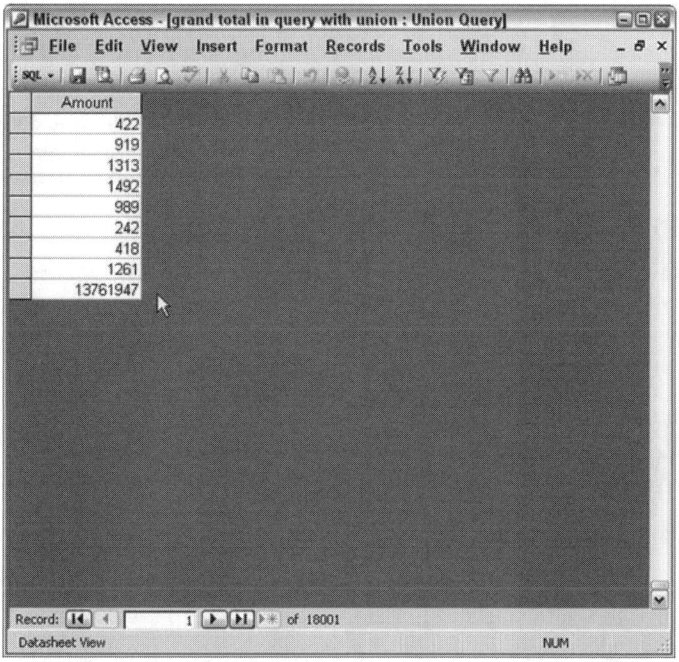

Amount
422
919
1313
1492
989
242
418
1261
13761947

Figure 5-11. Including the total with the data

Hacking the Hack

You can easily modify this query to return other aggregate values, such as a count or an average. For example, here is the SQL from before, but modified to return the average:

```
SELECT tblSales.Amount
FROM tblSales
UNION ALL SELECT Avg(tblSales.Amount) AS AvgOfAmount
FROM tblSales;
```

HACK #44 Sort Any Arbitrary String of Characters

The Access query grid is great for sorting your data, but you need to help it sort on characters in the middle of a field.

I love the query grid. It's very helpful for doing all sorts of sorts (pun intended). But did you ever notice that sorting on text data always occurs on the whole field, going left to right? This makes sense because this is the most common sorting requirement. Imagine, though, the problem of having to sort on, say, just the fifth character, or the last three characters, or in any other way that isn't the norm.

This is an issue especially when Access is used with data that comes from other systems. Accounting systems are notorious for this. They often lump together a bunch of disparate data into a fixed-width field. Here's another classic problem: you are given a list of people's names in one field, structured as first name/last name, but you need to sort on just the last name.

Sorting in the Middle

Figure 5-12 shows a table filled with sales records. The records follow a strict format comprising a two-character vendor code and a six-character date; the remaining digits are the sales amount, and the last two of those digits are the decimal part of the amount. Therefore, the first SalesData record (CT1023044595) breaks down like this:

- Vendor code is CT.
- The date is October 23, 2004.
- The amount is $45.95.

Let's say you need to sort the records by date. As shown in Figure 5-12, in each record, the date starts in position 3 and takes up six places.

Have you ever worked with data such as this? You need a record layout to go with the data; otherwise, you can't tell what kind of data it is. What if you had to guess which characters make up the date? Garbage in, garbage out, as the saying goes.

The best way to tackle a problem such as this is to use the Mid function. Mid is one of the functions that let you manipulate textual data. It works by isolating a part of a larger text string. You have to tell Mid three things: the string of data, the position you want to start from, and how many characters to include. The syntax looks like this:

```
Mid(string, starting position, length)
```

Even though we are conceptually working with dates in this example, the stored information is in text format. Therefore, it's easy to manipulate the date with standard string functions.

Figure 5-13 shows a query design in which the Mid function is used. The first column is the SalesData field itself, and the second column is a calculated field using the Mid function. Within the function, SalesData is enclosed in brackets. This is the standard way to put a field name in a function. Mid's

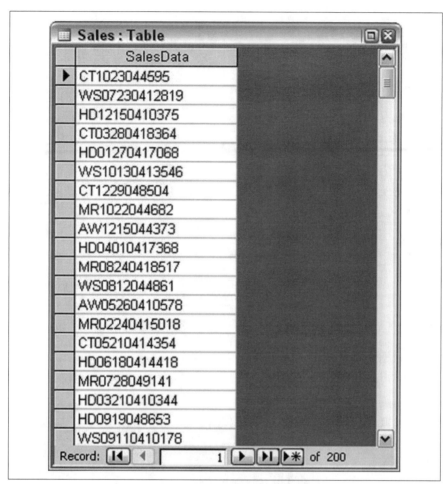

Figure 5-12. A vendor code, date, and amount, combined in one field

parameters are set to isolate six characters starting at position 3 (the date, in other words).

When the query runs, the second column has just the date in it because Mid does the job of grabbing the characters from positions 3 through 8. The second column receives the sort because, after all, the date is what we need to sort on. So, where the Sort row and the second column meet, set the choice to sort in ascending order by selecting Ascending from the drop-down menu.

Note in Figure 5-13 that the Show checkbox for the calculated field is unchecked. You don't have to actually display the column when the query is run. It is used just to make the sort happen, but it doesn't necessarily have to appear in the results.

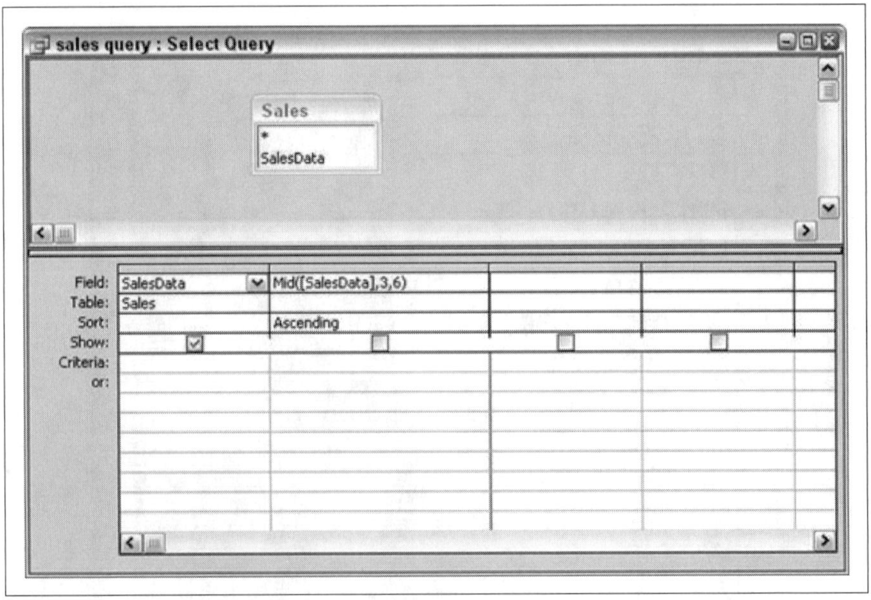

Figure 5-13. Using the Mid function to isolate the date for sorting

Figure 5-14 shows the result of running the query. Now the sales records are sorted by date. The first returned record (MR0104047011) contains 010404, the equivalent of January 4, 2004.

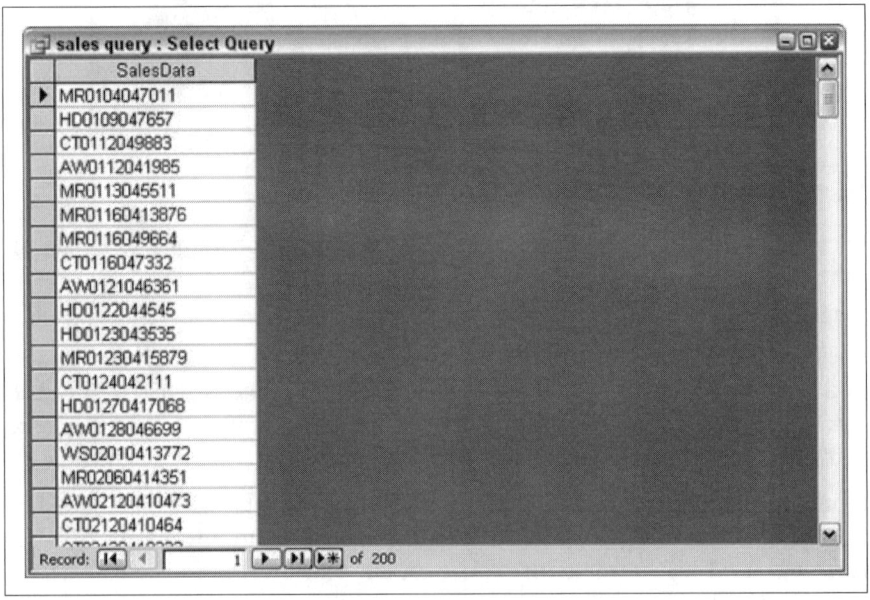

Figure 5-14. Records sorted by date

Sorting on Mixed Fixed Positions

What if you have to sort on both the date and the amount? What if the sort has to show the date in ascending order and the amount in descending order? This is a common requirement: to see money amounts sorted from high to low. Can you do this?

But of course! In this case, the technique is to have two columns with expressions, one each for the date and the amount. Figure 5-15 shows how you do this, with the amount starting in the ninth position. The length parameter for the Mid function that processes the amount is set to 5. Usually, a length is known, but not always. In this example, the amounts among the records might be four or five digits long, so setting the length to 5 works for all records.

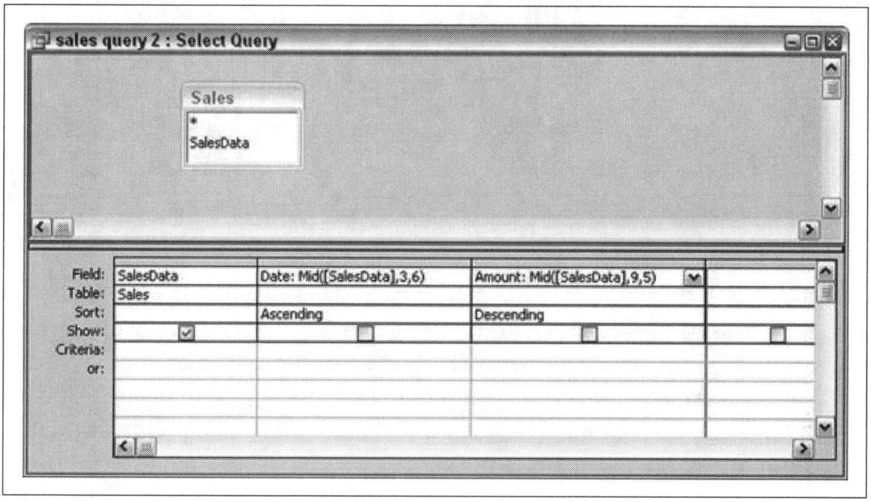

Figure 5-15. A query design for sorting on two subsections of the field

In this example, as before, only the actual SalesData field is shown when the query runs. Therefore, the second and third columns both have unchecked Show boxes. The second and third columns both use Mid to work on different substrings within the same full SalesData string.

Now the result is slightly different. Figure 5-16 displays the returned data. Comparing this result to the result shown in Figure 5-14, you can see that records 6 through 8 have been reordered. These records share the same date of January 16, 2004 (011604), but now the amounts are reordered based on the query specification.

```
sales query 2 : Select Query                                    _ □ ✕
                SalesData                                              ▲
  ▶  MR0104047011
     HD0109047657
     CT0112049883
     AW0112041985
     MR0113045511
     MR0116049664
     CT0116047332
     MR01160413876
     AW0121046361
     HD0122044545
     HD0123043535
     MR01230415879
     CT0124042111
     HD01270417068
     AW0128046699
     WS02010413772
     MR02060414351
     AW021204622
     HD0212044891
     CT02120418222
                                                                      ▼
  Record: [◄◄] [◄] [        1 ] [►] [►►] [►*] of 200
```

Figure 5-16. Sorting on date and amount, which returns a different order

Sorting on Characters When Their Position Is Unknown

Often, you need to manipulate data imported from external systems before you can use it in your application. This is a common issue with names. Your database table might have separate fields for first and last names. This of course makes it a no-brainer to sort on last name. But imagine the difficulty when you are given full names in one field. What if the names are in the order of first and then last name, with a space in the middle, and you need to sort on the last name? The difference here, compared to the previous sales information example, is that you can't know, record by record, in which position the last name starts.

The trick to sorting by last name is to first determine the position of the space. In this case, you use the InStr function with the Mid function. Instead of hard-coding the position of the space, InStr returns the position of the space.

The InStr function tells you the starting position of the first occurrence of a substring inside a larger string. In this example, the string being searched is the Client field, and the substring is a space. By itself, InStr looks like this:

```
InStr([Client]," ")
```

Here we use the `InStr` function to tell the `Mid` function the position from which it should start counting. `InStr` is embedded inside the `Mid` function. Together, they look like this:

```
Mid([Client],InStr([Client]," ")+1,10)
```

Note that although the `InStr` function returns the position of the space, we are interested in the starting position of the last name. This is one position to the right of the space, and for this reason, 1 is added after the `InStr` function. The returned value of `InStr` plus the value 1 is used as the starting position parameter in the `Mid` function.

Figure 5-17 shows how to set up a query using these nested functions. The value of 10 is arbitrarily used here as the length of the last name. Last names vary in length, but using 10 characters to sort on all but guarantees the sort will be in the right order.

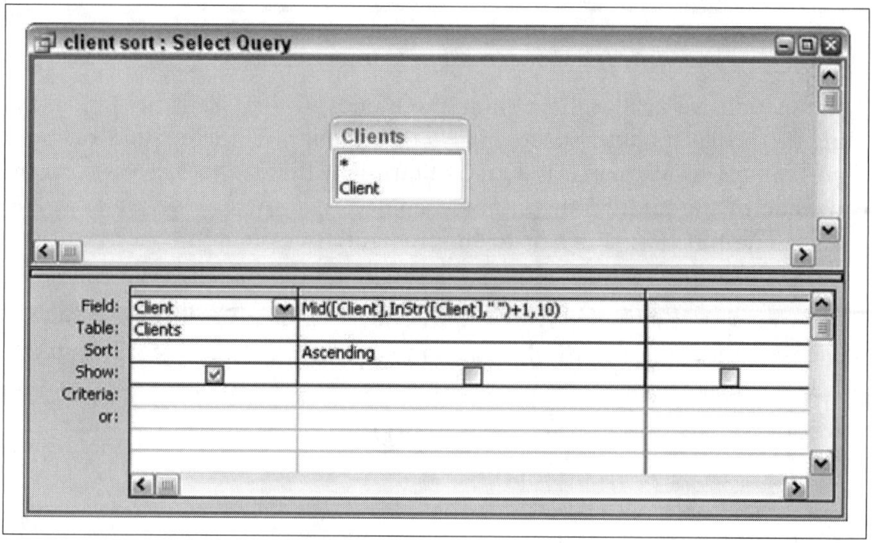

Figure 5-17. Using nested functions in a sort

Figure 5-18 shows the result of the query. Clients are sorted by last name, within a single field that contains full first and last names. Neat!

Hacking the Hack

Sorting on names isn't difficult when first and last names are all you have to work with. But what about middle names, titles, and suffixes? How can you handle these? Let's up the ante on this hack and include a custom function in the query.

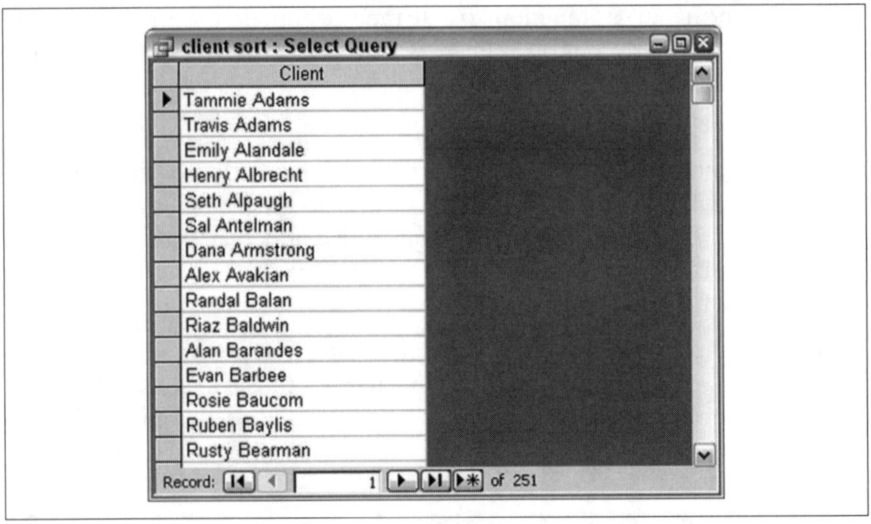

Figure 5-18. Clients sorted by last name

The function we need will examine the names in the Client field to determine the position of the space. Here's the catch: now there could be more than one space. My name is Ken S. Bluttman; that's two spaces—one on each side of the middle initial. Some names have three, four, or even five spaces. The function is meant to simply figure out the best space to use; it figures out the position of that space and tells the Mid function where it is.

First, you write the function in a VBA code module. To do this, from the database window, go to the Modules tab, and select to create a new module. Enter this code:

```
Function find_space(client_name As String)
Dim name_length As Integer
Dim space_loop As Integer
Dim space_count As Integer
Dim partial_name As String
Dim first_space_position As Integer
'count spaces in full name
space_count = 0
name_length = Len(client_name)
For space_loop = 1 To name_length
  If Mid(client_name, space_loop, 1) = " " Then
    space_count = space_count + 1
  End If
Next space_loop

'parse the full name using assumptions in each Case
Select Case space_count
   Case 0
      'no spaces found!
```

```
     'return 1 as the position
      find_space = 1
  Case 1
    'a first name and last name
    'split after first space
    find_space = InStr(client_name, " ")
  Case 2, 3
    'assume a first name, Middle name, and last name (2 spaces)
    'or a first name, Middle name, last name, and suffix (3 spaces)
    'split after second space
    find_space = InStr(client_name, " ")
    first_space_position = find_space
    partial_name = _
        Mid(client_name, find_space, name_length - find_space)
    find_space = InStr(partial_name, " ") + first_space_position - 1
  Case Else
    'difficult to make assumption on name structure
    'split after first space
    find_space = InStr(client_name, " ")
End Select
End Function
```

In a nutshell, the function takes a client name, counts how many spaces are in it, and then determines which space is best. The position of that space is used in the Mid function as before.

In the query grid, the call to the function, named find_space, is embedded in the Mid function, like this:

```
Mid([Client],find_space([Client])+1,10)
```

Figure 5-19 shows how to set up the query.

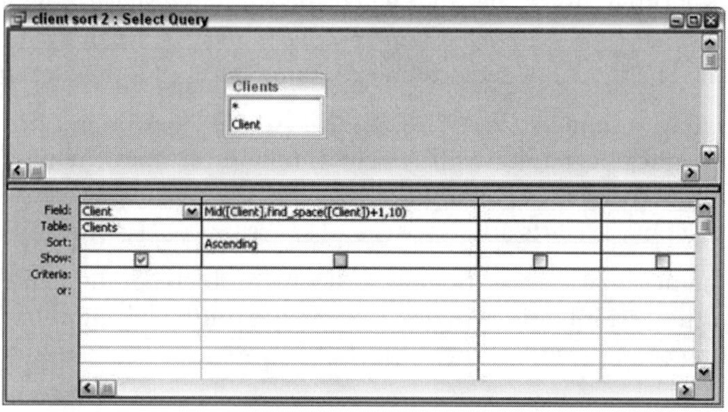

Figure 5-19. The Mid function, using the find_space function

When the query runs, each client name is examined in the find_space function. The function returns the best space position, and the names are sorted. Figure 5-20 shows the results of running the query.

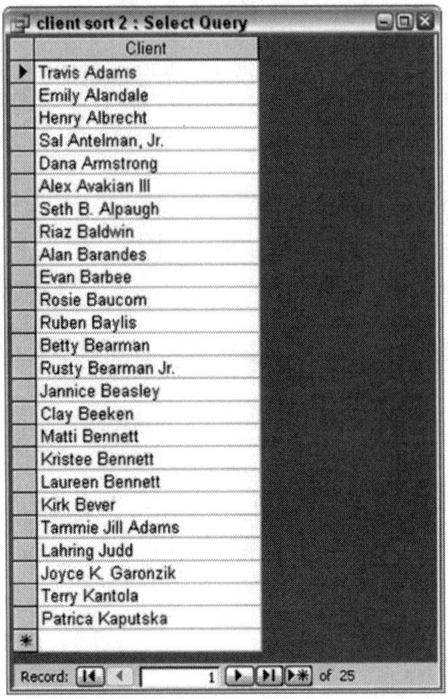

Figure 5-20. Sorting by last name when middle names and suffixes are present

Looking closely, you will see that the sort isn't without problems. The way the function is written, it assumes that when there are two spaces, the format of the name is *first name, last name, suffix*. This works for a name such as Alex Avakian III. The function assumes the last name starts after the first space.

Unfortunately, a name such as Tammy Jill Adams doesn't end up with the other last names beginning with A. The function assumes the best space is the first, and the name is sorted as though the last name starts with J. Tammy's last name starts after the second space. Sorry, Tammy!

Splitting names apart is traditionally a thorny problem. Some names always confound the best intentions of a name-parsing routine. That must be why I keep getting catalogs addressed to Mr. Ken.

See Also

- "Use a Custom Function in a Query" [Hack #48]

Summarize Complex Data

#45 Take advantage of Crosstab queries to get a view on multifaceted data.

When you need to aggregate data that has more than a simple grouping structure, Crosstabs are the way to go. "Create Conditional Subtotals" [Hack #29] shows you how to use groups and conditional summing on a report. That works as long as the conditions don't lead to an overwhelming number of possibilities.

The example in that hack uses five states and two years on which to create subtotals. The data model, though, has another table in play: a table of pets (the model is a simulation of a veterinary practice). This creates a large number of possibilities, such as all cat visits in New York in 2003, or all dog visits in Pennsylvania in 2004, and so on. Figure 5-21 shows the updated data model for this hack.

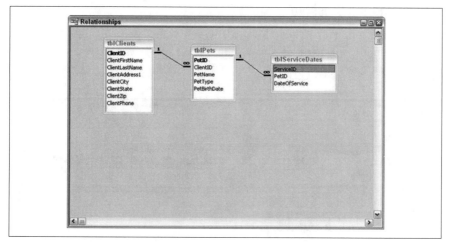

Figure 5-21. The pets data model

The data model includes seven types of pets (bird, cat, dog, ferret, horse, monkey, and snake), five states (CT, MA, NJ, NY, and PA), and two years of data (2003 and 2004). This makes 70 possible combinations. The best way to sum up the number of visits in which all these combinations of criteria are mixed and matched is to use a Crosstab query.

To get started, we must put together a Select query to join the different tables and return the fields needed in the Crosstab. Note that the Select query has a calculated field that isolates the year out of the DateOfService field. Figure 5-22 shows the design of the Select query.

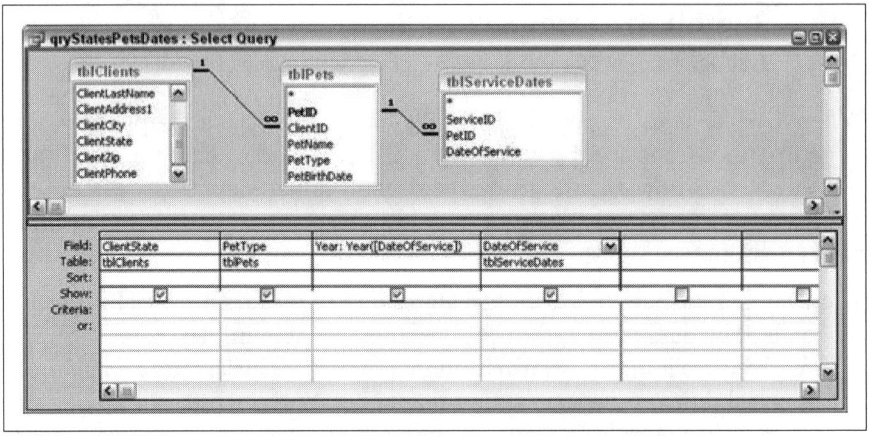

Figure 5-22. A Select query on which a Crosstab will run

Introducing the Crosstab

Access has a Crosstab Query Wizard, which walks you through creating a Crosstab query. Figure 5-23 shows the New Query dialog box in which a Crosstab query is initiated.

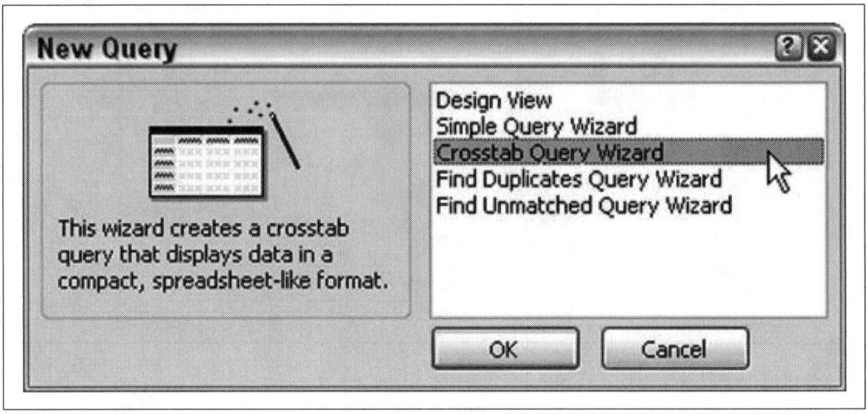

Figure 5-23. Starting up the Crosstab Query Wizard

In this example, select the qryStatesPetsDates query in the first screen of the wizard, as shown in Figure 5-24.

In the next screen, select two fields as the rows. In a Crosstab query, the rows act as groups. Note that at least two fields must remain after you select fields for the rows. Select the state and pet type fields to be the row headings.

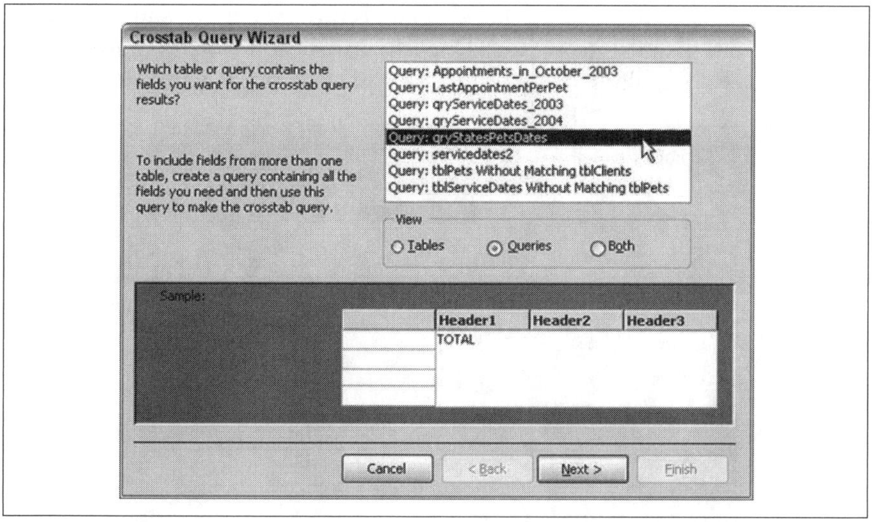

Figure 5-24. Selecting the Select query

In the next screen, select a field to be the column field. Crosstabs require at least one column field. Choose Year here, as shown in Figure 5-25 (note that this figure shows the third screen, not the second).

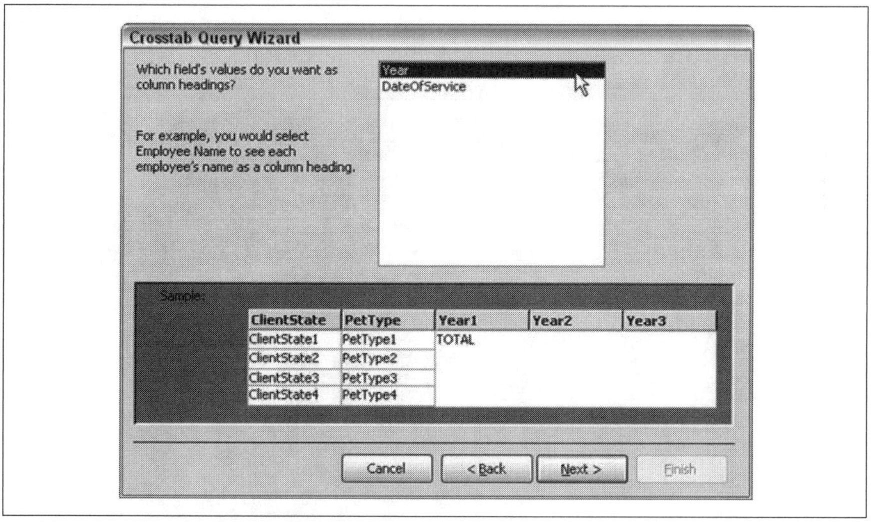

Figure 5-25. Selecting Year as the column heading

In the last field selection screen, one field remains. Select the type of aggregation—in this case, Count, as shown in Figure 5-26, because the purpose is to count visits. Also be sure to uncheck the "Yes, include row sums" checkbox on the left. Keeping this checked returns a field of sums based on just combinations of state and pet type (the row headings) and that isn't our focus here; we're looking for the combination of state, pet type, and year.

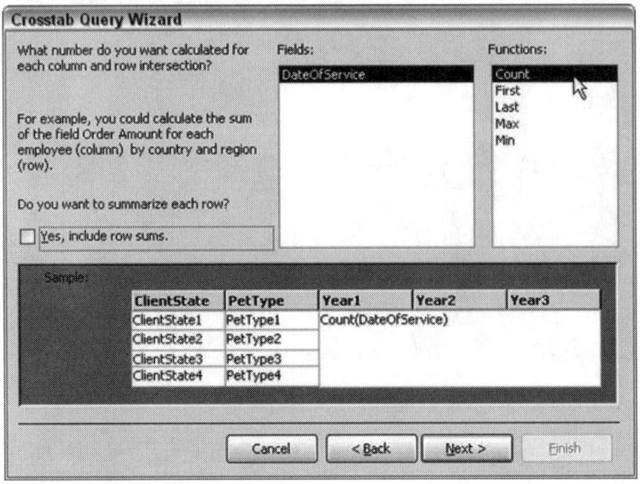

Figure 5-26. Selecting to return a count

When the query completes, all the counts are available. Figure 5-27 shows how the query presents sums in all combinations of state, pet type, and year.

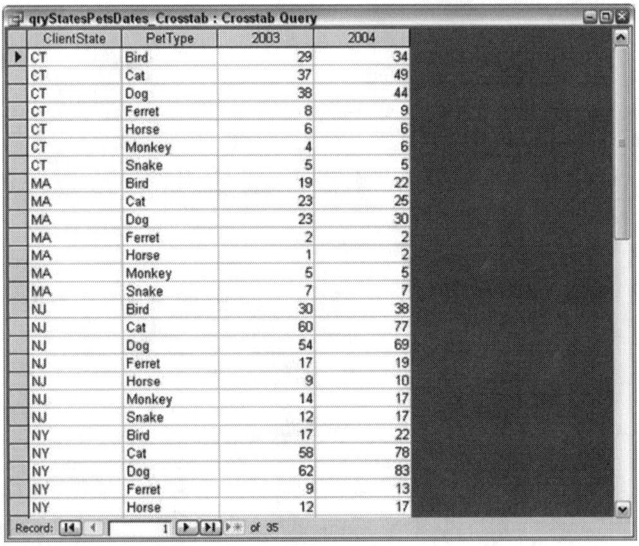

ClientState	PetType	2003	2004
CT	Bird	29	34
CT	Cat	37	49
CT	Dog	38	44
CT	Ferret	8	9
CT	Horse	6	6
CT	Monkey	4	6
CT	Snake	5	5
MA	Bird	19	22
MA	Cat	23	25
MA	Dog	23	30
MA	Ferret	2	2
MA	Horse	1	2
MA	Monkey	5	5
MA	Snake	7	7
NJ	Bird	30	38
NJ	Cat	60	77
NJ	Dog	54	69
NJ	Ferret	17	19
NJ	Horse	9	10
NJ	Monkey	14	17
NJ	Snake	12	17
NY	Bird	17	22
NY	Cat	58	78
NY	Dog	62	83
NY	Ferret	9	13
NY	Horse	12	17

Figure 5-27. The completed Crosstab query

There are 35 records by virtue of the fact that state and pet type are row headings, and year is a column heading. This still provides the 70 unique combinations because the two years, 2003 and 2004, each have their own column.

See Also

- "Create Conditional Subtotals" [Hack #29]

HACK #46 Get All Combinations of Data

Remove the Join clause in a SQL statement to return a Cartesian product (which returns all possible combinations).

Leaving the Join clause out of a SQL statement returns a number of records equal to the product of the number of records in the tables. Taking two tables, for example, as long as one field from either table is designated for output, the number of returned records in a Select query of this design is the product of the counts of the two tables.

Behind the scenes, the query is matching all combinations of the data. If each table has hundreds or thousands of records, the returned number of records can be in the millions. This can be disastrous—that is, unless returning records in this way is by design. Why would you do this? It makes sense to do it to explicitly return all the combinations. If you need such all-inclusive matching, you don't have to bother with any VBA code; just create a query that does it for you. Figure 5-28 shows a table with 12 people and another table with eight possible activities.

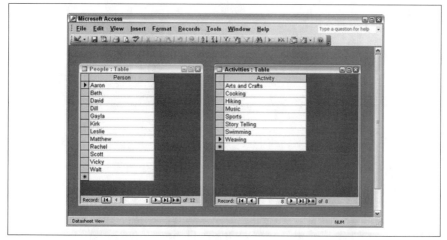

Figure 5-28. Two unrelated tables

Create a `Select` query with the two tables, and designate the single field from each table for output. Figure 5-29 shows the query design. Note that the lack of a relation line between the tables is intentional.

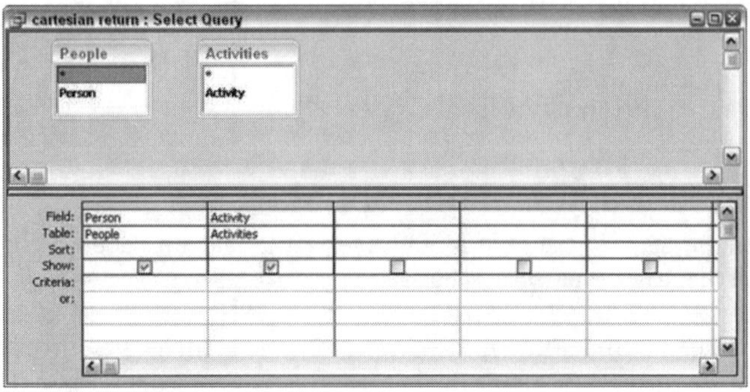

Figure 5-29. A Select query of unrelated tables

A little tip-tap on a calculator shows 96 combinations of person and activity. Running the query returns the 96 records, as shown in Figure 5-30.

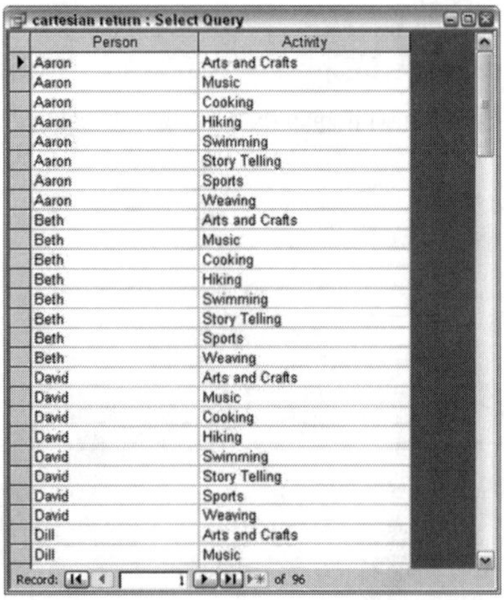
cartesian return : Select Query

Person	Activity
Aaron	Arts and Crafts
Aaron	Music
Aaron	Cooking
Aaron	Hiking
Aaron	Swimming
Aaron	Story Telling
Aaron	Sports
Aaron	Weaving
Beth	Arts and Crafts
Beth	Music
Beth	Cooking
Beth	Hiking
Beth	Swimming
Beth	Story Telling
Beth	Sports
Beth	Weaving
David	Arts and Crafts
David	Music
David	Cooking
David	Hiking
David	Swimming
David	Story Telling
David	Sports
David	Weaving
Dill	Arts and Crafts
Dill	Music

Record: 1 of 96

Figure 5-30. Returning the combined records

The query results can be copied, exported, and so on. This is a fast and easy way to get all combinations of data. Going one step further, a third table is added to the query. This new table contains parts of the day, in two records: morning and afternoon. Running the query returns the expected 192 records, which is the product of $12 \times 8 \times 2$. Figure 5-31 shows the result.

cartesian return : Select Query

Person	Activity	PartOfTheDay
Aaron	Arts and Crafts	Morning
Aaron	Arts and Crafts	Afternoon
Aaron	Music	Morning
Aaron	Music	Afternoon
Aaron	Cooking	Morning
Aaron	Cooking	Afternoon
Aaron	Hiking	Morning
Aaron	Hiking	Afternoon
Aaron	Swimming	Morning
Aaron	Swimming	Afternoon
Aaron	Story Telling	Morning
Aaron	Story Telling	Afternoon
Aaron	Sports	Morning
Aaron	Sports	Afternoon
Aaron	Weaving	Morning
Aaron	Weaving	Afternoon
Beth	Arts and Crafts	Morning
Beth	Arts and Crafts	Afternoon
Beth	Music	Morning
Beth	Music	Afternoon
Beth	Cooking	Morning
Beth	Cooking	Afternoon
Beth	Hiking	Morning
Beth	Hiking	Afternoon
Beth	Swimming	Morning
Beth	Swimming	Afternoon
Beth	Story Telling	Morning
Beth	Story Telling	Afternoon

Record: 1 of 192

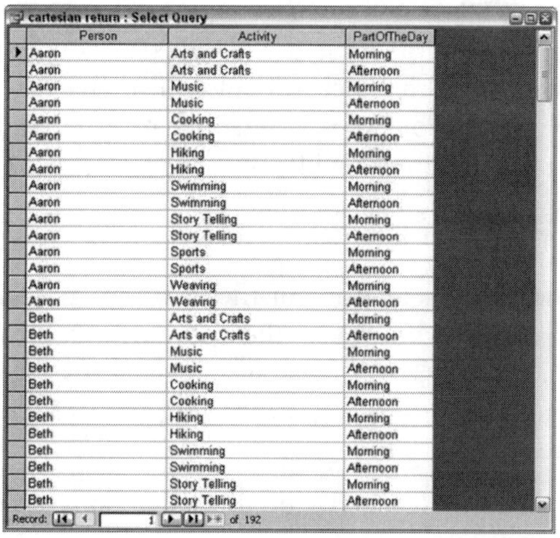

Figure 5-31. Returning combinations on three unrelated tables

Although it isn't efficient to handle data in this unrelated way, at least with regard to database work, a set of combinations such as this makes for useful reports, checklists, and so on.

HACK #47

Don't Let Nulls Ruin Data Summaries

When nulls are mixed in with valid data, incorrect results can occur. Here are some guidelines to tame the beast.

When you are dealing with values in Access, you might be tempted to think that a blank field is simply a blank field. However, there is a difference between a blank field that is filled in with an empty string and a blank field that is null. For example, when you are looking at number fields, there is a difference between a field with a `0` value and a field with a `null` value. This hack helps you work with these nonvalue values.

The first frustrating thing about nulls is that if you write a line such as this, every line will show up as `Not Blank`, even if you have `null` values:

```
IIF([Amount]=Null,"Blank","Not Blank")
```

This occurs because in a Boolean expression, any item compared to `Null` returns `False`.

There is an easy way to deal with this, using a function available in Access called `ISNULL`. This function returns a Boolean and allows you to perform your test. Here is how to rewrite the previous example:

```
IIF(ISNULL([Amount],"Blank","Not Blank")
```

That clinches it. Now, any encountered `null` is converted to `Blank`.

Nulls in Number Fields

Let's assume you have a table with a field called Amount. You are trying to determine the average of that field (assume also that the average doesn't need to be weighted). If you write a query that attempts to determine the average value, the SQL might look like this:

```
SELECT Avg(tbl_Amount.Amount) AS AvgOfAmount
FROM tbl_Amount;
```

This gives you the average amount of the values in that field. However, if you have nulls for any of the values, the query will ignore them. So, if your values are 8, null, 8, null, 8, null, the average is 8. If your values are 8, 0, 8, 0, 8, 0, the average is 4. Depending on the purpose of the query, you might want to see 4 instead of 8.

If you want to substitute 0 for null, you can try to do it with the ISNULL function by writing a line such as this:

```
IIF(ISNULL([Amount]),0,[Amount])
```

There is a much easier way, though. The NZ function available in Access requires two parameters: one for the value and the other for the value if it is null. You can use this for both number and string functions. Here is what the SQL of the query looks like using the NZ function:

```
SELECT Avg(NZ([Amount],0)) AS AverageofAmount
FROM tbl_Amount;
```

As you can see, this is more compact than writing out IIF statements to perform the same function.

Next, let's look at an example of a string function. Assume you live in an area where pine trees are popular, and you have a survey in which you input the type of tree only if it is something other than pine; otherwise, you just input the number of trees (bad design, but I've seen worse) and leave the tree type field null.

Now, assume that you have inherited this application, and you want to use it in other areas of the country. You want to update all the null Tree_Type fields with Pine Tree. You can do so with the NZ function. Here is what the SQL for this query looks like:

```
UPDATE tbl_TreeTypes SET tbl_TreeTypes.Tree_Type =
nz([Tree_Type],"Pine Tree");
```

This will work, but you have to update every record. So, if you can't use Tree_Type = Null, you might ask if you can use null for criteria in a query. You can, using one of two methods. The easiest way is to use IS NULL for the criteria. The previous query looks like this using IS NULL:

```
UPDATE tbl_TreeTypes SET tbl_TreeTypes.Tree_Type = "Pine Tree"
WHERE (((tbl_TreeTypes.Tree_Type) Is Null));.
```

Preventing Nulls

It might be necessary for you to prevent nulls and zero-length strings in your database in the first place. A good example for this might be a name field or a ZIP code field. You can do this through either your table design or your data entry forms.

Table design to prevent nulls and zero-length strings. When you design your table, you can set several properties to help you handle blank fields, as shown in Figure 5-32.

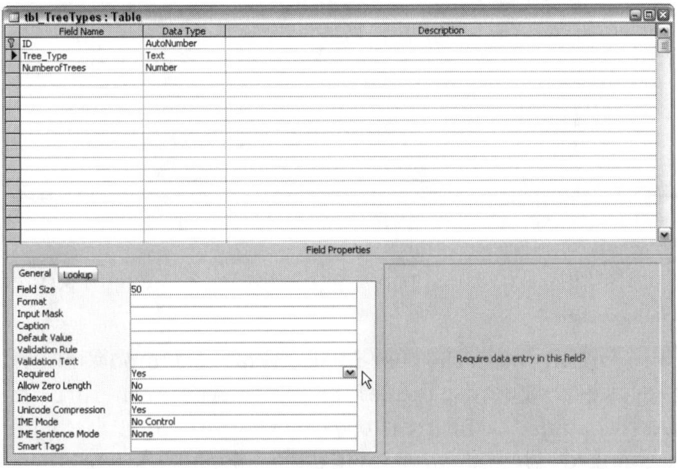

Figure 5-32. Setting field properties to control nulls and zero-length strings

The first is a property called Required. If you enter Yes for the Required property, you are telling Access a value must be entered in this field for it to be saved. This won't prevent someone filling it with a zero-length string. Setting the Allow Zero Length property to No forces an entry other than a zero-length string. If you say Yes, and you just want to eliminate nulls (test for blank by writing [Field]=""), you can set the Default Value property to "".

If you set these two properties correctly, you will have a value in each field, and you won't have to deal with nulls in your application. The same thing applies to number fields: there is a Required property you can set to Yes, and there is also a Default Value property. Normally, the Default Value property is set to 0 in a number field. However, if you want to ensure that users enter a value in this field and don't simply skip over it, you can remove the 0 in the default value field and set the Required property to Yes. This ensures that the record isn't saved until the user puts a value in the field (0 can be entered unless you have a validation rule in place).

Form design to prevent nulls and zero-length strings. If you don't have control over the table design, but you want to ensure the data entered is accurate, you can do so through Access forms. When you create a form in Access, several textbox properties are available that can help you ensure meaningful data, as shown in Figure 5-33.

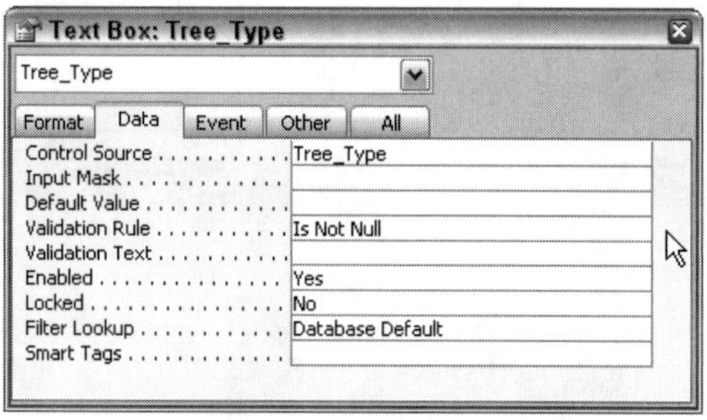

Figure 5-33. Controlling nulls through form control properties

You can set the Default Value property to allow a zero-length string if all you want is avoid a null.

You can also write code in the Lost Focus event. It is important to do this in the Lost Focus event because the Before Update event won't fire if the field is just tabbed through, and the After Update event fires after the field has actually been changed. Here is what that code might look like for a text box called TextBox1:

```
Private Sub TextBox1_LostFocus()
If IsNull(Me.TextBox1.Value) Then
  MsgBox "You must enter a value in this field", vbOKOnly, "Important"
  Me.TextBox2.SetFocus
  Me.TextBox1.SetFocus
End If
End Sub
```

You might be wondering why the Set Focus event is called twice. You must set the focus off of the text box and then back onto it; otherwise, it won't let you set the focus to the box. You might also be wondering why the code doesn't use the Validation Rule property. The validation rule run onlys when the field is changed, so if you simply skip a field, it won't run.

There is a limitation to using the Lost Focus event if a user uses the mouse and doesn't click each field. You can get around this limitation by setting the Cycle property on the Other tab of the Form Properties dialog box to Current Record (as shown in Figure 5-34) and then setting the Navigation Buttons property to No on the Format tab of the same dialog box (as shown in Figure 5-35).

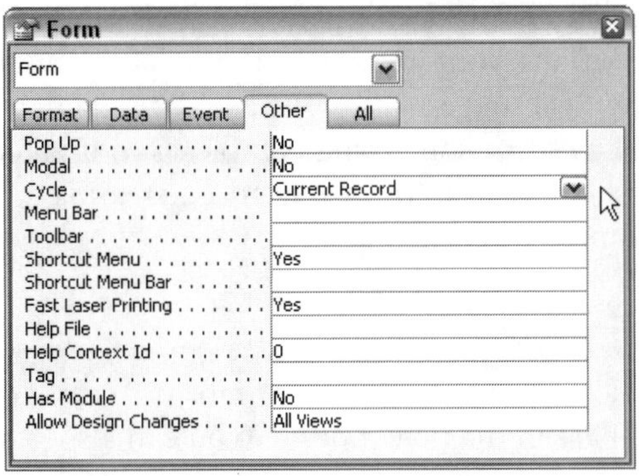

Figure 5-34. Setting the Cycle property to Current Record

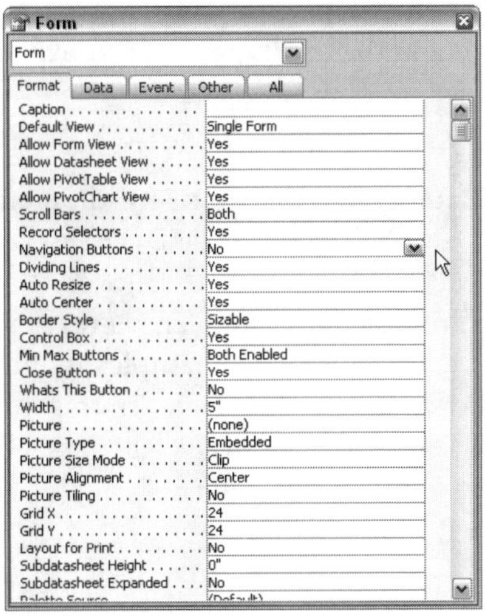

Figure 5-35. Setting the Navigation Buttons property to No

Once you have done this, you can create your own buttons to allow users to move to the next record, and you can put your validation text in there. In all cases, it is much easier to assign these settings during table design, but many times you don't have that control.

—Michael Schmalz

Use a Custom Function in a Query

#48   Write a custom function to manipulate multiple data formats.

When you need to perform complex manipulation of data in a query, it is often easier to write a function to perform the manipulation. You can avoid using complex functions inside a query and always write a user function. However, it is best to use your judgment. If you have a rather simple concatenation of a few fields, I suggest you write a user function within your query. But if you need to perform something complex and it is likely that you will need to do it in other places in the application, creating a new function will save you a lot of time.

Creating a New Function

To create a function, go to the Modules tab in Access, and create a new module. Once you are in the new module (you can also go into Design view in an existing module), select Insert → Procedure. Give it a name, select Function as the Type, and select Public as the Scope. Once you have your function, you can place variables between the parentheses. After the parentheses, give your function a type by typing As *datatype*; this ensures that your function is returned in the datatype that you expect.

Manipulating Dates

Dates come from different systems in many different formats, including YYYYMMDD, MM/DD/YYYY, and MMDDYYYY. The problem comes when you need to have the date in another format, as happens when you import data from a mainframe or a fixed-length text file in which the date is actually imported as text. This first example assumes the format being imported is YYYYMMDD or YYMMDD. In this function, the string is brought in as an argument and the Left, Right, and Mid functions are used with the CDate function to create the date:

```
Public Function GetDate(Dt As Variant) As Date
Dim MM As String
Dim DD As String
Dim YYYY As String
If VBA.InStr(1, Dt, "/") > 0 Then Dt = ""
Select Case VBA.Len(Access.Nz(Dt, ""))
  Case 8
    YYYY = VBA.Left(Dt, 4)
    MM = VBA.Mid(Dt, 5, 2)
    DD = VBA.Right(Dt, 2)
    GetDate = VBA.CDate(MM & "/" & DD & "/" & YYYY)
```

```
Case 6
  YYYY = VBA.Left(Dt, 2)
  MM = VBA.Mid(Dt, 3, 2)
  DD = Right(Dt, 2)
  GetDate = VBA.CDate(MM & "/" & DD & "/" & YYYY)
Case Else
  GetDate = #1/1/1900#
End Select
End Function
```

Notice that this function passes the string as a variant; this allows it to test for a null value or trap an actual date. If the variable is declared as a string, a null value results in an error. In this case, if a real date, null value, or anything other than YYMMDD or YYYYMMDD is passed, it returns a date of 1/1/1900. You can set that date to be something else. The If InStr ... Then line tests to see if a slash (/) is in the Dt variable. If it is, the procedure sets Dt to an empty string.

Now, let's assume you need to take it the other way. Assume you have a date field, and you need to turn it into a fixed-length string. Here is how the required function looks:

```
Public Function GetDateString(Dt As Date) As String
Dim MM As String
Dim DD As String
Dim YYYY As String

MM = VBA.Right(DatePart("m", Dt) + 100, 2)
DD = VBA.Right(DatePart("d", Dt) + 100, 2)
YYYY = VBA.DatePart("yyyy", Dt)

GetDateString = YYYY & MM & DD

End Function
```

This function passes the variable as a date. If a null or nondate is passed to the function, it returns #Error. This result simply shows how the function reacts when an inappropriate date is passed to it.

Also notice that the function uses the Right function along with DatePart and then adds 100 to it. This ensures that the month and date return two digits. If you didn't do this, it might work on your computer if you have dates set with leading zeros, but it could bomb on another computer. You can also use this logic anytime you need to put leading zeros in for a number. If you need five leading zeros, type right(x + 100000,5).

Your next question might be, "How do I use these functions?" You can call these functions from within a query, just like you would any other function. You can also use them in forms, reports, and so on. Let's assume you have a table called tbl_PersonalInformation, and you have a field called HireDate that is a date type. If you need to have a field in a query that formats the date as YYYYMMDD, write it in the query's Design view, like this:

```
TextHireDate: GetDateString([HireDate])
```

That is all you need to do. The date will be converted to a string in the format that you need. It is important to note that you could do the same thing the function does right in the query. However, by doing it that way, you have no way of easily reusing the logic elsewhere in the application.

—Michael Schmalz

HACK #49   Create Access Tables with SQL Server Scripts

SQL Server writes scripts that create tables. With a little editing, you can put them to work in Access.

So much attention is given to upsizing from Access to SQL Server. This makes sense because, after all, databases tend to grow, not shrink. However, this hack isn't concerned with data; it has to do with design. Every so often you might need to duplicate a SQL Server schema in Access. This could be for the very purpose of preparing your Access database for SQL Server.

If you are familiar with SQL Server, you already know SQL Server Enterprise Manager can write SQL *create table* scripts based on existing tables. If this is all new to you, come along for the ride!

Walking Through Enterprise Manager

Enterprise Manager, shown in Figure 5-36, is the utility you use to manage SQL Server.

The Pets database is accessed in the left pane. The database contains various objects. The tables of the Pets database are listed in the right pane. Most of the tables are system tables. The last three tables—tblAppointments, tblClients, and tblPets—are user tables. That means I created them; this is the same paradigm we use in Access.

To generate a SQL script, right-click the tblClients table, and select All Tasks → Generate SQL Script..., as shown in Figure 5-37. After you select a destination for the script, a file is created.

A text file is written with SQL Server–specific SQL statements. Figure 5-38 shows the generated script opened in Notepad.

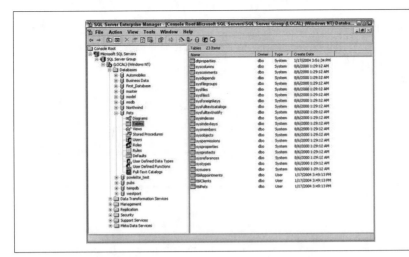

Figure 5-36. Exploring Enterprise Manager

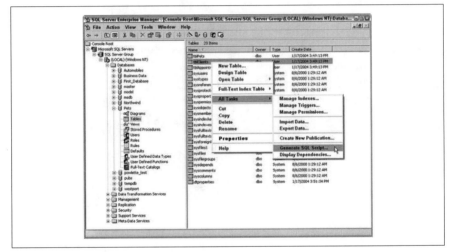

Figure 5-37. Preparing to generate a SQL script

As is, this script won't work if it's run inside an Access query. The pertinent part is in the middle, starting with the Create Table statement. Create Table is recognizable SQL in Access. Even so, the field types aren't correct in Access, so we still have to clean this up. Knowing what to do requires a little SQL knowledge, but if you haven't learned any yet, it's not a bad thing to get to know.

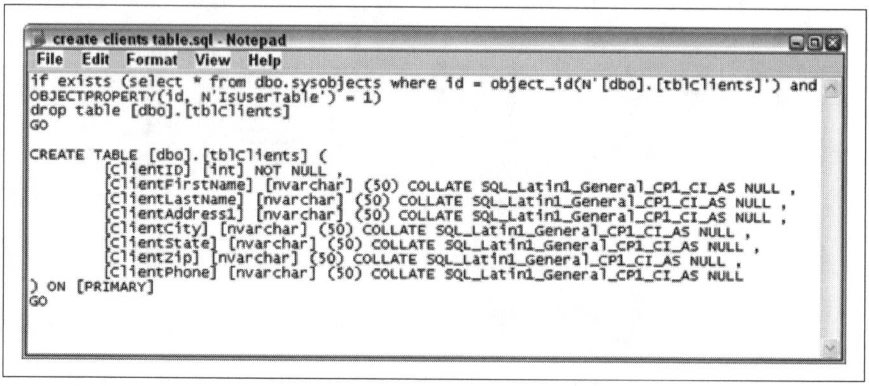

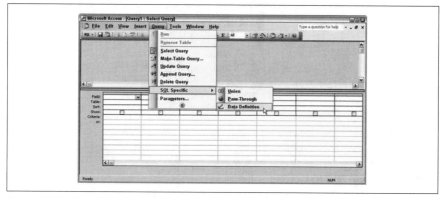

Figure 5-38. The generated script

Plenty of books are available on the subject of SQL. See the end of this hack for a short list.

Once you've cleaned up the SQL, and it's ready for Access, you need to call up a Data Definition query. Figure 5-39 shows where to access this special type of query in Access.

Figure 5-39. Creating a Data Definition query

Once you select the query type, you are left in a pane in which SQL is entered. Figure 5-40 shows the pane with the edited SQL script. Now it is ready to run in Access.

Sure enough, when this query runs, it creates a new tblClients table. So, essentially, not only is it possible to recreate a SQL schema in Access, but you also can edit a SQL Server–generated script to get the job done.

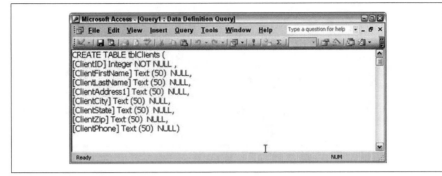

Figure 5-40. A SQL script, ready to run in Access

See Also

- *SQL Pocket Guide* (O'Reilly)
- *SQL in a Nutshell* (O'Reilly)

 ## Use Wildcards in Queries

The Like operator comes in handy when you don't quite remember how to spell a data item.

When you can remember only a partial amount of information, a great way to search through your database records is to use the SQL Like operator. Combining Like with wildcards makes for some powerful queries.

For example, imagine you have a database table filled with customer records. You need to look up someone whose last name starts with De, and that's all you can recall about her name.

Figure 5-41 shows a query that uses the asterisk (*) wildcard to find all customers whose last name starts with De. The asterisk is a placeholder for any number of characters. Therefore, running this query returns all customers with De as the first two characters in their last name.

Let's say instead that you remember the last name starts with D and is four characters long. In this case, the question mark (?) wildcard comes in handy. You use the question mark as a placeholder to represent a single character. Figure 5-42 shows three question marks being used to make up for three spaces after the letter D.

Figure 5-43 shows the result of running the query. All customers with four-character last names that start with D are returned.

Using wildcards lets you really get to your data in creative ways. You might recall the first and last letter of a name, or even just that a name is four characters long, but you don't remember any of the actual characters! In such as

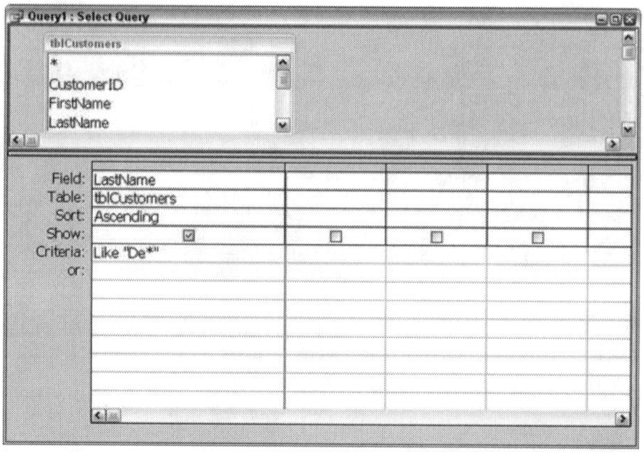

Figure 5-41. Finding customers with an asterisk wildcard

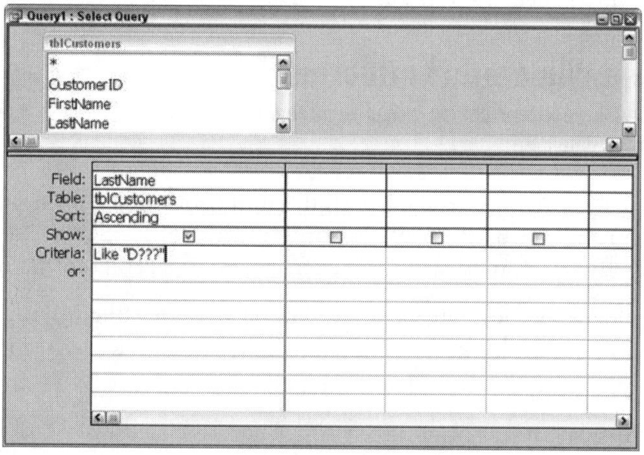

Figure 5-42. Finding customers using question marks

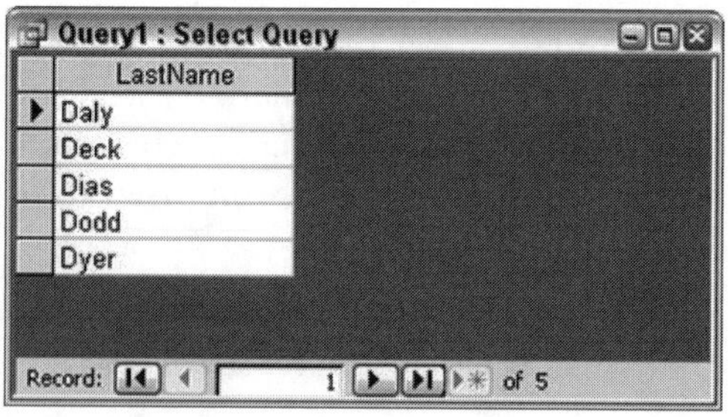

Figure 5-43. Returning records based on the wildcards

case, using a criterion of Like "????" returns all customers with last names that are four characters long, as shown in Figure 5-44.

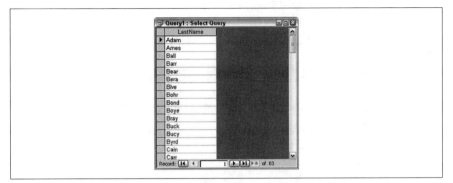

Figure 5-44. Returning all customers with a last name four characters long

Get Cleaner Or-Based Criteria

Avoid using multiple rows in the query grid by using the In operator.

The Access query grid is designed for easy query assembly, and it does a great job. Without a doubt, the grid has been an essential learning tool that helps us understand and use queries.

You can use the grid to create Or-based criteria in two ways. Figure 5-45 shows a typical way to set up a query. In this case, the query returns records in which the state is any of six possible values. As you can see, however, if a few more states were to be included, it would become necessary to start scrolling vertically to work on the list of states.

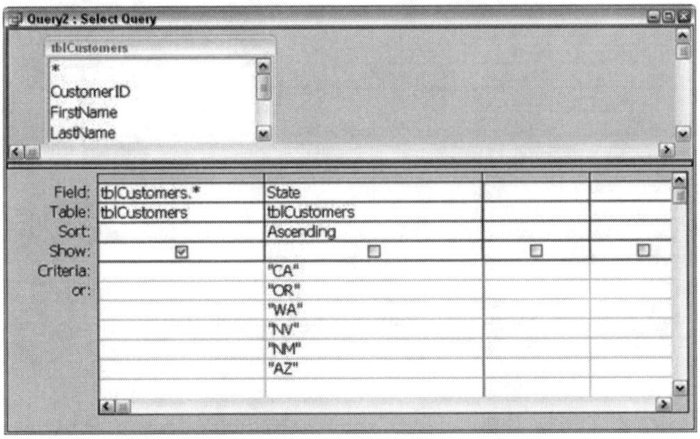

Figure 5-45. Creating Or-based criteria

Figure 5-46 shows an alternate way to set up the Or criteria. The specified states are put on one row, with Or statements throughout. However, this design also suffers from becoming unwieldy if more states are added. Each additional state being added also requires another Or operator, so the expression can become quite long.

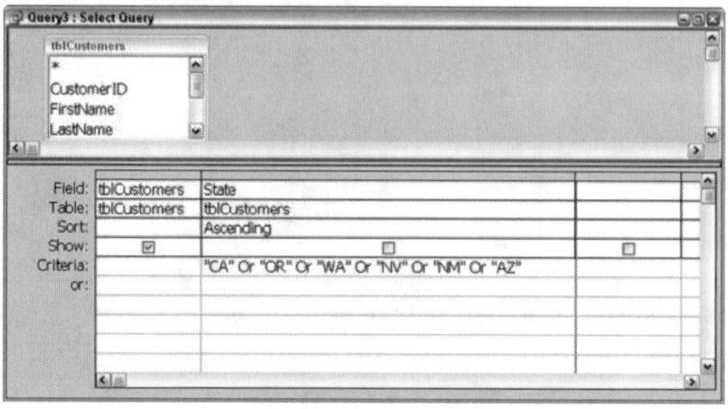

Figure 5-46. A long criteria statement

The In operator is the solution to this dilemma. The In operator is perfect for establishing Or-based criteria. Whereas in Figure 5-46 the inclusion of each state requires another Or operator, only one In operator is necessary, as shown in Figure 5-47.

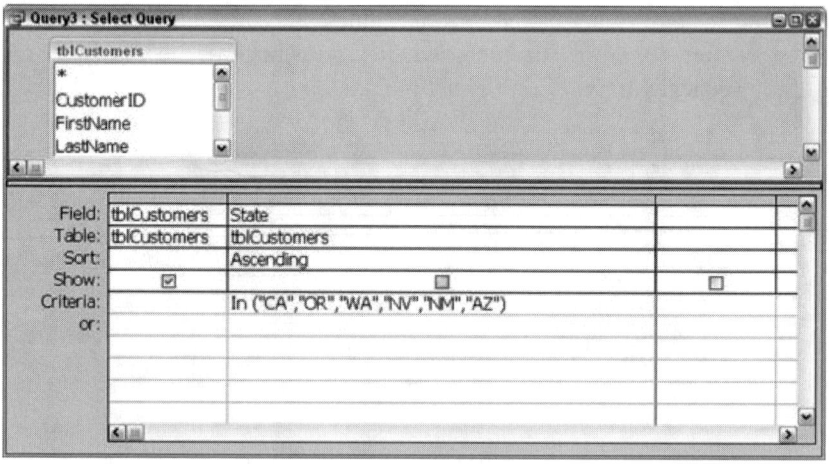

Figure 5-47. Using the In operator

Using the In operator makes it easy to add more states to the criteria. Just make sure you separate each state abbreviation with a comma.

Get Cleaner And-Based Criteria

Remove the need for multiple And statements by combining the In and Not operators.

Sometimes, criteria are set up to filter out certain records instead of including them. This reversal of logic makes sense in situations in which you want to return most of the records, but not all of them. "Get Cleaner Or-Based Criteria" [Hack #51] shows how to use the In operator to better manage Or-based criteria. When you set up criteria to be excluded, however, use the And operator. For example, you might ask, "Give me all states, except California *and* New Mexico."

Figure 5-48 shows a query design that excludes six states from the query results. As new states are added to this list, an additional And operator is required. Eventually, this method of writing multiple And operators becomes tiresome and you end up having to scroll to read through it all.

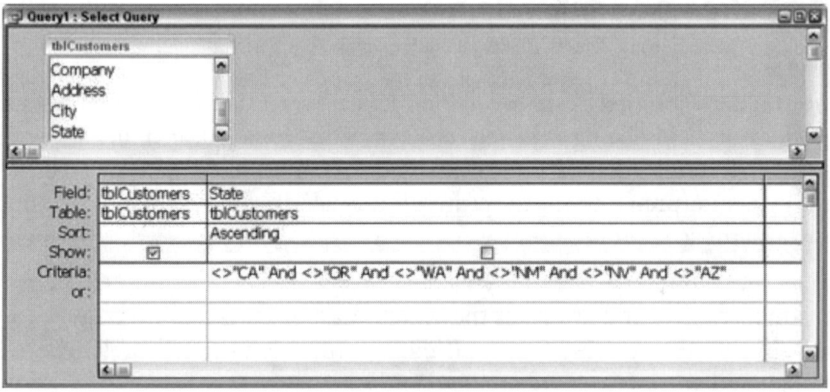

Figure 5-48. Using multiple And operators to filter out records

The In operator might come to mind as a way to reduce the long criteria statement. However, the point is to *not* include the criteria. The solution is to use both the In *and* the Not operators. Not is a logical operator: it reverses a condition. Including it with an In operator results in a list of items *not* to include, which works perfectly for this type of query.

Figure 5-49 shows the improved query, in which the multiple And statements are removed.

The query returns the same results, with a less-cluttered SQL statement.

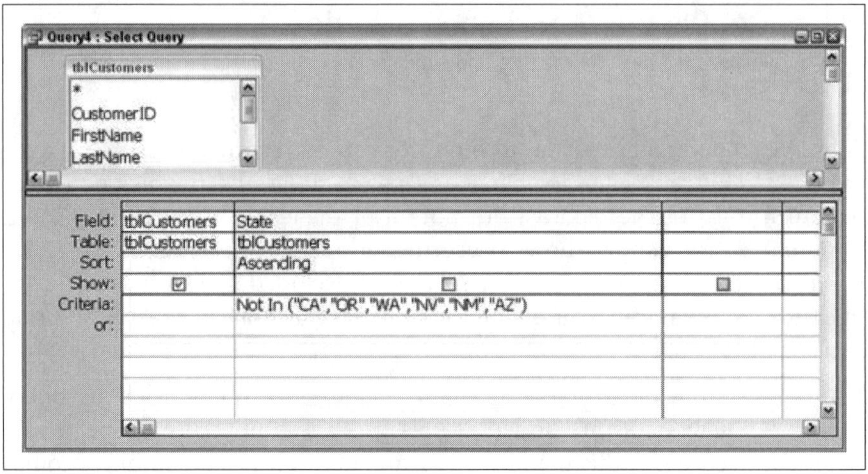

Figure 5-49. Using Not and In together

HACK #53   Create an Outer Join

Access doesn't support making an outer join; here's a workaround.

The standard join between two tables returns records that match based on the field or fields being selected as keys. This is called an *inner* join. For example, a statement such as "give me all customers and their sales records" usually is interpreted to mean return all the sales records and the customers to whom those records belong.

Sometimes, though, a *left* or *right* join is requested. For example, "give me all our customers and any sales they might have had" is really a request for a left join. In other words, return *all* the records from the left table (the customers) and any sales records that go with them.

Figure 5-50 shows how records returned from a left join query look. In this example, there are more customers than purchase date records. Some of the customers have no purchases and therefore have no data in the column on the right.

A right join returns all records from the table on the right and only those records from the table on the left that match on the key. The three types of joins—inner, left, and right—are easy to set up. The inner one is the default when two tables are related.

You can set the join type in either the Relationships window or in a query design by double-clicking directly on the line between the two tables. Figure 5-51 shows the Join Properties dialog box that appears when the line is double-clicked. The dialog contains options for the three join types.

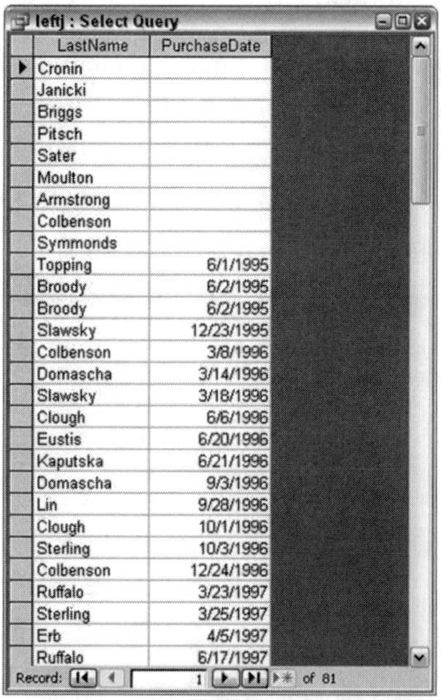

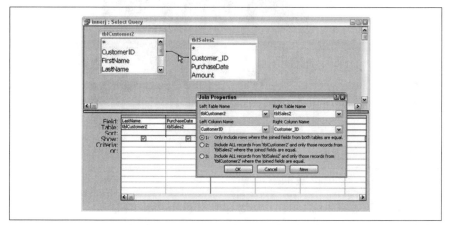

Figure 5-50. Returned records from a left join query

Figure 5-51. Setting join properties

As you can see, there is no option to create an *outer* join, which would return all the records that match, plus the records that don't match from *both* tables. The trick to doing this is to simply assemble the three types of available join queries into one query. This final query uses the Union operator to assemble the results from the other three queries.

A Union query works only with straight SQL statements. You can enter the SQL directly into a new query or, to make it easier, copy the generated SQL from the three join types and paste it into a new query. All you need to do is start the second and third mini-SQL Select statements with the Union operator in a new query, like this:

```
SELECT tblCustomer2.LastName, tblSales2.PurchaseDate
FROM tblCustomer2 INNER JOIN tblSales2 ON
tblCustomer2.CustomerID = tblSales2.Customer_ID
Union
SELECT tblCustomer2.LastName, tblSales2.PurchaseDate
FROM tblCustomer2 LEFT JOIN tblSales2 On
tblCustomer2.CustomerID = tblSales2.Customer_ID
Union
SELECT tblCustomer2.LastName, tblSales2.PurchaseDate
FROM tblCustomer2 RIGHT JOIN tblSales2 ON
tblCustomer2.CustomerID = tblSales2.Customer_ID;
```

Figure 5-52 shows the result of running the SQL.

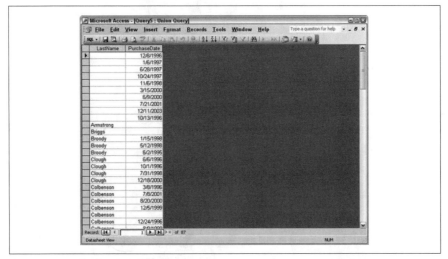

Figure 5-52. The results of an outer join

Both columns (each comes from a different table) have blanks—where there was no matching record in the other table—and the records that match are there as well.

Use Regular Expressions in Access Queries

#54 Sometimes wildcards aren't enough. With a little hacking, you can use regular expressions in your queries.

Although Access allows for some powerful string matching (see "Wildcard characters and the Like operator" in the Access Help system), sometimes you require an even more powerful solution. Microsoft added the ability to use regular expressions back in Version 5.0 of its Windows Scripting Engine, bringing it up to par with JavaScript. You can use this power inside an Access query as well.

Although the advanced details of regular expressions are beyond the scope of this hack, this example will get you started if you are new to the subject. If you need more information, I recommend the book *Mastering Regular Expressions* (O'Reilly).

In many cases it's possible to work around the lack of built-in regular expressions using Access's wildcard characters and multiple calls to different string functions, such as Left, Mid, Right, Len, and so on. However, once you see what you can do with a single custom function call, you can imagine the advanced possibilities and time savings.

Creating the Custom Function

The first thing we need to do is create a function that can be called from our Access query that ties into the Microsoft Scripting Runtime library.

This hack assumes the machine you are running has the latest version of Microsoft's Scripting Engine installed. If you are unsure, visit *http://www.microsoft.com/scripting*.

The following code uses the CreateObject function so that you don't have to check the Reference each time the code is placed in a new database:

```
Public Function RegExp(strString As String, _
    strRegExp As String, Optional bolIgnoreCase As Boolean = False) As
Boolean
    Dim re As Object
    Set re = CreateObject("vbscript.RegExp")
    re.Pattern = strRegExp
    re.IgnoreCase = bolIgnoreCase
    If re.Test(strString) Then
        RegExp = True
    Else
        RegExp = False
    End If
End Function
```

The function has two required parameters: the string being matched against and the string that contains the regular expression. The third, optional parameter tells the function whether to match the regular expression while ignoring the case; the default won't ignore the case.

Creating an Example Query

As an example, let's look at verifying part numbers by finding those that don't match a given criterion. Many times, you might receive data from multiple people and platforms that needs to be cleaned before going into a master database. Let's say that part numbers for a factory have the following criteria:

- They must start with a capital PN or a capital P.
- The next two positions must be numeric.
- The next position must be a capital letter (A–Z).
- The next three to four positions must be numeric.
- The next five to six positions must be capital letters (A–Z).

Examples of part numbers that meet the criteria include PN12W123ABCDE and P12W123ABCDE. Examples that don't meet the criteria include PN12W13ABCDE (only two digits after the W) and 12W123ABCDE (doesn't start with PN or P).

Given the set of criteria for the part number, here's the regular expression:

```
"^(PN|P)[0-9][0-9][A-Z][0-9]{3,4}[A-Z]{5,6}$"
```

As mentioned earlier, these regular expressions can become quite overwhelming until you get used to them. If you aren't familiar with them, I strongly recommend additional reading to learn the full power of these expressions. To better understand it, let's break down this expression:

^   Tells the expression to start at the beginning of the string

(PN|P)
    Says to match the characters PN or P

[0-9][0-9]
    Tells the expression to match two digits, both in the range 0 through 9

[A-Z]
    Says to match a single character A through Z

[0-9]{3,4}
    Says to match a single digit 0 through 9 at least three times and a maximum of four times

[A-Z]{5,6}

> Says to match a single character A through Z at least five times and a
> maximum of six times

Figure 5-53 shows the layout for a query to find part numbers that don't
match our criteria.

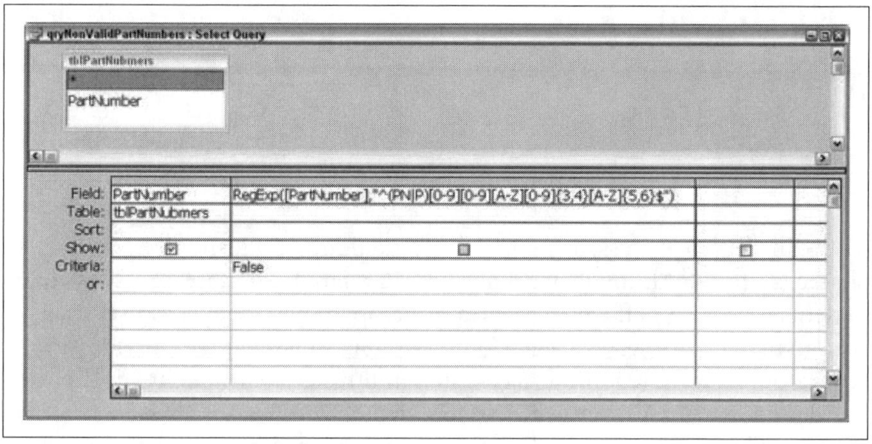

Figure 5-53. Calling the RegExp function from a query

Running the query in Figure 5-53 returns the part numbers that do *not* match
our given criteria so that you can review them before placing them into a
master database. Although you can do this without tapping into the power of
regular expressions, it requires a much more involved solution.

Hacking the Hack

As you discover the power of regular expressions, you will find them to be
very robust for all kinds of text processing. Another handy trick is to use
them to verify text input on a form. To do so, call the custom RegExp function from the BeforeUpdate event of the text box. If it returns false, set the
Cancel parameter variable to True, which clears the input on the text box.

You can even add an advanced feature to your application, which allows the
user to do searches based on her own regular expressions!

—*Steve Huff*

CHAPTER SIX

Multiuser Issues
Hacks 55–58

You can deploy Access databases as standalone applications as well as in shared systems. Although working with a shared database provides many benefits in terms of efficiency, issues can crop up with regard to users' activities getting in the way of each other's data. This chapter provides a few workarounds for integrating Access in a multiuser environment while ensuring data doesn't get trampled. "Build a Time-Out Feature" [Hack #57] catches and completes idle record edits, thereby allowing others to make changes. "Test for Duplication" [Hack #55] shows a way to validate data before users duplicate each other's entries. The chapter also covers a distribution method [Hack #56] that makes it easy to get a split database from your development machine to your clients, with the table links already matching the network.

HACK #55 Test for Duplication

Before you insert multiple entries into master tables in a busy data-entry environment, you'll need a custom validation process to avoid duplicated data.

Just because a database is deployed on the server doesn't mean the entire application must be in that server copy. A common approach is to put the data in the server database and distribute the forms to the local client computers, inside another Access file. This is a typical Access version of a client/server application.

Because the client installations are Access databases, using tables in the client databases opens up possibilities. One useful technique is to have *new* data entries go into local tables first, and later to bulk-insert them into the master table or tables on the server.

The heart of this technique is that entry operators have local tables that mirror the server tables. Their forms are bound to the local tables and all entry is done locally. At the end of the day, or at scheduled times throughout the day, a process runs that takes the data out of the local tables and moves it to the server tables.

Here is where the advantage lies. The insert process gathers the input from all the entry operators' client tables and tests for duplication before the actual insert into the server tables. Normally, such an interim validation would be overkill because data usually is validated upon entry. However, the point here isn't really to validate data in terms of correct content, but rather, to see if duplicate records were entered during input.

This is certainly a possibility in a busy customer service, sales, or telemarketing operation. For example, in an environment where phone calls come in, it is possible that Jane places an order for something and, an hour later, her husband Joe places an order for the same item. If different operators handled the husband and wife, no one would be the wiser that this is a duplicate order. Even the two created records might not be actual duplicates because the first name is different in each record. But if a custom-designed validation process is used, these two records can be flagged as duplicates because at least the address is the same in both records.

You also can test for near duplication on the server, so this begs the question: why bother with the separate table-entry approach? The answer is performance. If all entry goes straight to the server tables, *and* the custom duplication process runs on the larger tables, there could be some issues with speed.

Another issue to consider is how far back in time to look for duplicates. With the local approach, the test certainly is done at least at the end of the day, if not during scheduled times throughout the day, all for that day's processing. Involving older records in the server tables isn't necessary. An order placed twice in one day is probably a duplicate. An order that resembles one placed last week or last month is probably a repeat order.

—Andrea Moss

HACK #56 Distribute a Split Database with Predefined Table Links

If you follow this interesting distribution game plan, users will not have to link their local database files to the data tables on the system.

The technique known as *database splitting*, which involves a tables-only back-end Access file on a network share, copies of front-end Access files (with forms, reports, and so on) on each user's C:\ drive, and the use of linked tables, has been around for quite some time. The benefits of such client/server database configurations are widely known and documented.

However, it can be a challenge to deal with split databases during periods of frequent updates, especially during the development phase. For some users, their Office installation doesn't even include the Linked Table Manager, so they can get prompted for the Office installation CD when they attempt to refresh and change links. Other users might simply be uncomfortable or unfamiliar with how linked tables work. Frequent relinking, especially for users who were used to just sharing an MDB from one location, can be problematic.

When frequent rounds of revisions are being submitted to end users during the initial prototyping stage of development, it makes sense to keep the project in only one file. But once the data model is signed off, it's time to split the database. You can do this in two ways:

- Make a copy of the database so that you have two identical copies. In one copy, delete the tables. In the other copy, delete everything but the tables.

- Use the Database Splitter utility (Tools → Database Utilities). This automatically creates an Access file with just the tables and, at the same time, removes the tables from the database running the utility.

Then the back-end database (the one with the tables) goes on a network share, while the front-end database is distributed to users and is run from their PCs. The problem is that the front-end database must be linked to the tables in the back-end database. Simulating these links on your development PC before distributing the front end is the point here. If you can set the links so that they are the same as those in the production environment, users will not have to deal with establishing the links themselves from their PCs.

In other words, you can distribute the front end *prelinked*. All of this is based on the assumption that a drive-mapping standard is in place and that all users will have an identical map path.

Copying the Network Drive to Your Development Machine

The SUBST DOS command is all you need to copy the network drive to your development machine. On your development machine, you can use SUBST to create a map that matches the one users need.

First, create a directory on your computer that matches the folder on the share where the back-end database will go. If the network path includes subdirectories, create a path that matches that path structure on your development machine.

The syntax for using SUBST requires the new drive letter and the path it is set to, like this:

```
SUBST <New Virtual Drive Letter>:  <Path to map to that letter>
```

For example, if you have a subfolder named *XYZ_Corp* in your *C:\Clients* folder, and you want to map that folder to an *S:* drive, click Start/Run; type command (Windows 98, Me) or CMD (Windows NT, 2000, XP); click OK; and enter this at the command line:

```
SUBST S: C:\Clients\XYZ_Corp
```

Figure 6-1 shows how you do this in the Command Prompt box.

Figure 6-1. Using SUBST

If users are accessing a subfolder under the *S:* drive, create matching folder names under the folder that was substituted to the *S:* drive. Place the back-end database in the appropriate folder.

Now, when you are in the front-end database file and are linking the back-end tables, browse to your new *S:* drive to find the back-end database, thereby keeping the links the same as what the users need. When you send your users an update, they should not have to relink anything. This new drive letter will even show up when you open My Computer. The new virtual drive letter will last until the next time you restart. If you decide you no longer need a virtual drive, you can get rid of it with the /d switch:

```
SUBST S: /d
```

It's important to note that this removes the virtual mapping; it doesn't delete the folder or its files. Also, you can't use SUBST if you already have a drive using that letter, so if your keychain flash drive is using *G:*, you have to safely remove it before SUBSTing a folder to use the *G:* drive.

Of course, this technique works only in extremely stable environments, where all users have the same drive letter mapped to the given share. Although *S:* might work for your primary contact, other users of the application might have a different letter mapped to that location, or they might not have any letter mapped. They could be accessing the folder through its Universal Naming Convention (UNC) name (*\\ServerName\ShareName*). If this is the case, you can emulate this on your PC as well as long as you are willing to rename your PC to match the server's name (you can always change it back later).

Using UNC Instead

If you want to use UNC instead, you need to rename your computer. First, you need to know the server name at the client site and the full path of folders and subfolders to the share that will hold your back-end datafile. To rename your computer to match the server, bring up your PC's System Properties by right-clicking My Computer and clicking Properties, or by double-clicking the System icon in the Control Panel to open the System Properties dialog box. Select the Computer Name tab, and then click the Change button. When you see the Computer Name Changes dialog box, shown in Figure 6-2, type the desired name for the computer. It will require a reboot to take effect. Of course, this assumes you will be creating a name conflict on the network. The assumption is that your development machine isn't on the production network. If it is, you can disconnect your computer during this process.

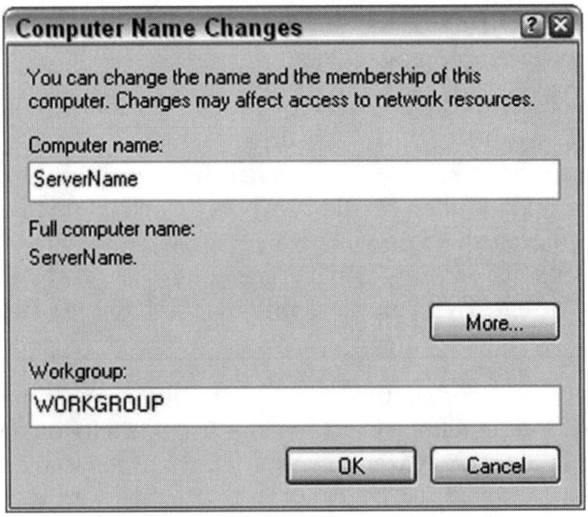

Figure 6-2. Changing the name of the computer

So, if XYZ Corp.'s server, called *ServerName*, has a *DeptShare* folder and a subfolder called *DataFolder* that will hold your datafile, change your computer's name to *ServerName*. Then, create a folder named *DeptShare* off the root of your *C:* drive, and create a subfolder called *DataFolder* inside the *DeptShare* folder.

Once the folder structure is in place, browse to the *DeptShare* folder, right-click in an empty area of the folder, and then click Properties. Select the Sharing tab, and make selections to share the folder, as shown in Figure 6-3.

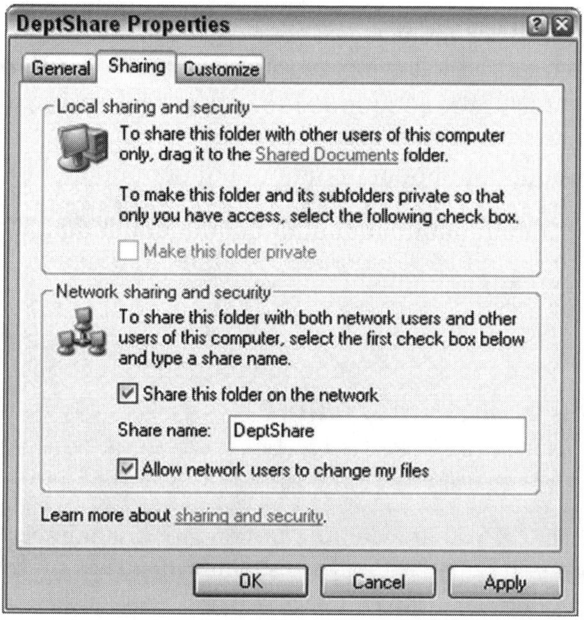

Figure 6-3. Sharing a folder

Now go to My Network Places, and click Add a Network Place. Click Next on the wizard's first screen, and the wizard will ask you where to create the new network place; select "Choose another network location." Click Next, and in the Internet or Network Address box, type \\ServerName\DeptShare. Click Next; Windows will ask what to call the share. If the name isn't already in the box, type DeptShare for ServerName. Click OK, and then click Finish.

Finally, back in your Access application file, delete all the linked tables. This time, when relinking the tables, make sure to go through My Network Places/Entire Network in the link dialog to browse to the datafile, or type \\servername\deptshare into the dialog to browse to the datafile. This causes Access to create the links to use the UNC naming convention. If you use the My Computer shortcut to your share, Access recognizes that it is local and uses the C: drive path to create the link. To ensure that your link is using UNC, type this in the debug window:

```
?Currentdb.TableDefs("<your table name>").Connect
```

Make sure to put the name of one of the linked tables in the code line where you see the *<your table name>* prompt. The response should look like this:

```
;DATABASE=\\Servername\DeptShare\DataFolder\Project_dat.mdb
```

Note that you will see the name of your database; you won't see *Project_ dat.mdb*. If you get the following response, you need to try again, making sure you go through the entire network, workgroup, computer name, and share name when browsing to your datafile:

```
;DATABASE=C:\DeptShare\DataFolder\Project_dat.mdb
```

Once this is correct, end users at the client site shouldn't need to relink, regardless of which drive letter (if any) they have mapped to the network location.

—Steve Conklin

HACK #57　Build a Time-Out Feature

Make sure your data is saved and available to others. Lock the records when they're not being updated.

The phone rings, or you are late to a meeting, or any number of other distractions pop up. It happens to all of us. Unfortunately, you sometimes forget to close out of the file open on your PC.

In a multiuser database, this can be a real nuisance. Depending on the record-locking scheme being used, if a record is left in the middle of an edit, other workers might not be able to make changes to that record. Figure 6-4 shows the dreadful message a user can get when attempting to make a change to a record someone else has left open.

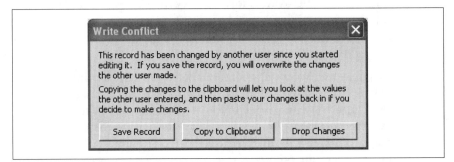

Figure 6-4. A record that has been left in an edited state

Although the message in Figure 6-4 gives the second user the options he needs, it is better to not even see this message, if it can be avoided. A productive measure for this situation is to close a form in which no activity is sensed after a period of time. In other words, if the first user has not completed any changes to the record within a specified time, the form should just close. Closing the form ends the record-editing process, and the changes are saved automatically. The alternative, to drop the changes, is discussed at the end of this hack.

It's About Time

Forms have an intrinsic timer control and Timer event. If you're familiar with Visual Basic, you know how to actually place a timer control on a form. In Access, the control is effectively already on the form, although you don't see it. Instead, you use the property sheet to set the Interval property and to indicate what occurs in the On Timer event.

To display the property sheet, open the form in Design mode, and press F4 on the keyboard. If necessary, make sure the property sheet is displaying properties about the form itself, not about one of the controls or sections. Select Form from the drop-down box at the top of the property sheet.

Figure 6-5 shows the property sheet set to display the properties for the form. The On Timer and Timer Interval properties are found on both the Event tab and the All tab.

 You can display the property sheet in a few ways. You can press F4, or you can press Alt-Enter. You can also use the View → Properties menu, or just click the Properties button on the Form Design toolbar.

The Interval property accepts values between 0 and 2,147,483,647 milliseconds. A setting of 1000 equals one second. The 10000 setting shown in Figure 6-5 is the equivalent of 10 seconds. By the way, the largest setting of 2,147,483,647 equals almost 25 days. Yes, you can schedule an Access event every 25 days!

The On Timer event property links to either a macro or a code procedure. In this example, a code procedure was written. I'll explain the code soon, but first, let's examine the form's design.

In Good Form

Figure 6-6 illustrates the form design, field list, and property sheet. Notice the text box control in the form header that isn't bound to a field. The

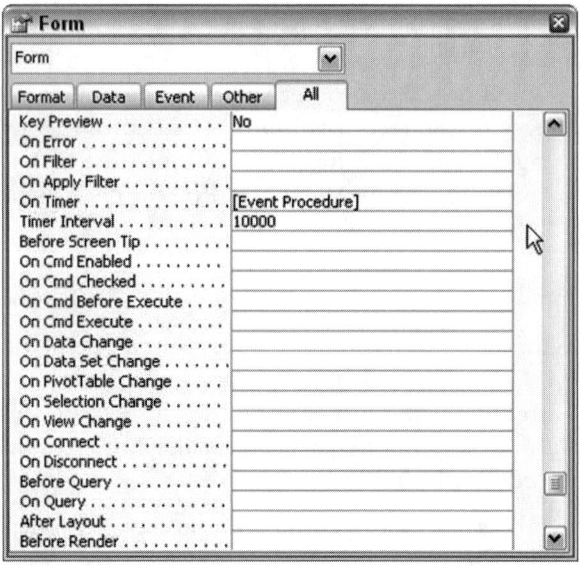

Figure 6-5. Setting the Timer Interval and On Timer event

property sheet is set to display the properties of the unbound box, txtTime, and its Visible property is set to No. In other words, when the form is in View mode, the txtTime text box won't be seen.

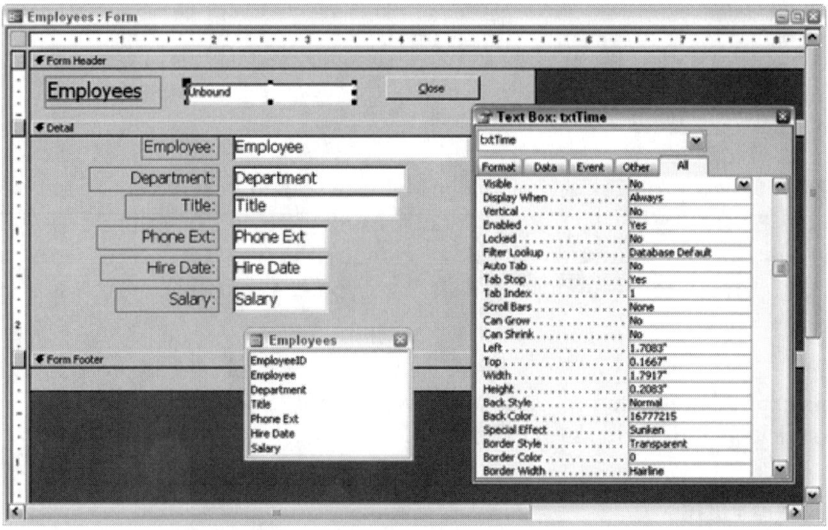

Figure 6-6. An unbound text box to hold a time reference

The txtTime text box isn't meant to be used for entry. Instead, it holds a snapshot of the computer's clock time, at the moment the form is activated. To make this happen, you need to enter a little code in the form's Activate event.

To get to the event code stub, select [Event Procedure] from the drop-down menu to the right of On Activate in the property sheet and then click the ellipses (...) button, as shown in Figure 6-7. This brings you to the form's code module, right at the start of the Activate event. How's that for convenience?

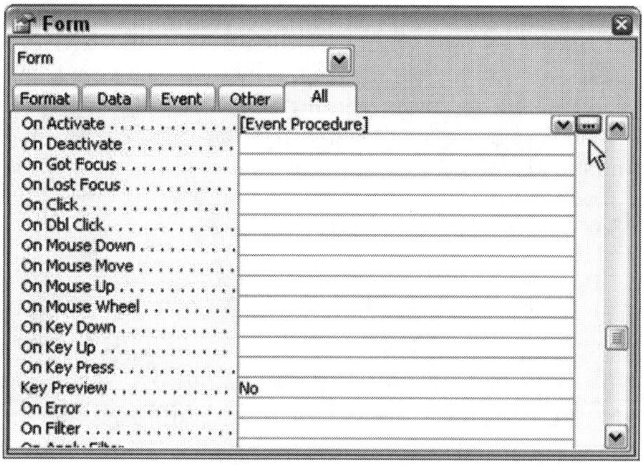

Figure 6-7. Getting to an event code stub from the property sheet

Here is the code to enter in the Activate event:

```
Private Sub Form_Activate( )
    Me.txtTime = Now
End Sub
```

The On Timer event contains the DateDiff function, set to test for the difference in seconds between the established form activation time and the current time. From the property sheet, select [Event Procedure] in the drop-down menu to the right of On Timer. Click the ellipses button and enter this code:

```
Private Sub Form_Timer( )
If DateDiff("s", Me.txtTime, Now) > 5 Then
    DoCmd.Close
End If
End Sub
```

The first parameter of the DateDiff function indicates which interval to test; in this case, s is for seconds. The function tests if more than five seconds have lapsed between the time stored in the txtTime text box and now. Bear in mind that there are two values to coordinate here: the timer interval and how many seconds to test for.

This example is set up to test every 10 seconds if there is a difference of five seconds, but you can change these numbers. For example, it might be easier on the user if the timer interval is 30 seconds. There is a balance of what makes sense here. If users are likely to edit the same records often, make the interval shorter.

> The Now( ) function returns the system time. Every computer keeps an internal clock running. When timing events, it's necessary to start with a baseline time. The Now( ) function takes a *snapshot* of the time, which is then compared to a later time (effectively another snapshot, but later in time). Subtracting the first snapshot from the second snapshot equals the elapsed time. Incidentally, the computer clock is also used in programs that allow you to enter "today's date." Sometimes, the clock needs to be reset.

If we stopped here, the form would close 10 seconds after being opened. That is, upon the first run of the On Timer event (which occurs 10 seconds after the form is opened) a difference greater than five seconds is found, and the DoCmd.Close line runs, closing the form. But our goal is to close the form only when there is no activity, not just for the heck of it.

The key to making this hack work is to add code to each change event for the various text entry boxes on the form. The form in this example has text boxes for editing employee name, department, title, and so on. The Change event for each text box receives a single line of code to update the txtTime text box with the current time. In other words, every time a change is made in an entry text box the txtTime text box (remember, this one is invisible) is reset to Now, like this:

```
Private Sub Department_Change( )
    Me.txtTime = Now
End Sub
```

The Change event fires each time a character is entered or backspaced out of the text box. Therefore, as a user types in one of the entry text boxes, the txtTime text box is constantly updated with the current time. Then, when the timer event fires, the DateDiff function returns a difference of less than five seconds, and the form stays open. Only when the form is left idle does a difference greater than five seconds occur, thereby closing the form.

Figure 6-8 shows how the form's code module should look after these routines have been entered. It's OK if your event routines aren't in the same order.

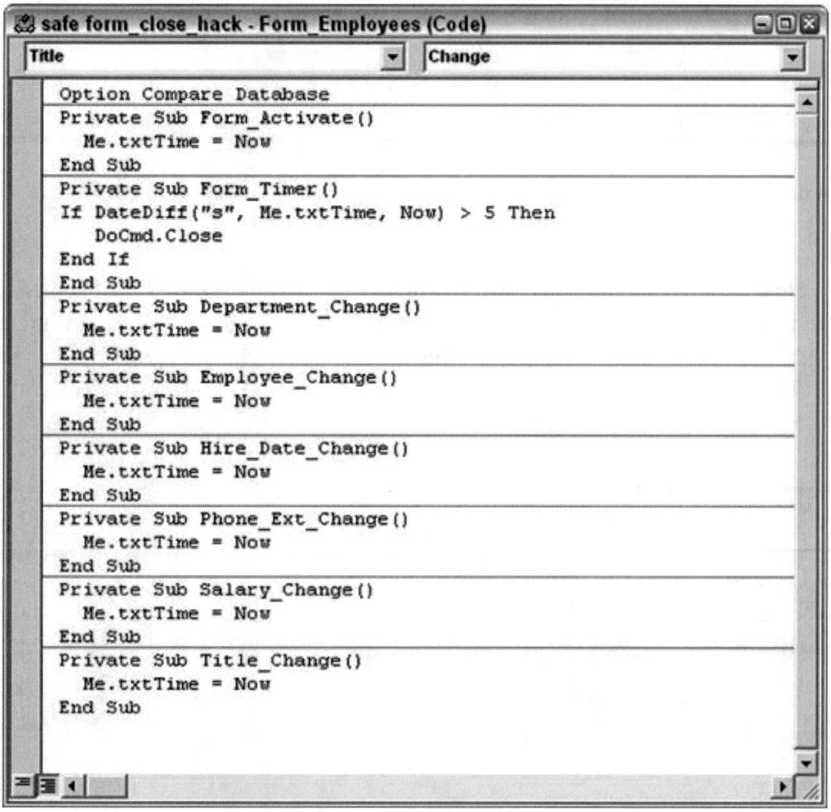
safe form_close_hack - Form_Employees (Code)
Title
Change
Option Compare Database
Private Sub Form_Activate()
Me.txtTime = Now
End Sub
Private Sub Form_Timer()
If DateDiff("s", Me.txtTime, Now) > 5 Then
DoCmd.Close
End If
End Sub
Private Sub Department_Change()
Me.txtTime = Now
End Sub
Private Sub Employee_Change()
Me.txtTime = Now
End Sub
Private Sub Hire_Date_Change()
Me.txtTime = Now
End Sub
Private Sub Phone_Ext_Change()
Me.txtTime = Now
End Sub
Private Sub Salary_Change()
Me.txtTime = Now
End Sub
Private Sub Title_Change()
Me.txtTime = Now
End Sub

Figure 6-8. The code that handles an inactive form

Hacking the Hack

You can implement this hack in many different ways. So far, all we know is how to reset the baseline time each time a character is entered with the keyboard. Also, the only action after a period of inactivity has been to close the form. Here are some other ideas.

Reset the time when the mouse is moved. In addition to capturing keyboard entries as a way to reset the time held in the invisible text box, it makes sense to do this whenever the mouse is moved as well. Some people are quick on the mouse, and just giving the mouse a push keeps the form open. In fact, I often do this to keep my screensaver from starting up.

Access forms can also use the `MouseMove` event. Insert code into the `MouseMove` event in the same manner explained earlier. The purpose of the code is the same, to reset the invisible text box to `Now`.

```
Private Sub Title_MouseMove(Button As Integer, _
    Shift As Integer, X As Single, Y As Single)
  Me.txtTime = Now
End Sub
```

As long as the mouse is moved at least once every 10 seconds, the form will stay open.

Let the user decide the timer interval. Each user has his own way of working, not to mention his own speed of working. So, instead of hardcoding the timer's interval value, why not let the user decide what is best? To do this, you have to build a way to let him select the interval into the form (or somewhere else, such as in a preferences area). Figure 6-9 shows how the form has been modified by adding a combo box. The combo box lets the user select from a list of possible values.

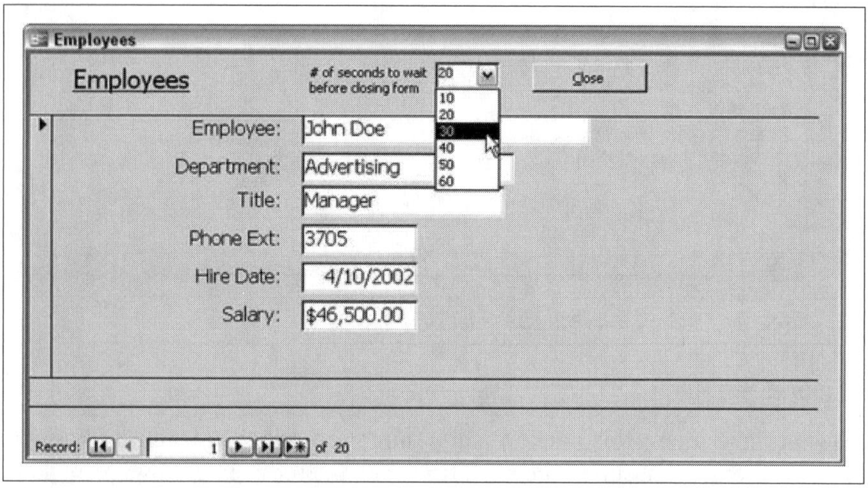

Figure 6-9. Letting the user decide how long to wait before closing the form

The code is updated as well. The combo box has been named cmbSeconds. Its Row Source Type is set to Value List, and the Row Source is set to the choices 10, 20, 30, 40, 50, and 60. When the user selects a value from the combo box, the combo box's Change event fires to update the invisible text box to the current time. Also, the form's Activate event now takes care of establishing a default time to wait—20 seconds in this case, as shown in Figure 6-10.

It's necessary to have a default value to use until or unless the user selects an interval. Finally, the number of elapsed seconds that are tested for is now always one fewer than the interval selected in the combo box. Figure 6-10 shows the updated code module.

```
safe form_close_hack - Form_Employees2 (Code)

Form                                    Activate

Option Compare Database
Private Sub Form_Activate()
   Me.txtTime = Now
   Me.cmbSeconds.DefaultValue = 20
End Sub
Private Sub cmbSeconds_Change()
   Me.TimerInterval = Me.cmbSeconds * 1000
End Sub
Private Sub Form_Timer()
If DateDiff("s", Me.txtTime, Now) > Me.cmbSeconds - 1 Then
   DoCmd.Close
End If
End Sub
Private Sub Department_Change()
   Me.txtTime = Now
End Sub
Private Sub Employee_Change()
   Me.txtTime = Now
End Sub
Private Sub Hire_Date_Change()
   Me.txtTime = Now
End Sub
Private Sub Phone_Ext_Change()
   Me.txtTime = Now
End Sub
Private Sub Salary_Change()
   Me.txtTime = Now
End Sub
Private Sub Title_Change()
   Me.txtTime = Now
```

Figure 6-10. Setting the Interval property with the combo box Change event

Save the record but leave the form open. Just because a record is displayed in a form doesn't necessarily mean it is being edited. The Dirty property is true if edits have been made or false if no data has changed. You can change the code in the form's Timer event to test the Dirty property. If it is true, the record is saved, and a message is presented, as shown in Figure 6-11. If Dirty is false, and no edit is occurring, nothing happens. Either way the form stays open.

The new code for the Timer event uses a pair of nested If statements. First, if the elapsed time is greater than the predetermined interval of the test, the

Figure 6-11. The saved-edits message

second If statement comes into play. The second If tests the Dirty property. If true, the record is saved, and the message is displayed:

```
Private Sub Form_Timer( )
If DateDiff("s", Me.txtTime, Now) > Me.cmbSeconds - 1 Then
   If Me.Dirty Then
      DoCmd.RunCommand acCmdSaveRecord
      MsgBox "Edits have been saved!"
   End If
End If
End Sub
```

If you started an edit and didn't complete it, the code completes it for you. If an edit is initiated, no harm is done.

Close the form without saving the record. So far, each approach in the hack has been based on saving the record that is in the middle of an edit. This is a judgment call because even if the person walked away from his work you don't know for sure whether to save his entry. To be on the safe side, the work is saved.

Of course, the argument exists to not save the edits. It's easy to drop the edits with an Undo action. Here is a snippet of modified code that goes into the Timer event:

```
Private Sub Form_Timer( )
If DateDiff("s", Me.txtTime, Now) > 10 Then
   If Me.Dirty Then
      DoCmd.RunCommand acCmdUndo
      DoCmd.Close
   End If
End If
End Sub
```

Essentially, if the record isn't in its pristine state (confirmed by the Dirty property), the code runs an Undo command and closes the form without saving the record. This is just one way to handle dropping a half-completed edit.

Another enhancement is to save the values out of the form and into a tempo-rary table or even a text file, and to leave a message box alerting the user that his entry was dropped but that he can find his unsaved efforts at the place where you saved them.

HACK #58 Implement Unique Usernames

Even when Access Security isn't active, you can implement unique usernames when all users are Admin.

Access Security is great in many multiuser situations because you can assign rights to groups and individuals. However, sometimes this is just a lot of overhead. In a small group of users who all use the same objects, you don't get much added value by implementing security.

The downside of not using security is that all users are given the name Admin. You can confirm this in an unsecured database by going to the Immediate window (Ctrl-G in the VB Editor) and typing the following:

```
?CurrentUser
```

The CurrentUser property contains the logged-in name of the user. When security is on, each user has a specific name. When security is off, all users are Admin.

An easy way to use specific names in an unsecured database is to first have users enter their names and then have the entered names available through-out the session. This technique makes sense only in a configuration in which each user works on a local database with the forms. The data tables remain on in a back-end database on the server.

When a user starts up her client-based front end, she is asked to enter her name. This is just an easy affair handled by an input box. A loop keeps test-ing for her entry, and when she is done, the entry is handed off to the Tag property of the main form. This works best if the main form opens automat-ically when the user starts up the database. This code goes into the main form's Open event:

```
Private Sub Form_Open(Cancel As Integer)
    Dim user_name As String
    user_name = ""
    Do Until user_name <> ""
      user_name = InputBox("Please enter your name", "Enter Name")
    Loop
    Me.Tag = user_name
End Sub
```

Implement Unique Usernames

Throughout the session, the person's name is always available via this simple reference back to the main form and its tag, assuming that the main form is named frmMain. Change the form name to match yours:

```
Forms!frmMain.Tag
```

Because the application is configured in the way that each user is using a local version of the main form, the reference to the Tag property always returns the user's unique name.

That's all it takes. By accessing the entered username in this way, you can use the name in reports, populate field text boxes with it, use it in queries; in other words, use the name wherever you need it in your application.

—Andrea Moss

External Programs and Data

Hacks 59–71

Access isn't an island of an application, not by a long shot. It integrates easily with many programs. Obviously, it shares characteristics with the other Office products, and it is relatively easy to include Word, Excel, Outlook, and PowerPoint files in your Access solutions. Several hacks in this chapter do just that. For example, "Import Noncontiguous Ranges of Data from Excel" [Hack #59] and "Use Excel Functions Inside Access" [Hack #61] involve integration with Excel. "Manage Word Documents from Access" [Hack #67] shows you how to use Word's object model to create a programmatic solution, and "Use Word to Compare Data in Two Access Tables" [Hack #62] shows you a neat way to use Word independently to test your data.

This chapter also includes hacks on using XML data, integrating with MySQL, and using SQL Server stored procedures. All in all, the chapter offers quite a bit, and using the techniques presented here will certainly gain you an edge in your development efforts.

Import Noncontiguous Ranges of Data from Excel

HACK #59

A standard import lets you get only one data range at a time. Here are a couple of workarounds to get you more.

When importing data from an Excel workbook into Access, you can select to import a worksheet or a range. You can select a range only when the workbook includes established named ranges. Figure 7-1 shows the first screen of the Import Spreadsheet Wizard. This wizard appears after you select File → Get External Data and select to import from an Excel file.

Whether you're importing a worksheet or a range, the problem is that you can select only one item in the list. Usually, single worksheets are imported because a wealth of data can sit on a single worksheet. Ranges are a different

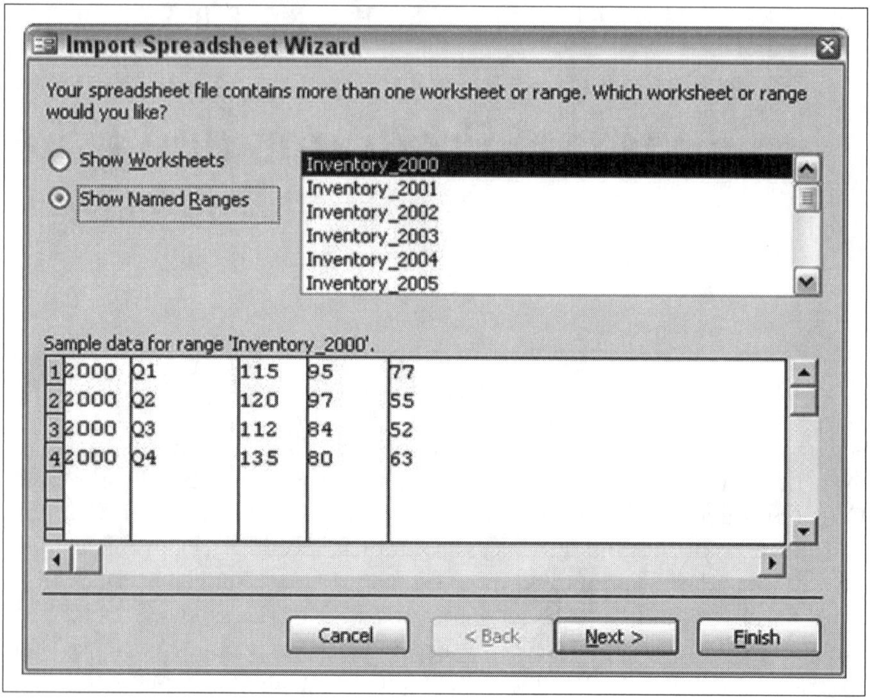

Figure 7-1. Importing data from Excel

story. You might need to import more than one range. It's tedious to run the Import Spreadsheet Wizard over and over again.

Using Macros for Multiple Imports

An easy way around the one-range-at-a-time import is to create a macro that uses multiple TransferSpreadsheet actions. Each occurrence of this action imports a single range, but you can create a sequence of them in a single macro. You should consider whether the ranges are to be imported as new tables, or whether the ranges are to be accumulated into a single table.

Import Excel data into separate tables.   Figure 7-2 shows a macro that imports five ranges into five tables. Each import puts data into a separate Access table. Each table name is specified in the Table Name argument of each TransferSpreadsheet action. The first five actions of the macro delete the existing tables just before the imports. The imports place the Excel data into tables with the same name as the tables being deleted.

Here is a potential problem: if you don't delete the tables first, the data is appended to the tables because they already exist. Most likely you don't

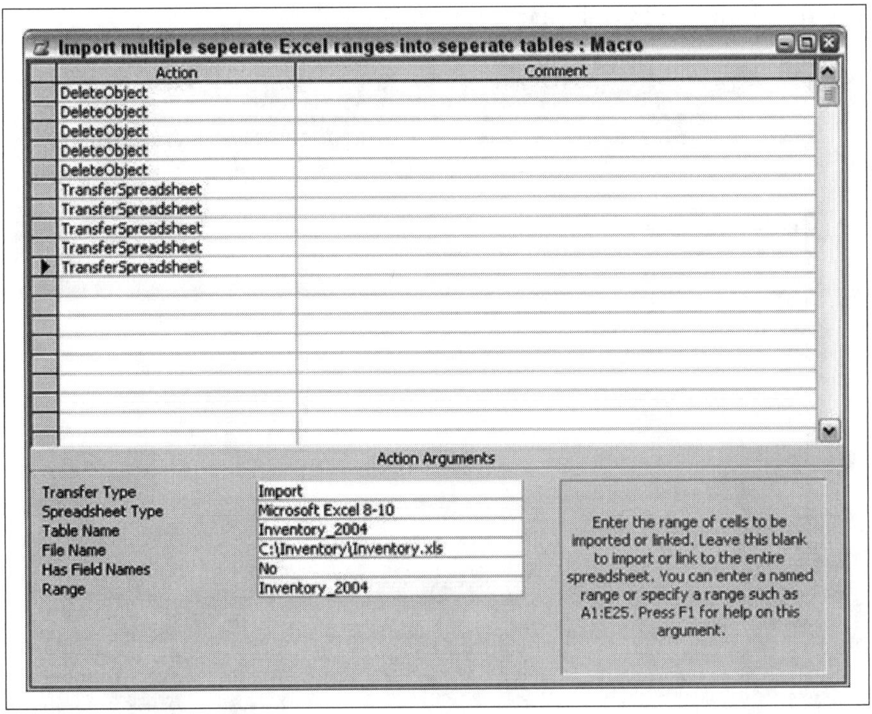

Figure 7-2. A macro that creates separate Access tables

want to do this. Deleting the Access tables first guarantees that the tables are recreated with just the newly imported data.

You set the actual TransferSpreadsheet actions such that each addresses a different range in the Excel data. You set this in the Range argument, shown in Figure 7-2; it's an acceptable way to gather data from different Excel ranges.

Import Excel data into a single table. If you want to combine the data from different Excel ranges into one Access table, the Table Name argument of each TransferSpreadsheet action should be identical. You still must empty the destination table first. In this macro, you do so with the RunSQL action, which runs a simple Delete operation:

```
Delete * From Inventory_All
```

Prior to this, turn off warnings so that the process isn't interrupted with a confirmation message.

After the Delete operation, the TransferSpreadsheet actions fill the now-empty Inventory_All table. All the data is appended to the table.

Figure 7-3 shows how this macro is structured.

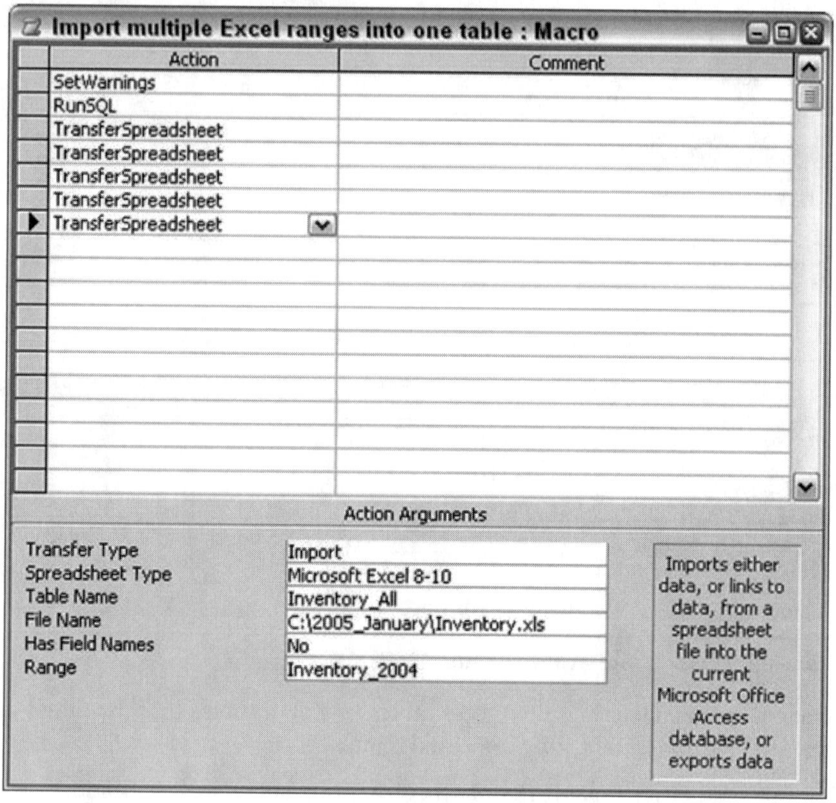

Figure 7-3. A macro that populates one Access table

Importing Noncontiguous Data from Excel Without Using Ranges

Macros are handy but are limited in power. As shown in the previous section, you can import ranges easily enough. You can even import areas of a workbook by address. In other words, you can enter A1:D15 to import part of an Excel worksheet. That's about it, though. A macro can't do anything much more sophisticated than that. This is where some VBA comes in handy.

Figure 7-4 shows an Excel worksheet. The data consists of product amounts broken out by years and quarters.

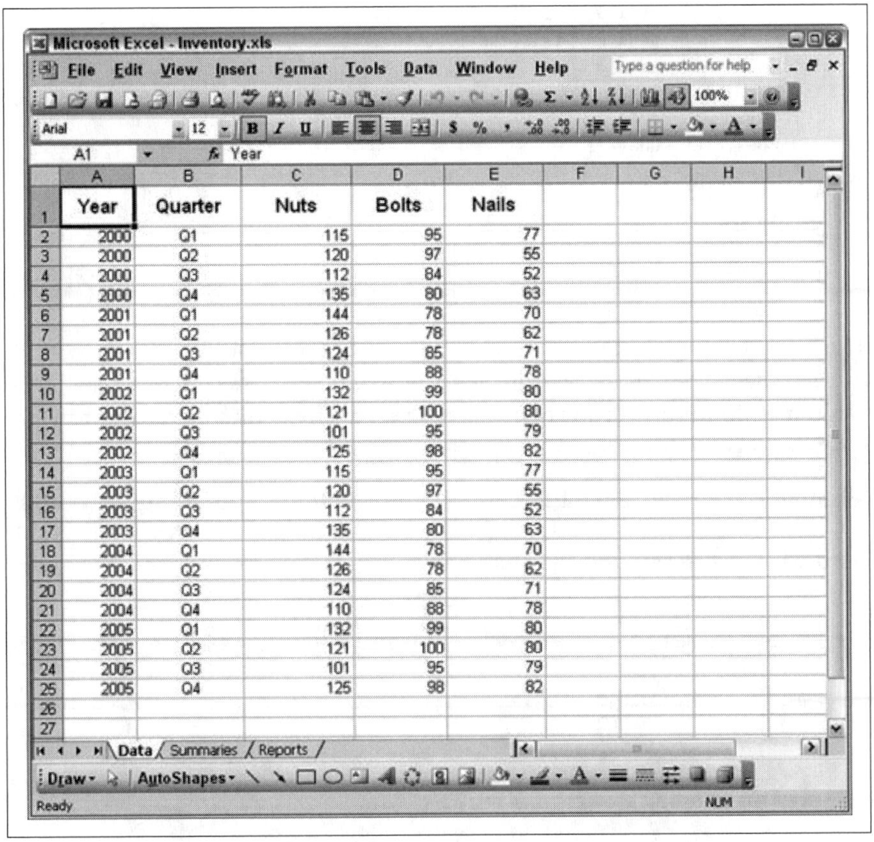

Figure 7-4. Excel data to be imported

To import, say, just the second-quarter figures for each year requires a process that tests each row to see if the quarter is Q2. Here is a code routine that does just that:

```
Sub get_excel()
Dim test_quarter As Integer
Dim conn As ADODB.Connection
Set conn = CurrentProject.Connection
Dim xl As Object
Set xl = GetObject("C:\Inventory\Inventory.xls")
'first delete existing records
conn.Execute "Delete * From Inventory_All"
With xl
  With .Worksheets("Data")
    For test_quarter = 2 To 25 'known row numbers on worksheet
      If .Cells(test_quarter, 2) = "Q2" Then
        ssql = "Insert Into Inventory_All Values("
        ssql = ssql & .Cells(test_quarter, 1) & ", "
        ssql = ssql & "'" & .Cells(test_quarter, 2) & "', "
```

```
      ssql = ssql & .Cells(test_quarter, 3) & ", "
      ssql = ssql & .Cells(test_quarter, 4) & ", "
      ssql = ssql & .Cells(test_quarter, 5) & ")"
      conn.Execute ssql
    End If
  Next test_quarter
End With
End With
xl.Close
Set xl = Nothing
MsgBox "done"
End Sub
```

This code uses automation to create an Excel object and sets the workbook to the object. It then cycles through the worksheet rows. A test sees if the value in column 2 is Q2. When this is true, all five columns of the row are inserted into the Inventory_All Access table.

Of course, you can alter the code to test on other conditions. Also, you don't have to hardcode the Q2 test. Figure 7-5 shows the Access table populated with just the second-quarter records.

F1	F2	F3	F4	F5
2000	Q2	120	97	55
2001	Q2	126	78	62
2002	Q2	121	100	80
2003	Q2	120	97	55
2004	Q2	126	78	62
2005	Q2	121	100	80

Record: |◄| |◄| 7 |►| |►I| |►*| of 7

Figure 7-5. Populating the table with portions of the Excel workbook

A little code can go a long way. Setting the reference to the Excel workbook is a simple process with the GetObject function. Once the routine is connected to a workbook, you can do many things with a little knowledge of Excel's programmatic model.

H A C K   Use Excel to Reorient Access Data
#60   Use Excel's Paste Special Transpose feature to turn data on its ear.

Here's an easy way to change columns to rows (or rows to columns; I guess it all depends on how you look at it). Figure 7-6 shows a table filled with some data. The table contains 8 fields and 100 rows of data.

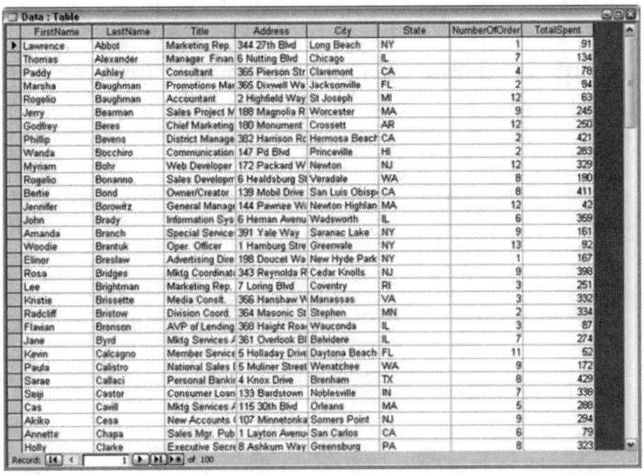

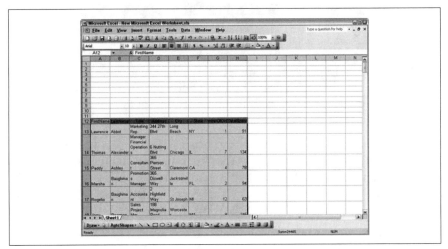

Figure 7-6. Eight columns of data in a table

Perhaps your user wants to view the data so that each person's record is displayed vertically, which isn't an uncommon request with Excel users. This hack shows how to do just that: put this data in Excel, but turn it sideways.

First, select all the data in the Access table; then, pop over to an open Excel workbook. Find an empty worksheet, and paste the data. Note that for this example, I have purposely pasted the data in row 12. You will see why in a moment. Figure 7-7 shows how the data landed in Excel.

Figure 7-7. Access data pasted in Excel

Upon being pasted, the data is in a selected state. That's great! Just leave it as is, but if you lose the selection, just select it again. The next step is to copy the data, by either selecting Edit → Copy or pressing Ctrl-C. Copying the data is a necessary step. It might seem that the data is already on the clipboard. It is, but not in the way we need; therefore, the extra copy from within Excel is necessary.

Now that the data is copied in an Excel format, click in cell A1. This removes the selected state from the data, but that's okay at this point. In fact for the next step, the data must be deselected, and a single cell must be active.

Use the Edit → Paste Special menu to open the Paste Special dialog box, as shown in Figure 7-8.

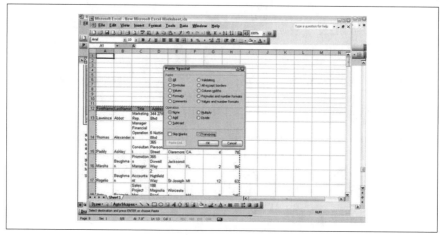

Figure 7-8. The Paste Special dialog box

There are few things to note in Figure 7-8. As already noted, the data is deselected. Cell A1 is the active cell. The Paste Special dialog will paste the copied data in the next operation, but the critical point is that the Transpose box is checked. This checkbox is near the bottom of the dialog box.

Clicking the OK button completes the process. Figure 7-9 shows how the data sits at the top of the worksheet. Earlier, I made the first paste in row 12 to give enough room for the second paste. We already knew there were eight fields of data, and now they occupy eight worksheet rows. Although not visible in Figure 7-9, the data goes 100 columns to the right.

The data in the first paste is no longer needed, so you can delete it. A few formatting changes will make the data presentable and ready for work. Figure 7-10 shows how the data looks after a facelift and how analysis is already being run on the data.

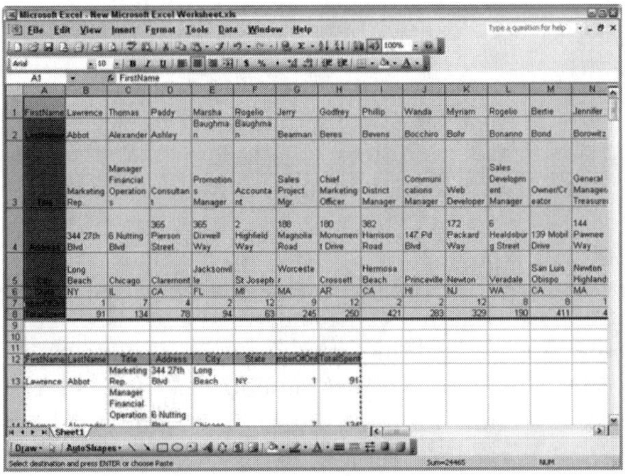

Figure 7-9. The transposed data

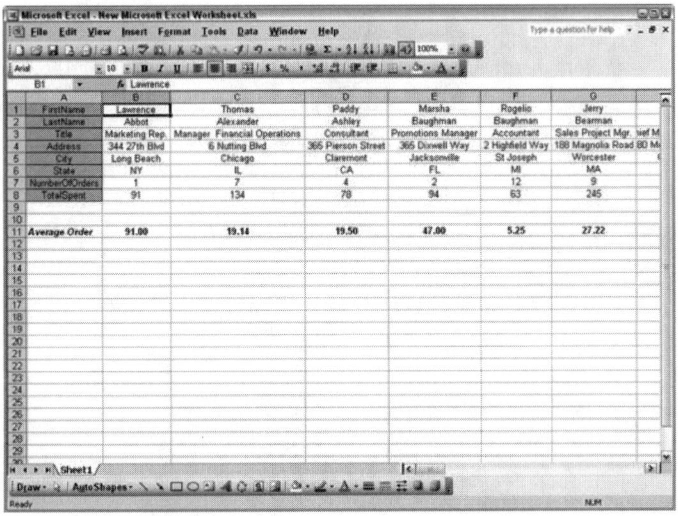

Figure 7-10. Working with the transposed data

Use Excel Functions Inside Access

HACK #61

Expose powerful functions available in Excel to your Access application.

Excel has many powerful built-in functions for such things as financial and statistical analysis. If you want to do the same type of analysis in Access, you can do one of the following three things: purchase an off-the-shelf code solution, write your own code for analysis, or use automation to tap into Excel's

Use Excel Functions Inside Access

functions from inside Access. This hack shows you how to tap into Excel via automation and use spreadsheet functions, saving you time and money over the other options.

This hack involves Access working hand in hand with Excel, so you need to make sure Excel is installed on the machine on which your database will be running. This is a safe assumption in most corporate environments.

A Simple Excel Function

Excel's FV (future value) function calculates the value of an investment at some time in the future based on periodic, constant payments and on a constant interest rate. The following VBA function takes the same parameters as Excel's FV worksheet function and returns the same result as if you were using the future value function right in Excel:

```
Public Function FV(dblRate As Double, intNper As Integer, _
            dblPmt As Double, dblPv As Double, _
            intType As Integer) As Double
    Dim xl As Object
    Set xl = CreateObject("Excel.Application")
    FV = xl.WorksheetFunction.FV(dblRate, intNper, dblPmt, dblPv, intType)
    Set xl = Nothing
End Function
```

The WorksheetFunction property of Excel's Application object is key to calling Excel functions from code, whether in Access or even directly in Excel's VBA environment. With this property, nearly every Excel worksheet function is available to build into a solution.

Figure 7-11 shows a form that takes input from a user and calls the FV function from the Calculate Future Value button.

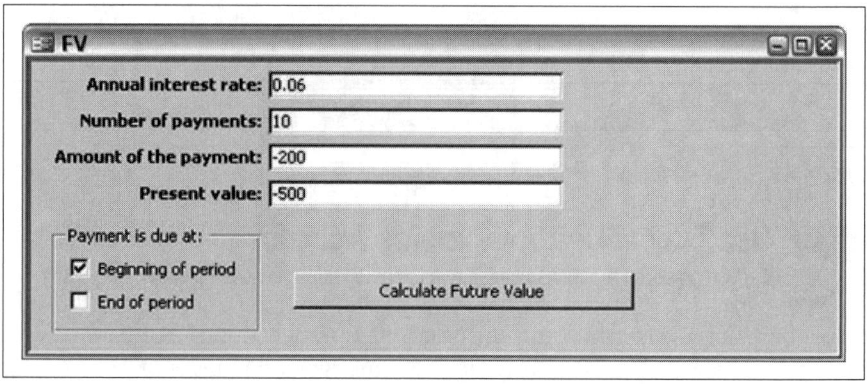

Figure 7-11. Calling the FV function from a form

Clicking the Calculate Future Value button executes the following code:

```
Private Sub cmdFV_Click()
    Dim dblFV As Double
    dblFV = FV(txtRate / 12, txtNper, txtPmt, dblPv, frmType)
    MsgBox "FV = " & dblFV, vbInformation, "Future Value"
End Sub
```

The cmdFV_Click event calls the FV function and displays the message box shown in Figure 7-12. You can modify the code to write the solution back to a table or to display it elsewhere on the form object as needed.

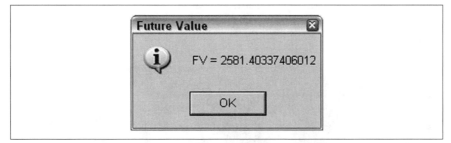

Figure 7-12. Message box displayed from the cmdFV_Click event

An Excel Function with an Array Parameter

The example of calculating a future value required five parameters to be passed into Excel, and with the magic of automation, we got the result back. However, what would happen if one of those parameters were an array, as many are in Excel?

If an Excel function requires an array or table array, you can pass it an array or a multidimensional array created in Access and get back the needed result. Let's look at the code you'd use to call Excel's percentile worksheet function, which returns the kth percentile of values that you specify from a given array of values:

```
Public Function Percentile(strTbl As String, strFld As String, k As Double)
As Double
    Dim rst As ADODB.Recordset
    Dim dblData() As Double
    Dim xl As Object
    Dim x As Integer
    Set xl = CreateObject("Excel.Application")
    Set rst = New ADODB.Recordset
    rst.Open "Select * from " & strTbl, CurrentProject.Connection,
adOpenStatic
    ReDim dblData(rst.RecordCount - 1)
    For x = 0 To (rst.RecordCount - 1)
        dblData(x) = rst(strFld)
        rst.MoveNext
```

```
      Next x
      Percentile = xl.WorksheetFunction.Percentile(dblData, k)
      rst.Close
      Set rst = Nothing
      Set xl = Nothing
   End Function
```

With this function, we pass the table name and field name to be read into the Access array, which in return is passed into Excel's percentile function along with the kth percentile value that we are looking for in the array of values. It's worth noting that you can pass the function a query name instead of a table, depending on the application's requirements.

Figure 7-13 shows a form that displays a subform that is bound to the tblData table and displaying the SampleData field in datasheet mode.

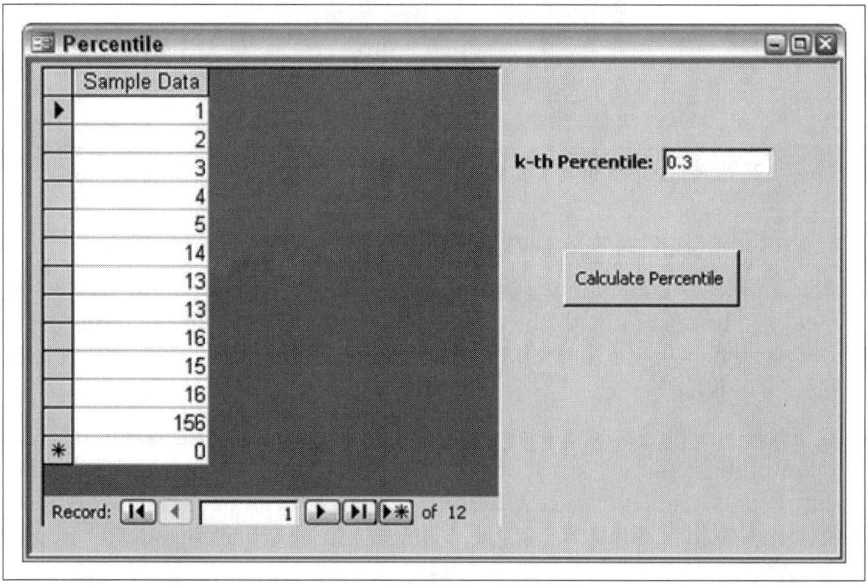

Figure 7-13. Calling the percentile function from a form

This sample calculates the 30th percentile from the list 1, 2, 3, 4, 5, 14, 13, 13, 16, 15, 16, 156 when the user clicks the Calculate Percentile button. Clicking the Calculate Percentile button executes the following code:

```
   Private Sub cmdPercentile_Click( )
      Dim dblPercentile As Double
      dblPercentile = Percentile("tblData", "SampleData", txtK)
      MsgBox "Percentile = " & dblPercentile, vbInformation, "Percentile"
   End Sub
```

This code produces the message box in Figure 7-14.

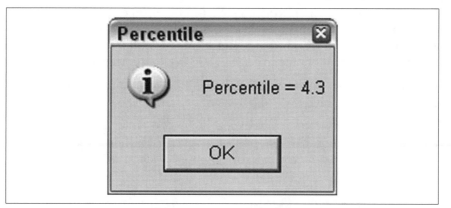

Figure 7-14. The message box displayed from the cmdPercentile_Click event

As noted previously with the FV function, you can write this return value back to a table or display it on the form. You can also call the FV function or Percentile function from a query or use it on a report.

Other Excel Spreadsheet Functions

You can call more than 100 functions using the WorksheetFunction method of the Excel object via automation. Keep in mind that some are redundant with built-in Access functions, such as Excel's ISNUMBER and Access's ISNUMERIC, and others, such as ISERR and ISNA, aren't of much use unless you are doing some other advanced spreadsheet automation.

You also have to consider whether the overhead of automation is acceptable in your application. It might not be as efficient as a well-written custom function. However, it can be a huge timesaver if you don't have time to write your own custom functions such as the Percentile function.

—Steve Huff

HACK #62 Use Word to Compare Data in Two Access Tables

Look for discrepancies the easy way, using Word's Document Compare utility.

Sometimes, you have to compare data in two Access tables. Usually you do this when you have one table that derives from two different copies of the database. The data might differ between the tables; for example, some data has been updated in one table, and now you need to uncover the discrepancies.

You can do this in a couple of ways. You can use some queries, but if there are many fields, query design could be difficult. Another option is to write code to read through both tables and identify the differences. This works but it also takes a bit of time to get the code working correctly.

Here's a great alternative: Word has a built-in feature that compares two documents and highlights the differences.

The first thing you need to do is export the Access tables as text files. Word then uses these to run a comparison. Figure 7-15 shows the two tables already saved as text. As you can see, they appear identical.

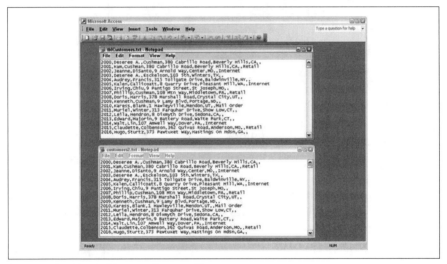

Figure 7-15. Two tables saved as text files

In Word, open one of the text files. Then, use the Tools → Compare and Merge Documents menu item to browse to the second text file. As shown in Figure 7-16, you have options for how to compare and merge the documents. I always choose "Merge into new document." That way, I know the original files aren't altered.

A new document is created, but you immediately run into a problem. Word's spellchecker and grammar checker will flag nearly everything as incorrect because the export from Access creates records with no space breaks. This is correct for the data, but not as far as Word is concerned. So, the next thing to do is turn off the spellchecker and grammar checker in Word's Options dialog, as shown in Figure 7-17. By the way, the first opened text file didn't flag any errors because it was still a text file. The new merged document, on the other hand, is a proper Word document.

Figure 7-16. *Setting up the document comparison*

Figure 7-17. *Turning off spellchecker and grammar checker in Word*

Once you can see the document for what it is, you can see places where the data doesn't match because the data is formatted with strikethroughs, as shown in Figure 7-18.

Scrolling through this data is a breeze. You can quickly see where the data is different and decide what to do about it.

—*Andrea Moss*

Figure 7-18. Identifying unmatched data

Import Varied XML Data into Access

Access is pretty good at importing simple XML data, but sometimes you want to import data that isn't precisely the way Access expects it to be.

Access lets you import data from XML files into its tables. For example, let's consider a database containing a table that defines a list of books. Figure 7-19 shows the Design view for this table. It includes six fields of three different types.

To begin, the table contains a few books, as shown in Figure 7-20.

The easiest way to see the XML format Access expects to receive when it imports data to this table is to export some of the data, which you can do by selecting a table in the database and then selecting Export... from the File menu. In this case, the XML format we'll need to let Access import automatically looks like the data that was just exported as XML. In other words, exporting records into XML shows the XML node structure any XML data being imported back in should have. Example 7-1 shows the exported data.

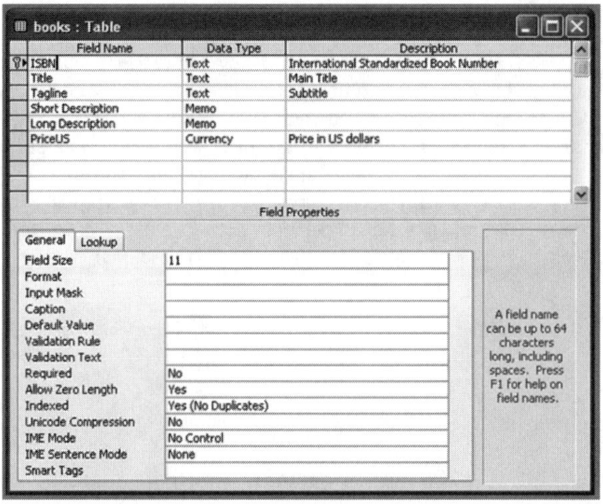

Figure 7-19. A simple table to which we'll import data

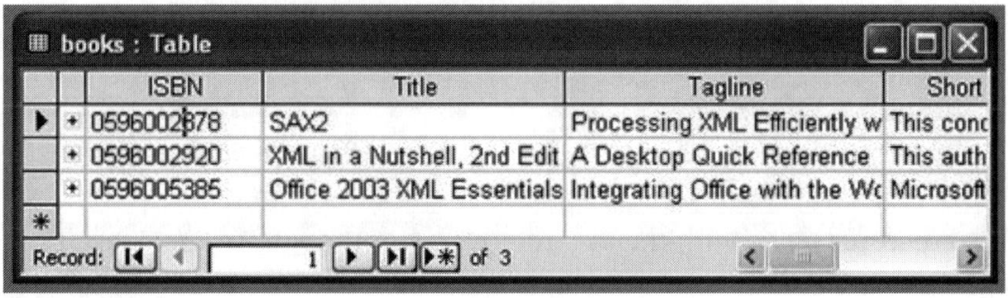

Figure 7-20. Test data in the books table

Example 7-1. New data for import

```
<?xml version="1.0" encoding="UTF-8"?>
<dataroot>
<books>
<ISBN>0596002637</ISBN>
<Title>Practical RDF</Title>
<Tagline>Solving Problems with the Resource Description Framework</Tagline>
<Short_x0020_Description>The Resource Description Framework (RDF) is a structure
for describing and interchanging metadata on the Web.</Short_x0020_Description>
<Long_x0020_Description>The Resource Description Framework (RDF) is a structure
for describing and interchanging metadata on the Web - anything from library
catalogs and worldwide directories to bioinformatics, Mozilla internal data
structures, and knowledge bases for artificial intelligence projects.</Long_
x0020_Description>
<PriceUS>39.95</PriceUS>
</books>
<books>
<ISBN>0596003838</ISBN>
```

Example 7-1. New data for import (continued)

```
<Title>Content Syndication with RSS</Title>
<Tagline>Sharing Headlines and Information Using XML</Tagline>
<Short_x0020_Description>RSS is sprouting all over the Web, connecting weblogs
and providing news feeds.</Short_x0020_Description>
<Long_x0020_Description>RSS is sprouting all over the Web, connecting weblogs and
providing news feeds.  Originally developed by Netscape in 1999, RSS (which can
stand for RDF Site Summary, Rich Site Summary, or Really Simple Syndication) is
an XML-based format that allows Web developers to create a data feed that
supplies headlines, links, and article summaries from a web site</Long_x0020_
Description>
<PriceUS>29.95</PriceUS>
</books>
<books>
<ISBN>0596002912</ISBN>
<Title>XPath and XPointer</Title>
<Tagline>Locating Content in XML Documents</Tagline>
<Short_x0020_Description>Referring to specific information inside an XML document
can be like looking for a needle in a haystack: how do you differentiate the
information you need from everything else?</Short_x0020_Description>
<Long_x0020_Description>Referring to specific information inside an XML document
can be like looking for a needle in a haystack: how do you differentiate the
information you need from everything else?  XPath and XPointer are two closely
related tools that play a key role in XML processing by allowing developers to
find these needles and manipulate embedded information.</Long_x0020_Description>
<PriceUS>24.95</PriceUS>
</books>
</dataroot>
```

The structure begins with the dataroot element, though Access doesn't actually care what that container element's name is. The books element tells Access this information goes into the books table, and the ISBN, Title, Tagline, and other elements inside each books element go to fields in the books table. The only trick is in the Short Description and Long Description fields, which, because XML won't accept spaces in tag names, Access prefers to see as Short_x0020_Description and Long_x0020_Description. Access doesn't care what order the fields come in, but it will recognize them only if they're child elements, not attributes.

To get started, select Get External Data from the File menu, and then select Import. The dialog box shown in Figure 7-21 will appear.

You might need to select XML from the "Files of type" drop-down menu at the bottom because the dialog initially defaults to Access formats. Select a file, and click Import. The Import XML dialog box shown in Figure 7-22 will appear.

You can click the plus sign to the left of the books if you want to inspect their structure. If you just click OK, Access creates a new table called books1

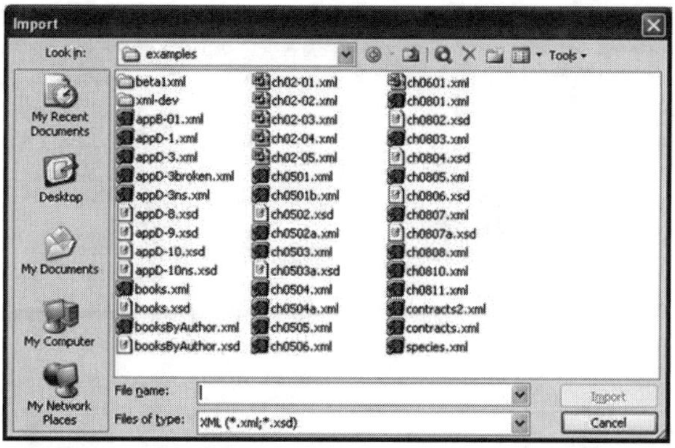

Figure 7-21. Initial Import dialog box

Figure 7-22. Import dialog box showing structure of XML documents

(or whatever number avoids a conflict) to import the XML into Access without conflicting with the prior XML table.

That might be perfectly fine because it gives you a chance to compare the new data with the old before merging the two. Access provides two more options, however: one that lets you just create a new table based on the structure of the XML file, and another that lets you append the data in the XML file to an existing table. In this case, we know the new books are different from the old books, so click Options, and select Append Data to Existing Table(s), as shown in Figure 7-23.

If you click OK now, the extra books will be added to the existing books table, as shown in Figure 7-24.

Access refuses to import XML data, which causes a conflict with existing key relationships. For example, if you import that same document again in

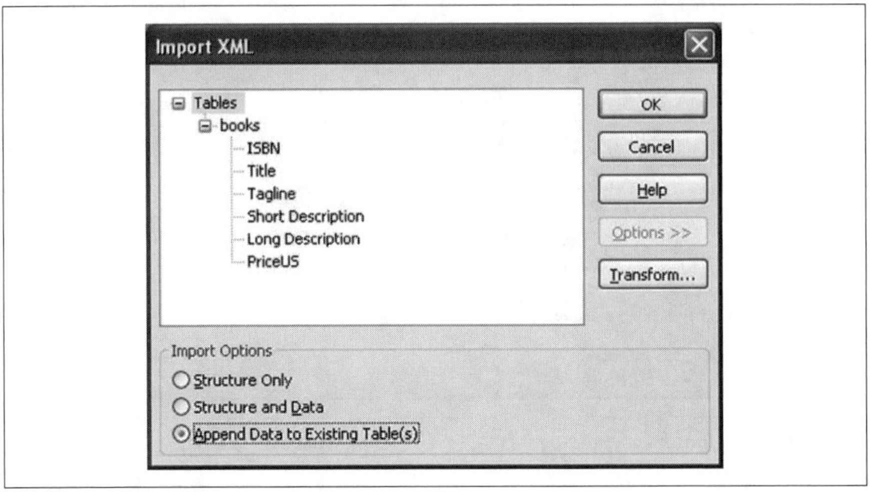

Figure 7-23. *Import dialog box showing more complex structure of XML documents and append options*

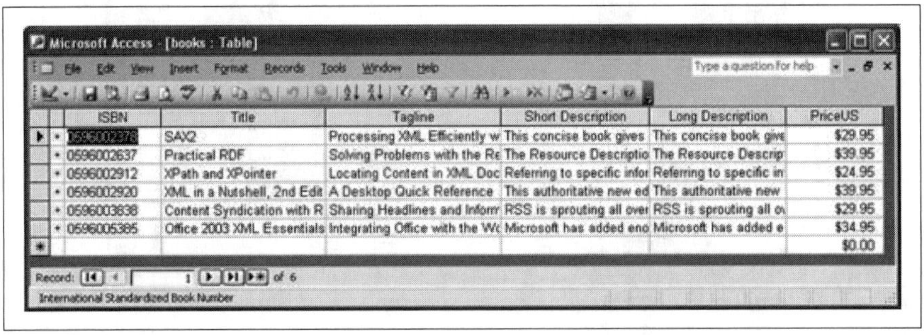

Figure 7-24. *The results of importing a document and appending its data*

the same way, you'll be rewarded with the ImportErrors table shown in Figure 7-25.

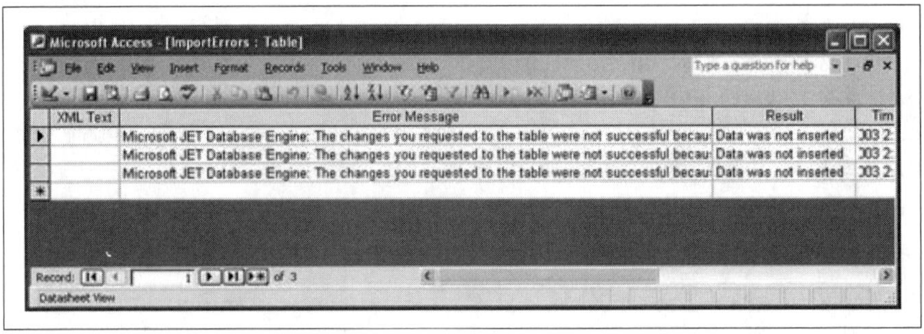

Figure 7-25. *The results of importing a document and appending its data when the data is already there*

Using the Transform... button shown in Figure 7-23, you can also perform conversions, which make it easier to import data that doesn't arrive in a form that meets Access's expectations. For example, suppose information about a new book arrived in the form shown in Example 7-2.

Example 7-2. ch0812.xml, an attribute-based XML document for import

```
<update>
<books ISBN="0596003277" Title="Learning XSLT" Tagline="A Hands-On
Introduction to XSLT and XPath" Short_x0020_Description="A gentle
introduction to the complex intricacies of XSLT" Long_x0020
_Description="A gentle introduction to the complex intricacies of
XSLT and XPath, walking through the spec from simple work to
complex." PriceUS="34.95" />
</update>
```

In Example 7-2, all data is stored in attributes, and Access won't even look at attributes during an import. To get this information into Access, you need to use a transformation, such as the generic one shown in Example 7-3, which converts all attributes to child elements.

Example 7-3. ch0813.xsl, a stylesheet for transforming attributes into elements

```
<?xml version="1.0" encoding="UTF-8"?>
<xsl:stylesheet version="1.0" xmlns:xsl="http://www.w3.org/1999/XSL/Transform">
<!--Derived from recipe 6.1 of Sal Mangano's XSLT Cookbook-->

<xsl:output method="xml" version="1.0" encoding="UTF-8" indent="yes"/>

<xsl:template match="@*">
  <xsl:element name="{local-name(.)}" namespace="{namespace-uri(..)}">
    <xsl:value-of select="."/>
  </xsl:element>
</xsl:template>

<xsl:template match="node()">
  <xsl:copy>
    <xsl:apply-templates select="@* | node()"/>
  </xsl:copy>
</xsl:template>

</xsl:stylesheet>
```

When applied to Example 7-2, the stylesheet in Example 7-3 produces the result shown in Example 7-4, which Access can import easily.

> Again, Access doesn't care what the root element's name is; update is an appropriate description for human consumption.

Example 7-4. An "elementized" version of the data in Example 7-2

```
<?xml version="1.0" encoding="UTF-8"?>
<update>
<books>
<ISBN>0596003277</ISBN>
<Title>Learning XSLT</Title>
<Tagline>A Hands-On Introduction to XSLT and XPath</Tagline>
<Short_x0020_Description>A gentle introduction to the complex intricacies of
XSLT</Short_x0020_Description>
<Long_x0020_Description>A gentle introduction to the complex intricacies of XSLT
and XPath, walking through the spec from simple work to complex.</Long_x0020_
Description>
<PriceUS>34.95</PriceUS>
</books>
</update>
```

If you tell Access to import *ch0812.xml*, the file shown in Example 7-2, you won't have much to choose from in the Import XML dialog box, as shown in Figure 7-26.

Figure 7-26. Access's initial reaction to the document that stores data in attributes

If you choose Options → Transform…, you canadd the stylesheet, much as you did for the export transformation. Add the stylesheet to the list of transformations, and select ch0813, as shown in Figure 7-27.

When you click OK, Access applies the transformation to the document, modifying the display of components you see and producing the result in Figure 7-28.

In this case, the table already exists, so be sure to select Append Data to Existing Table(s). When you click OK, the data from Example 7-1 is added to the books table, as shown in Figure 7-29.

Transformations are a powerful tool in pretty much any area of XML development. Using a bit of XSLT—admittedly, a bit challenging to learn—you can convert the structures you have into the structures Access expects.

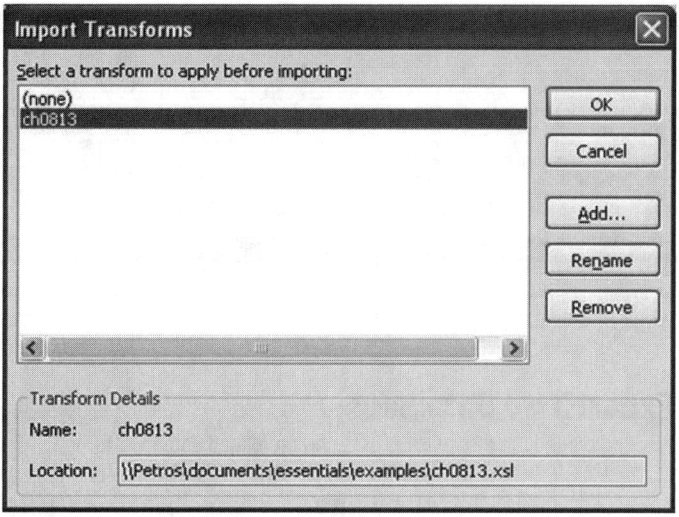

Figure 7-27. Selecting a stylesheet for transformation

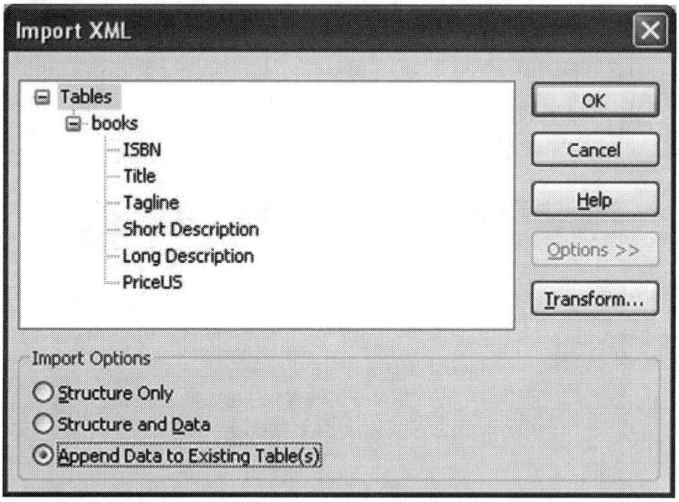

Figure 7-28. A transformed document ready for import

See Also

- "Export XML Data Sanely" **[Hack #64]**
- "Break Through VBA's Transformation Barrier" **[Hack #65]**

—Simon St. Laurent

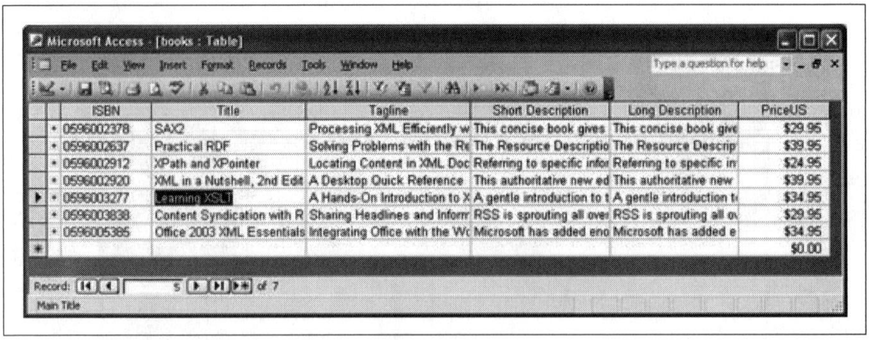

Figure 7-29. *The result of importing a transformed document*

Export XML Data Sanely

HACK #64

Working around the thorny issue of exporting related data to XML.

Exporting a single table to XML produces some easily reusable data. Exporting multiple tables to XML, however, might not produce data that other applications can use; it all depends on how you structured your tables and relationships. You can solve this problem in two ways: restructure your data or use a query to export data that's been unnormalized.

For our initial example, we'll start with a database containing a table that defines a list of books. Figure 7-30 shows the Design view for that table. It includes six fields of three different types.

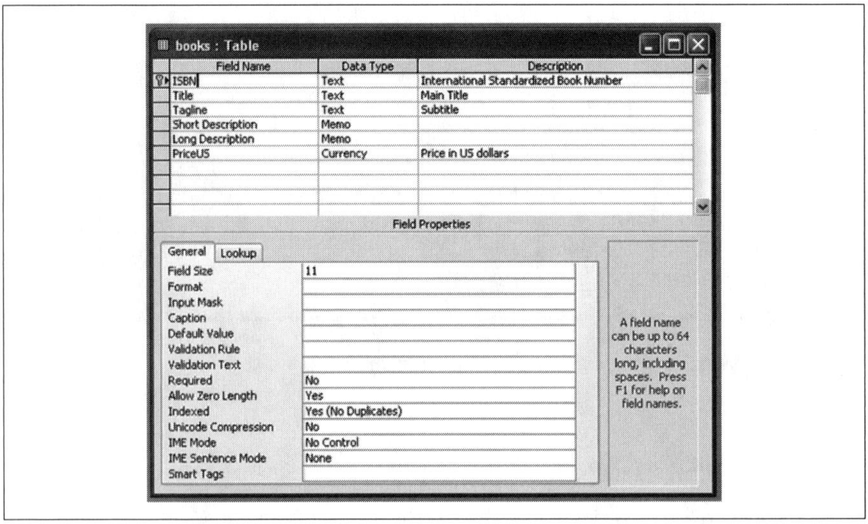

Figure 7-30. *A simple table for export*

For the initial tests, this table contains just a little bit of information. Exporting mature tables with thousands of records can quickly produce large XML files—definitely useful in real life but difficult for initial analysis. Figure 7-31 shows a partial view of the content in the test table.

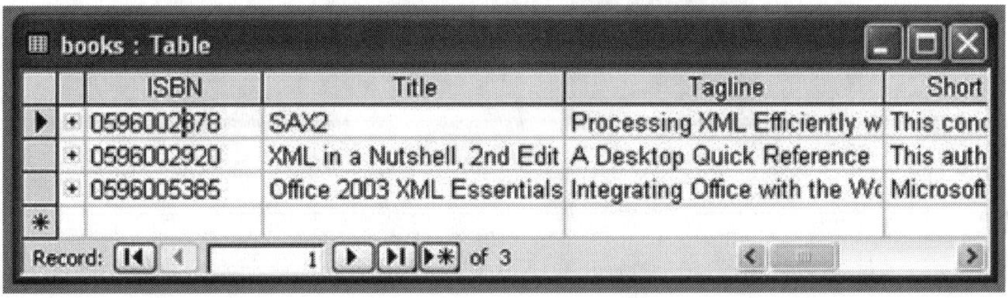

Figure 7-31. Test data in the books table

Exporting this table to XML involves a few steps, most of which will be familiar to developers who have exported information from Access databases before. The process starts by selecting the books table in the database, then selecting Export... from the File menu. The dialog box shown in Figure 7-32 will appear, and you'll need to select XML (*.xml) from the "Save as type" drop-down box.

Figure 7-32. Selecting the destination for the export

When you perform the export, Access might actually create more files than just the XML file, but they'll all appear in the same directory together with the XML. Once you click the Export button, a small dialog box with basic options, shown in Figure 7-33, appears.

Figure 7-33. Basic export options

For now, we'll accept the defaults and just click OK. This results in two files: *books.xml* and *books.xsd*. The *books.xml* file contains the information from the table, and *books.xsd* contains an XML Schema description of that content, annotated with a bit of information specific to Access and its Jet database engine.

The *books.xml* file, shown in Example 7-5, reflects the structure and content of the original table closely.

Example 7-5. A simple table export

```
<?xml version="1.0" encoding="UTF-8"?>
<dataroot xmlns:od="urn:schemas-microsoft-com:officedata" xmlns:xsi="http://www.
w3.org/2001/XMLSchema-instance"  xsi:noNamespaceSchemaLocation="books.xsd"
generated="2003-03-26T13:49:17">
<books>
<ISBN>0596005385</ISBN>
<Title>Office 2003 XML Essentials</Title>
<Tagline>Integrating Office with the World</Tagline>
<Short_x0020_Description>Microsoft has added enormous XML functionality to Word,
Excel, and Access, as well as a new application, Microsoft InfoPath.  This book
gets readers started in using those features.</Short_x0020_Description>
<Long_x0020_Description>Microsoft has added enormous XML functionality to Word,
Excel, and Access, as well as a new application, Microsoft InfoPath.  This book
gets readers started in using those features.</Long_x0020_Description>
<PriceUS>34.95</PriceUS>
</books>
<books>
<ISBN>0596002920</ISBN>
<Title>XML in a Nutshell, 2nd Edition</Title>
<Tagline>A Desktop Quick Reference</Tagline>
<Short_x0020_Description>This authoritative new edition of XML in a Nutshell
provides developers with a complete guide to the rapidly evolving XML space.</
Short_x0020_Description>
```

Example 7-5. A simple table export (continued)

```
<Long_x0020_Description>This authoritative new edition of XML in a Nutshell
provides developers with a complete guide to the rapidly evolving XML space.
Serious users of XML will find topics on just about everything they need,
including fundamental syntax rules, details of DTD and XML Schema creation, XSLT
transformations, and APIs used for processing XML documents.  Simply put, this is
the only references of its kind among XML books.</Long_x0020_Description>
<PriceUS>39.95</PriceUS>
</books>
<books>
<ISBN>0596002378</ISBN>
<Title>SAX2</Title>
<Tagline>Processing XML Efficiently with Java</Tagline>
<Short_x0020_Description>This concise book gives you the information you need to
effectively use the Simple API for XML, the dominant API for efficient XML
processing with Java.</Short_x0020_Description>
<Long_x0020_Description>This concise book gives you the information you need to
effectively use the Simple API for XML, the dominant API for efficient XML
processing with Java.</Long_x0020_Description>
<PriceUS>29.95</PriceUS>
</books>
</dataroot>
```

This document's root element, dataroot, is the only piece of this document
specific to Access:

```
<dataroot xmlns:od="urn:schemas-microsoft-com:officedata" xmlns:xsi="http://
www.w3.org/2001/XMLSchema-instance"  xsi:noNamespaceSchemaLocation="books.
xsd" generated="2003-03-26T13:49:17">
```

It makes a namespace declaration for the od prefix, which isn't actually used in
this document, and it includes a pointer to the XML Schema describing this
document's structure. Because the element names used here aren't in any
namespace, the document uses the xsi:noNamespaceSchemaLocation attribute
to identify the schema that should be used for all the elements in this document that have no namespace. It also includes one small bit of metadata in the
generated attribute, that identifies the time and date when this XML document was created.

The dataroot element contains three child books elements, each indicating a
row in the books table. Their contents map fairly simply to the names and
values of the table columns:

```
<books>
<ISBN>0596002920</ISBN>
<Title>XML in a Nutshell, 2nd Edition</Title>
<Tagline>A Desktop Quick Reference</Tagline>
<Short_x0020_Description>This authoritative new edition of XML in a Nutshell
provides developers with a complete guide to the rapidly evolving XML space.
</Short_x0020_Description>
```

```
<Long_x0020_Description>This authoritative new edition of XML in a Nutshell
provides developers with a complete guide to the rapidly evolving XML space.
Serious users of XML will find topics on just about everything they need,
including fundamental syntax rules, details of DTD and XML Schema creation,
XSLT transformations, and APIs used for processing XML documents.  Simply
put, this is the only references of its kind among XML books.</Long_x0020_
Description>
<PriceUS>39.95</PriceUS>
</books>
```

The only significant variation here involves the column names, which include spaces. Instead of Short Description, now we have Short_x0020_Description, following a convention Microsoft developed for representing spaces in XML element names.

> XML forbids spaces in element names because they make it difficult to separate the element name from the attributes, so Access uses _x0020_, the Unicode hex number, for the space.

Exporting individual tables is useful, but sometimes you might want to export multiple tables and preserve the relationships between them. Access allows you to export a set of tables, though it works most easily when only two tables are involved.

Exporting from Tables in a One-to-Many Relationship

For our first example, we'll add a table that contains information about (very fictional) promotions for various books. Figure 7-34 shows what this table looks like.

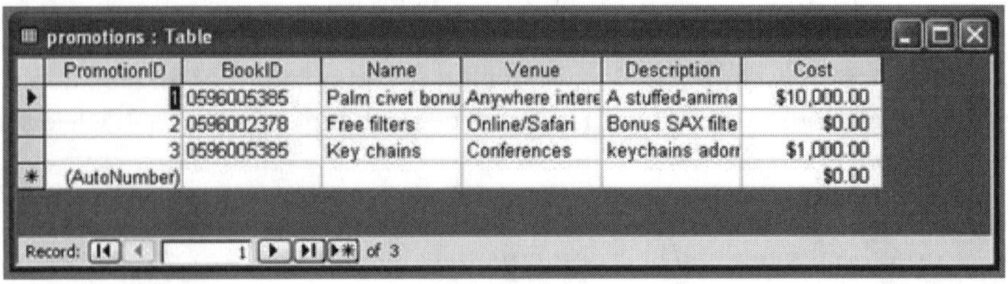

	PromotionID	BookID	Name	Venue	Description	Cost
▶	1	0596005385	Palm civet bonu	Anywhere intere	A stuffed-anima	$10,000.00
	2	0596002378	Free filters	Online/Safari	Bonus SAX filte	$0.00
	3	0596005385	Key chains	Conferences	keychains ador	$1,000.00
*	(AutoNumber)					$0.00

Record: ◄◄ ◄ 1 ► ►► ►* of 3

Figure 7-34. The promotions table

The promotions table links to the books table through its BookID field, as shown in Figure 7-35.

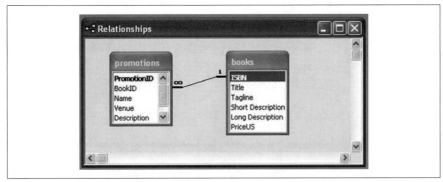

Figure 7-35. Relationship between the books and promotions tables

Exporting this pair of tables takes a few more steps because Access lets you choose how the export works. The choice of which table is the base table makes a big difference in the export results, so the following examples will export it both ways.

We'll start by exporting the books table again, but this time, we'll select More Options from the dialog box shown in Figure 7-36.

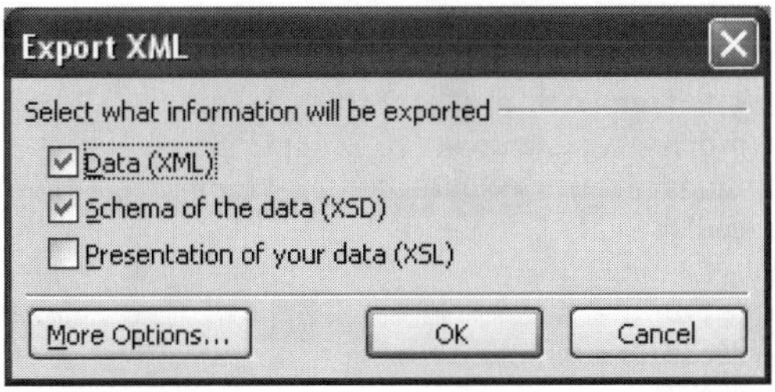

Figure 7-36. Basic export options

Clicking More Options brings up a larger dialog with a lot more choices, as shown in Figure 7-37.

In this case, all the information we need is on the first (Data) tab. Checking the Promotions box and clicking the OK button tells Access to export both the books table and the linked records of the promotions table—in this case, all of them. Example 7-6 shows an abbreviated version of the export, with the new content from the promotions table in bold.

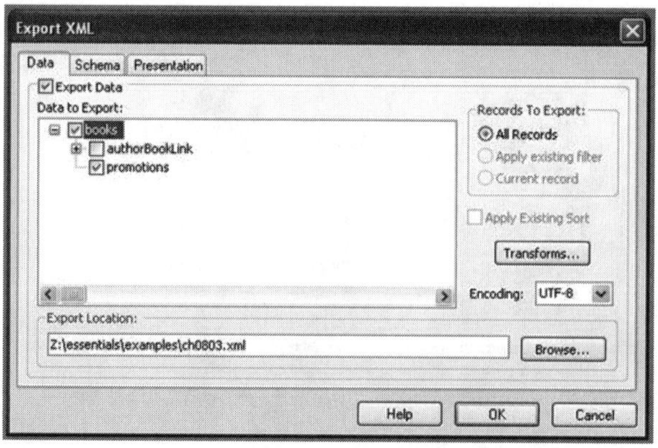

Export XML Data Sanely

Figure 7-37. The full version of the Export XML dialog box

Example 7-6. Exported linked tables

```
<?xml version="1.0" encoding="UTF-8"?>
<dataroot xmlns:od="urn:schemas-microsoft-com:officedata" xmlns:xsi="http://www.
w3.org/2001/XMLSchema-instance"  xsi:noNamespaceSchemaLocation="ch0804.xsd"
generated="2003-03-31T16:37:01">
<books>
<ISBN>0596005385</ISBN>
<Title>Office 2003 XML Essentials</Title>
<Tagline>Integrating Office with the World</Tagline>
<Short_x0020_Description>...</Short_x0020_Description>
<Long_x0020_Description>...</Long_x0020_Description>
<PriceUS>34.95</PriceUS>
<promotions>
<PromotionID>1</PromotionID>
<BookID>0596005385</BookID>
<Name>Palm civet bonus</Name>
<Venue>Anywhere interested</Venue>
<Description>A stuffed-animal palm civet,
lovingly screen-printed to match the cover,
with every copy of the book.</Description>
<Cost>10000</Cost>
</promotions>
<promotions>
<PromotionID>3</PromotionID>
<BookID>0596005385</BookID>
<Name>Key chains</Name>
<Venue>Conferences</Venue>
<Description>keychains adorned with lovely palm civets
and the title of the book.</Description>
<Cost>1000</Cost>
</promotions>
</books>
<books>
```

Example 7-6. Exported linked tables (continued)

```
<ISBN>0596002920</ISBN>
<Title>XML in a Nutshell, 2nd Edition</Title>
<Tagline>A Desktop Quick Reference</Tagline>
<Short_x0020_Description>...</Short_x0020_Description>
<Long_x0020_Description>...</Long_x0020_Description>
<PriceUS>39.95</PriceUS>
</books>
<books>
<ISBN>0596002378</ISBN>
<Title>SAX2</Title>
<Tagline>Processing XML Efficiently with Java</Tagline>
<Short_x0020_Description>...</Short_x0020_Description>
<Long_x0020_Description>...</Long_x0020_Description>
<PriceUS>29.95</PriceUS>
<promotions>
<PromotionID>2</PromotionID>
<BookID>0596002378</BookID>
<Name>Free filters</Name>
<Venue>Online/Safari</Venue>
<Description>Bonus SAX filters, open source-licensed,
for developers who visit the SAX2 book site.</Description>
<Cost>0</Cost>
</promotions>
</books>
</dataroot>
```

The general pattern here is much like the original export of the books table, except that zero or more promotions elements—whose BookID holds the same value as the containing books element's ISBN element—now appear inside each books element. This works the same way that zero or more books elements appeared inside the dataroot element. All the table columns are listed inside each promotions element, making it easy to reconstruct the information in the promotions table or to treat the information as a complete set of information about each book. There's no need to reconstruct the original tables and calculate primary key/foreign key links.

As soon as you step beyond the one-to-many relationship, however, this kind of simple containment will fail you.

Exporting from Tables in a Many-to-Many Relationship

A many-to-many relationship, implemented with an intermediary table, as shown in Figure 7-38, produces XML that most likely will be useful only if someone reimports it into Access and works with it there.

Access lets you traverse this relationship in an XML export, as shown in Figure 7-39. This time, the export uses a [Lookup Data] element to indicate that simply nesting the data in the XML document structures isn't going to

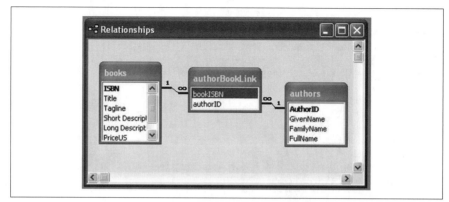

Figure 7-38. Related tables with a many-to-many relationship, expressed as two one-to-many relationships

work. One-to-many relationships are represented using containment, and many-to-one relationships are represented as separate pieces. In this case, the many-to-many relationship includes both of those choices.

Figure 7-39. Exporting related tables with a many-to-many relationship

[Lookup Data] provides a warning that reassembling some of these relationships is going to require extra lookup work on the part of the consuming application.

> If you reimport this data into Access, it'll do that work, so this might not be a problem.

Example 7-7 shows the results of this export.

Example 7-7. A many-to-many export combining containment and lookup

```
<?xml version="1.0" encoding="UTF-8"?>
<dataroot xmlns:od="urn:schemas-microsoft-com:officedata" xmlns:xsi="http://www.
w3.org/2001/XMLSchema-instance"  xsi:noNamespaceSchemaLocation="ch0806.xsd"
generated="2003-04-01T21:01:50">
<books>
<ISBN>0596005385</ISBN>
<Title>Office 2003 XML Essentials</Title>
<Tagline>Integrating Office with the World</Tagline>
<Short_x0020_Description>...</Short_x0020_Description>
<Long_x0020_Description>...</Long_x0020_Description>
<PriceUS>34.95</PriceUS>
<authorBookLink>
<bookISBN>0596005385</bookISBN>
<authorID>1</authorID>
</authorBookLink>
</books>
<books>
<ISBN>0596002920</ISBN>
<Title>XML in a Nutshell, 2nd Edition</Title>
<Tagline>A Desktop Quick Reference</Tagline>
<Short_x0020_Description>...</Short_x0020_Description>
<Long_x0020_Description>...</Long_x0020_Description>
<PriceUS>39.95</PriceUS>
<authorBookLink>
<bookISBN>0596002920</bookISBN>
<authorID>3</authorID>
</authorBookLink>
<authorBookLink>
<bookISBN>0596002920</bookISBN>
<authorID>4</authorID>
</authorBookLink>
</books>
<books>
<ISBN>0596002378</ISBN>
<Title>SAX2</Title>
<Tagline>Processing XML Efficiently with Java</Tagline>
<Short_x0020_Description>...</Short_x0020_Description>
<Long_x0020_Description>...</Long_x0020_Description>
<PriceUS>29.95</PriceUS>
<authorBookLink>
<bookISBN>0596002378</bookISBN>
<authorID>2</authorID>
</authorBookLink>
</books>
<authors>
<AuthorID>1</AuthorID>
<GivenName>Simon</GivenName>
<FamilyName>St.Laurent</FamilyName>
<FullName>Simon St.Laurent</FullName>
</authors>
<authors>
```

Example 7-7. A many-to-many export combining containment and lookup (continued)

```
<AuthorID>2</AuthorID>
<GivenName>David</GivenName>
<FamilyName>Brownell</FamilyName>
<FullName>David Brownell</FullName>
</authors>
<authors>
<AuthorID>3</AuthorID>
<GivenName>Elliotte</GivenName>
<FamilyName>Harold</FamilyName>
<FullName>Elliotte Rusty Harold</FullName>
</authors>
<authors>
<AuthorID>4</AuthorID>
<GivenName>Scott</GivenName>
<FamilyName>Means</FamilyName>
<FullName>W. Scott Means</FullName>
</authors>
</dataroot>
```

Now each books element contains one or more authorBookLink elements, each holding an authorID element. The value of that authorID element maps to an authorID element inside an authors element. If the data is going back into Access, this is fine, but if it's going to another application—Excel, perhaps, or an XSLT transformation into HTML for a browser—this isn't much fun.

This might feel like a case in which it would make sense to store repetitive (nonnormalized) data in the tables, but fortunately, there's a better option: exporting a query instead of a table.

Using a Query to Tame the Export

By themselves, queries don't provide nested views, but they certainly make it easier to present some kinds of information—notably, many-to-many relationships. The mechanics of exporting queries are much like those of exporting single tables, and the results are similar.

> Access supports SQL queries, obviously, because that's at the heart of its functionality. Access doesn't, however, support other standards for querying, such as XQuery.

To demonstrate, let's export a SQL query named booksByAuthor, which uses the books, authors, and authorBookLink tables to create a list of books sorted by author. The SQL for the query expresses the relationships an XML processor working with the linked table export would otherwise have to deal with:

```
SELECT authors.GivenName, authors.FamilyName, books.ISBN, books.Title
FROM books INNER JOIN (authors INNER JOIN authorBookLink ON authors.AuthorID
= authorBookLink.authorID) ON books.ISBN = authorBookLink.bookISBN
ORDER BY authors.FamilyName;
```

The interface for exporting a query is the same as the interface for a table, except there is no option for exporting linked information. When you export a query, all the information you want to export must be in that query. Exporting the query produces the result shown in Example 7-8.

Example 7-8. An exported query

```
<?xml version="1.0" encoding="UTF-8"?>
<dataroot xmlns:od="urn:schemas-microsoft-com:officedata" xmlns:xsi="http://www.
w3.org/2001/XMLSchema-instance"  xsi:noNamespaceSchemaLocation="booksByAuthor.
xsd" generated="2003-04-02T14:47:59">
<booksByAuthor>
<GivenName>David</GivenName>
<FamilyName>Brownell</FamilyName>
<ISBN>0596002378</ISBN>
<Title>SAX2</Title>
</booksByAuthor>
<booksByAuthor>
<GivenName>Elliotte</GivenName>
<FamilyName>Harold</FamilyName>
<ISBN>0596002920</ISBN>
<Title>XML in a Nutshell, 2nd Edition</Title>
</booksByAuthor>
<booksByAuthor>
<GivenName>Scott</GivenName>
<FamilyName>Means</FamilyName>
<ISBN>0596002920</ISBN>
<Title>XML in a Nutshell, 2nd Edition</Title>
</booksByAuthor>
<booksByAuthor>
<GivenName>Simon</GivenName>
<FamilyName>St.Laurent</FamilyName>
<ISBN>0596005385</ISBN>
<Title>Office 2003 XML Essentials</Title>
</booksByAuthor>
</dataroot>
```

Just as in a tabular representation of the query, information repeats—notably, the ISBN and title of *XML in a Nutshell*, which has two authors. If you're sending data to an application that lacks Access's appreciation for relations between tables, this approach will probably work much more easily.

See Also

- "Import Varied XML Data into Access" [Hack #63]
- "Break Through VBA's Transformation Barrier" [Hack #65]

—Simon St. Laurent

Break Through VBA's Transformation Barrier

Strange but true: Access supports XSLT transformation on input when you use the GUI, but not when you automate the process with VBA. The same goes for output. Fortunately, you can work around this by calling the MSXML parser directly.

The examples in "Import Varied XML Data into Access" [Hack #63] give some ideas for how to get information into your Access tables even if the data arrives in a format other than the simple element-only form Access expects. However, if such data arrives on a regular basis, you probably don't want to be clicking through forms every time you need to import more data.

Unfortunately, converting these steps to an automated VBA process is a challenge because the ImportXML function doesn't provide a place for any transformations. As it turns out, neither does the ExportXML function.

The syntax of the ImportXML function looks like this:

```
Application.ImportXML (DataSource, ImportOptions)
```

It takes only a data source, the name and path of the XML file to import, and an options constant—acAppendData, acStructureAndData (the default), or acStructureOnly. There is no option for an XSLT transformation. Similarly, the ExportXML function looks like this:

```
Application.ExportXML (ObjectType, DataSource, DataTarget, SchemaTarget,
PresentationTarget, ImageTarget, Encoding, OtherFlags)
```

The PresentationTarget argument does have something to do with transformation, but it's only for output. It identifies where Access will put a stylesheet for turning the XML into HTML based on its own expectations, not yours.

You can get around these problems in two ways. First, you can write some custom code. The import version will instantiate an XML parser (probably MSXML), read the content from the document however you deem appropriate, and then use ADO, DAO, or SQL Update queries to put the data in the database. The export version will read data from the database and write it to an MSXML DOM tree as necessary.

This might be appropriate if you have complicated cases, but it's a lot of code for what's most likely a simple problem, and you can't test how it works (or reuse that work) outside of Access.

A more likely approach, if you can stand working with XSLT, is to add a step before the import or after the export that performs an extra transformation. Because Access doesn't let you pass objects to the import or get objects from the export, you need to work with temporary files to produce the results you want. Conveniently, you can use the same function for both cases.

A simple version of this function looks like this:

```
Private Sub Transform(sourceFile, stylesheetFile, resultFile)

Dim source As New MSXML2.DOMDocument30
Dim stylesheet As New MSXML2.DOMDocument30
Dim result As New MSXML2.DOMDocument30

' Load data.
source.async = False
source.Load sourceFile

' Load style sheet.
stylesheet.async = False
stylesheet.Load stylesheetFile

If (source.parseError.errorCode <> 0) Then
   MsgBox ("Error loading source document: " & source.parseError.reason)
   Else
If (stylesheet.parseError.errorCode <> 0) Then
      MsgBox ("Error loading stylesheet document: " & _
         stylesheet.parseError.reason)
   Else
      ' Do the transform.
      source.transformNodeToObject stylesheet, result
      result.Save resultFile
End If
End If

End Sub
```

The Transform function takes three arguments: the path of a source file holding the original XML, the path of a stylesheet file holding the XSLT that will be used to transform it, and the path to which the resulting document should be saved. Typically, you'll want to call Transform before using Access's native ImportXML function or after you've used the ExportXML function.

For example, you might import XML files to a table directly with this call:

```
Application.ImportXML "http://simonstl.com/ora/updateBook.xml", acAppendData
```

But if that XML file stored the data as attributes, and you wanted to apply a transformation to that data before you imported it into Access, you might do this instead:

```
Transform "http://simonstl.com/ora/updateBook.xml", _
    "C:\xslt\attsToElem.xsl", _
    "C:\temp\tempImport.xml"
Application.ImportXML "C:\temp\tempImport.xml", acAppendData
```

Similarly, you can apply a transformation after you exported data, turning it into HTML:

```
Application.ExportXML acExportTable, "books", "C:\temp\tempExport.xml"
Transform "C:\temp\tempExport.xml", _
    "C:\xslt\booksToHTML.xsl", _
    "C:\export\exportedBooks.html"
```

Writing XML documents out to files and then reparsing them isn't efficient by any means, but it patches a gap left by the Access API for importing and exporting XML. Unless you're dealing with huge volumes of data, or doing this processing constantly, users of your databases aren't likely to notice a big difference. Import and export are usually pretty slow operations anyway.

See Also

- "Import Varied XML Data into Access" **[Hack #63]**
- "Export XML Data Sanely" **[Hack #64]**

—Simon St. Laurent

HACK #66 Leverage SQL Server Power by Calling Stored Procedures

Get a leg up on performance when using SQL Server data.

Developers creating Access applications that are front ends to SQL Server databases have two choices for their application type. The Microsoft-recommended choice is to use an Access data project (ADP), which is directly tied to the SQL Server database. This native-mode OLE DB connection results in a lighter-weight, better-performing front end that can directly use SQL views, stored procedures, and user-defined functions. It also lets developers design objects directly on the server (no need to use Enterprise Manager).

Despite these advantages, many situations force developers to use ODBC linked tables in a traditional Access MDB file. Not the least of these is the ability to create local tables in the MDB (in an ADP, even the Switchboard Items table must be on the server) and the ability to connect to other data sources (such as other Access databases, Excel spreadsheets, text files, and so on). Just because you choose to use an MDB as a front end doesn't mean you have to give up the server-side processing power of SQL Server stored procedures.

Hooking Up with ODBC

When an Access MDB is using ODBC links to SQL Server, all data processing is done on the client side—that is, within Access on the workstation. If a listbox on a form gets filtered by a combo box selection, all the records are returned over the network to Access and Access applies the filter. Alternatively, the use of stored procedures can increase performance in your Access MDBs by shifting the filtering to the server. Stored procedures are powerful because they combine the data-joining capabilities of Access queries or SQL views with the ability of VBA procedures to accept parameters and to loop and process data.

T-SQL, Microsoft SQL Server's version of the SQL language, is somewhat different from the Jet (Access's) flavor of SQL. It is also much different from VBA. However, if you can create Access queries and write VBA functions, you can learn to write SQL stored procedures. It isn't difficult to become good enough in T-SQL to increase the performance of your applications. Whether you install MSDE (the *lite* version of SQL Server that ships with Microsoft Office) or SQL Server itself, you can look at the stored procedures within the Northwind database to get started.

The ADO library is one way to execute stored procedures in Access. You do this in VBA by executing a `Command` object whose command text is the stored procedure name. First it is necessary to open a `Connection` object on the SQL Server database. The code in Example 7-9 executes the `CustOrdersOrders` stored procedure that ships with Northwind, sending in the much-abused customerid `ALFKI` to fill an ADO recordset with all the orders belonging to Alfreds Futterkiste.

Example 7-9. Running a stored procedure

```
Dim cn As ADODB.Connection
Dim sp As ADODB.Command
Dim rs As ADODB.Recordset
Set cn = New ADODB.Connection
cn.ConnectionString = CurrentDb.TableDefs("dbo_customers").Connect
cn.Open
Set sp = New ADODB.Command
sp.ActiveConnection = cnSQL
sp.CommandType = adCmdStoredProc
sp.CommandText = "CustOrdersOrders"
```

Example 7-9. Running a stored procedure (continued)

```
sp.Parameters.Refresh
sp.Parameters("@customerid") = "ALFKI"
Set rs = sp.Execute
```

Access, however, can't use ADO recordsets in certain situations. Although Access uses ADO more and more with every new version release, Access 2003 still has deep ties to DAO, so much so that Microsoft put back a default reference to DAO in VBA, after not including it in Access 2002 (XP). A data-entry form bound to a linked table will have an underlying recordset that isn't ADO, but rather, is DAO. Controls such as combo boxes or list-boxes, on unbound or DAO-bound forms, require their recordsets to be DAO as well.

Creating a Pass-Through Query

Access can tap into stored procedure power and get a DAO recordset filled with data via a stored procedure using an underutilized feature known as a Pass-Through query. Creating a Pass-Through query is relatively straightforward, and the results returned are in a DAO recordset, appropriate for use in any Access object or control that can use a query as its data source.

To create a Pass-Through query, select Queries in the Database window, and click New. Click Design View, and then click OK. Click Close on the Table list to go directly into Design view. On the Query menu, click SQL-Specific, and then click Pass-Through, as shown in Figure 7-40.

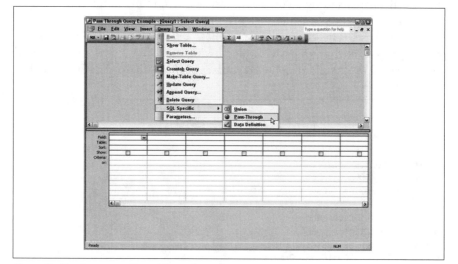

Figure 7-40. Creating a Pass-Through query

The query designer will switch to SQL view and allow only SQL statements to be entered. Enter CustOrdersOrders 'ALFKI' in the SQL view of the query designer. Click Save, and name the query qry_CustOrdersOrders_pt.

At this point, Access doesn't know where to pass this query. On first execution, you are prompted for the data source connection to use: cChoose the same data source you used to link your SQL tables. After choosing the appropriate data source, Access sends the SQL string contained in the query to the server, and SQL runs the stored procedure and returns the results to Access, as shown in Figure 7-41.

OrderID	OrderDate	RequiredDate	ShippedDate
10643	8/25/1997	9/22/1997	9/2/1997
10692	10/3/1997	10/31/1997	10/13/1997
10702	10/13/1997	11/24/1997	10/21/1997
10835	1/15/1998	2/12/1998	1/21/1998
10952	3/16/1998	4/27/1998	3/24/1998
11011	4/9/1998	5/7/1998	4/13/1998

qry_CustOrdersOrders_pt : SQL Pass-Through Query

Record: 1 of 6

Figure 7-41. Data returned from SQL Server via a stored procedure

—*Steve Conklin*

Manage Word Documents from Access
Tap into the Word object library to copy Access data directly into a Word document.

As is the case with all Microsoft Office products, Word has a significant number of exposed objects and methods to work with, and becoming familiar with a decent number of these is a challenge worth undertaking.

This hack creates a procedure that places data from Access into a table in a Word document. The concepts here also apply to other Word manipulations. Perhaps this will be your springboard into a new avenue of Office development.

Hooking into Word

In an Access code module, we're going to place a routine to work with an existing Word document. To make this a little easier, we'll set a reference to Word's object library. We'll do this inside the Access VB Editor, using the Tools → References menu and the References dialog box, as shown in

Figure 7-42. Note that your version number of the Word library might differ, so use whatever you have.

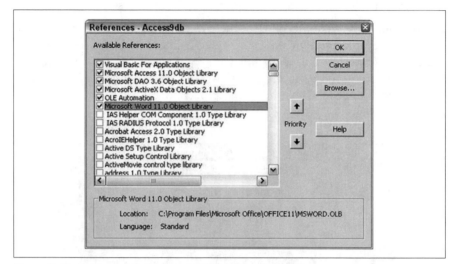

Figure 7-42. Setting a reference to the Word object library

The Code

The next thing to do is enter the code. This must go into an Access code module:

```
Sub Access_to_Word( )
Dim conn As ADODB.Connection
Set conn = CurrentProject.Connection
Dim recset As ADODB.Recordset
Set recset = New ADODB.Recordset
Dim row_num As Integer
Dim col_num As Integer
Dim word_doc As Object
'Assumes Word doc is in same path - change name and path as needed
Set word_doc = GetObject(Application.CurrentProject.Path & "\Customers.doc")

'get data from Access table
recset.Open "Select * From Customers Where State='OR'", _
    conn, adOpenKeyset, adLockOptimistic
'get the record count - used to create Word Table
recset.MoveLast
recset.MoveFirst

With word_doc
    'navigate to Word bookmark and create table
    'the number of table rows matches the recordset row count
    'the number of table columns matches the number of recordset fields
    .Bookmarks("Customers").Select
```

```
    .Tables.Add Range:=Selection.Range, _
        NumRows:=recset.RecordCount, NumColumns:=recset.Fields.Count
    For row_num = 1 To recset.RecordCount
      For col_num = 1 To recset.Fields.Count
        .Tables(.Tables.Count).Cell(row_num, col_num).Select
        Selection.TypeText recset.Fields(col_num - 1)
      Next col_num
    'next database record
    recset.MoveNext
    Next row_num
  End With
  recset.Close
  Set recset = Nothing
  Set word_doc = Nothing
  MsgBox "done"
  End Sub
```

Here are some highlights of this code:

- The Access data is gathered into a recordset.

- The GetObject function is referenced to the existing Word document. Note that this example assumes the database and the document are in the same directory. Also, the name of the document is hardcoded, but you can change this as necessary.

- The document has a preestablished bookmark named Customers. This is used as a guide to where to create the table.

- A Word table is created, and its row and column dimensions match those of the recordset. This ensures the new Word table is exactly the correct size to house the data.

- The Word table is populated cell by cell by looping through the record-set. An outer loop cycles through the recordset rows, and in each row an inner loop cycles through each field.

The Data Has Landed Intact

After running this code, the document has a table with the data, as shown in Figure 7-43. Note that there is no connection back to Access; the data is just essentially part of the Word document.

Note that this simplistic example assumes a number of things: the bookmark exists, there is no existing table, and the Access table isn't too large in terms of rows and fields to make the Word table too densely packed.

Nonetheless, this hack serves as a brief introduction to tapping into Word objects. Because the reference has been set to the library, you can now use the Object Browser in Access to review Word's objects.

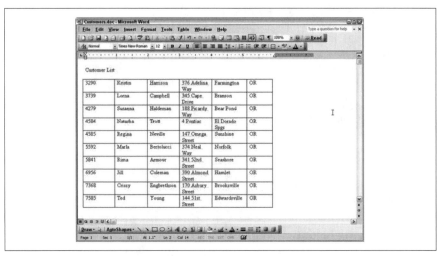

Figure 7-43. The Access data in a Word table

Use Access as a Front End to MySQL

MySQL is a widely used open source database program that often runs on Linux web servers, and Access makes a great front end for data entry and reporting.

MySQL is a wildly successful open source SQL database that runs on most Linux-based web servers. It's the perfect database to store information for use in database-driven web sites because you can use the PHP programming language to read the data from MySQL and display it on web pages. In fact, the combination of Linux, Apache (an open source web server that runs on Linux), MySQL, and PHP is so popular that it's known by its initials: LAMP.

However, MySQL doesn't hold a candle to Access when it comes to forms and reports. MySQL has no built-in form editor or report writer. Instead, you type commands at a command line or write programs (usually as part of PHP-based web pages) to enter, edit, and display information.

But who wants to create programs that display data entry forms for each table? This is where Access comes in. Access can add a friendly face to your MySQL database. In the same way an Access database can link to tables in another Access database, you can link to tables in a MySQL database on your web server over a LAN or the Internet. Once the tables are linked, you (or your users) can use Access forms to enter or edit the MySQL data and Access reports to display it.

Installing the MySQL Tools

MySQL does have a Windows-based utility you can use for creating and editing the structure of the tables in your MySQL databases. The older version of the program is called MySQL Control Center, and it has been replaced by MySQL Query Browser. You can download either program from the MySQL web site (*http://dev.mysql.com/downloads/*) for free. The manual for MySQL Query Browser is available online at *http://dev.mysql.com/doc/query-browser/en/*, or you can download it as a PDF or Windows Help file.

When you start MySQL Query Browser, you specify the server on which MySQL runs, your MySQL username, and your password. Once connected, you see a list of the tables for which you have access permission, and you can view or edit the data or structure of the tables, as shown in Figure 7-44.

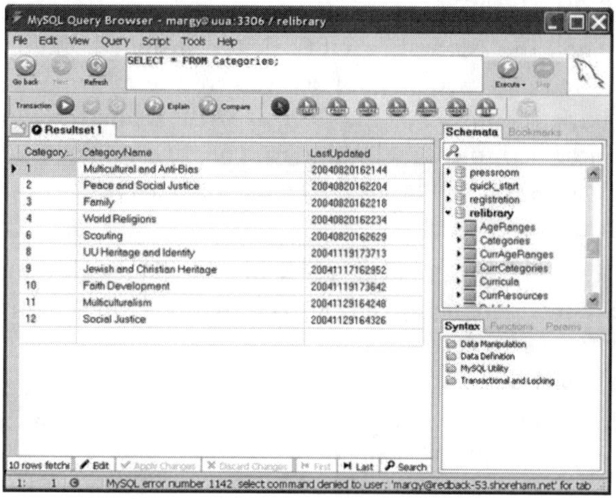

Figure 7-44. MySQL Query Browser

MySQL Query Browser is useful, but it's not the tool to give to your database users. For example, you can't create forms with data validation, combo boxes, or subforms, and you can't create formatted reports. For this, you need Access.

For Access to connect to a MySQL database, you need to install the MySQL Connector/ODBC driver (also called the MySQL ODBC or MyODBC driver). This driver lets Access communicate with MySQL via Open Database Connectivity (ODBC). You can download the MySQL ODBC driver from *http://dev.mysql.com/downloads/* for free. After you install it, a new option appears when you link to external tables from an Access database.

You don't need to install MySQL Query Browser on every computer on which your Access database will run; you need it only if you plan to use it to look at or change the structure of the tables in your MySQL database. But every computer on which your Access database runs needs the MySQL ODBC driver installed because Access uses the driver every time you open a linked MySQL table.

If you plan to connect to a MySQL database over the Internet, your requests will probably need to pass through one or more firewalls. The MySQL ODBC driver communicates over port 3306, so this port must be open on all the firewalls between your computer and the MySQL server. You can specify a different port when you create the link from Access to MySQL, in case your MySQL server is configured to use a nonstandard port number.

Linking to MySQL Tables

Once you've got the MySQL ODBC driver installed, linking Access to MySQL tables requires two steps: making sure the tables contain the right fields and making the link. For the Access/MySQL link to work right when editing data into the tables, each table to which you link needs to have the following two fields (the names of the fields don't matter):

AutoNumber
   In MySQL, this is an INT (integer) field of size 11 with the UNSIGNED and AUTO INC (auto increment) options selected. This field must be the primary key for the table.

Date
   This field is updated automatically any time the record is edited. In MySQL, this is a TIMESTAMP field.

Most tables have these two fields anyway; good database design suggests using an AutoNumber field as the primary key for most tables. However, if your MySQL tables don't have these fields, you need to use MySQL Query Browser or some other tool to add them.

Creating the links in Access is a snap. Choose File → Get External Data → Link Tables to display the Link dialog box. Set the file type to ODBC Databases, and you see the Select Data Source dialog box, which lists ODBC databases you've used before, in the form of Data Source Name (DSN) files that contain the connection information for the database. If you are opening a table in a database you've used before, choose the DSN file for the database, click OK, and choose the tables to link.

If you are linking to a MySQL database for the first time, click the New button in the Select Data Source dialog box, choose MySQL ODBC Driver from the driver list (it's near the end), click Next, specify a name for the DSN file you are creating to store the connection information, and click Finish. You'll see the MySQL ODBC Driver DSN Configuration dialog box, shown in Figure 7-45.

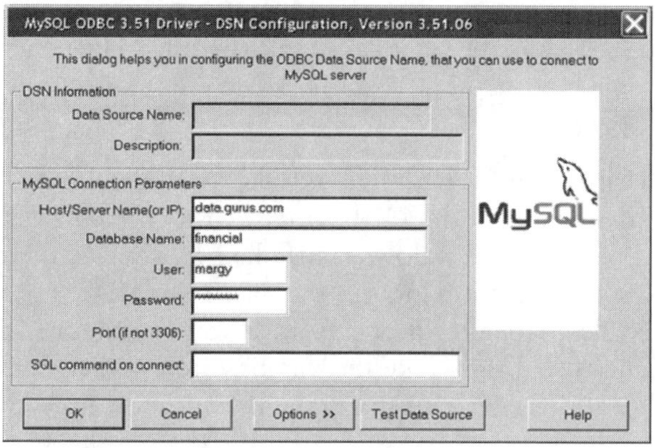

Figure 7-45. Specifying connection information for a MySQL database

Fill in the hostname of the MySQL server, the name of the database that contains the tables to which you want to link, and your MySQL username and password. If your MySQL server doesn't communicate over port 3306 (the default), enter the port number, too. If you want to make sure your connection information is correct, click Test Data Source, and Access will try to connect to the MySQL database and tell you whether it succeeded.

When you click OK, Access displays the Link Tables dialog box (the same dialog box you use when linking to tables in other Access databases). However, in addition to the list of tables, you can select the Save Password checkbox. This option is misnamed because Access stores the MySQL password no matter what; this checkbox actually controls whether it stores the MySQL username. If you don't select this option, you have to enter the MySQL username each time your Access database makes its initial connection to the MySQL database.

> If you have any security concerns about the information in the table, don't check the Save Password checkbox when you create a link to a MySQL table. If you save both the MySQL username and password in the Access database, anyone who can open the Access database can make changes to the information in your MySQL database.

Linked tables from MySQL databases appear on the Tables list in the Access Database window with a blue-green globe icon rather than the usual box icon. You can't change the structure of linked tables, and you can't create relationships that enforce referential integrity between tables, but otherwise, you can use the data just as if it were in your Access database. If you change the structure of a table in the MySQL table, be sure to relink it by choosing Tools → Database Utilities → Linked Table Manager.

Hacking the Hack

When you specify the information about a MySQL database, Access creates a DSN file and stores it in the C:\Program Files\Common Files\ODBC\Data Sources folder (assuming Windows is installed on your C: drive). Strangely, Access also stores the information in the database (MDB) file, so it doesn't read this DSN file again after it creates it. If you set up an Access database with MySQL links and then take the database to another machine, all you need is the MySQL ODBC driver installed. You don't need to bring along the DSN file, too.

Access stores the MySQL connection information as a connection string that looks like this (the line breaks after each semicolon are included for readability only):

```
ODBC;
DRIVER={MySQL ODBC 3.51 Driver};
DESC=;
DATABASE=financial;
SERVER=data.gurus.com;
UID=odbc-margy;
PASSWORD=ziasti;
PORT=;
OPTION=;
STMT=;
TABLE=Categories
```

To see the connection string for a linked table, select the table in the Database window, click Design, click Yes when Access points out that the table structure will be read-only, right-click anywhere in the Design window, and choose Properties from the menu that appears. As you can see, both the username and the password (if you have chosen to save the password) appear in plain text—so much for security. You can't edit the connection string because the table structure can't be edited.

If you open a DSN file with Notepad or another text editor, you see the same connection string, but without the semicolons. You can edit the DSN file, but it won't affect existing linked tables; it affects only tables that you link using the DSN file in the future.

See Also

- MySQL documentation at *http://dev.mysql.com/doc/*
- MySQL Connector/ODBC driver documentation at *http://dev.mysql.com/doc/mysql/en/ODBC_Connector.html*
- PHP documentation at *http://www.php.net/docs.php*

— Margaret Levine Young

HACK #69 Send Access Data Through Outlook Automatically

Implement bulk emailing of your data by tapping into Outlook objects.

The purpose of most databases is to store and report information. Often, it is necessary to send the reports that are generated by a database to multiple users. This doesn't have to be a manual process. By automating Microsoft Outlook from Access VBA, it is possible to automatically generate reports and send them via email.

The first item you need to determine is whether you are going to send emails only through your address book. If you decide to do that, you don't need to adjust any of the default settings in Outlook. If, however, you want to send to any address through your application, you need to make a change in Outlook.

By default, Outlook automatically checks the email addresses when you send an email. When you are doing this in an automated fashion, you will have errors to deal with if an email address doesn't exist in your address book. To shut off this feature in Outlook, go to the Tools → Options dialog.

On the Options dialog, shown in Figure 7-46, click the E-mail Options button in the Preferences tab, and then click the Advanced E-mail Options button shown in Figure 7-47.

This action brings up a dialog box with three sections: "Save messages," "When new items arrive in my Inbox," and "When sending a message," as shown in Figure 7-48.

The "When sending a message" section contains a checkbox for "Automatic name checking," as shown in Figure 7-48. Check the box if you want Outlook to check addresses, and uncheck it if you want to simply send the messages without checking.

Now that you have determined how you want Outlook to handle addresses, you are ready to build email functionality into your application. Although you will eventually want to have reports based on parameterized queries that

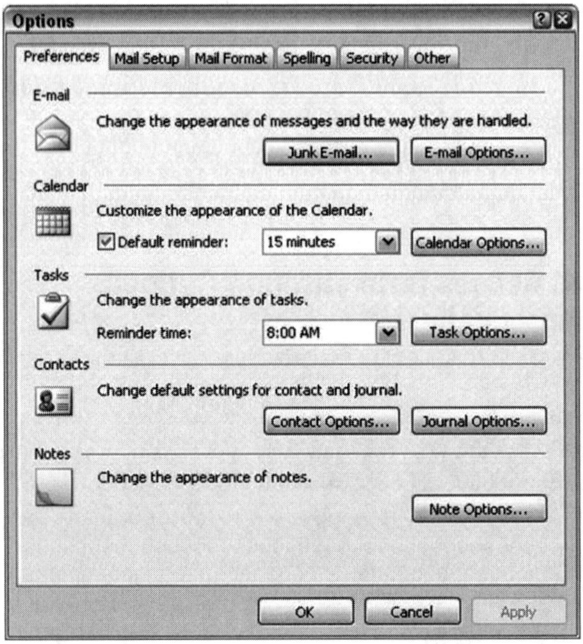

Figure 7-46. Outlook's Options dialog

go to different users, this example shows how to send individual reports to multiple recipients.

It should be noted that to deal with the increasing number of problems with viruses, Outlook prompts the user to allow access to the address book and to send the messages. Although this prevents you from sending email unattended, it is certainly much easier than doing everything manually every time. In older versions of Outlook, you can send multiple emails unattended.

To accomplish the email task, create a table called tbl_Email with two text fields: Email_Address (50 characters) and Report_Name (25 characters). You can make the fields larger if it is warranted. If you use automatic name checking, you just need to put in the display name of the people you want to send the messages to in the Email_Address field. If you aren't using automatic name checking, you need to enter the full email address. Put in two or three records for your test.

In a normal application environment, you would want this to be driven from a form; however, this example simply sends all the emails through a procedure.

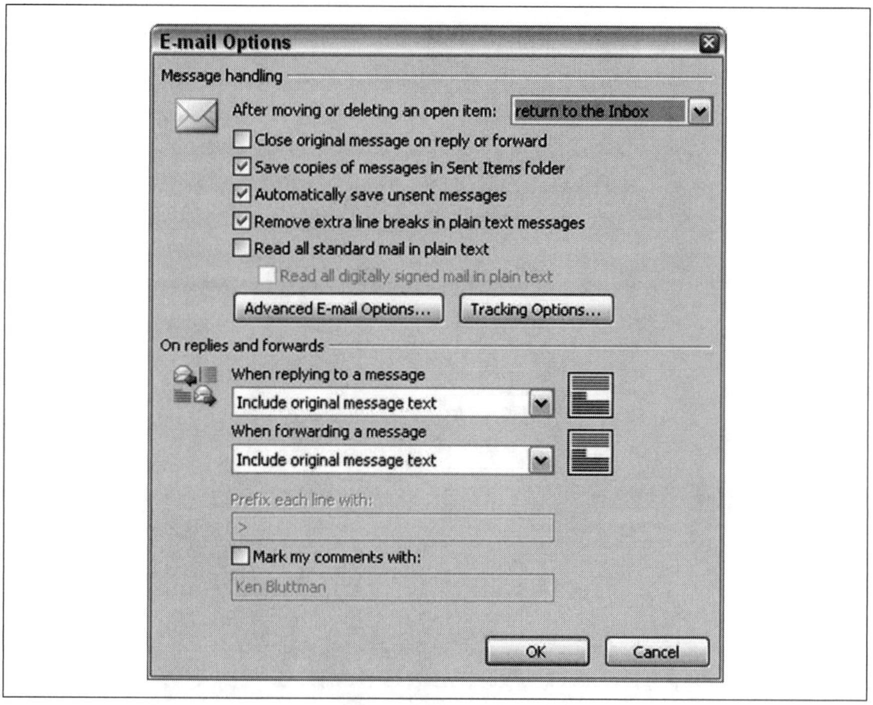

Figure 7-47. The Advanced E-mail Options dialog

To create the procedure, go to the Modules tab in Access, and click New. Once you are in a blank module, go to Insert → Procedure, make sure the radio boxes for Sub and Public are selected, and fill in SendOutlookEmail in the Name text box. This creates the shell for your procedure.

Now you need to create a reference to Microsoft Outlook. Do this by going to Tools → References and checking the box for the version of Outlook that you have. Now you can reference the Outlook object model. If you use a version of Access other than Access 2003, you might need to check the box for Microsoft Data Access Objects (mine is Microsoft DAO 3.6 Object Library). Now you are ready to begin coding.

The Code

The code is shown in Example 7-10.

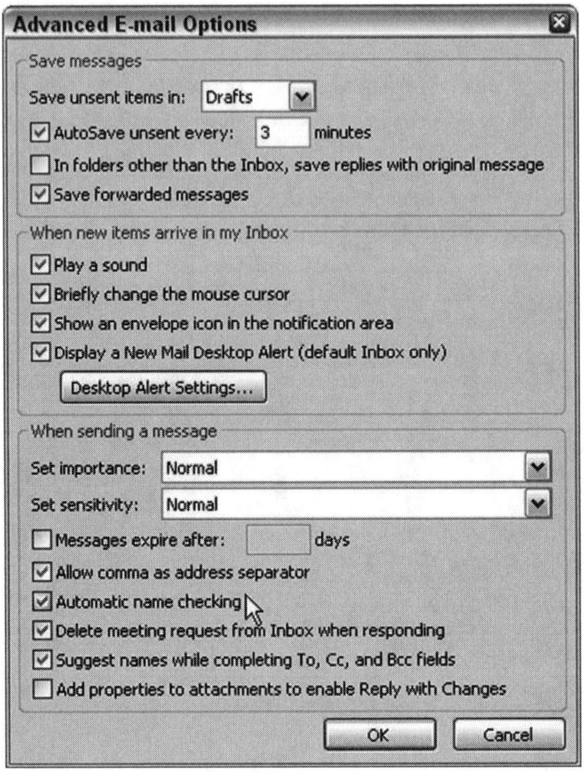

Figure 7-48. Changing how Outlook handles names and email addresses

Example 7-10. Access VBA code to send email

```
Public Sub SendOutlookEmail( )
Dim db As DAO.Database
Dim ReportRs As DAO.Recordset
Dim EmailRS As DAO.Recordset

Dim olApp As Outlook.Application
Dim olMail As Outlook.MailItem

Dim EmailColl As Collection
Dim varEmail As Variant
Dim FileName As String

' Outlook only allows one instance to be open at a time,
' so you can call it with New and it will use the instance
' that you already have open.  I suggest having Outlook open
' already so you are not prompted for user name or password.
Set olApp = New Outlook.Application
```

Example 7-10. Access VBA code to send email (continued)

```
Set db = CurrentDb
Set ReportRs = db.OpenRecordset( _
    "Select Report_Name from tbl_Email Group by Report_Name")

ReportRs.MoveFirst

While Not ReportRs.EOF
  Set EmailColl = New Collection
  Set EmailRS = db.OpenRecordset( _
    "Select Email_Address from tbl_Email Where Report_Name = " & """" & _
      ReportRs.Fields(0).Value & """" & ";")
  EmailRS.MoveFirst
  While Not EmailRS.EOF
    EmailColl.Add EmailRS.Fields(0).Value
    EmailRS.MoveNext
  Wend

  EmailRS.Close
  Set EmailRS = Nothing

  Set olMail = olApp.CreateItem(olMailItem)
  olMail.subject = "Monthly Report"
  For Each varEmail In EmailColl
    olMail.Recipients.Add varEmail
  Next
  olMail.Body = "Your Monthly Report is attached"
  FileName = "C:\Reports\" & ReportRs.Fields(0).Value & ".rtf"
  DoCmd.OutputTo acReport, ReportRs.Fields(0).Value, _
      acFormatRTF, FileName
  ' If you had multiple attachments, you could add them one at a time
  olMail.Attachments.Add FileName, olByValue, 1, "Monthly Report"
  olMail.Send

  Set olMail = Nothing
  Set EmailColl = Nothing

  ReportRs.MoveNext
Wend

  ReportRs.Close
  Set ReportRs = Nothing

  Set olApp = Nothing
  ' You can close Outlook with olApp.Quit - but since I suggested
  ' that you keep it open I am not closing it here

  Set db = Nothing
End Sub
```

When you run the code, you will quickly become annoyed at the number of prompts you receive. As stated earlier, this is much better than doing it manually, but there has to be a better way.

> The code requires several variables for the Outlook objects and data objects; see Example 7-10 for these items. This example also takes advantage of the Collection object; however, you can skip that step and just use the recordset. The main reason the code uses the Collection object is that, in my production-automated email applications, I pass Collections to the email procedure for the report names and the email addresses. This lets me use that same procedure in other Microsoft Office applications such as Excel or Word, where I might not be using recordsets. The procedure saves the reports in a directory called *C:\Reports*; if this directory doesn't exist on your system, you can create the directory, or you can place the reports in a different directory.

An Easier Way

Now that you are familiar with the items to send emails through Outlook, here is an easier way to handle it. Most likely this will be helpful only for large jobs because it requires two steps.

The adjusted Access procedure in Example 7-11 changes the original code from Example 7-10 to save the email instructions in an *ADO.Recordset* XML file. Outlook then processes this file. You will need to create a reference to ADO in both the Outlook and Access VBA environments.

Example 7-11. Creating an XML file from an ADO recordset

```
Public Sub CreateOutlookXML( )
Dim db As DAO.Database
Dim ReportRs As DAO.Recordset
Dim EmailRS As DAO.Recordset

Dim saveRS As ADODB.Recordset
Set saveRS = New ADODB.Recordset

saveRS.Fields.Append "Email_Address", adVarChar, 50, adFldFixed
saveRS.Fields.Append "File_Name", adVarChar, 50, adFldFixed
saveRS.Open
Dim FileName As String

Set db = CurrentDb
Set ReportRs = db.OpenRecordset( _
    "Select Report_Name from tbl_Email Group by Report_Name")

ReportRs.MoveFirst
```

Example 7-11. Creating an XML file from an ADO recordset (continued)

```
While Not ReportRs.EOF
  FileName = "C:\Reports\" & ReportRs.Fields(0).Value & ".rtf"

  Set EmailRS = db.OpenRecordset( _
    "Select Email_Address from tbl_Email Where Report_Name = " & """" & _
      ReportRs.Fields(0).Value & """" & ";")
  EmailRS.MoveFirst
  While Not EmailRS.EOF
    saveRS.AddNew
      saveRS.Fields(0).Value = EmailRS.Fields(0).Value
      saveRS.Fields(1).Value = FileName
    saveRS.Update
    EmailRS.MoveNext
  Wend

  EmailRS.Close
  Set EmailRS = Nothing

  DoCmd.OutputTo acReport, ReportRs.Fields(0).Value, _
    acFormatRTF, FileName

  ReportRs.MoveNext
Wend

  saveRS.Save "C:\Reports\EmailFile.xml", adPersistXML
  saveRS.Close
  Set saveRS = Nothing
  ReportRs.Close
  Set ReportRs = Nothing

  Set db = Nothing
End Sub
```

This procedure takes advantage of a disconnected ADO recordset. With ADO, you can create a recordset on-the-fly without connecting to a database. In addition, you might also notice that this procedure creates all the files Outlook will send later. If you want to, you can have a step that runs at the beginning of the process to create the XML file with no records and then have multiple procedures run that continue to add to the XML file to be processed by Outlook at a particular time.

Macros in Outlook

Next, you need to create the Outlook procedure. To make this work, you need to add a macro to your Outlook environment. In Outlook, select Tools → Macros → Visual Basic Editor, and click the ThisOutlookSession object in the Project Explorer. Once there, enter the code in Example 7-12.

Example 7-12. Processing the ADO recordset in Outlook

```
Public Sub EmailTest( )
Dim mi As MailItem
Dim varitm As Variant
Dim adors As ADODB.Recordset
Set adors = New ADODB.Recordset
adors.Open "C:\Reports\EmailFile.xml"
adors.MoveFirst
While Not adors.EOF
Set mi = Application.CreateItem(olMailItem)
mi.Recipients.Add adors.Fields(0).Value
mi.Subject = "Monthly Report"
mi.Body = "Your monthly report is attached."
mi.Attachments.Add adors.Fields(1).Value, olByValue, 1, "Monthly Report"
mi.Send
Set mi = Nothing
adors.MoveNext
Wend
adors.Close
Set adors = Nothing
End Sub
```

This sends all your emails without prompting you each time. Although it creates a two-step process, you will appreciate not having to click through each message. This is particularly useful if you have a significant number of emails to send. If necessary, you can store additional fields for Subject and Body in the recordset and have those also become dynamic.

The one downside of this procedure is that it sends an individual email for each record. You can update it to go through the recordset and determine if emails can be grouped; however, this is unlikely to be necessary. In addition, you can also create multiple XML files for each email to be sent and have the procedure cycle through all the XML files and then move them when it is completed (I implemented such a procedure for a client once).

You will need to save this procedure using the Save icon from the Visual Basic Environment if you want to use it again. Also, depending on your security settings, you might be prompted to enable this macro each time you open Outlook and attempt to use it.

Using either approach will certainly help you tackle your Access projects and help automate sending emails. If you need to send just a message to users, you can use the first procedure and eliminate the lines related to attachments. In either case, the power of using VBA in Microsoft Office applications should be evident.

—Michael Schmalz

Create Access Tables from Outside Access
#70   You don't have to be in Access to use Access.

Here's the scenario: you have an Excel solution that needs to populate an Access table. The table will be a new table in the database. You might think the table needs to exist before you can populate it via ADO or some other means, so you manually create the table and then go back to Excel and run the routine that populates the table.

Actually, you don't have to go to Access and create the table. Just create it directly from code while in Excel. It's a simple matter, really; you just need to work with the ADOX library.

In Excel, set a reference to ADOX by using the Tools → References menu and setting the references in the References dialog box, as shown in Figure 7-49.

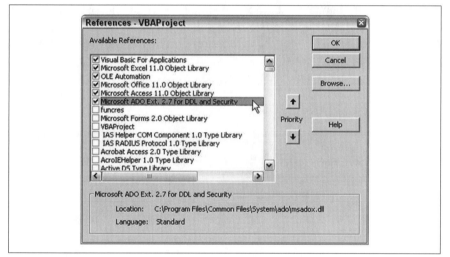

Figure 7-49. Setting a reference to ADOX

The Code

It's now just a matter of whipping up a little code that uses the ADOX programmatic model. In an Excel code module, enter this code:

```
Dim cat As New ADOX.Catalog
Dim tbl As New ADOX.Table
Dim db_file_path As String
'change path and database!
db_file_path = ActiveWorkbook.Path & "\abc.mdb"
```

```
'connect to the Access database
cat.ActiveConnection = "Provider=Microsoft.Jet.OLEDB.4.0;" & _
    "Data Source=" & db_file_path

'Create a table
With tbl
.Name = "Prospects"
' First, fields are appended to the table object
' Then the table object is appended to the Tables collection
.Columns.Append "Name", adVarWChar
.Columns.Append "Company", adVarWChar
.Columns.Append "Phone", adVarWChar
.Columns.Append "Address", adVarWChar
End With

cat.Tables.Append tbl

Set cat = Nothing
MsgBox "Table created!"
```

Just be sure to change the hardcoded database name and path. This code creates the Prospects table in the Access database. The table will have four fields. The Append method of the Columns property takes the name of the field and the field type as a constant. The constants for the field types differ from what you see in Access, although they serve the same purpose. To see all the constants, use the Object Browser and filter it to just show the ADOX library, as shown in Figure 7-50.

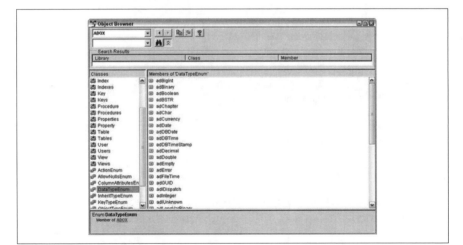

Figure 7-50. Displaying ADOX constants

Hacking the Hack

This hack uses ADOX, which is an available external library. You just as easily can run the code in this hack from Word, PowerPoint, Outlook, and other programs. The point is that you can create and manipulate Access database tables even when Access isn't running.

Write VBA with the Macro Recorder in Word #71 and Excel

Take advantage of autogenerated code to speed up your coding efforts.

Let's say you need to work with Word or Excel from within Access. And let's say the project involves writing VBA for Word or Excel that will be used from Access via automation. Well, you don't have to climb as steep a learning curve as you might think. That's because both Word and Excel can generate VBA code automatically.

To make this work, you first turn on the Macro Recorder, perform certain actions in the application, and then stop the recorder. Just select Tools → Macro → Record New Macro to start the recorder, as shown in Figure 7-51.

Figure 7-51. Starting to record an Excel macro

With the recorder running, you can perform a few actions of entering data and creating a chart. After stopping the recorder (while it is recording, a toolbar with a Stop button is visible), the code is in an Excel code module. Figure 7-52 shows an example of the code Excel generates.

Usually, you'll need to work with the generated code. It will have hard-coded cell references that might not make sense for your application.

Figure 7-52. Excel autogenerated VBA code

However, using the Macro Recorder, you can generate most of what you need and then just edit it to make it work right. Code such as this that works in Excel will run fairly well from Access when a reference is set to the Excel library (everything said here also applies to Word). You will need to make some changes, but this is still a big timesaver.

—Kirk Lamb

CHAPTER EIGHT

Programming
Hacks 72–91

VBA, ADO, DAO, SQL, XML: developers subsist in a world of acronyms. The great thing about all these technologies is how well they work together in our custom solutions. You might be familiar with just a handful of these technologies, but when you finish reading this chapter, you will walk away with a bit more knowledge than when you started.

In this chapter, you'll find hacks that optimize code by reducing the number of lines and reducing repetitive routines. "Substitute Domain Aggregate Functions for SQL Aggregate Functions" [Hack #74] shows you how to reduce code by avoiding SQL functions. Other hacks show you how to protect your code and keep users out of the design elements. One of these, "Protect Programming Code from Curious Users" [Hack #77], shows you how to apply password protection to your code.

The chapter also contains hacks that enhance the user experience. For example, "Help Users Drill Down to a Record" [Hack #79] helps users quickly find a desired record from a large number of records. And "Save Values from Unbound Controls for Later Recall" [Hack #84] gives users a way to recreate form selections from earlier sessions.

HACK #72 Store Initial Control Selections for Later Recall

The Tag property is a great place to store data about controls. Here's how to put it to good use.

Combo boxes and listboxes are great for presenting users with choices. As the user makes selections in a combo box or listbox, the value is available to use in code simply by referring to the control's Value property:

```
If IsNull(cmbLevel) Then
    MsgBox "No Value Selected"
Else
```

```
    MsgBox cmbLevel.Value
  End If
```

You can even refer only to the control itself and leave the Value property off, like this:

```
  If IsNull(cmbLevel) Then
    MsgBox "No Value Selected"
  Else
    MsgBox cmbLevel
  End If
```

Note that both code snippets begin with a test for a null. The listbox or combo box might initially be null, so it is good practice to include a way to avoid bombing out if this is the case.

As users click away and make selections, a listbox or combo box's value changes to reflect the user's last selection. But what if you have to recall an earlier selection or perhaps the first selection the user made? A user might have forgotten what he first selected and wants to return to that value. You can build into your application a way to do this, but it will be for naught unless you stored the initial value.

Of course, you can keep the initial value stored in a table, but that's extra work. Instead, this hack shows you how to store a control's initial value—right in the control itself! Both the listbox and the combo-box controls have a Tag property. This property has no purpose other than to act like a little comment area for Access objects.

> In case you are wondering about the OldValue property, here is the skinny on that. OldValue stores the unedited value while the value is being edited. This is like a before-and-after picture of an edit, but it works only for the most recent change. You can't use OldValue to recall a value from several changes back.

Figure 8-1 shows a form with a combo box, a listbox, and a button. Both the combo box (cmbLevel) and the listbox (listRegion) have their Row Source Type set to Value List. The combo box has four Row Source items: Beginner, Intermediate, Advanced, and Expert. The listbox has five Row Source items: East, West, North, South, and Central. Original selected values for these controls are stored in the Tag property.

These controls are unbound. When the form opens, they are blank. In the form's Open event, the Tag property of each control is set to a zero-length string. Here is the complete code:

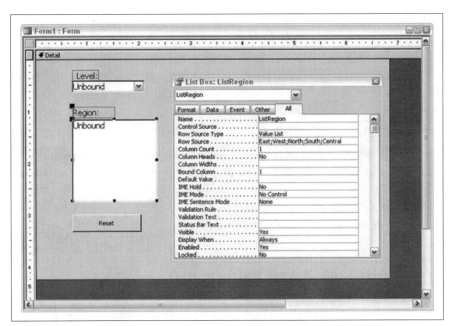

Figure 8-1. A form with a combo box, listbox, and button

```
Private Sub Form_Open(Cancel As Integer)
  cmbLevel.Tag = ""
  listRegion.Tag = ""
End Sub

Private Sub cmbLevel_AfterUpdate()
  If cmbLevel.Tag = "" Then
    cmbLevel.Tag = cmbLevel
  End If
End Sub

Private Sub listRegion_AfterUpdate()
  If listRegion.Tag = "" Then
    listRegion.Tag = listRegion
  End If
End Sub

Private Sub cmdReset_Click()
  cmbLevel = cmbLevel.Tag
  listRegion = listRegion.Tag
End Sub
```

The first time a selection is made in either cmbLevel or listRegion, the Tag property is tested to see if it is a zero-length string. If it returns true, the Tag property updates to the control's current value. This activity occurs in the

AfterUpdate event because the new latest value is required. The latest value is the current one after the update.

The test for a tag with a zero-length string is successful only the first time it is run. Every time after that, a new selection is made in a control; therefore, the test fails because the Tag property has a value—the original selected value.

The Reset button, when clicked, simply sets both the combo box and the listbox to the original selections by setting them to their own Tag properties.

This hack shows you only how to store the initial selections. What you actually do with them is a function of your application. The great thing about this hack is that it is easily portable. Because no tables are involved, you can copy the code into other controls' event stubs and just change the name of the control reference in the code.

HACK #73 Write Code Faster by Turning Off Syntax-Checking

Make sure Access doesn't pester you with warning messages while you're writing code.

If you're like me, sometimes your fingers can't keep up with your brain. Often, when I am writing code, I am several lines ahead in my thoughts, and I'm typing as fast as I can to keep up. The last thing I want is to lose my train of thought, but if I make a few typing errors or leave out a keyword or variable, Access pops up a scolding message.

The error message in Figure 8-2 is a perfect example. I am in the midst of coding a Select Case statement. I don't know what the expression is yet, but I do have in mind what the actual cases are, and I want to get them down fast. But no, Access hangs me up on the Select Case line.

I know I left something out! I did this on purpose, and I will return and enter it in a little while! This interruption is just annoying.

So, I have learned to turn off these annoying messages as I enter lengthy chunks of code. Figure 8-3 shows the Options dialog. In the VB editor, use Tools → Options to display the dialog box.

On the Editor tab of the dialog, uncheck the Auto Syntax Check checkbox. Doing so is the key to fast coding. When you turn off the syntax check, you can type without interruption. Errors will still be flagged by their color coding (lines with errors will change color), but no more pesky message boxes will appear that you have to clear.

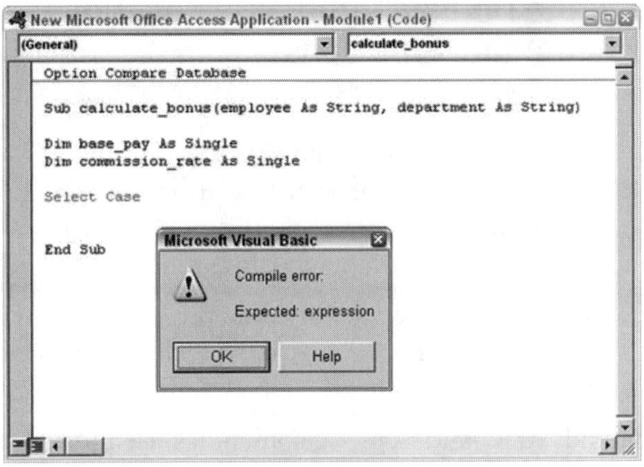

Figure 8-2. *A pesky warning message*

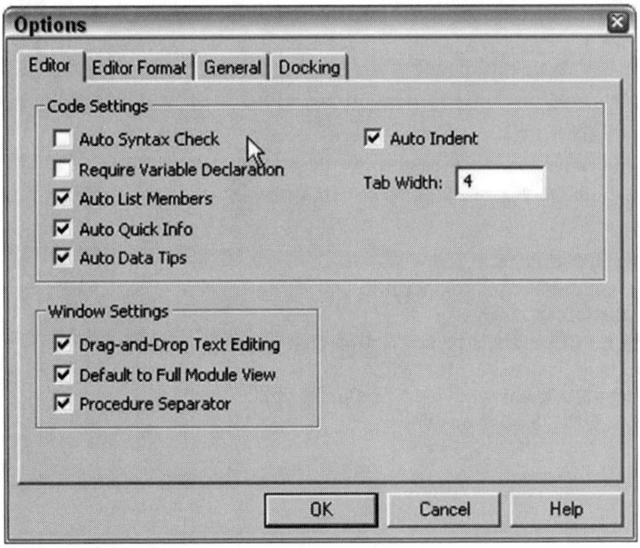

Figure 8-3. *Turning off Auto Syntax Check*

Of course, it's a good idea to turn syntax-checking back on when you finish entering code!

Substitute Domain Aggregate Functions for SQL Aggregate Functions

HACK #74

Reduce the amount of code you enter and still get the same results.

Within VBA code, it is a common practice to tap into the ADO objects and use some SQL to query data in the database. Because SQL is the de facto standard for querying data, following this route is understandable. However, sometimes you don't need to query data in this way.

For example, if you need to process individual records, using ADO and SQL makes sense. A recordset is created that is typically scrolled through using the MoveNext method within a Do Until loop or similar construct.

On the other hand, ADO and SQL are sometimes used just to get an aggregate value from a set of records. In this situation, the individual records are of no concern. Instead, you're looking for a summary, such as a sum, a count, or an average.

The Code

Example 8-1 shows a routine that uses ADO and SQL to return the sum of some invoice amounts.

Example 8-1. Using ADO and SQL to return a sum

```
Sub get_SQL_Sum( )
  Dim conn As ADODB.Connection
  Set conn = CurrentProject.Connection
  Dim rs As New ADODB.Recordset
  rs.Open "Select Sum(Amount) As SumOfAmount From Invoices" & _
    " Where InvoiceDate=#12/10/04#", _
          conn, adOpenKeyset, adLockOptimistic
  MsgBox rs.Fields("SumOfAmount")
  rs.Close
  Set rs = Nothing
  Set conn = Nothing
End Sub
```

The SQL statement includes the SQL aggregate Sum function. Also, the sum of the amounts is from a set of records filtered to a single invoice date of 12/10/04. The code in Example 8-1 requires creating ADO objects and then destroying them afterward (by setting them to Nothing).

You can boil down all this to a single line using a *domain aggregate function*.

Boiling Down the Code

Domain aggregate functions provide the same results as SQL aggregate functions. However, whereas you need to somehow embed SQL aggregate functions into a SQL statement, you can code domain aggregates independently.

Example 8-2 shows how a short routine using the DSum domain aggregate function replaces the code in Example 8-1.

Example 8-2. Using DSum to return the sum

```
Sub get_Domain_Sum( )
  Dim amount As Single
  amount = DSum("[Amount]", "Invoices", "[InvoiceDate] = #12/10/04#")
  MsgBox amount
End Sub
```

Other than dimensioning the amount variable and using a message box to display the result, the code requires just one statement:

```
      amount = DSum("[Amount]", "Invoices", "[InvoiceDate] = #12/10/04#")
```

The arguments handed to DSum are the field to sum, the domain (a table or Select query), and any filtering. The third argument works in the same manner as the SQL Where clause.

You can even enter complex criteria for the third argument. For example, this line of code returns the sum of amount when the invoice date is 12/10/04, the customer is Anderson, and the location is either Chicago or Dallas:

```
      amount = DSum("[Amount]", "Invoices", "[InvoiceDate] = #12/10/04# And
      [Customer]='Anderson' And ([Location]='Chicago' or [Location]='Dallas')")
```

Domain Aggregate Functions

There are several domain aggregate functions:

DAvg
> Returns the average of the values in the field in the first argument.

DCount
> Returns the count of records.

DLookup
> Returns the value of the first field in the first record that matches based on the criteria in the third argument.

DFirst *and* DLast
> Returns the value of the field in the first argument from the first or last record.

DMin *and* DMax
> Returns the minimum or maximum value of the field in the first argument from among the records.

DStDev *and* DStDevP
> Returns the standard deviation of the values in the field in the first argument. You use DStDev with a sample from a population. You use DStDevP with the full population.

DSum
> Returns the sum of the values in the field in the first argument.

DVar *and* DVarP
> Returns the variance among the values in the field in the first argument. You use DVar with a sample from a population. You use DVarP with the full population.

All the domain aggregate functions work with the same three arguments: the field being evaluated, the domain, and the criteria. Look up these functions in the Access Help system if you want more information. Integrating them into your procedures is a great way to retrieve quick summaries of data with just single lines of code.

HACK #75   Shrink Your Code with Subroutines

Say goodbye to long and difficult-to-maintain code by placing repetitive processing into subroutines.

All applications live and grow. Functionality begets functionality. As users start banging away at your first delivered application, they scream for more features. As you add these features, the amount of code can grow. Often, routines get copied, and then a couple of literals, variable names, or criteria get changed. You end up with code that has a number of similar routines.

Example 8-3 shows three identical routines, with the exception that each addresses a different state.

Example 8-3. Multiple nearly identical routines

```
Sub get_NY_records()
'
'get New York customers
'
Dim conn As ADODB.Connection
Set conn = CurrentProject.Connection
Dim recset As ADODB.Recordset
Set recset = New ADODB.Recordset
recset.Open "Select * From Customers Where State='NY'", conn
Do Until recset.EOF
```

Example 8-3. Multiple nearly identical routines (continued)

```
      ''Process records here
   recset.MoveNext
   Loop
   recset.Close
   Set recset = Nothing
End Sub

Sub get_CT_records( )
   '
   'get Connecticut customers
   '
   Dim conn As ADODB.Connection
   Set conn = CurrentProject.Connection
   Dim recset As ADODB.Recordset
   Set recset = New ADODB.Recordset
   recset.Open "Select * From Customers Where State='CT'", conn
   Do Until recset.EOF
      ''Process records here
   recset.MoveNext
   Loop
   recset.Close
   Set recset = Nothing
End Sub

Sub get_MA_records( )
   '
   'get Massachusetts customers
   '
   Dim conn As ADODB.Connection
   Set conn = CurrentProject.Connection
   Dim recset As ADODB.Recordset
   Set recset = New ADODB.Recordset
   recset.Open "Select * From Customers Where State='MA'", conn
   Do Until recset.EOF
      ''Process records here
   recset.MoveNext
   Loop
   recset.Close
   Set recset = Nothing
End Sub
```

The code in Example 8-3 is frightfully redundant. You can optimize code
such as this by creating a subroutine that takes an argument. You place the
code that is identical in all the routines into the subroutine and then use the
argument to pass the particular individual value to the subroutine to run the
process.

In Example 8-3 the only differentiating item in the code is the state, such as
in this statement, which selects Massachusetts (MA) records:

```
   recset.Open "Select * From Customers Where State='MA'", conn
```

Example 8-4 shows how to change the code by using a subroutine. Now the repetitive code is placed in a separate subroutine named get_state_records. The subroutine takes a string argument, named state.

Example 8-4. The repetitive code placed into a subroutine

```
Sub get_NY_records( )
   'get New York customers
   get_state_records "NY"
End Sub

Sub get_CT_records( )
   'get Connecticut customers
   get_state_records "CT"
End Sub

Sub get_MA_records( )
   'get Massachusetts customers
   get_state_records "MA"
End Sub

Sub get_state_records(state As String)
  Dim conn As ADODB.Connection
  Set conn = CurrentProject.Connection
  Dim recset As ADODB.Recordset
  Set recset = New ADODB.Recordset
  recset.Open "Select * From Customers Where State='" & state & "'", conn
  Do Until recset.EOF
     ''Process records here
  recset.MoveNext
  Loop
  recset.Close
  Set recset = Nothing
End Sub
```

Now, each individual routine, such as get_MA_records, simply calls the generic subroutine and passes the state initials as the argument. This is done in a single line of code:

```
      get_state_records "MA"
```

The generic get_state_records subroutine takes the passed argument and uses it in the SQL statement that opens the recordset:

```
      recset.Open "Select * From Customers Where State='" & state & "'", conn
```

You can easily see that the code in Example 8-4 is shorter than the code in Example 8-3.

Years ago, programmers would boast about how many thousands of lines of code they had written. I suppose now the fashion is for programmers to talk about how many lines of code they avoided writing!

Shrink Your Code with Optional Arguments

Put subroutines to even more general use by accepting different numbers of arguments.

"Shrink Your Code with Subroutines" **[Hack #75]** shows you how to reduce code by using a generic subroutine. This hack takes that concept a step further. Subroutines can take optional arguments. Calling routines are required only to supply arguments that aren't optional. The optional ones are, well, optional.

Example 8-5 shows a handful of routines and the subroutine they call.

Example 8-5. A set of routines that call a subroutine

```
Sub get_NY_records( )
   'get New York customers
   get_state_records "NY"
End Sub

Sub get_CT_records( )
   'get Connecticut customers
   get_state_records "CT"
End Sub

Sub get_MA_records( )
   'get Massachusetts customers
   get_state_records "MA", "Boston"
End Sub

Sub get_state_records(state As String, Optional city As String)
   Dim conn As ADODB.Connection
   Set conn = CurrentProject.Connection
   Dim recset As ADODB.Recordset
   Set recset = New ADODB.Recordset
   If state = "MA" Then
      recset.Open "Select * From Customers Where State='" & state _
         & "' And City='" & city & "'", conn
   Else
      recset.Open "Select * From Customers Where State='" & state & "'", conn
   End If
   Do Until recset.EOF
   ''Process records here
   recset.MoveNext
   Loop
   recset.Close
   Set recset = Nothing
End Sub
```

The subroutine takes two arguments: state, which is required, and city, which is optional. The Optional keyword is placed in front of the argument name:

```
Sub get_state_records(state As String, Optional city As String)
```

> No keyword is available for specifying that an argument is required. All arguments are required unless you specifically set them as optional with the Optional keyword. Note also that optional arguments must come after all the required arguments. You can have multiple optional arguments, but you must precede each one with the Optional keyword.

Let's assume the requirements have changed; now, any NY or CT records can be used, but for Massachusetts (MA), we need only records for which the city is Boston.

One way to accommodate this new requirement is to use subroutines: one that accepts a single state argument and one that accepts two arguments, for the state and the city. The functionality would work, but there would be more code.

However, by incorporating the city as an optional argument, you can use the single subroutine for all the states. Massachusetts records are accessed by the two arguments being passed:

```
get_state_records "MA", "Boston"
```

New York and Connecticut records are accessed with the single required state argument:

```
get_state_records "CT"
```

We've modified the subroutine to handle two types of queries, one with a single criterion and one that uses both criteria:

```
If state = "MA" Then
    recset.Open "Select * From Customers Where State='" & state _
      & "' And City='" & city & "'", conn
Else
    recset.Open "Select * From Customers Where State='" & state & "'", conn
End If
```

And that's it! By just altering the existing subroutine a bit, we don't need to create a second subroutine.

Protect Programming Code from Curious Users

Your code is valuable. Add password protection to your modules.

I think you'll agree that developed code is valuable, in terms of the time and expense it took to create it as well as what would be involved to recreate it. So, like any valuable asset, a little protection goes a long way. Of course, I would be remiss if I didn't mention that the first thing you should do is have a backup system in place. But even if you do have a back-up system, if the code in a production system gets trampled somehow, it still costs the company to take down the system to fix the code.

Luckily, there is an easy way to protect your code. This hack prevents all but those who know the password from seeing your code. To add this protection, you must access the Tools → Properties menu in the VB editor, as shown in Figure 8-4. In this example, the menu item is Customers Properties because my code project is named Customers. Your menu item will reflect the name of your code project.

> Initially, the name of the code project is set to the name of the database. You can change this in the General tab on the Project Properties dialog box (Tools → Properties).

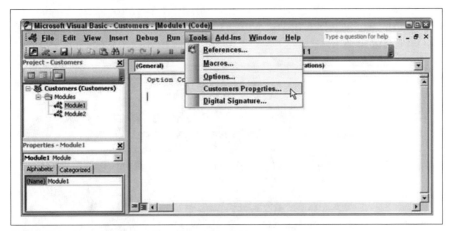

Figure 8-4. Accessing the project properties

On the Protection tab in the Project Properties dialog box, select the option to protect the project and establish a password. Enter a password, and click OK, as shown in Figure 8-5. Don't forget that passwords are case-sensitive.

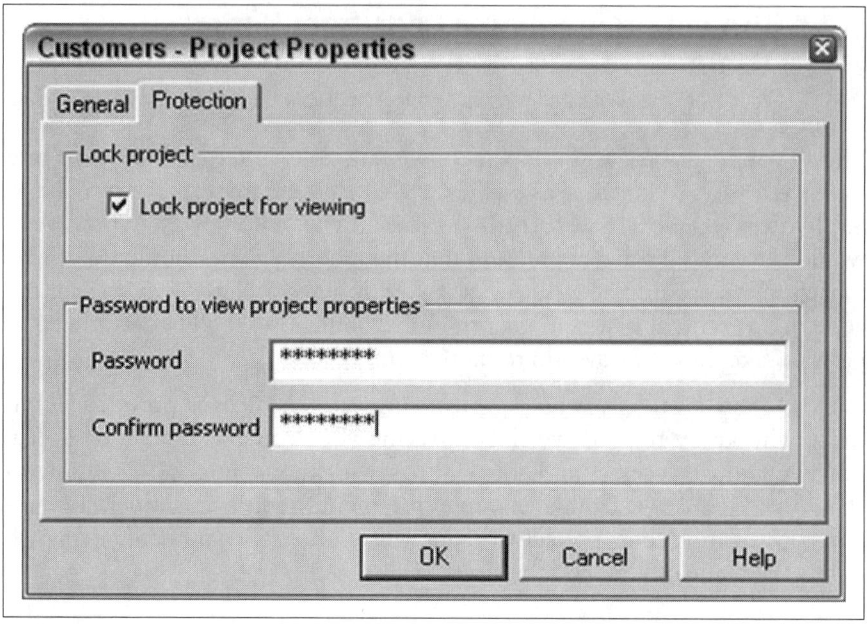

Figure 8-5. *Protecting the project*

You won't see any change until you close the database and then reopen it. When you go to the VB editor, the list in the Project window will be collapsed to the top level of the project itself. If you try to open the list (by clicking the plus sign), a box in which to enter the password will pop up, as shown in Figure 8-6.

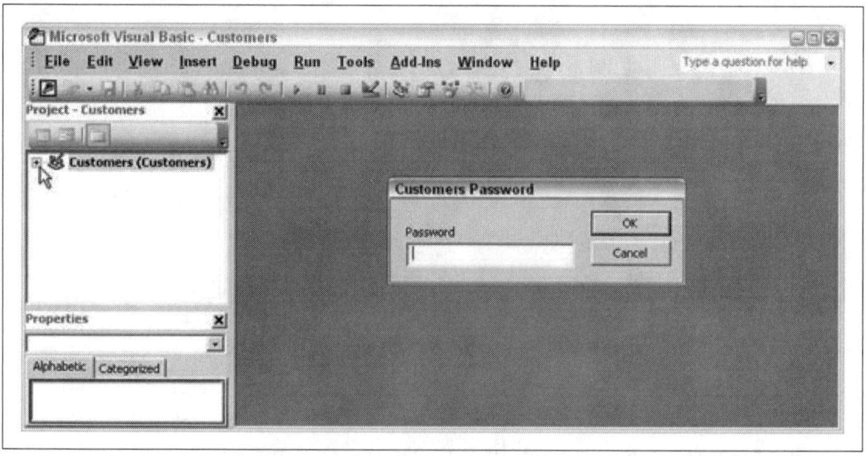

Figure 8-6. *Requiring a password to see the code*

This is as far as you can get without knowing the password. The protection actually helps in two ways: not only is the code protected from tampering, but also it is invisible. Therefore, your code is protected in terms of intellectual rights as well. If you developed some excellent routines that you hold dear, you can relax knowing that others can't even view them, much less copy them.

HACK #78 Build a Secret Developer Backdoor into Your Applications

Keep users out of your design while letting yourself in the easy way.

Some users are a little too curious for their own good. Left to their own devices, they will explore your database's design. A few approaches exist to combat this. You can turn on security, convert the database to a read-only *.mde* version, or just remove the ability to get to the design elements.

This last option, although not as robust as using Access security, is a common way to keep users on the up and up. Setting the following options in Startup Options, shown in Figure 8-7, helps make it hard for users to get into the database design:

- Set the opening form.
- Uncheck the Display Database Window checkbox.
- Uncheck the Allow Built-in Toolbars checkbox.
- Uncheck the Allow Toolbar/Menu Changes checkbox.

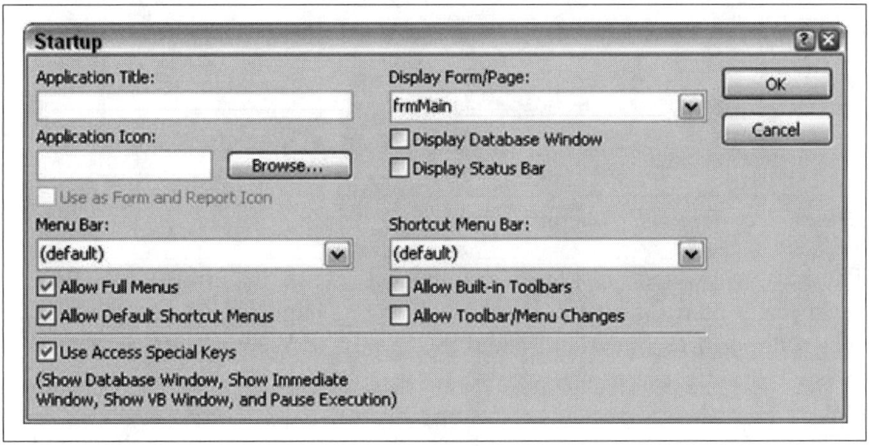

![Startup dialog box]

Figure 8-7. *Changing startup options*

In the form design, you can implement the following additional settings:

- Set the Shortcut Menu property to No.
- Set Allow Design Changes to Design View Only.
- Assign a custom menu bar that doesn't provide a way to access design elements.

This will keep most users focused on their work. Unfortunately, it might also mean you just made it more difficult for you to get into the database design. This hack builds a hidden shortcut that only you, the developer, know about. This shortcut takes you directly to the database's design elements.

Figure 8-8 shows a form in Design mode. A command button is strategically placed where you wouldn't think to click. You can see it in the upper-left corner of the form. It doesn't look like a regular button, although it is. The Transparent property has been set to Yes, which makes it look flat. Any caption disappears as well when the button is transparent. Therefore, it really appears as just the outline of a rectangle.

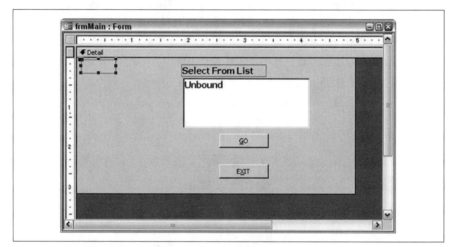

Figure 8-8. A form with a transparent button

The button has code inside its double-click event. A double-click event is never really used for buttons because everyone expects that a single button click will perform an action. When the form is in View mode, the button is invisible. Its Visible property is set to true, but the transparency overrides that.

Note that the mouse pointer doesn't change when the user passes it over the invisible button. The button is enabled, though. A user could accidentally click it without knowing it. Therefore, using the double-click event instead of the single-click event serves as a safeguard. This approach isn't foolproof, but it does keep stray clicks from running any code.

The Code

When you double-click the transparent button, the following code runs to ask for a password:

```
Dim pw As String
pw = InputBox$("Enter Password", "Password")
If pw = "Access Rocks!" Then
  DoCmd.SelectObject acTable, , True
Else
  MsgBox "Incorrect Password"
End If
```

If the password entered is correct, the database window is displayed.

Figure 8-9 shows the form in View mode after the button has been double-clicked. The button itself isn't visible; you need to know where it is to double-click it.

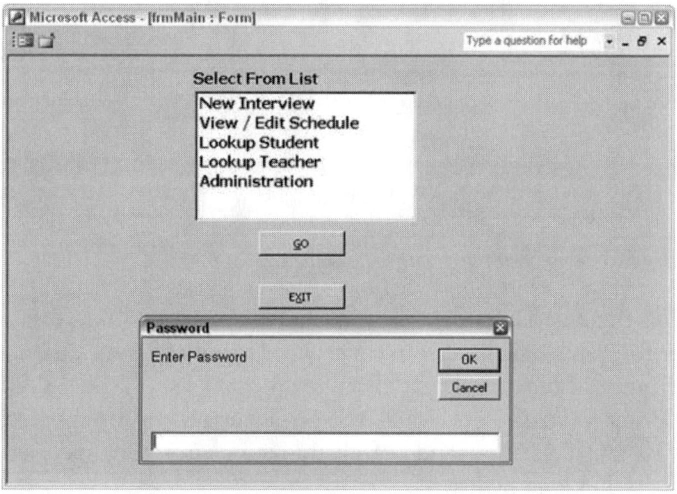

Figure 8-9. Entering a password to open the database window

—Kirk Lamb

Help Users Drill Down to a Record

Facilitate browsing through a lengthy customer database by first grouping customers.

Sometimes users need to spend a lot of time finding a specific customer from a long list of customer records. For example, loading customer names into a combo box or a listbox requires your users to do a lot of scrolling.

Here's a technique that removes some of this drudgery. The first step is to provide a way to list smaller groups of customers. Figure 8-10 shows a form in which four buttons (on the left, inside the Browse Customers frame) lead to customers whose last names start with A–F, G–L, M–R, and S–Z.

Figure 8-10. Browsing customers within alphabetic groupings

Segregating the customers into four groups is subjective. You can apply this technique to even single letters; in other words, you can have 26 buttons. The more customers there are, the smaller the groupings should be. Keep in mind that the point is to present smaller lists of customers for users to browse through. If you have thousands of customers, a grouping such as A–F still results in a rather lengthy list.

Clicking any of the four buttons opens a form that is filtered to customers whose last name falls into the indicated grouping. For example, the code in the Click event for the A–F button looks like this:

```
Private Sub cmdAF_Click()
  DoCmd.OpenForm "frmBrowseCustomers", acNormal, , _
  "CustomerLastName Like'A*' or CustomerLastName Like 'B*' or " & _
  "CustomerLastName Like'C*' or CustomerLastName Like 'D*' or " & _
  "CustomerLastName Like'E*' or CustomerLastName Like 'F*'"
End Sub
```

The OpenForm method opens the frmBrowseCustomers form filtered to the appropriate customers. Figure 8-11 shows the form opened with the A–F customers.

Figure 8-11. A filtered set of customers on a form

The form in Figure 8-11 really serves just as a browse feature. Users still don't see the full customer record. To see the full record, the user must double-click any record shown on the browse form, which opens the full customer record. The form that displays customer details is filtered to the particular record selected in the form shown in Figure 8-11.

To make this happen, the *key* is necessary. The key, an AutoNumber type named CustomerID in this example, is on the browse form, but it is hidden. Figure 8-12 shows the design of the browse form. In Design mode, you can see the key field.

All the fields in the browse form have code in their double-click events. The code calls a subroutine named open_customer, which opens the customer detail form. This time, the OpenForm method uses the key to open the detail form. Figure 8-13 shows the code behind the browse form.

Double-clicking a record in the browse form pulls up the customer's details. Figure 8-14 shows the customer detail form.

To summarize, when working with a large number of customers (or with other types of data, for that matter), users can get to the desired detail records pretty quickly by grouping the records into smaller browsable sets. Then, from the interim browse form, they can view the full details. Using

Figure 8-12. The design of the browse form

Figure 8-13. The code behind the browse form

this technique makes it easy to get to a detail record with just a few clicks, without having to scroll through a long list.

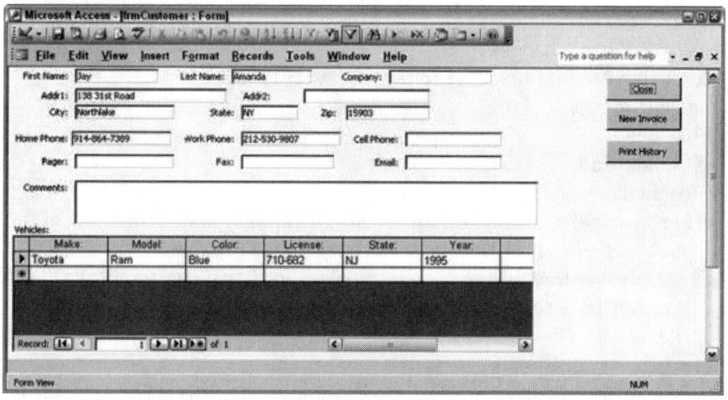

Figure 8-14. A form with the customer detail

HACK #80 Prevent Users from Disabling Your Startup Options

Stop users from being able to hold down the Shift key to get to the database window.

After spending all that time developing your database application and then setting the startup options, the last thing you want is for someone to be able to simply hold down the Shift key during startup and then mess around with your application. This hack explores two different ways to prevent this: disabling the Shift key code for Access databases (MDBs) and disabling the Shift key code for Access Data Projects (ADPs).

Access MDB

With MDB files, the hack works by adding a property called `AllowBypassKey` to the database object. Setting the property to `False` disables the Shift key, and changing it back to `True` enables it again. You need to decide on an event to trigger the value change. It could be when a specific user logs into the database or, as in this code example, when a file named *AllowByPass.txt* is in the same directory as the database:

```
Public Function DetermineByPass()
    If Len(Dir(CurrentProject.Path & "\AllowByPass.txt")) = 0 Then
        ChangeProperty "AllowBypassKey", DB_BOOLEAN, False, True
    Else
        ChangeProperty "AllowBypassKey", DB_BOOLEAN, True, True
    End If
End Function
Public Function ChangeProperty(strPrpName As String,_
                        varPrpType As Variant, _
                        varPrpValue As Variant, _
                        bolDDL as Boolean) As Boolean
```

```
        Dim prp As Variant
        Const conPrpNotFoundError = 3270
        On Error GoTo ChangePrp_Err
        CurrentDb.Properties(strPrpName) = varPrpValue
        ChangeProperty = True
    ChangePrp_Bye:
        Exit Function
    ChangePrp_Err:
        If Err = conPrpNotFoundError Then   'Property not found
            Set prp = CurrentDb.CreateProperty(strPrpName, _
                                        varPrpType, varPrpValue, bolDDL)
            CurrentDb.Properties.Append prp
            Resume Next
        Else
            'Unknown Error
            MsgBox Err.Description
            ChangeProperty = False
            Resume ChangePrp_Bye
        End If
    End Function
```

After the code checks for the *AllowByPass.txt* file, it calls the ChangeProperty function and sets it to False if the file isn't found or to True if it is found.

First the ChangeProperty function attempts to set the value passed to it in varPrpValue to the strPrpName property, which in this case is AllowBypassKey. An error number (3270) occurs the first time this function is called with a new property because that property has not yet been appended to the database's properties collection. The function traps for this error number and creates the property with the error-handling routine.

This example uses CurrentDB so that you don't need to manually set a reference to the DAO library for Access 2000 and 2002 (Access 2003 has the reference set by default). It is worth noting that the CurrentDB method establishes a hidden reference to the Microsoft DAO 3.6 object library when used in a 2000 or 2002 MDB file.

The last parameter to the ChangeProperty function (bolDDL) sets the DDL parameter of the AllowBypassKey property. The DDL parameter determines if the property can be altered via automation. By setting this parameter to True, you prevent someone with VBA coding experience from resetting the parameter by automation.

Once the code is in place in an Access module, you need to make sure it gets run when the database starts up. The best way to do this is to use the AutoExec macro. The AutoExec macro is nothing more than a regular macro with a special name. Access automatically runs it based on its name. You should note that the AutoExec macro gets executed after any form is opened from the Startup properties. This is something to consider if you are using the Startup properties and you place any events in the macro other than a call to the `DetermineByPass` function.

Once you've set up the `AutoExec` macro to call your function and the startup form is in place (called from either the `AutoExec` macro or the Startup properties), open the database without holding down the Shift key. This allows the `AllowBypassKey` property to be added to the database for the first time.

If you open the Access database with the *AllowByPass.txt* file in the same directory as the Access MDB, it sets the `AllowBypassKey` property to `True` but doesn't allow the bypass the first time the database is opened. The Access database must be opened a second time while holding down the Shift key to bypass the Startup properties, including the `AutoExec` macro, because now the `AllowBypassKey` internal property is set to `True`. Removing the *AllowBy-Pass.txt* file from the database's directory resets the property to `False` the next time the database is started up without holding down the Shift key, thereby preventing the next user from bypassing the Startup properties and the `AutoExec` macro.

If you use Access 2003, and you don't have your macro security setting set to Low, you need to hold down the Shift key when clicking the Open command button of the Access Security Warning screen shown in Figure 8-15.

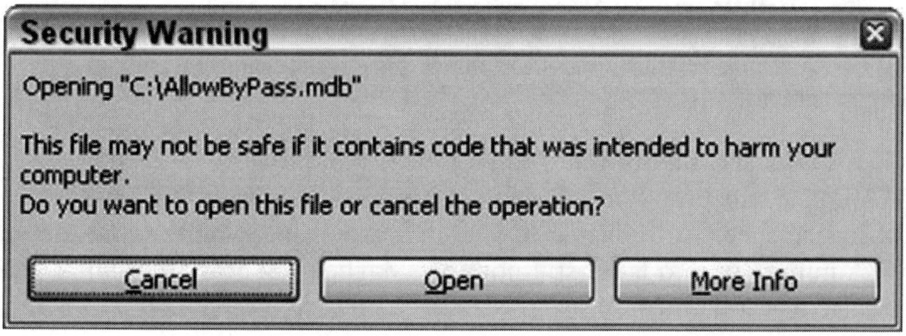

Figure 8-15. Access 2003 security warning

Access ADP

Because most ADPs use ADO only, the developers at Microsoft provided a way to disable the Shift key without referencing a DAO library directly or indirectly. This method of adding the `AllowBypassKey` is much simpler, but unfortunately, it works only with ADP projects. The following sample code works identically to the code for an Access MDB, without the need for a function such as `ChangeProperty`:

```
Public Function DetermineByPass()
    If Len(Dir(CurrentProject.Path & "\AllowByPass.txt")) = 0 Then
```

```
          CurrentProject.Properties.Add "AllowBypassKey", False
      Else
          CurrentProject.Properties.Add "AllowBypassKey", True
      End If
  End Function
```

Although this method for setting the AllowBypassKey property is much shorter and arguably easier to use with an ADP, it does have a drawback. You have no way of setting the DDL parameter to prevent someone from changing your AllowBypassKey property with automation.

Be Careful

This technique of disabling the Shift key is powerful; make sure you don't lock yourself out of your database. You might want to consider changing the DDL parameter in the sample code for the Access MDB to False so that you can use remote automation to reset it if you need to. If you do lock yourself out, you can always create a new database and import all the objects over to the new database, then reset your Startup properties and replace the database you got locked out of with the new copy you just made.

—*Steve Huff*

HACK ## Inform Users of a Long Process

#81   While your code is conquering a long looping process, users might think their system has crashed, unless you provide some visual clue that a process is running.

When a user clicks a button to run a process, and that process takes a while to complete, the user won't know if the process is still running or if the system has crashed. Just imagine it: you click a button on a form and ... nothing. A minute or two later, still nothing. Maybe even 5 or 10 minutes later, the system is still unresponsive.

This is nerve-wracking for the user sitting in front of his computer. He has to weigh whether he should try the break key or let the system continue to look like it is hung up. On the other hand, if he stops a process that was running smoothly after all, he will just have to start it all over again. Ugh!

Don't leave your users in this predicament. You know that 100,000 records are being processed and it takes a while. But your users might not know this and get frustrated waiting.

This hack takes advantage of the SysCmd method. With SysCmd, you can write messages in the status bar during CPU-intensive processing, even with screen refresh turned off. Figure 8-16 shows a form (a rather simple one, I admit). The button has been clicked, and the process is chugging away. Notice the status bar in the lower-left corner of the screen; a continuously updated message is being generated there.

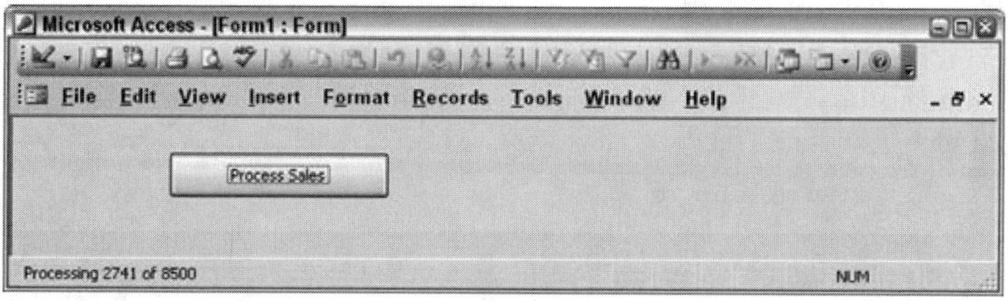

Figure 8-16. Providing a feedback message in the status bar

The message in the status bar says, "Processing 2741 of 8500." Thinking like a programmer, you probably realize that to have the total number of records being processed in the message means a record count property is being used.

The Code

Here is the code behind the button:

```
Private Sub cmdProcessSales_Click( )
  Dim conn As ADODB.Connection
  Set conn = CurrentProject.Connection
  Dim recset As New ADODB.Recordset
  Dim total_records As Long
  Dim record_num As Long
  record_num = 0
  recset.Open "Select * From SalesRecords", conn, adOpenKeyset,
adLockOptimistic
  total_records = recset.RecordCount
  Do Until recset.EOF
    recset.Fields("NetSales") = recset.Fields("Sales") - recset.
Fields("Costs")
    record_num = record_num + 1
    feedback_msg = "Processing " & record_num & " of " & total_records
    SysCmd acSysCmdSetStatus, feedback_msg
  recset.MoveNext
  Loop
  recset.Close
  Set recset = Nothing
  SysCmd acSysCmdClearStatus
End Sub
```

The code creates a recordset and loops through it. Prior to the looping, the RecordCount property populates the total_records variable. During the looping, another variable, record_num, is incremented. These two variables are used to create the message:

```
feedback_msg = "Processing " & record_num & " of " & total_records
```

Then the message is used in the SysCmd method:

```
SysCmd acSysCmdSetStatus, feedback_msg
```

Finally, at the end of the processing, the code clears the status bar by giving SysCmd a clear status flag:

```
SysCmd acSysCmdClearStatus
```

Hacking the Hack

Providing a feedback message of the type described here is helpful in gauging the length of a process. If the feedback consisted of just the number of records processed without indicating the total number to be processed, you still would not know how long the process will take to complete. For example, a simple message of "Processing 2471" doesn't let you know if you are halfway done, are nearly done, or have hardly even begun.

Of course, the message format of "Processing X of XX" works only in a loop. Other long processes might not be based on a loop. A complex query can take time, especially when it needs to work on many records. It isn't possible to break into a query in the same way, so the thing to do is to put the time that the process started in the status bar.

The Now function returns the time from the system clock. By displaying that in the status bar, you're at least telling users when the process started so that they can compare the start time to the clock time in the system tray at the right of the Windows taskbar.

H A C K   Allow Users to Choose a Back-End Database
#82   Store ODBC connection strings in a table so they are ready to go when needed.

Certain system applications provide more than one database you can interact with. As long as the structure of the various databases and/or their tables is based on a common schema, it is possible to swap the back ends in and out. An easy way to do this is to provide the available connections in a list in which users select the database to use.

Figure 8-17 shows a table that simply contains ODBC connection strings.

On the form in which users select a connection, they just see the friendly names, provided in the table's second column (the first column serves as a

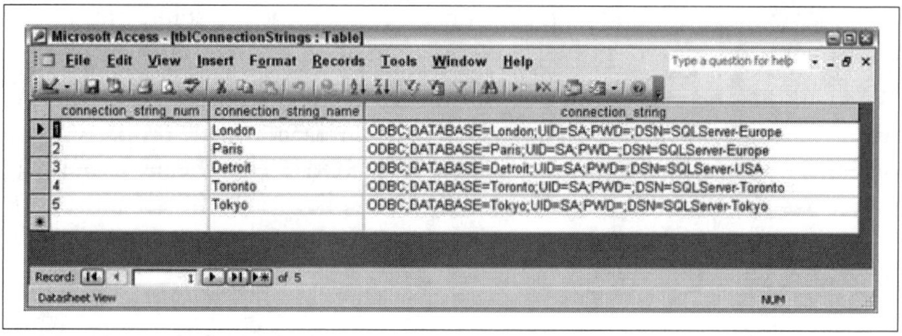

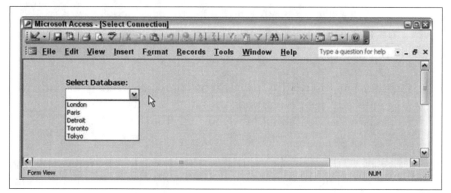

Figure 8-17. A table filled with ODBC connection strings

way to sort the list). Figure 8-18 shows the form and the combo box from which a connection is selected.

Figure 8-18. Selecting a database connection

The value of the combo box is used in code to set the Connection property for an ADO connection object, like this:

```
Dim conn As ADODB.Connection
Set conn = New ADODB.Connection
conn.ConnectionString = Me.cmbConnections
conn.Open
```

In this manner, users can easily change the database they are working with at will.

HACK #83 Override the Timeout Interval

In a busy network environment, a little patience is sometimes necessary.

When using Access to connect to an external database, performance depends on a number of factors. One of these is the network—specifically in regard to bandwidth and traffic. Bandwidth might be constant, but add in the dynamic of network traffic, and you often don't know what to expect.

To be on the safe side of having your processing complete, even if it takes a while longer, you can turn off the ADO CommandTimeout property. The default is for a timeout to occur after 30 seconds. This means that if the server has not communicated back to your application in 30 seconds, your application assumes a response isn't coming. You might then see a timeout message such as the one shown in Figure 8-19.

Figure 8-19. A timeout expired error message

Setting the timeout interval to 0 turns off this property. Your application will then wait indefinitely for a response. Assuming an ADO connection object named conn is being used, this is how you apply the setting:

```
conn.CommandTimeout = 0
```

The drawback to this approach is that you really might wait forever. By the very nature of turning off the timeout, you have no specific period of reasonable time to expect for the processing to complete. If someone pulled the plug on the server, you might not know it. If it makes sense, though, you can experiment with different settings. Note that the value used is in seconds, so a value of 300 sets the timeout interval to five minutes. Knowing the wait is no more than five minutes for success or failure might make more sense than waiting indefinitely.

HACK #84 Save Values from Unbound Controls for Later Recall

Give users a way to automatically recreate the way a form was set up so that they don't have to reenter information

Every time a form is closed, the values in unbound controls are lost (this isn't always strictly true, but it generally is).

Imagine a form that is filled with many unbound controls. A user makes several selections and expects to need to reuse the same selections another time. Saving the values in the unbound controls, and making them identifiable and recallable, can be a big timesaver. Let's call this a *scheme*.

Saving the values from unbound controls doesn't make them bound to anything. The values are saved to a table but only by creating code to do so. Figure 8-20 shows a form with three unbound listboxes.

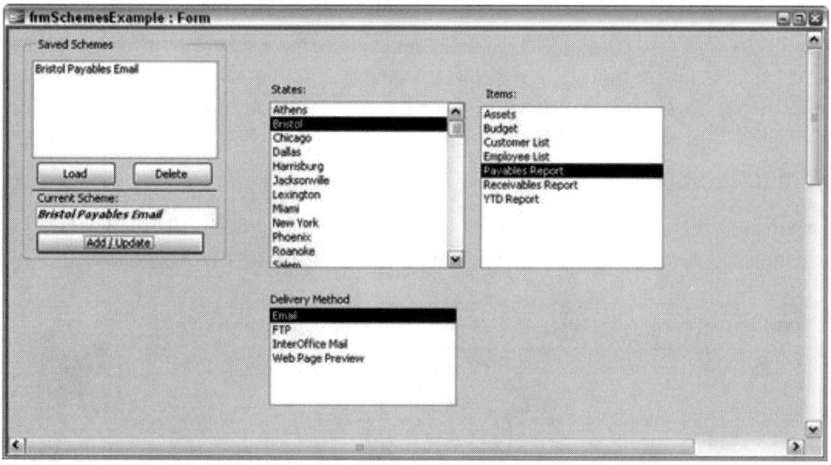

Figure 8-20. A form in which schemes of control values are saved

A selection has been made in each listbox, a scheme name has been entered, and the Add/Update button has been clicked. This has created a scheme that stores the values from the listboxes.

The Code

The code behind the Add/Update button looks like this:

```
Dim conn As ADODB.Connection
Set conn = CurrentProject.Connection
Dim rs As ADODB.Recordset
Set rs = New ADODB.Recordset

ssql = "Insert into tblSchemes Values("
ssql = ssql & "'" & Me.txtSchemeName & "', "
ssql = ssql & "'" & Me.listOffices & "', "
ssql = ssql & "'" & Me.listItems & "', "
ssql = ssql & "'" & Me.listDeliveryMethod & "')"

'delete scheme first
delete_ssql = "Delete * From tblSchemes Where Scheme='" & schemename & "'"
conn.Execute (delete_ssql)
```

```
'now insert scheme
conn.Execute (ssql)

conn.Close
Set conn = Nothing

Me.lstSchemes.Requery
Exit Sub
err_end:
MsgBox Err.Description
```

Note that some of the code has been removed. Checking for nulls and such isn't shown here, to keep the focus on the point of the hack.

Running the Code

The values in the listboxes, along with the supplied name of the scheme, are inserted as a record into the tblSchemes table shown in Figure 8-21.

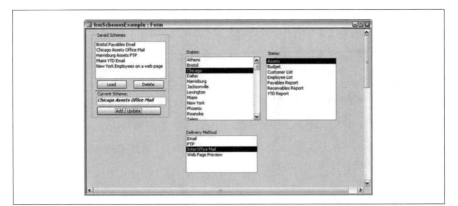

Figure 8-21. The control values stored in a table

As more and more schemes are saved, the listbox of schemes (on the left) fills up. From this list, a scheme can be reentered on the form. Figure 8-22 shows the numerous schemes now available.

Figure 8-22. Many schemes to choose from

The Load and Delete buttons work with the table records and the form. Load populates the unbound controls with values stored in the table for whichever scheme is selected in the scheme listbox. Delete simply deletes the appropriate record from the table.

Hacking the Hack

The final thing to consider is what to do when unbound listboxes and combo boxes are set to multiselect. This allows more than one item to be selected. In this situation, you're storing relational data. For example, one scheme can have more than one selection in a listbox. To handle this, you literally create a set of related tables. One holds the general scheme information, and the other holds a record for every value in the listbox. The tables relate on a key—the scheme name.

Figure 8-23 shows how this works.

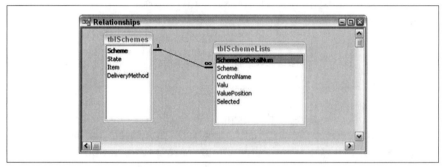

Figure 8-23. Saving schemes that have multiple selections per control

The secondary table stores the scheme name, the name of the control, the value of the control, the item's position in the list, and whether the item is selected. Every list item is stored, along with its position and its selected state. When a scheme is reloaded, the various parameters are needed to recreate the list and to reflect which items were selected.

HACK
#85

Sort Records Randomly

Get a unique sort of records whenever you need one.

Records in a table are always in some kind of order. A primary key or other index might have been applied. Even when all indexes are removed, the records are in the order in which the table received them.

A hack is available for getting a true random sort of the records. Literally sort them on random values! To get this to work, you add an extra field to the table. You then populate the field with randomly generated values. Let's look at some code:

```
Sub random_sort_field( )
    Dim conn As ADODB.Connection
    Set conn = CurrentProject.Connection
    Dim ssql As String
    Dim recset As New ADODB.Recordset
    Dim tbl As String
    tbl = "tblCustomers" ' the table name could be passed as an argument

    ssql = "Alter Table " & tbl & " Add Column RandomSort Long"
    'may already have field so trap error
    On Error Resume Next
    conn.Execute ssql

    Randomize
    recset.Open "select * From " & tbl, conn, adOpenDynamic, adLockOptimistic
    Do Until recset.EOF
        recset.Fields("RandomSort") = Int(Rnd( ) * 50000)
        recset.MoveNext
    Loop
    recset.Close
    Set recset = noting
    conn.Close
    MsgBox "done"
End Sub
```

The table—tblCustomers in this example—receives a new field named Random-Sort. However, the field might already be there from the last time this code was run, so an On Error statement precedes the operation:

```
ssql = "Alter Table " & tbl & " Add Column RandomSort Long"
'may already have field so trap error
On Error Resume Next
conn.Execute ssql
```

The code then cycles through the table, and the RandomSort field is populated with random values using the RND function:

```
recset.Fields("RandomSort") = Int(Rnd( ) * 50000)
```

Now, the tblCustomers table can be sorted on the RandomSort field, as shown in Figure 8-24.

Each time the routine runs, the values in the RandomSort field change, thereby providing a new sort.

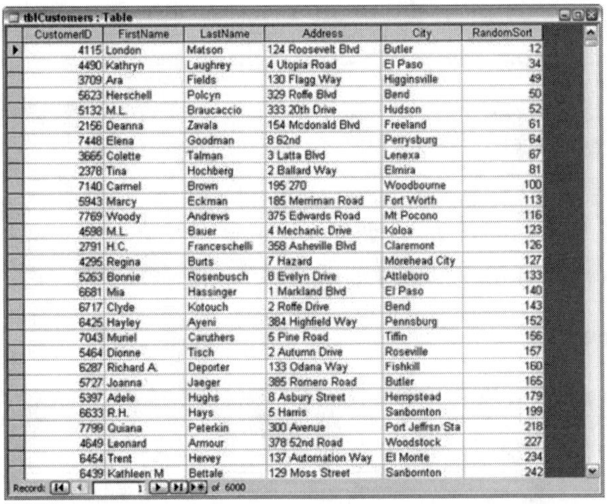

tblCustomers : Table

CustomerID	FirstName	LastName	Address	City	RandomSort
4115	London	Matson	124 Roosevelt Blvd	Butler	12
4490	Kathryn	Laughrey	4 Utopia Road	El Paso	34
3709	Ara	Fields	130 Flagg Way	Higginsville	49
5623	Herschell	Polcyn	329 Roffe Blvd	Bend	50
5132	M.L.	Braucaccio	333 20th Drive	Hudson	52
2156	Deanna	Zavala	154 Mcdonald Blvd	Freeland	61
7448	Elena	Goodman	8 62nd	Perrysburg	64
3665	Colette	Talman	3 Latta Blvd	Lenexa	67
2378	Tina	Hochberg	2 Ballard Way	Elmira	81
7140	Carmel	Brown	195 270	Woodbourne	100
5943	Marcy	Eckman	185 Merriman Road	Fort Worth	113
7769	Woody	Andrews	375 Edwards Road	Mt Pocono	116
4598	M.L.	Bauer	4 Mechanic Drive	Koloa	123
2791	H.C.	Franceschelli	358 Asheville Blvd	Claremont	126
4295	Regina	Burts	7 Hazard	Morehead City	127
5263	Bonnie	Rosenbusch	8 Evelyn Drive	Attleboro	133
6681	Mia	Hassinger	1 Markland Blvd	El Paso	140
6717	Clyde	Kotouch	2 Roffe Drive	Bend	143
6425	Hayley	Ayeni	384 Highfield Way	Pennsburg	152
7043	Muriel	Caruthers	5 Pine Road	Tiffin	156
5464	Dionne	Tisch	2 Autumn Drive	Roseville	157
6287	Richard A.	Deporter	133 Odana Way	Fishkill	160
5727	Joanna	Jaeger	385 Romero Road	Butler	165
5397	Adele	Hughs	8 Asbury Street	Hempstead	179
6633	R.H.	Hays	5 Harris	Sanbornton	199
7799	Quiana	Peterkin	300 Avenue	Port Jeffrsn Sta	218
4649	Leonard	Armour	378 52nd Road	Woodstock	227
6454	Trent	Hervey	137 Automation Way	El Monte	234
6439	Kathleen M	Bettale	129 Moss Street	Sanbornton	242

Record: 1 of 6000

Figure 8-24. Randomly sorted records

HACK #86 Bulk-Update Controls on a Form

Tap the Controls property to make fast property changes.

When working with a form's design, typically you set properties for controls with the property sheet. You can select single controls one by one and set properties, or you can select a handful of controls and update them together. When you use the latter method, the number of properties listed on the property sheet shrinks to just those that are common to all the selected controls.

This works fine for the most part—that is, setting properties to multiple controls isn't difficult. But what if you had to see what a property is before deciding whether to change it? In this situation, the property sheet won't help you. When multiple controls are selected, the property sheet can't display individual control properties. It displays a property's value if all the selected controls have the same value for the property, but that isn't always the case.

Accessing Control Properties in Code

Luckily, Access has a `Controls` property that belongs to the form object, and a `Properties` property for the controls themselves. This makes it possible to read and write control properties. To start, Example 8-6 shows a routine that reads control properties.

Bulk-Update Controls on a Form

Example 8-6. Reading control properties

```
Sub list_control_properties()
Dim form_name As String
Dim ctl As Control
Dim list_type As Integer
Dim prop_num As Integer

form_name = "frm1" ' change as needed!
DoCmd.OpenForm (form_name), acDesign

list_type = 2 ' change to use with Select Case below

Select Case list_type
  Case 1
  ' list names and values of properties for single control
  With Forms(form_name).Controls(1)
    For prop_num = 0 To .Properties.Count - 1
      Debug.Print .Name & ":   " & _
      .Properties(prop_num).Name & ":   " & _
        .Properties(prop_num).Value
    Next
  End With
  Case 2
  ' list value of entered property for all controls on form
  With Forms(form_name)
    For Each ctl In Forms(frm_name).Controls
      On Error Resume Next
      Debug.Print ctl.Name & ":  Caption=" & _
        ctl.Properties("Caption")
    Next
  End With
End SelectEnd Sub
```

The routine in Example 8-6 has two variations of reading control properties, which you can choose by setting the list_type variable to 1 or 2. A Select Case statement uses this number to run one or the other code snippet. When the list_type variable is set to 1, the properties of a single control are read. In particular, each property's name and value are written to the Immediate window. The single control is referenced in Example 8-6 simply as .Controls(1). You can enter the name of an actual control instead by putting the name in quotes.

Figure 8-25 shows the results of returning all the property names and values for a single control.

When the list_type variable is set to 2, all the controls on the form are tapped. A single property that is entered into this line indicates which property to return:

```
Debug.Print ctl.Name & ":  Caption=" & ctl.Properties("Caption")
```

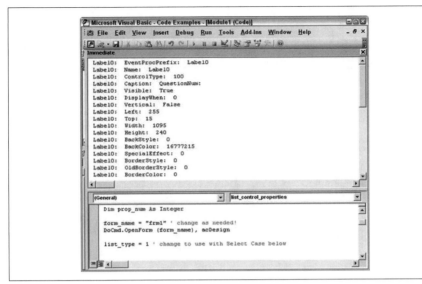

Figure 8-25. Returning a list of control properties

Also note the `On Error Resume Next` statement before this line. This line is included because not all properties exist for all controls. In this example, the `Caption` property is being accessed, but some controls, such as text boxes, don't have captions. The error trap keeps the procedure going, and only controls that have the indicated property make it into the Immediate window, as shown in Figure 8-26.

Note that the routine in Figure 8-26 addresses a form in the code. The form must be open for the code to work, presumably in Design mode because the point of this hack is to make bulk design changes. The `DoCmd` statement takes care of opening the form in Design mode; just provide the name of your form. In the following line, replace *frm1* with the name of your form:

```
form_name = "frm1" ' change as needed!
```

Changing Properties the Easy Way

Example 8-7 shows a routine that changes the `ForeColor` property to red for all text boxes on the form. To work with a single type of control, the code tests the `ControlType` property. If the control type matches the enumeration value, the property is updated.

Bulk-Update Controls on a Form

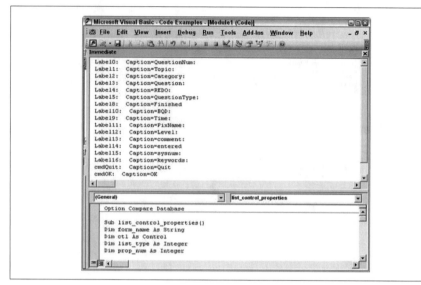

Figure 8-26. Returning the Caption property for controls that have one

Example 8-7. Working with a single control type

```
Sub update_controls( )
Dim ctl As Control
Dim form_name As String
form_name = "frm1"
DoCmd.OpenForm (form_name), acDesign
  With Forms(form_name)
    For Each ctl In Forms(frm_name).Controls
      If ctl.ControlType = acTextBox Then
        ctl.Properties("ForeColor") = vbRed
      End If
    Next
  End With
End Sub
```

You can choose to change a property for all the controls on a form or for particular control types. If you're working with the full set of controls, it's a good idea to use an On Error Resume Next statement so that the process won't bomb when a control doesn't have the particular property.

The code in Example 8-7 addresses text boxes only. Figure 8-27 shows how to use the Object Browser to find the members of the acControlType enumeration.

Figure 8-27. Reviewing control-type constants

Provide Complete XML Control to Any Version of Access

Use the MSXML Parser to make XML native to your applications.

Support for XML has been growing through successive Access releases, but complete XML control still isn't available. For instance, Access 2003 supports importing and exporting XML, but even so, the level of functionality is limited. For example, you can't import attributes (a type of XML data).

Referencing an external XML parser not only improves the XML support, but also provides the same level of support to any version of Access. This is possible because the parser is an independent piece of technology. As long as you can reference it, you can use it to its fullest.

Referencing the Parser

In the Access VB editor, use the Tools → References menu to open the References dialog box, shown in Figure 8-28.

Scroll through the list, and find Microsoft XML. The reference will include a version number; any version will do. If you are curious how the parser versions differ, visit Microsoft's web site (*http://www.microsoft.com*).

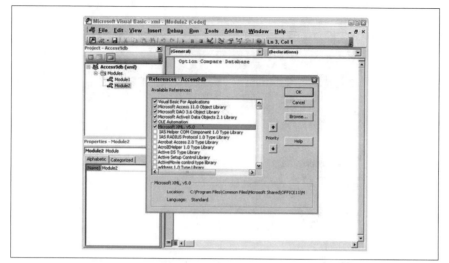

Figure 8-28. Adding a reference to the XML parser

 If you don't find the Microsoft XML reference on your computer, download the MSXML parser from Microsoft (*http:// www.microsoft.com/xml*).

With the reference set, you can work with XML in many sophisticated ways. This hack isn't the place to learn how to use the parser (see the end of the hack for some resources). Instead, we'll preview using the parser to load XML data and insert it into an Access table. Along the way, we'll accomplish a couple of tricks: filtering XML data and loading attributes.

An XML file filled with employee information has been prepared, as shown in Figure 8-29.

The Code

In an Access code module, the following code has been entered. This code uses objects available from the parser reference:

```
Sub read_xml( )
    On Error GoTo err_end
    Dim conn As New ADODB.Connection
    Set conn = CurrentProject.Connection
    Dim xmlobj As DOMDocument
    Dim xml_list As IXMLDOMNodeList
    Dim xml_node As IXMLDOMNode
    Set xmlobj = New DOMDocument
    xmlobj.async = False
    xmlobj.Load "C:\Employees.xml"
```

Figure 8-29. The Employees.xml file

```
Set xml_list = xmlobj.selectNodes _
  ("Employees/Department/Employee")
For Each xml_node In xml_list
   ssql = "Insert Into tblEmployees Values (" & _
      xml_node.childNodes(0).Text & ", '" & _
      xml_node.childNodes(1).Text & "', '" & _
      xml_node.parentNode.Attributes(0).Text & "')"

 conn.Execute ssql
 Next
 MsgBox "done"
err_end:
 MsgBox Err.Description
End Sub
```

The XML file is loaded into the xmlobj object variable:

```
xmlobj.Load "C:\Employees.xml"
```

Typical XML objects are nodes and node lists. A *list* is a collection of nodes. The actual nodes are the employee elements, which are children of the department nodes:

```
Set xml_list = xmlobj.selectNodes _
    ("Employees/Department/Employee")
```

Employee nodes have two children: EmployeeID and Name. These child elements and the parent department element are the basis from which a SQL Insert statement is created.

```
ssql = "Insert Into tblEmployees Values (" & _
  xml_node.childNodes(0).Text & ", '" & _
  xml_node.childNodes(1).Text & "', '" & _
  xml_node.parentNode.Attributes(0).Text & "')"
```

After the routine runs, the tblEmployees table is populated with the XML data, as shown in Figure 8-30.

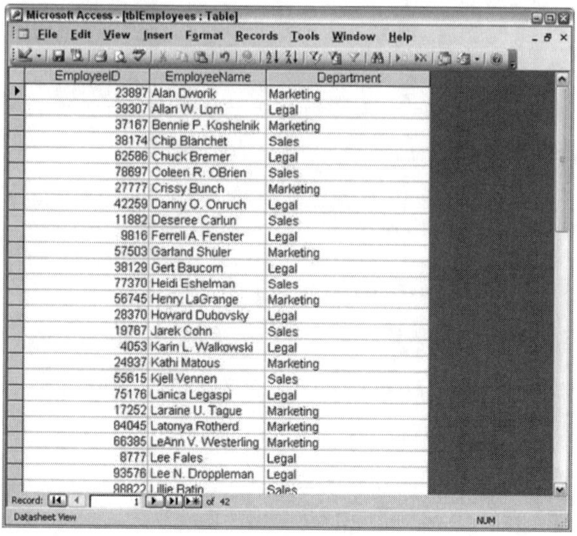

Figure 8-30. The XML data now in Access

So, in just a short routine, we've accomplished two things that are typically taken for granted as being impossible. One is that now, only Access 2003 can work with XML in a robust way, and the other is that attributes can't be imported. The routine in this hack will work with any version of Access that references the parser and clearly has no problem putting an attribute's value into an Access table.

See Also

- "Use Access as an XML Database" [Hack #95]
- *XML Hacks* (O'Reilly)
- *Office 2003 XML* (O'Reilly)

Use Custom Enumerations

HACK #88

Use familiar names, instead of memorizing equivalent numbers, to avoid errors and speed up coding.

Having a list of properties and methods appear while typing really helps when you're coding. For example, entering Application in a code module and then entering a period opens up a list of methods and properties that belong to the Application object.

You can use this same helpful facility to provide you with constants that are particular to your project or business. Take, for example, an application that has to take the department code into account for some specific processing. Each department has a unique code number, but the numbers themselves are meaningless. This makes the code numbers difficult to remember.

That is where a set of enumerated variables comes in handy. Not only can you give names to the numerical code numbers, but the names become available in a list while typing.

Figure 8-31 shows a VBA code module. In the declaration section, I used the Enum statement to create the variables. I gave a name to the block (DepartmentCodes in this example) and used the End Enum statement to end the block.

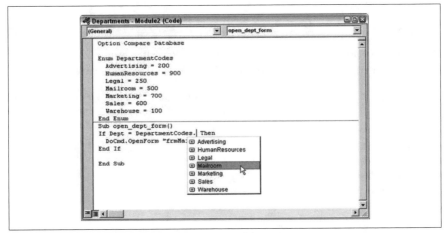

Figure 8-31. Using Enum for more efficient coding

Within the Enum block, I assigned each department's code number to its name. Now, when coding within a procedure, all I have to do is type DepartmentName and enter a period. The enumerated variables appear, and I can select the one I need. By selecting one, I'm really selecting the department code number, but I no longer have to memorize the numbers. This reduces errors because honestly, up until I used this technique I could not remember if Advertising was 200 or 600. Thankfully, by using Enum, I'm able to let go of remembering such things and can concentrate on the more important aspects of my projects.

HACK #89 Convert Text to the Desired Case

Have any text string be returned in uppercase, lowercase, or proper case.

One of the occasional requirements thrown at a developer is the ability to change the case of the text. This isn't a really difficult problem. All you have to do is use the UCase or LCase functions, which return a text string as all capital letters or all lowercase letters, respectively.

However, no function is available for returning *proper case* (a.k.a. *mixed case* or *sentence case*): text in which each word starts with an uppercase letter, with the rest of the word in lowercase.

Microsoft Word has the ability to return proper case, but Access doesn't. While you're waiting for the two development teams at Microsoft to get together on this, here is a function that returns all three case types: upper, lower, and proper. The function takes two arguments: the text to be converted and the type of treatment to apply.

The Code

When converting to upper- or lowercase, the function simply uses the respective built-in UCase or LCase function. Why reinvent the wheel?

To convert text to proper case requires a looping process. If you think about it, all you need to do is apply UCase or LCase to each character in the text. The trick is to know which letters get which treatment.

```
Function change_case(txt As String, case_type As String) As String
  Select Case case_type
  Case "Upper"
    change_case = UCase(txt)
  Case "Lower"
    change_case = LCase(txt)
  Case "Proper"
    'create proper case
    Dim space_flag As Boolean
    space_flag = False
    'first letter is alway uppercase
    change_case = UCase(Left(txt, 1))
    For test_case = 2 To Len(txt)
      If Mid(txt, test_case, 1) = " " Then
        space_flag = True
```

```
          change_case = change_case & LCase(Mid(txt, test_case, 1))
        Else
          If space_flag = True Then
            change_case = change_case & UCase(Mid(txt, test_case, 1))
            space_flag = False
          Else
            change_case = change_case & LCase(Mid(txt, test_case, 1))
          End If
        End If
      Next test_case
  End Select
End Function
```

To start, the first letter of the string becomes uppercase. That one is a given. Then, a loop cycles through the rest of the text string. A character can be a space. When a space is encountered, a flag is set to true. When a nonspace character is encountered, one of two things can happen:

If space_flag *is true*
> The character comes directly after a space, so change the character to uppercase, and set space_flag to false.

If space_flag *is* false
> The character followed another nonspace character. Therefore, the character being evaluated isn't the first letter of a word, so change it to lowercase.

Note that you don't need to test whether a character is upper- or lowercase while it is being evaluated. If it follows a space, it ends up as uppercase, regardless of the case in which it was typed. The same approach holds true for characters that don't follow a space: they are set to lowercase regardless.

Running the Code

The change_case function needs two arguments. You can specify them from field controls, from code, or even from within the Immediate window. Figure 8-32 shows how the function is called from a form.

A text box contains the string of text, a listbox offers the three case types, and a command button calls the function with this little snippet of code:

```
Private Sub Command2_Click()
  Dim z As String
  z = change_case(Me.Text1, Me.List1)
  MsgBox z
End Sub
```

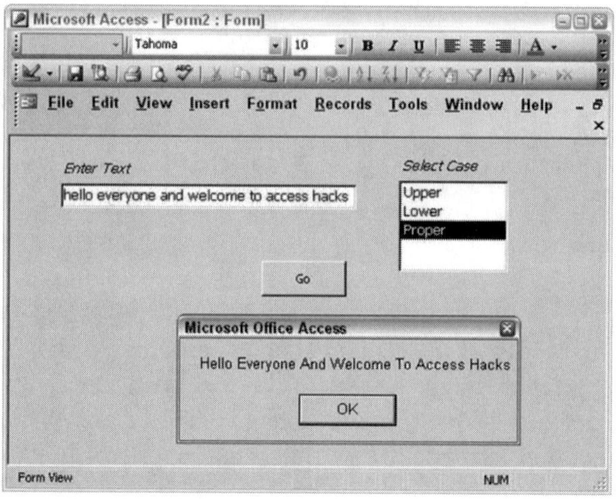

Figure 8-32. *Returning text in a selected case*

HACK #90   Create a Code Library

Make your favorite custom functions available in all your databases.

As a developer, I find I often create and use the same functions on a number of different projects. Too many times I have had to hunt down some code I wanted to reuse. This has taken a good amount of time because not only do I have to recall where I used the code before, but I also need to remember which computer it is on!

The solution to this chaos is to put all the code in one database and use the database as a code library. A good way to do this is to clean up the code and assemble it in one or more code modules, in a single database. Make all the code routines be functions so that they return values. Then, just save the database and close it. Finally, change the extension of the database to *.mda*.

Figure 8-33 shows a module filled with functions. This module is in the Access file that has the extension changed to *.mda*.

With a changed extension, now the file is recognized as an add-in, as shown in Figure 8-34.

From a regular Access database, the code library is referenced. In the VB editor, use Tools → References to open the References dialog box. From the dialog, browse to the location of the saved code library. It might be necessary to change "Files of type" in the Add Reference dialog to Add-ins, as shown in Figure 8-35.

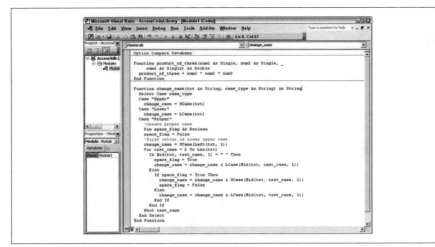

Figure 8-33. A module of code functions

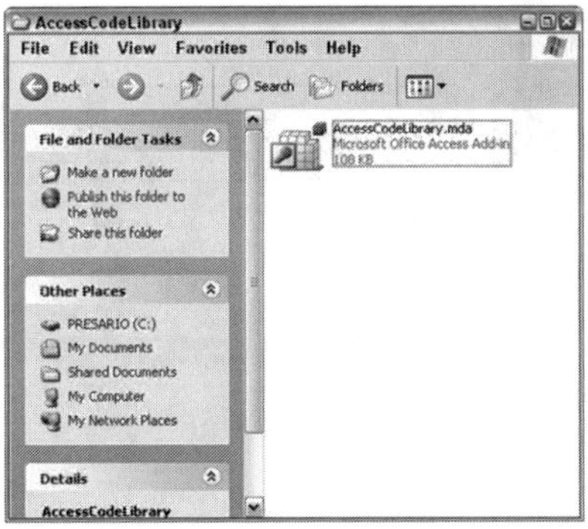

Figure 8-34. Recognizing the file as an add-in

Now, the functions in the code library are available in the regular database. Figure 8-36 shows how they are listed in the Object Browser.

Over time, as you create more and more routines, the value of keeping them in one place becomes a real timesaver. You never know when you will need to use an algorithm you created years ago.

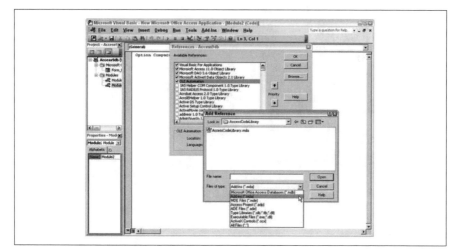

Figure 8-35. Referencing the add-in

Figure 8-36. Viewing the custom functions in the Object Browser

HACK #91 Automatically Check for Database Table Updates

Pull updated objects from a master database when your database opens.

One of the issues you face with a distributed application is how to propagate updated tables to the user community. This happens when you must process new data or when lookup lists have new values that have table data as the source. Redistributing the entire database is one way to go, although that disrupts the workflow. In that scenario, users must stop what they are doing, get the new file, and save it somewhere. Even when that process is automated, you can't be sure someone is currently using the database you are about to overwrite.

Instead, here's a great way to have users' applications update themselves. The update occurs when a user starts up her local copy of the database. A code routine checks the database's tables against those in a master database on the network. When a table in the master database is found to be newer, it is copied into the user's database.

Running Code at Startup

Each user's locally installed database contains a table named tblTableVersions that has two fields: one contains the names of the tables in the database, and the other has the last modified date of each table. When the database is opened, a code routine opens the master database and compares the modified date of the tables in the master database with the records in the tblTableVersions table.

You might wonder why we don't just compare the modified dates of the tables themselves in the local database. Why is a table kept with the modified dates? The reason is a safeguard: users might alter the tables locally, thereby changing the last modified date on local tables. The point is to check if the master database contains updated tables that have not been used yet. The dates in the local tblTableVersions table are the modified dates of tables in the master database—from the last time any particular table was copied.

Figure 8-37 shows the tblTableVersions table. Two tables have dates that are in December 2004.

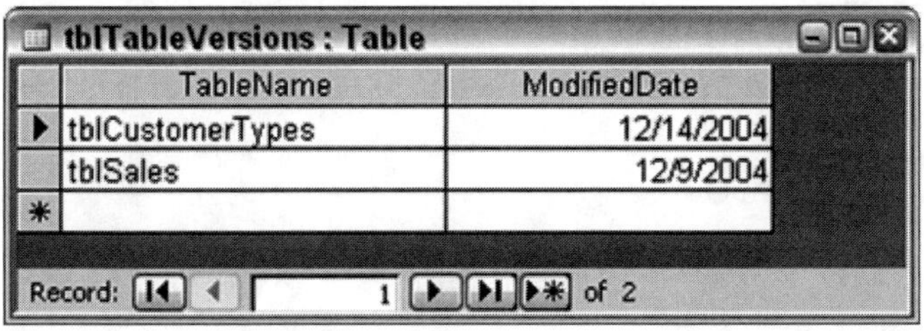

TableName	ModifiedDate
tblCustomerTypes	12/14/2004
tblSales	12/9/2004

Record: 1 of 2

Figure 8-37. Keeping track of the last modified date

The Code

When the local database opens, the AutoExec macro calls the following get_ updates function, which therefore runs upon startup:

```
Function get_updates()
On Error GoTo err_end
Dim update_db As String
update_db = "G:\UpdateDB.mdb"

Dim cat As New ADOX.Catalog
Dim tbl As New ADOX.Table
Dim conn As ADODB.Connection
Set conn = CurrentProject.Connection

Dim local_tbl As String
Dim current_object_date As Date
' Open the catalog
cat.ActiveConnection = "Provider=Microsoft.Jet.OLEDB.4.0;" & _
    "Data Source=" & update_db
For Each tbl In cat.Tables
  If Left(tbl.Name, 4) <> "MSys" Then
      current_object_date = _
        DLookup("[ModifiedDate]", "tblTableVersions", _
          "[TableName] = '" & tbl.Name & "'")
      If tbl.DateModified > current_object_date Then
        DoCmd.DeleteObject acTable, tbl.Name
        DoCmd.TransferDatabase acImport, "Microsoft Access", _
        update_db, acTable, tbl.Name, tbl.Name
        'store new date
        conn.Execute ("Update tblTableVersions Set ModifiedDate=#" & _
          tbl.DateModified & "# Where TableName='" & tbl.Name & "'")
      End If
  End If
Next
Set cat = Nothing
Set conn = Nothing
MsgBox "done"
Exit Function
err_end:
MsgBox Err.Description
End Function
```

Running the Code

A mixture of VBA, ADOX, and ADO works together to check for updates. An ADOX catalog object is created and is set to the master database—*G:\ UpdateDB.mdb* in this example. All the tables in the master database are examined; however, system tables aren't included. All system tables start with MSys [Hack #15].

The DateModified property of each table in the master database is checked against the locally stored date for the same named tables. When it finds that a master database table has a newer modified date, DoCmd deletes the table in the local database and imports the new table from the master database. Then, a SQL Update statement updates the date for the table in the tblTable-Names table.

After the routine completes, the user can go about her business as usual. The application works as always because the table names have not changed.

The only caveat with this hack is that it is useful to update tables that don't share in a relationship. Related tables need to have the relationship broken before you delete and then reestablish them. Therefore, this hack is perfect for tables that contain the source for lookup lists or that don't participate in a relationship. You can develop additional code to test for relationships and handle them appropriately.

Third-Party Applications
Hacks 92–95

Much of the focus in Access books involves how to manage building an application—working with tables, queries, forms, and reports—and applying solutions with macros and code. However, once you've completed all that work, you might need a tool to document your database **[Hack #92]**. Similarly, when you create an application, you might not be considering all the management, functionality, and utilities that can go into your database. Fortunately, a product is available that fleshes this out for you **[Hack #93]**.

Of course, data is the point of a database. How often have you designed a database and then had to find some data to test it with? You can enter data manually, or you can use a product that creates data for you **[Hack #94]**.

In addition to all this, this chapter also shows you how to build an application without any tables. "Use Access as an XML Database" **[Hack #95]** shows how to run an XML database from Access, reading from and writing to an external XML file.

HACK #92 Document Your Database with Total Access Analyzer

Get the full nuts-and-bolts skinny on your database.

Even a simple Access database has a lot in it. Just take a table of data, a form, a few controls, and a report, and the number of properties is in the hundreds. A large database has an unimaginable number of items in it.

Now, imagine a utility that lets you drill down anywhere in your database and uncover nuggets of information you probably didn't even know about. Enter the Total Access Analyzer by FMS, Inc. (*http://www.fmsinc.com*). This outstanding product tells you everything about your database. It leaves nothing out.

Running the Analyzer

After you install the Analyzer, it is available as an add-in. Regardless of which database you have open, just go to the Tools → Add-Ins menu to find the Analyzer. The Analyzer runs from a main form, shown in Figure 9-1.

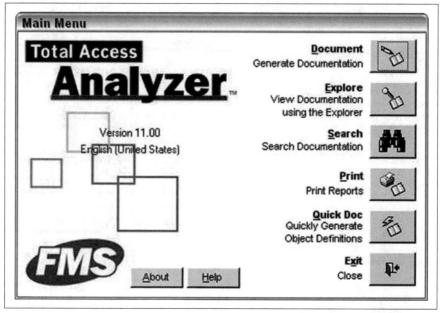

Figure 9-1. Total Access Analyzer

To get started, click the Document button. This runs the Documentation Wizard, which walks you through selecting which items to document. Figure 9-2 shows the first screen of the Documentation Wizard.

After making a selection, click the Next button to bring up the wizard's second screen, shown in Figure 9-3.

On this screen, you can select to document relationships, document security, and generate field cross references that show you where fields are used throughout the database, among other things. Generating field cross references is a great feature because although it's good to get details about a field, it's even better to know where the field's data is presented (on forms and reports).

The documentation process works by writing the results to an external file. In the third wizard screen, shown in Figure 9-4, you can select where this external file goes (or just accept the default location) and then schedule the documentation.

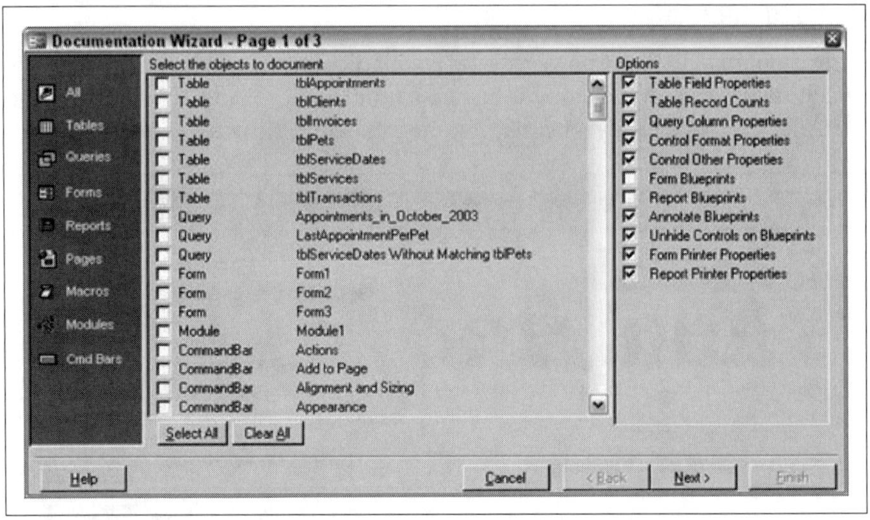

Figure 9-2. Documentation Wizard, step 1

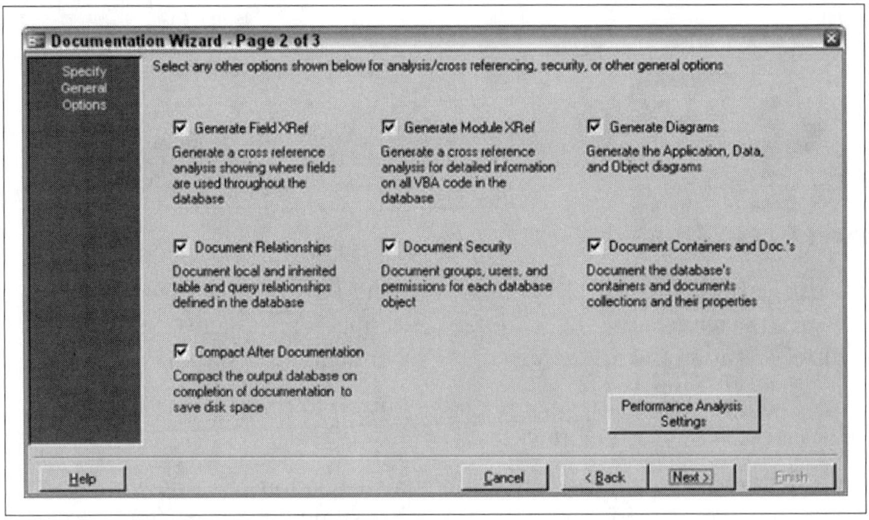

Figure 9-3. Documentation Wizard, step 2

The documentation process begins when you click the Finish button. It can take a moment or two, depending on the size of the database.

Viewing the Documentation

To view the documentation, click the Explore button back on the main form, shown in Figure 9-1. The Documentation Explorer opens, as shown in

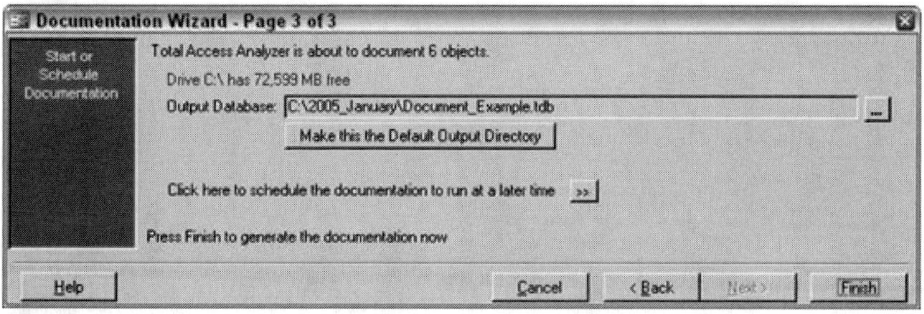

Figure 9-4. *Documentation Wizard, step 3*

Figure 9-5. In the Explorer, you select objects in the left explorer pane, and the details are shown in the right pane.

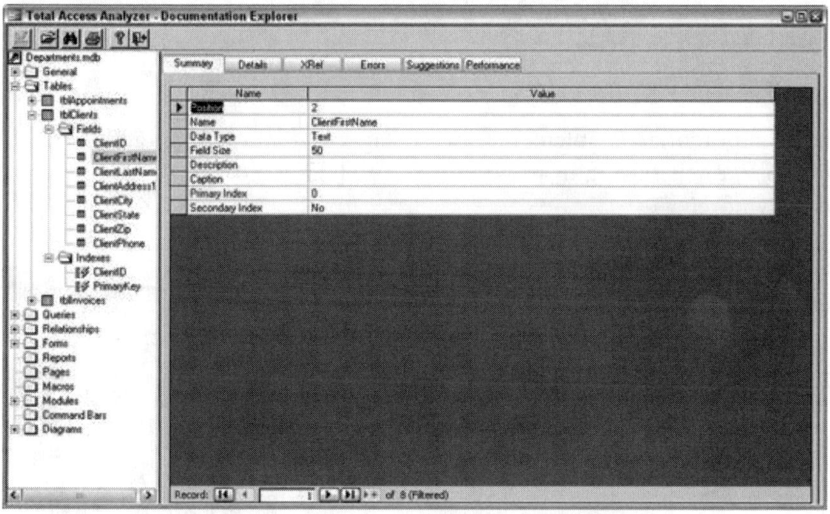

Figure 9-5. *Exploring the documentation*

At this point you have a wealth of information to sift through. You can look up everything about your database and its objects; the Explorer's layout makes this easy. For example, as shown in Figure 9-6, you can see all the procedures in a module and their declarations—all next to each other and easy to compare. Just try doing *that* in a code module.

Errors and Suggestions

Not only does Total Access Analyzer document the database, but it also goes further to identify problems and offer suggestions. Figure 9-7 shows

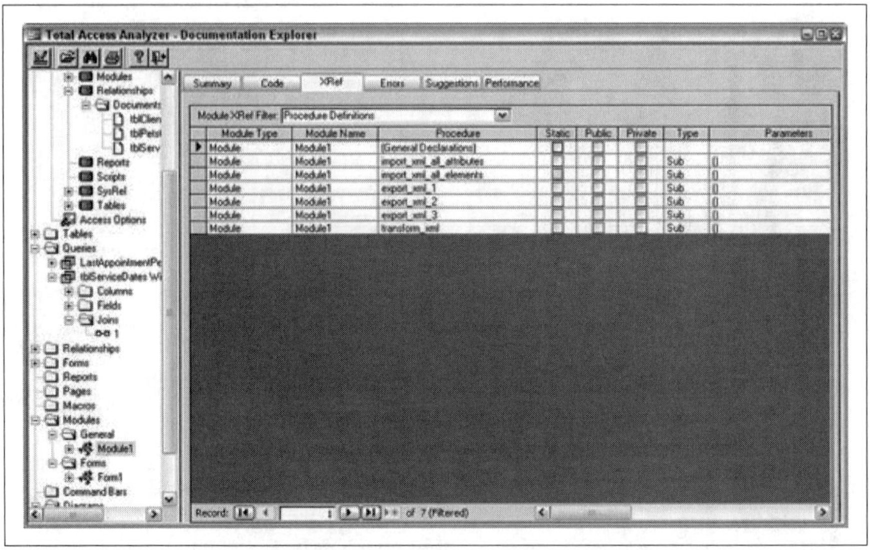

Document Your Database with Total Access Analyzer

Figure 9-6. Exploring a module

where a potential problem has been flagged. I tend to forget to set the
Option Explicit setting in my modules. Well, I guess I can't get away with
that anymore!

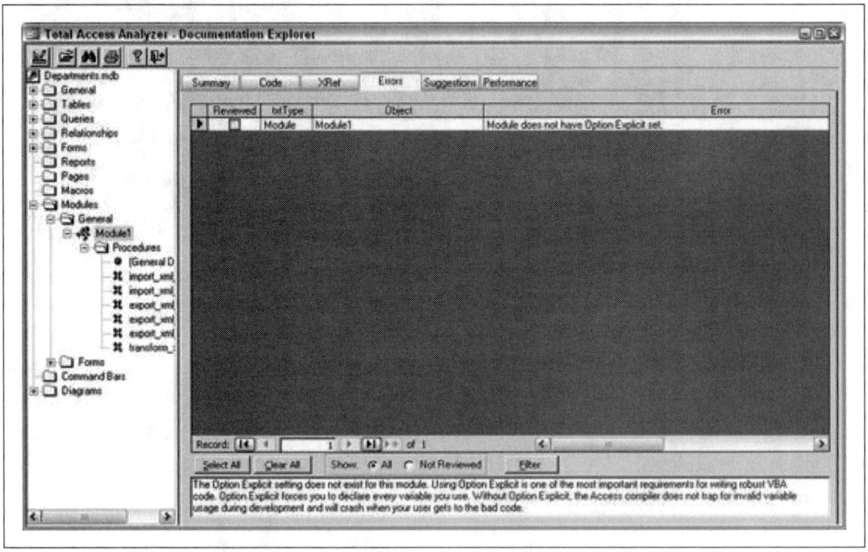

Figure 9-7. Exploring an error

Figure 9-8 shows a list of suggestions the Analyzer has assembled. Such suggestions are really useful for making an application the best it can be.

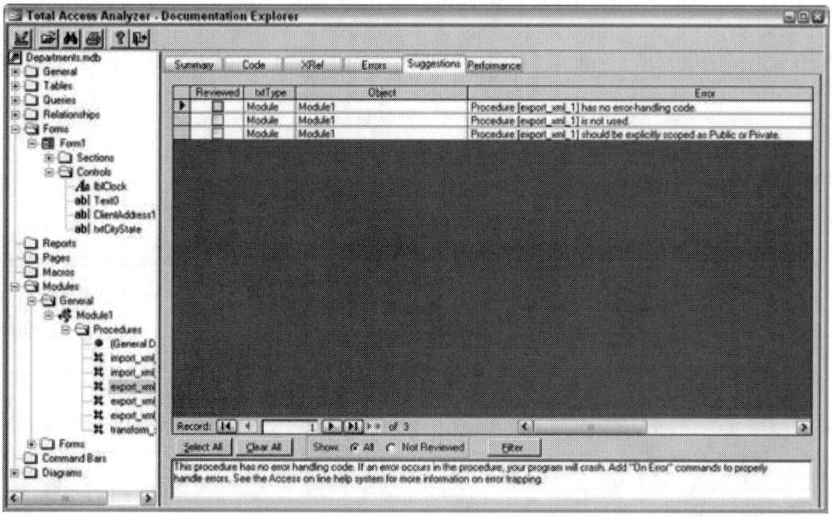

Figure 9-8. Exploring suggestions

Total Access Analyzer is a great product not only for listing all the objects, properties, methods, and attributes about a database, but also for finding out what you can do to improve them. Other options from the main form include searching for particular items in the documentation and printing the documentation.

HACK #93 Build an Application Shell with EZ Application Generator

Let your fingers do the walking through the process of creating an Access application.

Why go through the drudgery of putting together a database from scratch—creating a splash screen, integrating security and help, creating a report generator, and more—when a great product is available that can do it for you? EZ Application Generator by Database Creations, Inc. (*http://www.databasecreations.com*) creates a framework for an application. You still create your data tables, forms, and other database objects, but in the end, you will have a complete application that has it all, from A to Z.

The EZ Application Generator Wizard runs through nearly a dozen screens that cover all the bases, from adding application information, logos, and other graphics, right through to setting up security, error trapping, and advanced search features.

To get started, create a new database. You can create your tables, forms, reports, and other database objects now, or anytime after the application shell is completed. The EZ Application Generator starts when you select it from the Add-Ins list.

The first screen, shown in Figure 9-9, accepts the application title and other general information.

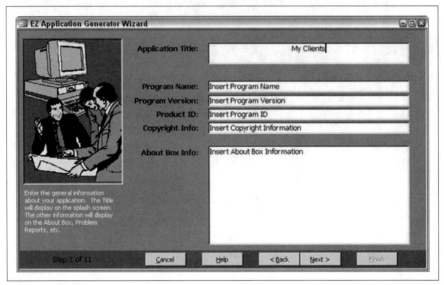

Figure 9-9. Entering general application information

In the next screen, shown in Figure 9-10, you select the images to use for the splash screen, the logo, and the icon.

In the next screen, shown in Figure 9-11, you select a theme for the switch-board. Boy, is this easy! To think of all those years I did this by hand!

Several more screens follow, in which you can set up titles, tips of the day, legal agreements, and other useful application items. Along the way, security and error handling are initiated.

The screen in Figure 9-12 lets you select to include a calendar, clock, and calculator, as well as scheduling options.

When the EZ Application Generator Wizard finishes, the database is populated with the objects needed to run your application. You can access and run all tasks, including your own database objects, from a switchboard. All the utilities you selected in the EZ Application Generator Wizard are available from the switchboard as well, as shown in Figure 9-13.

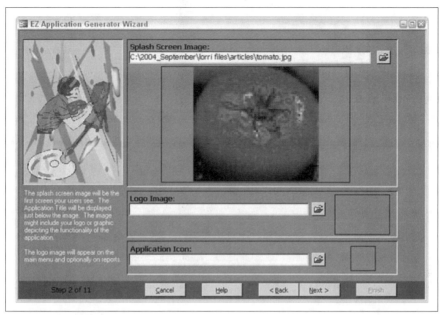

Figure 9-10. Selecting graphics

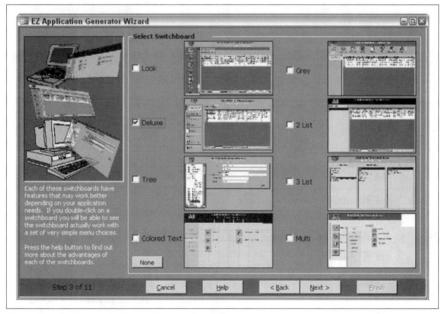

Figure 9-11. Selecting a switchboard theme

Database Creations offers other developer-friendly products as well. Visit the company's web site for more information.

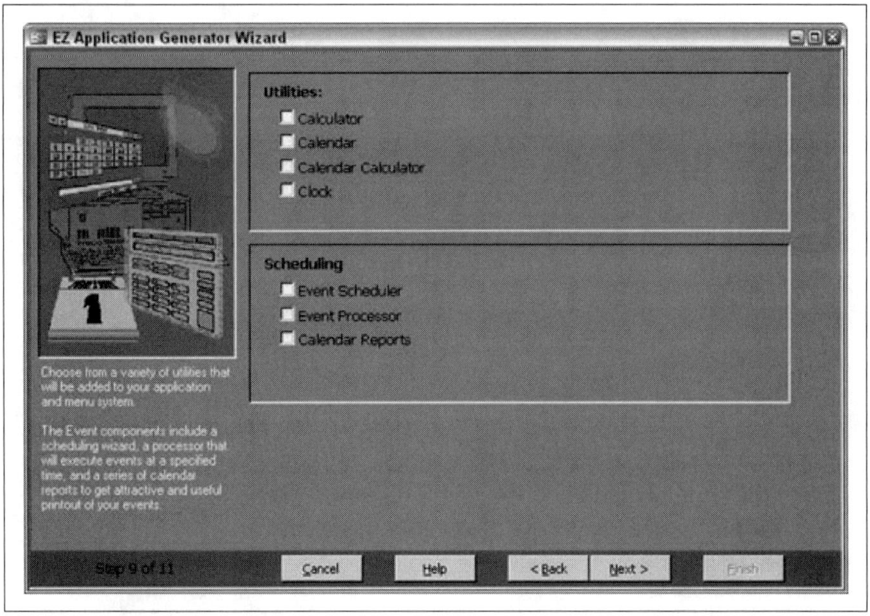

Figure 9-12. Selecting utilities

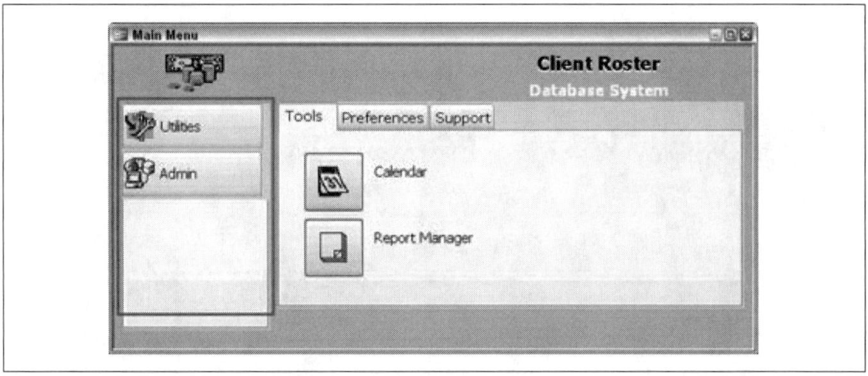

Figure 9-13. Running the application in a switchboard

Load Your Database with Test Data

#94   Use predesigned test data that matches your tables and fields.

Building a database application is one thing, but testing it is another. Sometimes you can get your hands on archived production data and use it to test
an application before it is released. Other times, though, you have to create
your own test data.

Although putting a few records into your tables to make sure everything works accordingly can reassure you that your database application works, loading it with hundreds or thousands of records lets you *really* see how your application will perform when it's released.

Records2Go (*http://www.records2go.com*) is a data-generation product that lets you define schemas and then produces data to your specifications. The created data is saved into an external text or XML file, which you can import into Access. You can make any number of records using this tool; I have used Records2Go to make records numbering in the hundreds of thousands.

Figure 9-14 shows how Records2Go works. You have a handful of settings to input, including how many records to make, what the created file is named, and where it will be saved. The form's main focus is the grid in which you define a table layout.

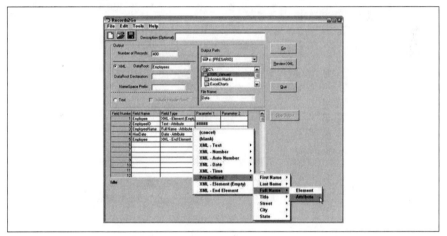

Figure 9-14. Creating an XML data set

You can create two types of files: text and XML. Figure 9-14 shows an XML schema being set up. Whether you're creating a text file or an XML file, each row in the grid represents a field. On each row, you enter the field name, field type, and other parameters. You can use standard field types—such as numbers, dates, and text—or you can use field types from a set of predefined data. The predefined data offers name and address field type information.

You can use wildcards to control how data is created. For example, when you select the Text type, you can enter a phrase, which will be created as is, or you can use specific wildcards to represent random numbers or characters. In the specification in Figure 9-14, pound signs (#) indicate random number creation.

Figure 9-15 shows the XML data generated from the specification shown in Figure 9-14. The predefined Full Name attribute created just that: XML attributes of names. The EmployeeID field is filled with random numbers, and the hire dates fall within the range in the specification.

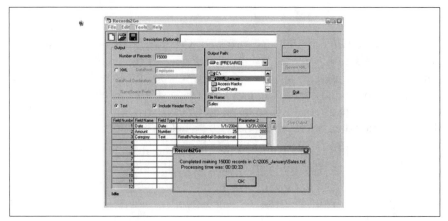

Figure 9-15. The created XML data

Records2Go is great for producing large sets of data. Figure 9-16 shows a specification for making 15,000 text records. The task was completed in 33 seconds.

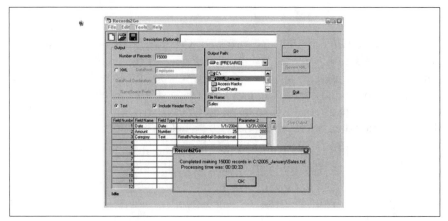

Figure 9-16. 15,000 records in 33 seconds

Figure 9-17 shows the created text file. One of the options is whether to include a header row. Other options include selecting the delimiter and the text qualifier.

```
Sales.txt - Notepad
File   Edit   Format   View   Help
Date,Amount,Category
2/2/2004,127,Wholesale
4/22/2004,58,Mail Order
6/26/2004,186,Wholesale
5/10/2004,107,Wholesale
8/14/2004,144,Internet
5/18/2004,96,Mail Order
10/11/2004,143,Retail
7/18/2004,183,Wholesale
8/30/2004,122,Wholesale
12/16/2004,48,Mail Order
8/22/2004,154,Wholesale
4/25/2004,104,Retail
4/15/2004,72,Mail Order
8/26/2004,148,Mail Order
1/11/2004,81,Retail
11/14/2004,116,Mail Order
12/17/2004,114,Mail Order
5/25/2004,129,Retail
4/4/2004,27,Internet
4/10/2004,148,Mail Order
3/21/2004,176,Retail
12/5/2004,26,Mail Order
1/5/2004,64,Retail
6/18/2004,95,Internet
4/6/2004,71,Retail
1/15/2004,71,Mail Order
11/16/2004,75,Retail
3/26/2004,145,Mail Order
2/26/2004,58,Internet
3/15/2004,78,Wholesale
4/5/2004,177,Retail
1/20/2004,28,Mail Order
2/4/2004,64,Wholesale
12/12/2004,59,Retail
6/29/2004,123,Mail Order
6/15/2004,189,Retail
2/1/2004,161,Wholesale
```

Figure 9-17. Test data ready to be imported into Access

A great facet of the product is that you can save and load specifications. In other words, when you create a data specification in the grid, you can save it so that you can use it whenever you need it. You can move rows around in the grid, add rows, delete rows, and so on. You even can use just some of the rows and leave others out—without having to delete them.

HACK #95 Use Access as an XML Database

Have Access work as a front end to your XML data.

A few hacks throughout this book (see the list at the end of this hack) explore XML usage with Access. This hack presents the crowning achievement: a complete XML database. To clarify, this hack shows you how Access can read from and write to XML files and have the data appear on a form for viewing and editing. The form has the requisite database function-ality: browse, add a record, update a record, and delete a record.

The power behind making this work is to incorporate the MSXML parser from Microsoft. Visit *http://www.microsoft.com/xml* and see "Provide Complete XML Control to Any Version of Access" **[Hack #87]** for an introduction to getting and using the parser. The parser is the key to getting Access to do more than simple XML imports and exports.

Figure 9-18 shows the form used in the application. The displayed record is from an XML file. The form has Previous and Next buttons for navigating through records, as well as Update and Delete buttons. The New button is for entering new records, and the Save button is used for saving new records to the file.

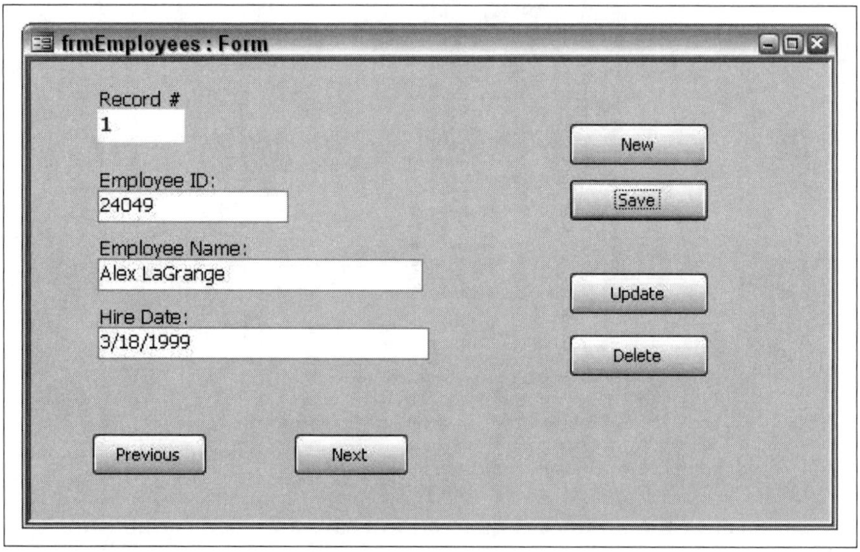

Figure 9-18. Displaying data from an XML file

The data is completely external, but it doesn't come from a table. This application contains no tables, whether linked or connected with ADO or ODBC. In fact, this application contains nothing except this one form.

The Code

The following code behind the form takes care of all data management:

```
Option Compare Database
  Public xmlobj As DOMDocument
  Public xml_list As IXMLDOMNodeList
  Public record_num As Integer
  Public file_name As String
```

```
Private Sub cmdDelete_Click()
  Dim xml_node As IXMLDOMElement
  Set xml_node = xmlobj.documentElement.childNodes(record_num)
  xmlobj.documentElement.removeChild xml_node
  xmlobj.Save file_name
  reload_file
End Sub

Private Sub cmdNew_Click()
  Me.txtEmployeeID = ""
  Me.txtEmployeeName = ""
  Me.txtHireDate = ""
  Me.txtRecordNum = ""
End Sub

Private Sub cmdNext_Click()
  If record_num < xml_list.length - 1 Then
    record_num = record_num + 1
  Else
    record_num = 0
  End If
  load_record
End Sub

Private Sub cmdPrevious_Click()
  If record_num > 0 Then
    record_num = record_num - 1
  Else
    record_num = xml_list.length - 1
  End If
  load_record
End Sub

Private Sub cmdSave_Click()
  Dim xml_node As IXMLDOMElement
  If Me.txtEmployeeID = "" Or Me.txtEmployeeName = "" Or _
    Me.txtHireDate = "" Then
    MsgBox "Must fill in all three fields"
    Exit Sub
  End If
  Set xml_node = xmlobj.createElement("Employee")
  xml_node.setAttribute "EmployeeID", Me.txtEmployeeID
  xml_node.setAttribute "EmployeeName", Me.txtEmployeeName
  xml_node.setAttribute "HireDate", Me.txtHireDate
  xmlobj.documentElement.appendChild xml_node
  xmlobj.Save file_name
  reload_file
End Sub

Private Sub cmdUpdate_Click()
  xmlobj.documentElement.childNodes(record_num) _
    .Attributes(0).nodeValue = Me.txtEmployeeID
  xmlobj.documentElement.childNodes(record_num)
```

```
        .Attributes(1).nodeValue = Me.txtEmployeeName
    xmlobj.documentElement.childNodes(record_num) _
        .Attributes(2).nodeValue = Me.txtHireDate
    xmlobj.Save file_name
    reload_file

End Sub

Private Sub Form_Open(Cancel As Integer)
    file_name = "C:\EmployeeData.xml"
    Set xmlobj = New DOMDocument
    xmlobj.async = False
    xmlobj.Load file_name
    Set xml_list = xmlobj.selectNodes _
        ("Employees/Employee")
    'load first record
    record_num = 0
    load_record
End Sub

Sub load_record( )
    Me.txtEmployeeID = _
        xml_list.Item(record_num).Attributes(0).nodeValue
    Me.txtEmployeeName = _
        xml_list.Item(record_num).Attributes(1).nodeValue
    Me.txtHireDate = _
        xml_list.Item(record_num).Attributes(2).nodeValue
    Me.txtRecordNum = record_num + 1
End Sub

Sub reload_file( )
    xmlobj.Load file_name
    Set xml_list = xmlobj.selectNodes _
        ("Employees/Employee")
    'load first record
    record_num = 0
    load_record
End Sub
```

Loading the XML File

When the form opens, a public XML variable (xmlobj) is set to the loaded
XML file, which resides in memory. A list of nodes (xml_list) holds the
Employee records, and the first record is displayed in the form:

```
Private Sub Form_Open(Cancel As Integer)
    file_name = "C:\EmployeeData.xml"
    Set xmlobj = New DOMDocument
    xmlobj.async = False
    xmlobj.Load file_name
    Set xml_list = xmlobj.selectNodes _
        ("Employees/Employee")
```

```
'load first record
  record_num = 0
  load_record
End Sub
```

Browsing Records

In XML lingo, the length property is the same as the count property in VB. When the Next or Previous buttons are clicked, a public variable, record_num, is compared with the number of XML records. If the record_num variable hits the total count as a result of clicking Next, it resets to 0. If the record_num variable hits 0 as a result of clicking Previous, it resets to the number of records. Clicking Next or Previous completes with a call to the load_record routine:

```
Private Sub cmdNext_Click( )
  If record_num < xml_list.length - 1 Then
    record_num = record_num + 1
  Else
    record_num = 0
  End If
  load_record
End Sub

Private Sub cmdPrevious_Click( )
  If record_num > 0 Then
    record_num = record_num - 1
  Else
    record_num = xml_list.length - 1
  End If
  load_record
End Sub
```

The load_record routine simply fills the controls on the form with the data from the XML record that is positioned at the record_num number:

```
Sub load_record( )
  Me.txtEmployeeID = _
    xml_list.Item(record_num).Attributes(0).nodeValue
  Me.txtEmployeeName = _
    xml_list.Item(record_num).Attributes(1).nodeValue
  Me.txtHireDate = _
    xml_list.Item(record_num).Attributes(2).nodeValue
  Me.txtRecordNum = record_num + 1
End Sub
```

Updating a Record

When data is changed while on the form, the Update button must be clicked to save the changes back to the original file. The process here is to update the node (the employee record) in the file with the form values. The

Employee node is a child of documentElement Employees. The values aren't saved until the Save method runs on xmlobj. After that, the file is reloaded, and this last step resets the form back to the first record (an alternative is to leave the form displaying the updated record):

```
Private Sub cmdUpdate_Click( )
    xmlobj.documentElement.childNodes(record_num) _
        .Attributes(0).nodeValue = Me.txtEmployeeID
    xmlobj.documentElement.childNodes(record_num) _
        .Attributes(1).nodeValue = Me.txtEmployeeName
    xmlobj.documentElement.childNodes(record_num) _
        .Attributes(2).nodeValue = Me.txtHireDate
    xmlobj.Save file_name
    reload_file

End Sub
```

Deleting a Record

To delete a record set a node variable (xml_node) to the employee record. Then, the removeChild method of its parent deletes it:

```
Private Sub cmdDelete_Click( )
    Dim xml_node As IXMLDOMElement
    Set xml_node = xmlobj.documentElement.childNodes(record_num)
    xmlobj.documentElement.removeChild xml_node
    xmlobj.Save file_name
    reload_file
End Sub
```

As with other file changes, the Save method is necessary.

Adding a New Record

The New and Save buttons work together to add a record to the XML file. The New button simply clears the form, and new employee information can be entered. The Save button runs the code that saves a new record.

After validating that all text boxes contain data, a new element is created. Attributes are set to the form values, and the element, along with its attributes, are saved using the appendChild method. The Save method follows, and the file is reloaded (now it contains the new record):

```
Private Sub cmdSave_Click( )
    Dim xml_node As IXMLDOMElement
    If Me.txtEmployeeID = "" Or Me.txtEmployeeName = "" Or _
        Me.txtHireDate = "" Then
        MsgBox "Must fill in all three fields"
        Exit Sub
    End If
    Set xml_node = xmlobj.createElement("Employee")
    xml_node.setAttribute "EmployeeID", Me.txtEmployeeID
```

```
    xml_node.setAttribute "EmployeeName", Me.txtEmployeeName
    xml_node.setAttribute "HireDate", Me.txtHireDate
    xmlobj.documentElement.appendChild xml_node
    xmlobj.Save file_name
    reload_file
End Sub
```

See Also

- "Import Varied XML Data into Access" **[Hack #63]**
- "Export XML Data Sanely" **[Hack #64]**
- "Break Through VBA's Transformation Barrier" **[Hack #65]**
- "Provide Complete XML Control to Any Version of Access" **[Hack #87]**

CHAPTER TEN

The Internet
Hacks 96–100

Web technologies and the Internet are ingrained in so much of what we do that extending the Web to work with our database applications makes perfect sense. Although at first Access might not seem like a web-savvy product, with a few hacks Access can work well with the Web.

This chapter begins by showing how to save a report as HTML [Hack #96]. This lets you post your data to a web site. Better yet, how about bringing the Internet into your database? "Use a Browser Inside Access" [Hack #97] shows you how to use a web browser right within your Access forms. Need to get data from a web site? Just FTP it over [Hack #99].

HACK #96 Export a Report as HTML

Preview your reports on web pages to reach a larger audience.

Previewing summarized data is a key business need, and Access handles it quite well. To reach a large audience, you can print, email, save to Word, and so on. Another option is to save a report to a web page.

When you open an Access report, one of the selections on the File menu is Export. A handful of output types are available, and one of them is HTML. Figure 10-1 shows a report being exported as HTML.

Saving the report as an HTML file opens up a number of possibilities. The likely action is to view the report in a web browser. Figure 10-2 shows the report previewed in Internet Explorer. The HTML file is no longer a part of the database, so you must open it in the browser using the File → Open menu.

You can upload the HTML file to a web server and make it available publicly, or you can upload it to a controlled intranet group. Opening the file in

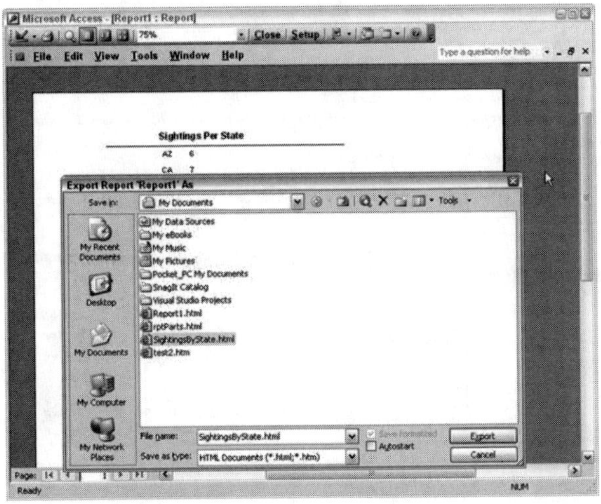

Figure 10-1. Selecting to export a report as HTML

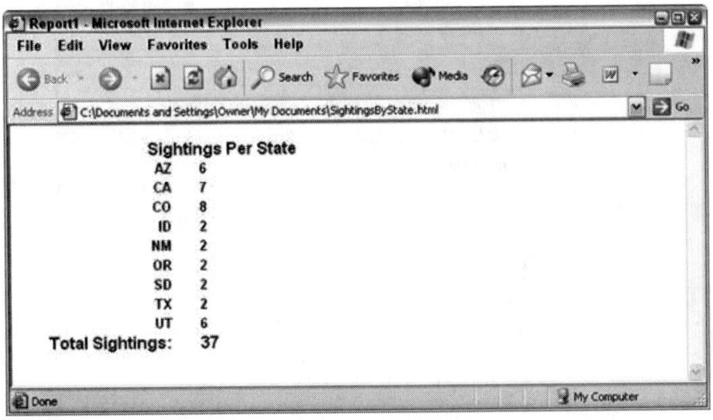

Figure 10-2. Viewing the exported data in a web browser

Notepad or another plain-text editor reveals the actual HTML code, as shown in Figure 10-3.

Note the highlighted contents of the HTML title tag. Referring back to Figure 10-2, you can see that the HTML file is named *SightingsByState.html*. But the title in Figure 10-3 just says Report1. Report1 was the name of the report in Access, so that's the title used in the Internet Explorer titlebar in Figure 10-2. We'll have to change the title in Notepad and display the file again in the browser.

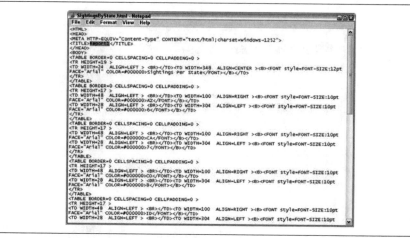

Figure 10-3. Viewing the source HTML

Figure 10-4 shows a slightly edited version of the HTML report. The title has been changed, and a few formatting changes are in place.

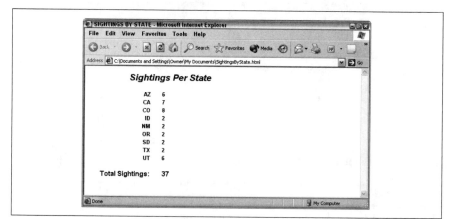

Figure 10-4. An updated view

Though the HTML code was edited directly in Notepad, you can open the HTML file with any HTML editor, such as Dreamweaver or FrontPage.

Use a Browser Inside Access

Place the Microsoft web browser on a form to coordinate data and the Web.

Access tables have a hyperlink field type, which stores a URL that, when clicked, opens your computer's browser and displays the site. This is useful, but to view the database information and the web site together is a challenge. You might have to reduce the size of both Access and the browser so that they fit together on your computer screen.

This hack puts the browser right on the Access form. To view the web site at the stored URL, you just load the browser with the URL address, and the web site appears on the form.

Figure 10-5 shows a form in Design mode. The Microsoft Web Browser control (one of the items in the list of More Controls that is available from the button on the toolbox) has been placed on the form.

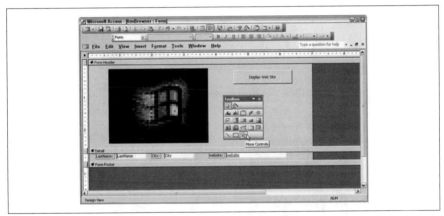

Figure 10-5. Selecting the Microsoft Web Browser control

Figure 10-6 shows the form in View mode.

The browser control displays the web site listed in the current record. This occurs when you click the Display Web Site button, which has this line of code in its Click event:

```
Me.WebBrowser1.Navigate URL:=Me.website
```

The web browser control has the Navigate method, and it navigates to the supplied URL. In this example, the URL comes from the web-site field on the form, from the current record. Of course, you can feed a URL to the web browser control in other ways. This is just one example.

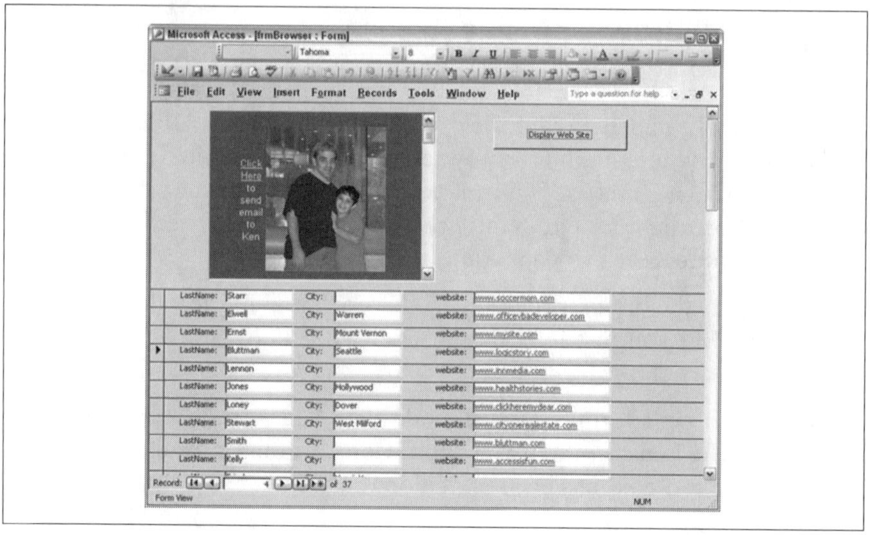

Figure 10-6. Viewing a web site on the form

Just like any control, you can place multiple web browser controls on a form. Figure 10-7 shows such an arrangement.

Figure 10-7. Multiple browsers on a form

This might seem excessive, but actually, you might have a good reason for using multiple browsers. For example, an application that integrates with current events can use this. Financial applications could keep tabs on different securities markets. The browser controls could even be displaying the output of webcams.

Pull the HTML Source Code from a Web Site
#98   Integrate web data into your application.

"Use a Browser Inside Access" **[Hack #97]** shows you how to use the Microsoft Web Browser control to display a web page. This hack takes that functionality a step further and shows how to get to the source code. Being able to access the source code makes it possible to extract data from a web site.

Figure 10-8 shows a web site being displayed in the browser control, and a message box displays the site's HTML.

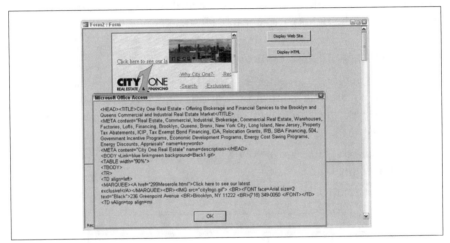

Figure 10-8. Reading the HTML source from a web site

> The Microsoft Web Browser control has an extensive programmatic model. Visit *http://msdn.microsoft.com/library/default.asp?url=/workshop/browser/prog_browser_node_entry.asp* for more information.

The HTML is returned with this line of code:

```
MsgBox Me.WebBrowser1.Document.documentElement.innerhtml
```

The programmatic model for the web browser control follows the document object model (DOM). As the browser displays a web site, documentElement and its child nodes become available. In this example, the full HTML is accessed with the innerhtml property. Because the HTML is accessible, you can pass it to any routine you want. For example, you can have a routine that looks for HTML tables from which to pull data or that searches through the HTML for keywords, and so on.

HACK #99 Download Files Using the Web Browser Control

FTP files without ever leaving your database.

"Use a Browser Inside Access" [Hack #97] and "Pull the HTML Source Code from a Web Site" [Hack #98] show you how to browse the Web from an Access form and how to retrieve the source HTML code. This hack shows you how to use the Web Browser control to pull files from an FTP site.

The File Transfer Protocol (FTP) is commonly used to move files to and from a web server. Often, the site is password-protected, so to try out this hack, you need the rights to access an FTP site.

Placing the Web Browser Control on a Form

As discussed in "Use a Browser Inside Access" [Hack #97], you can place the Microsoft Web Browser control on a form. The Navigate method takes a URL address to navigate to. In this hack, an FTP URL is supplied instead of an HTTP URL.

Using a line of code such as the following, the Web Browser control opens a login dialog (shown in Figure 10-9):

```
Me.WebBrowser0.Navigate URL:="ftp.logicstory.com"
```

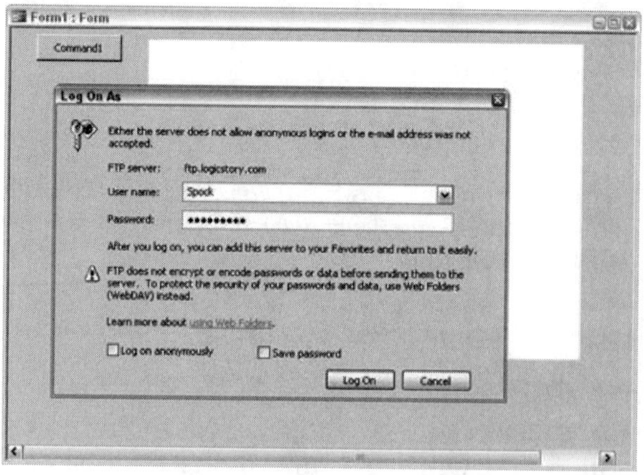

Figure 10-9. Entering a username and password for the FTP site

After the login is complete, the Web Browser control displays the site's contents. You can view, copy, delete, and rename objects depending on your user permissions, as shown in Figure 10-10.

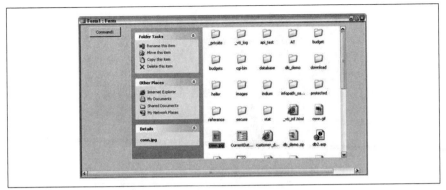

Figure 10-10. Viewing contents of the web site

When you select a file to copy, the Copy Items dialog displays the filesystem on the local computer. A directory is selected where the copied file will be pasted, as shown in Figure 10-11.

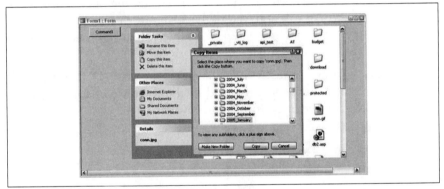

Figure 10-11. Selecting the local directory to save the copied file

Uploading Files

As noted earlier, when selecting a file to download, the "Copy this item" link opens the Copy Items dialog box. Although no equivalent link is available for initiating an upload, you can upload files to the FTP site. All you have to do is select the file on the local machine, and then click once in the Web Browser control and use the paste keyboard shortcut (Ctrl-V). Figure 10-12 shows the progress of a copy operation, confirming that a file is being copied to the site.

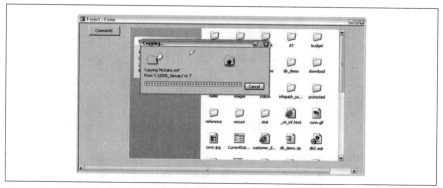

Figure 10-12. Copying a file to the remote server

 ## Use a Smart Tag to Open a Web Page

Quickly review web information when you need to see it.

Developers have mixed feelings about smart-tag technology. Some create sophisticated smart-tag solutions, and others shun their use. If you're open to using smart-tag technology, here is a simple way to use a smart tag to open a web page.

First, a smart tag is associated with a table field. Figure 10-13 shows a smart tag being associated with the Cost field in the tblServices table. After the smart tag is selected, the field's smart tag is available to click.

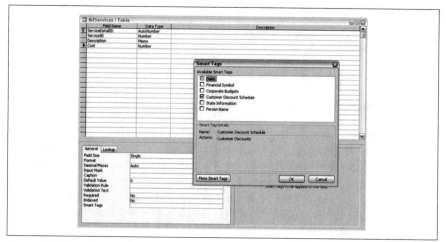

Figure 10-13. Selecting smart tags

Figure 10-14 shows the table open in Datasheet view. In each row, the Cost field displays a small purple triangle in the lower-right corner. Hovering your mouse pointer over the triangle opens the link to the smart tag.

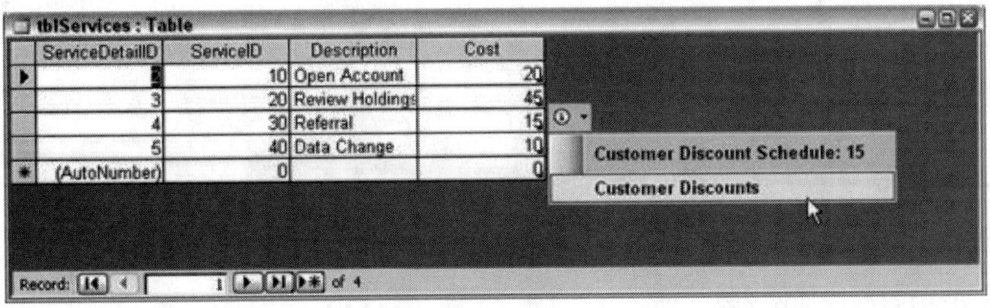

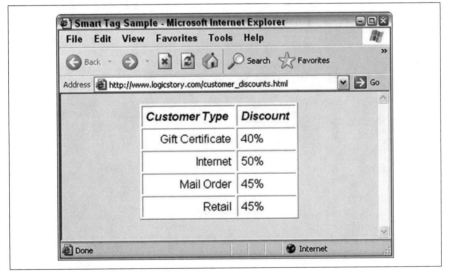

Figure 10-14. Accessing the smart tag from the Cost field

Clicking the smart tag initiates the action associated with the smart tag. In this example, the action is to open a web page to display some additional business information.

Figure 10-15 shows the web page that opens when the smart tag is clicked.

Figure 10-15. A web site accessed from a smart tag

In most database applications, users don't work directly with tables; instead, they do all their work through forms. Figure 10-16 shows that the smart tag in the underlying table is available on a form as well. From here, too, clicking the smart tag opens the web page.

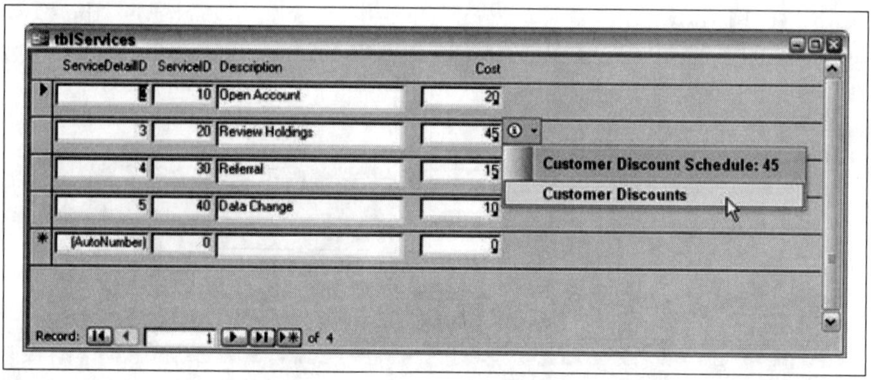

Figure 10-16. Smart tags at work on a form

To summarize, a smart tag can bring information from the Web to the Access application. The mechanics of creating smart tags are beyond our scope here, but if you visit *http://www.microsoft.com* and search for *smart tags*, you will turn up many articles on their development and use.

Index

We'd like to hear your suggestions for improving our indexes. Send email to *index@oreilly.com*.

properties (*continued*)
Row Source, populating lists and, 68
Running Sum, 92
counters, 116
SelStart, 61
Tag, control details and, 249

Q

queries
Action, 123
Crosstab, views and, 145
Data Definition, 160
functions, custom, 156
pass-through, 228
regular expressions in, 169
Select, 123
totals, 134
Union queries, 134
joins, 168
listbox population, 69
wildcards in, 161
XML exports and, 222
query grid
And-based criteria, 165
Or-based criteria, 163
sorting on any character, 135–144

R

randomly sorting records, 279
read-only command-line switch, 21
records
Admin user, 5
appending
log table, 18
preventing failure, 127
grouping, 266
locking, 178
sampling, 123
sorting, 279
separate alphabetically, 84–90
unmatched, 130
updates, confirm before save, 75
Records2Go, 306
references, ADOX library, 49
regular expressions in queries, 169
relationships
cascading updates, 12
many-to-many
exporting to XML and, 219
junction tables, 27

remember, 11
reports
counters, 116
embedded, viewing, 113
exporting, as HTML, 316
line numbers, 116
lines, shaded, 117
personalization and, 4
printing, close report, 99
watermarks, 99
whitespace, 119
Response argument, 65
right join, 166
RIGHT JOIN, sorting and, 89
Rnd function, 126
Row Source property, populating lists
and, 68
rows, query grid, 163
RunCode action, AutoExec macro, 7
Running Sum property, 92
counters, 116
running sums, 92

S

sampling records, 123
scripts, SQL Server in Access table
creation, 158
scrolling
Page Break controls, 54
Page Down key, 57
Page Up key, 57
security
backdoor building, 263
hiding data, 41
user edits, 21
usernames, 187
watermarks, 99
Select queries, 123
SelStart property, text entry and, 61
sending Access data through
Outlook, 237–244
SendKeys statement, 58
separate sorted records
alphabetically, 84–90
shaded lines in reports, 117
shortcut keys, AutoKeys macro, 10
shortcuts
deleting, 3
desktop to databases, 97
function keys, 11

tracking object use, 18
triggers
    audit logs and, 45
    form events and, 45
    simulating, 45

U

unbound controls, saving values, 276
UNC (Universal Naming
        Convention), 175
    renaming computer, 176
Union query
    joins, 168
    listbox population, 69
    totals, 134
unmatched records, 130
unused objects, identifying, 19
updates
    cascading, 11
        relationships and, 12
    controls, bulk updates, 281
    records, confirm before save, 75
    tables, check automatically, 294
uppercase text, 290
usernames, 187
users
    editing data, 21
    process length, 272
USys, hiding objects and, 41

V

validation, duplication prevention, 172
values
    custom, AutoNumber field, 31
    null values, 151
VBA
    conditional formatting and, 94
    macro recorder, Word and
        Excel, 247
    XSLT transformation and, 224
versions, data transfer, 14

video, Windows Media Player and, 110
viewing
    Crosstab queries and, 145
    Snapshot Viewer Control and, 114

W

watermarks, 99
Web browsers, 319
    file download, 322
Web pages, smart tags and, 324
whitespace in reports, 119
wildcards in queries, 161
Windows Media Player, video in
        forms, 110
wizards
    Crosstab Query Wizard, 146
    Export Text, 15
    Find Unmatched Query, 130
Word
    documents, 229
    macro recorder, writing VBA, 247
    table comparison and, 201
works, 128
WorksheetFunction property
        (Excel), 198
worksheets (Excel), importing, 189

X

XML
    data transfer and, 14
    exporting to, 212–223
        many-to-many relationships, 219
        queries and, 222
    importing data, 204–212
    MSXML parser and, 285
XSLT transformation, 224

Z

zero-length strings, preventing, 153

Colophon

Our look is the result of reader comments, our own experimentation, and feedback from distribution channels. Distinctive covers complement our distinctive approach to technical topics, breathing personality and life into potentially dry subjects.

The tool on the cover of *Access Hacks* is a flour sifter. Ever since humans first produced flour, they have constructed sifters to refine it. The Vikings used round, cup-shaped sieves utilizing horsehair fiber. In preindustrial times, whole wheat was ground in a mill, then sifted through successively finer bolting cloths to get various grades of flour, from dark whole-wheat to almost white for the wealthy. The bran removed while bolting was used by the miller to feed his livestock or was sold to others as feed.

Something similar to this process is still used in modern mills. Wheat first gets broken and separated by plain sifters and purifiers—two advanced sifting mechanisms. During this process the course outer bran skins are sifted from the inner white portions, called endosperm or semolina. Gradually the semolina is milled down into smooth, powdery flour. The clean bran, wheat feed, and flour are each collected in separate channels by a large number of different machines. No hand even touches the wheat until it leaves the mill.

Today flour is generally presifted, but sifting with a hand rotary crank or electric sifter is recommended before baking to remove lumps and further aerate flour, making it livelier for kneading.

Mary Anne Weeks Mayo was the production editor and proofreader, and Audrey Doyle was the copyeditor for *Access Hacks*. Darren Kelly provided quality control. Johnna Dinse wrote the index.

Hanna Dyer designed the cover of this book, based on a series design by Edie Freedman. The cover image is an original photograph by PhotoSpin Power Photos. Karen Montgomery produced the cover layout with Adobe InDesign CS using Adobe's Helvetica Neue and ITC Garamond fonts.

David Futato designed the interior layout. This book was converted by Keith Fahlgren to FrameMaker 5.5.6 with a format conversion tool created by Erik Ray, Jason McIntosh, Neil Walls, and Mike Sierra that uses Perl and XML technologies. The text font is Linotype Birka; the heading font is Adobe Helvetica Neue Condensed; and the code font is LucasFont's TheSans Mono Condensed. The illustrations that appear in the book were produced by Robert Romano and Jessamyn Read using Macromedia FreeHand MX and Adobe Photoshop CS. This colophon was written by Lydia Onofrei.